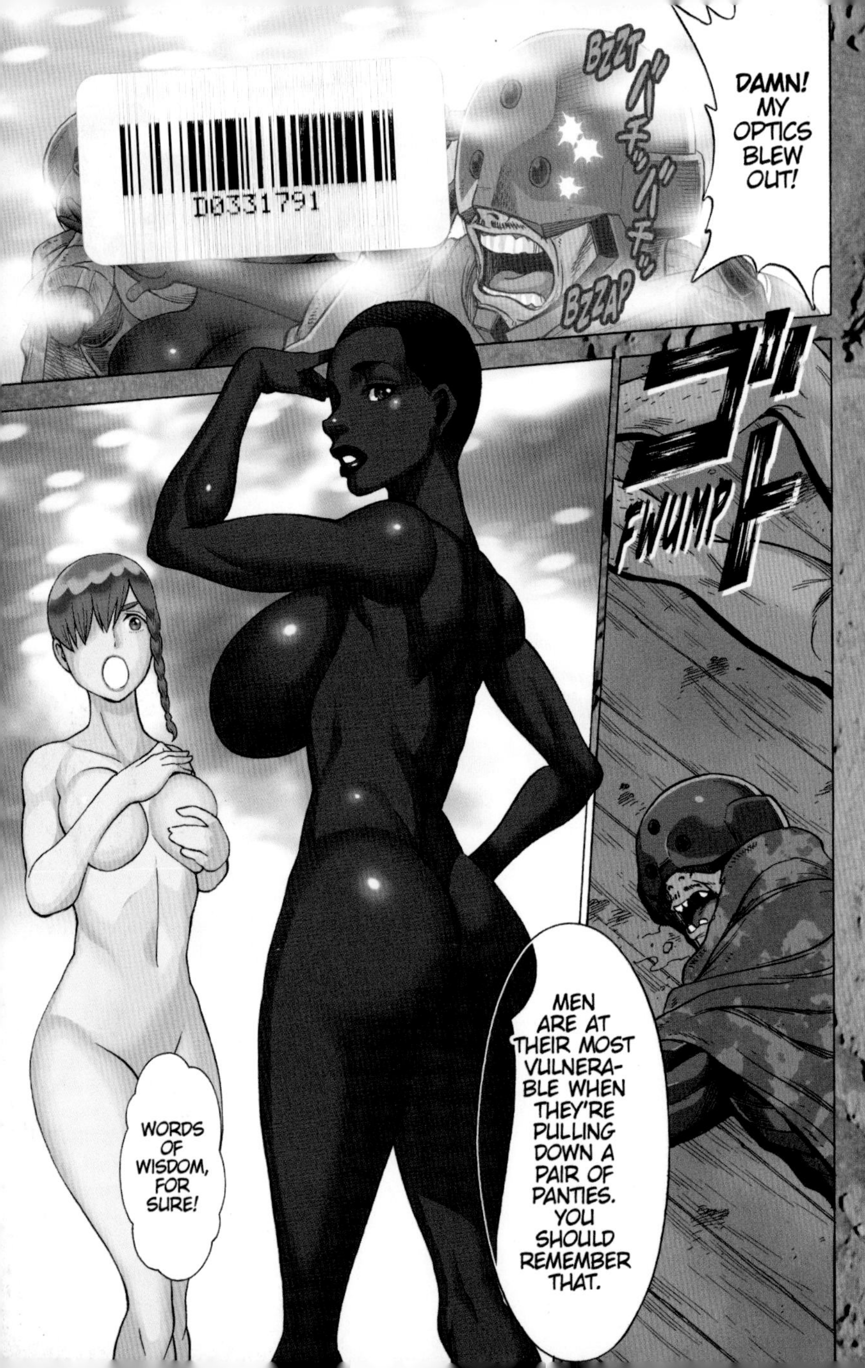
DAMN! MY OPTICS BLEW OUT!
BZZT
BZZAP
FWUMP
MEN ARE AT THEIR MOST VULNERA-BLE WHEN THEY'RE PULLING DOWN A PAIR OF PANTIES. YOU SHOULD REMEMBER THAT.
WORDS OF WISDOM, FOR SURE!

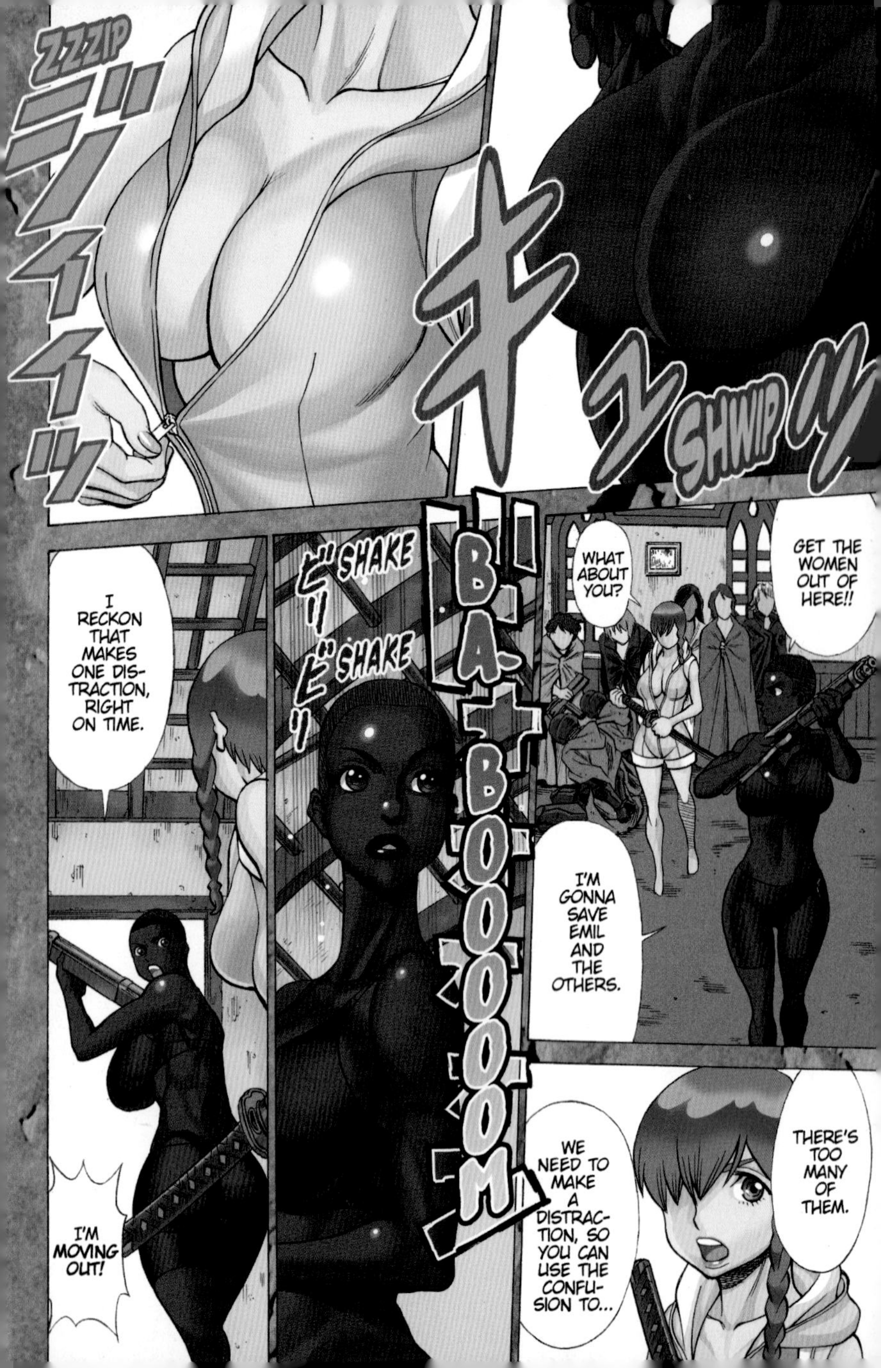
キュッ
SHWIP
ZZZIP
ジィィィッ
GET THE WOMEN OUT OF HERE!!
WHAT ABOUT YOU?
I'M GONNA SAVE EMIL AND THE OTHERS.
THERE'S TOO MANY OF THEM.
WE NEED TO MAKE A DISTRACTION, SO YOU CAN USE THE CONFUSION TO...
BA-BOOOOOOM
ビリ SHAKE
ビリ SHAKE
I RECKON THAT MAKES ONE DISTRACTION, RIGHT ON TIME.
I'M MOVING OUT!

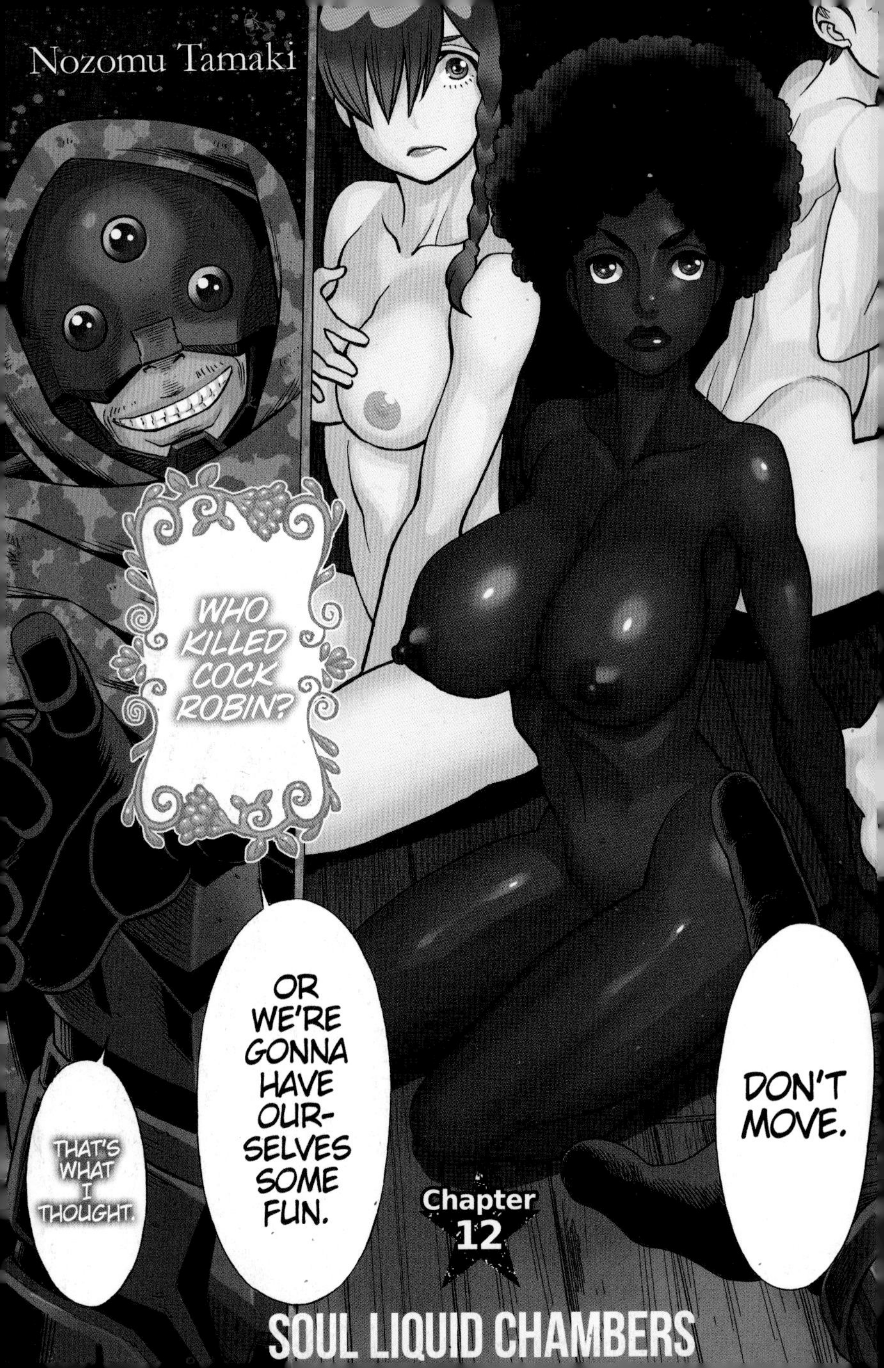

Nozomu Tamaki
WHO KILLED COCK ROBIN?
DON'T MOVE.
OR WE'RE GONNA HAVE OURSELVES SOME FUN.
THAT'S WHAT I THOUGHT.
Chapter 12
SOUL LIQUID CHAMBERS

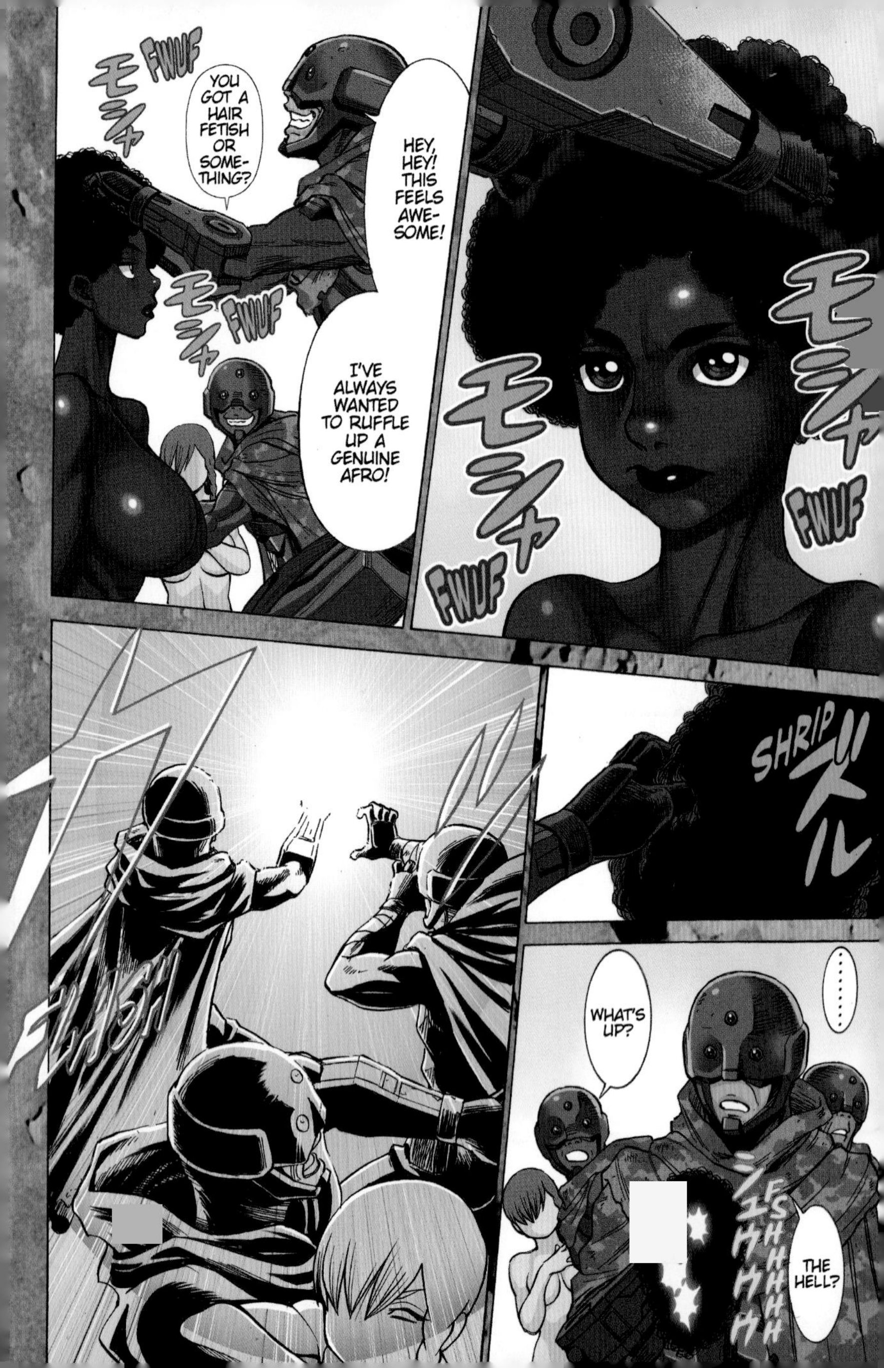
モシャ
FWUF
モシャ
FWUF
HEY, HEY! THIS FEELS AWE-SOME!
YOU GOT A HAIR FETISH OR SOME-THING?
モシャ
FWUF
I'VE ALWAYS WANTED TO RUFFLE UP A GENUINE AFRO!
モシャ
FWUF
ズル
SHRIP
......
WHAT'S UP?
シュウウウ
FSHHHHH
THE HELL?
FLASH

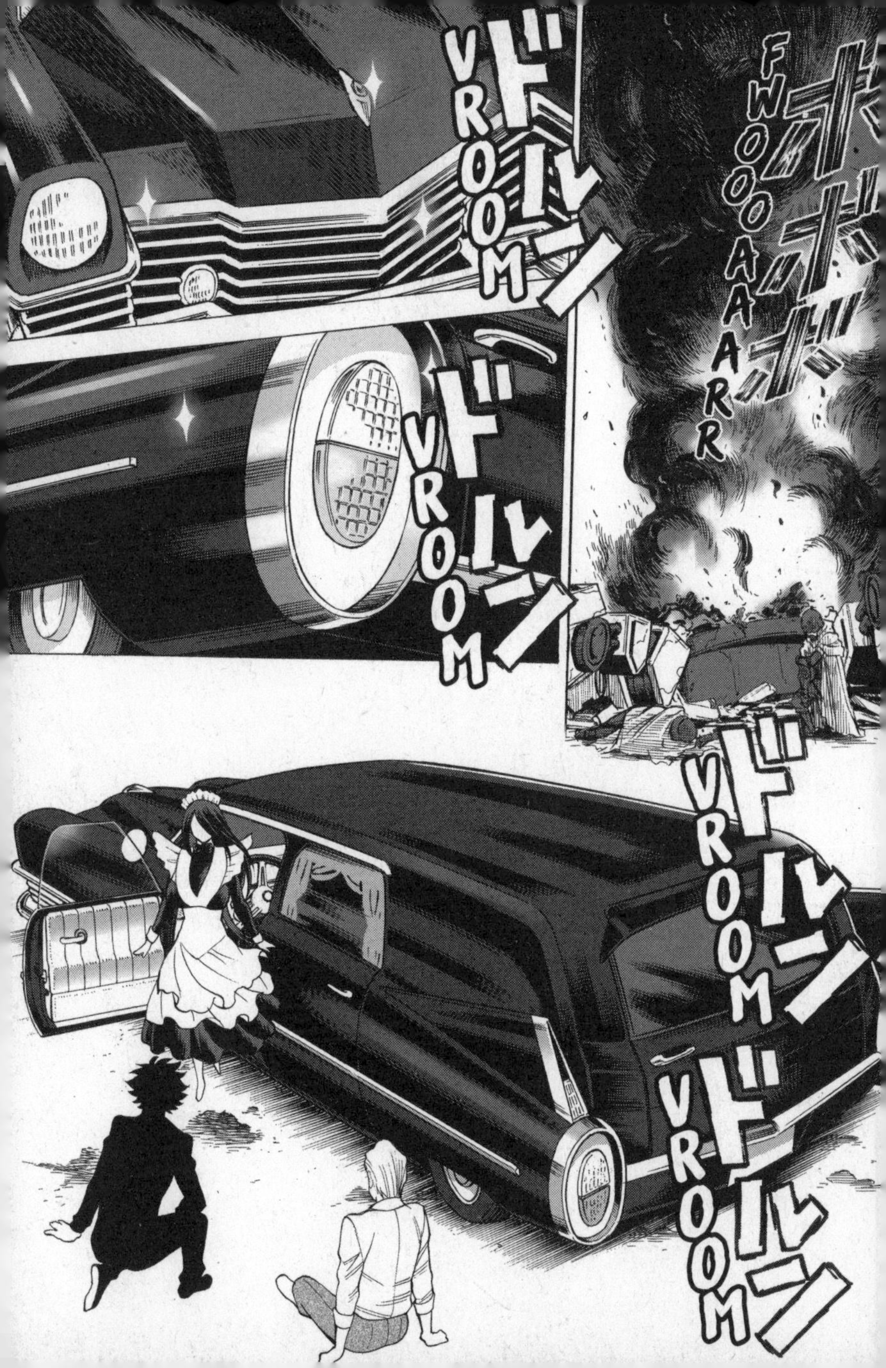

FWOOOAAARR
VROOM
VROOM
VROOM
VROOM

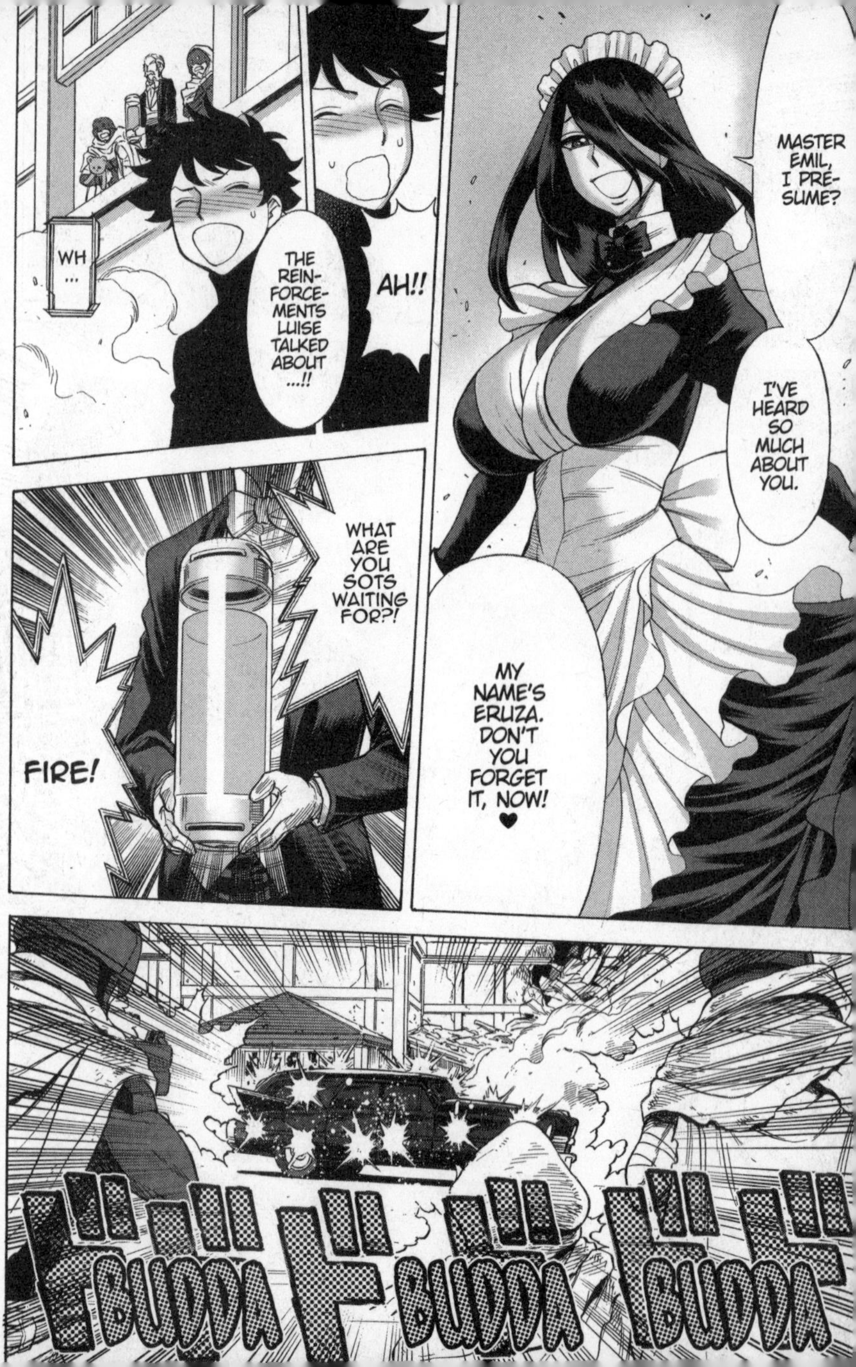
MASTER EMIL, I PRE-SUME?
I'VE HEARD SO MUCH ABOUT YOU.
MY NAME'S ERUZA. DON'T YOU FORGET IT, NOW! ♥
AH!!
THE REIN-FORCE-MENTS LUISE TALKED ABOUT ...!!
WH ...
WHAT ARE YOU SOTS WAITING FOR?!
FIRE!
BUDDA BUDDA BUDDA

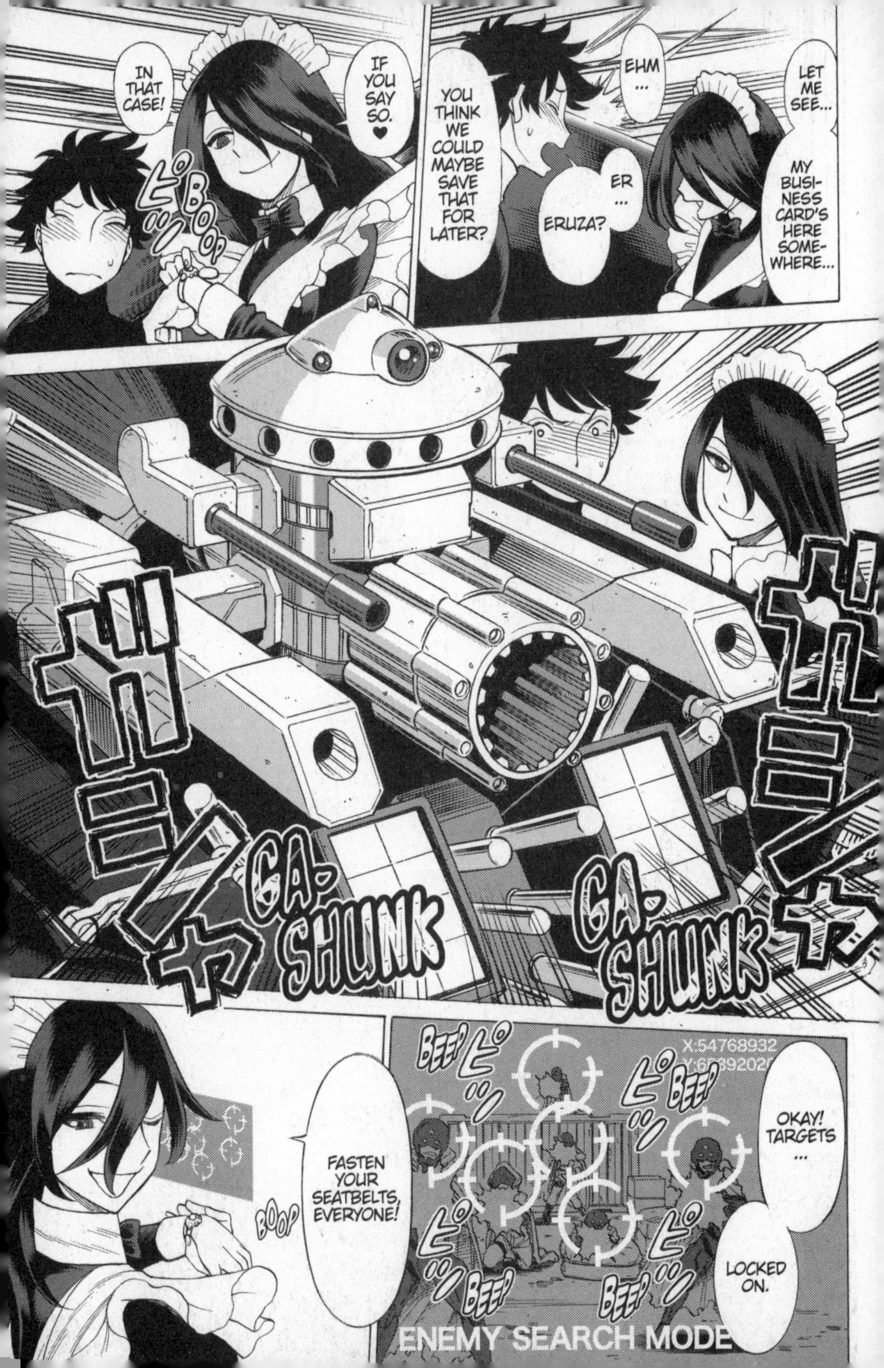
LET ME SEE...
MY BUSINESS CARD'S HERE SOMEWHERE...
EHM ...
ER ...
ERUZA?
YOU THINK WE COULD MAYBE SAVE THAT FOR LATER?
IF YOU SAY SO. ♥
IN THAT CASE!
BOOP
GA-SHUNK
GA-SHUNK
X:54768932
BEEP
BEEP
BEEP
BEEP
OKAY! TARGETS ...
LOCKED ON.
ENEMY SEARCH MODE
FASTEN YOUR SEATBELTS, EVERYONE!
BOOP

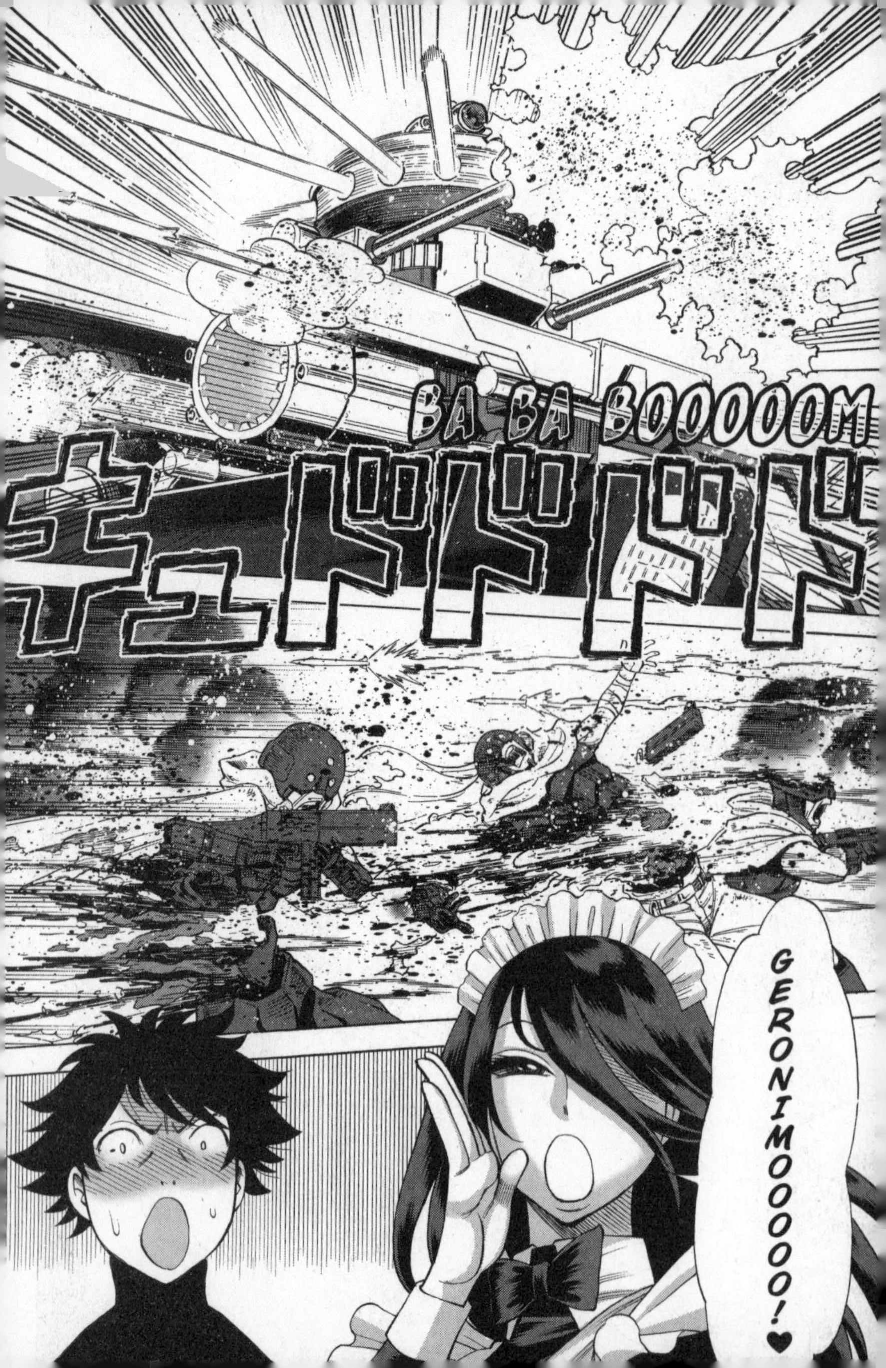
BA BA BOOOOOM
ギュドドドド
GERONIMOOOOOO!♥

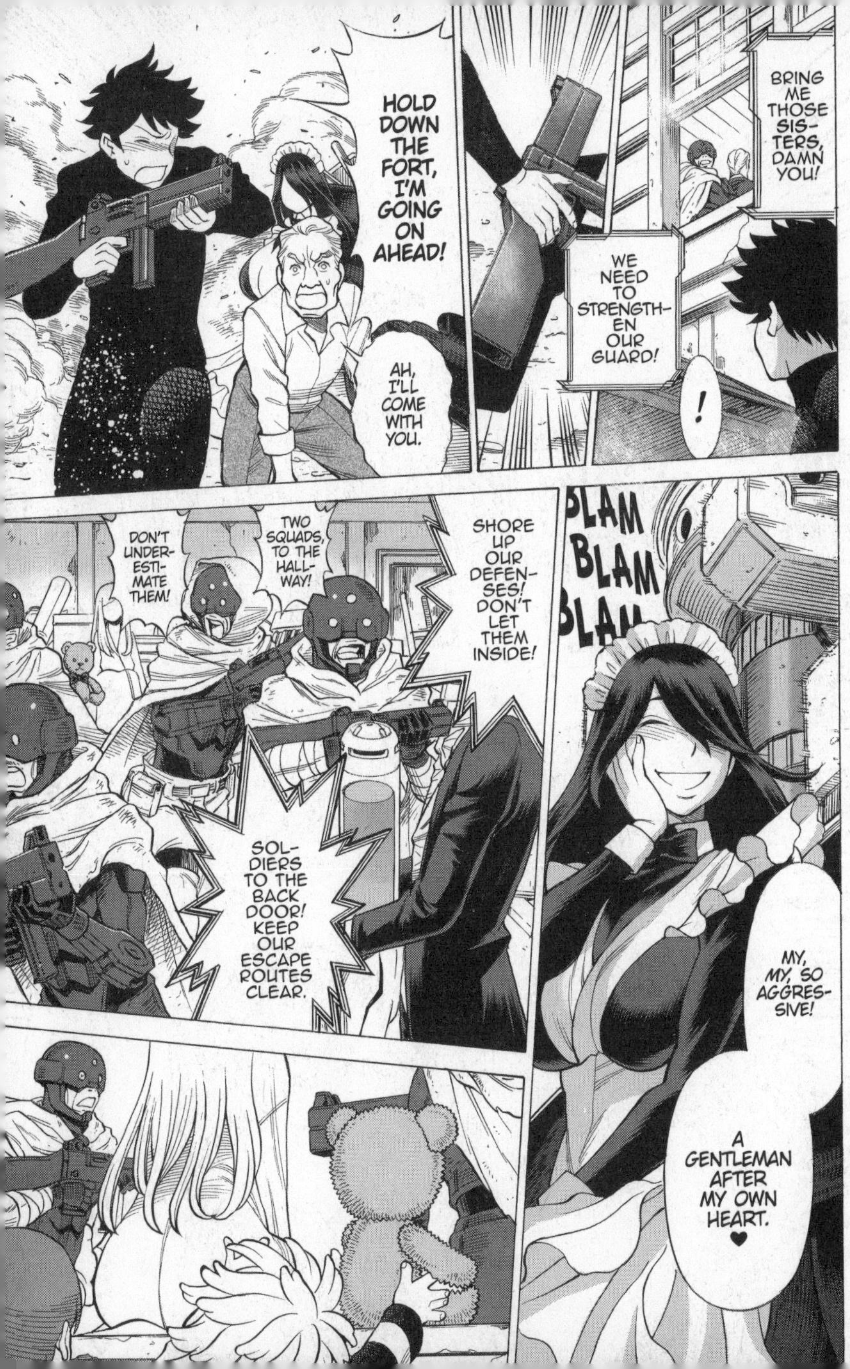
BRING ME THOSE SISTERS, DAMN YOU!
WE NEED TO STRENGTHEN OUR GUARD!
!
HOLD DOWN THE FORT, I'M GOING ON AHEAD!
AH, I'LL COME WITH YOU.
BLAM BLAM BLAM
MY, MY, SO AGGRESSIVE!
A GENTLEMAN AFTER MY OWN HEART. ♥
SHORE UP OUR DEFENSES! DON'T LET THEM INSIDE!
TWO SQUADS, TO THE HALLWAY!
DON'T UNDERESTIMATE THEM!
SOLDIERS TO THE BACK DOOR! KEEP OUR ESCAPE ROUTES CLEAR.

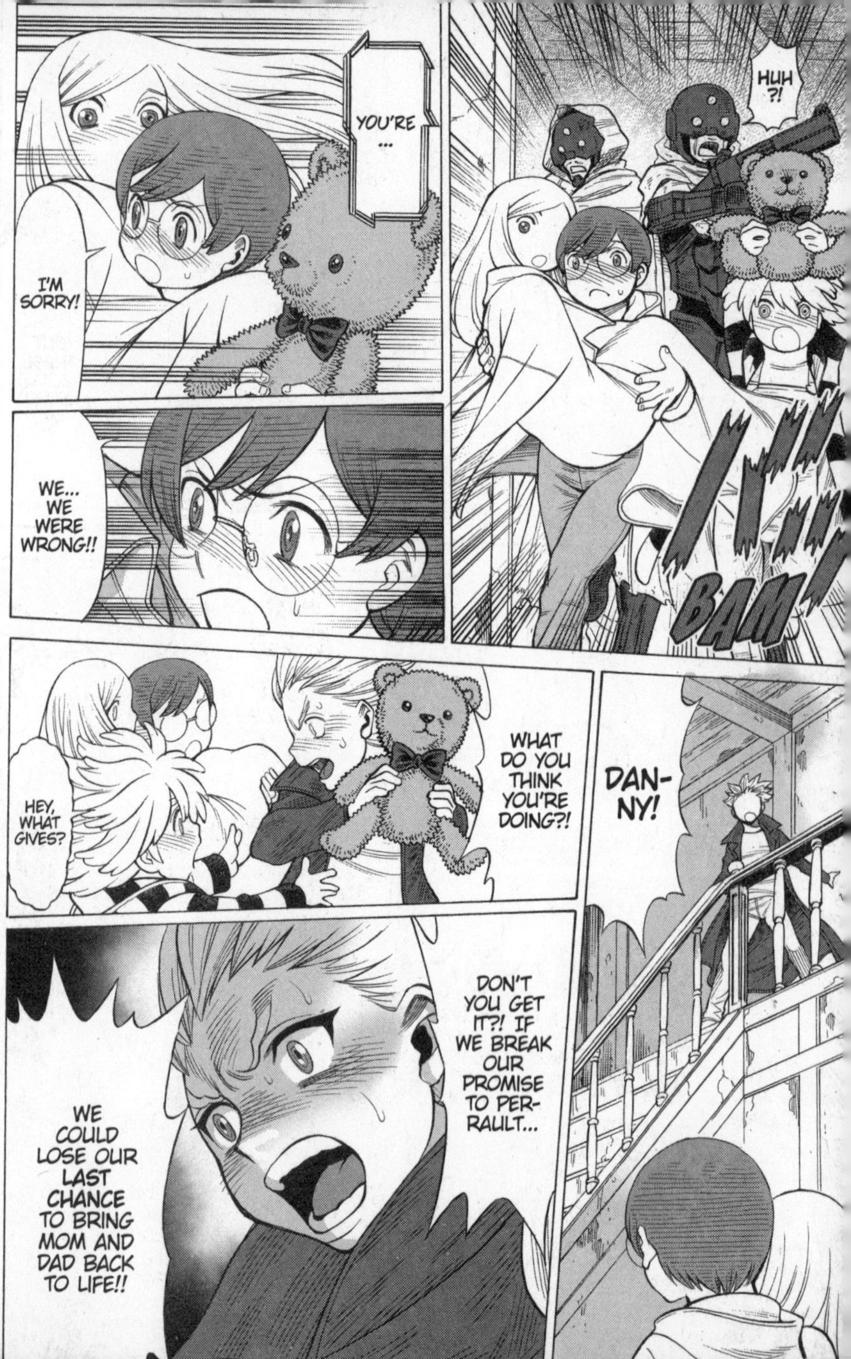
HUH ?!
BAM
YOU'RE ...
I'M SORRY!
WE... WE WERE WRONG!!
DAN-NY!
WHAT DO YOU THINK YOU'RE DOING?!
HEY, WHAT GIVES?
DON'T YOU GET IT?! IF WE BREAK OUR PROMISE TO PER-RAULT...
WE COULD LOSE OUR LAST CHANCE TO BRING MOM AND DAD BACK TO LIFE!!

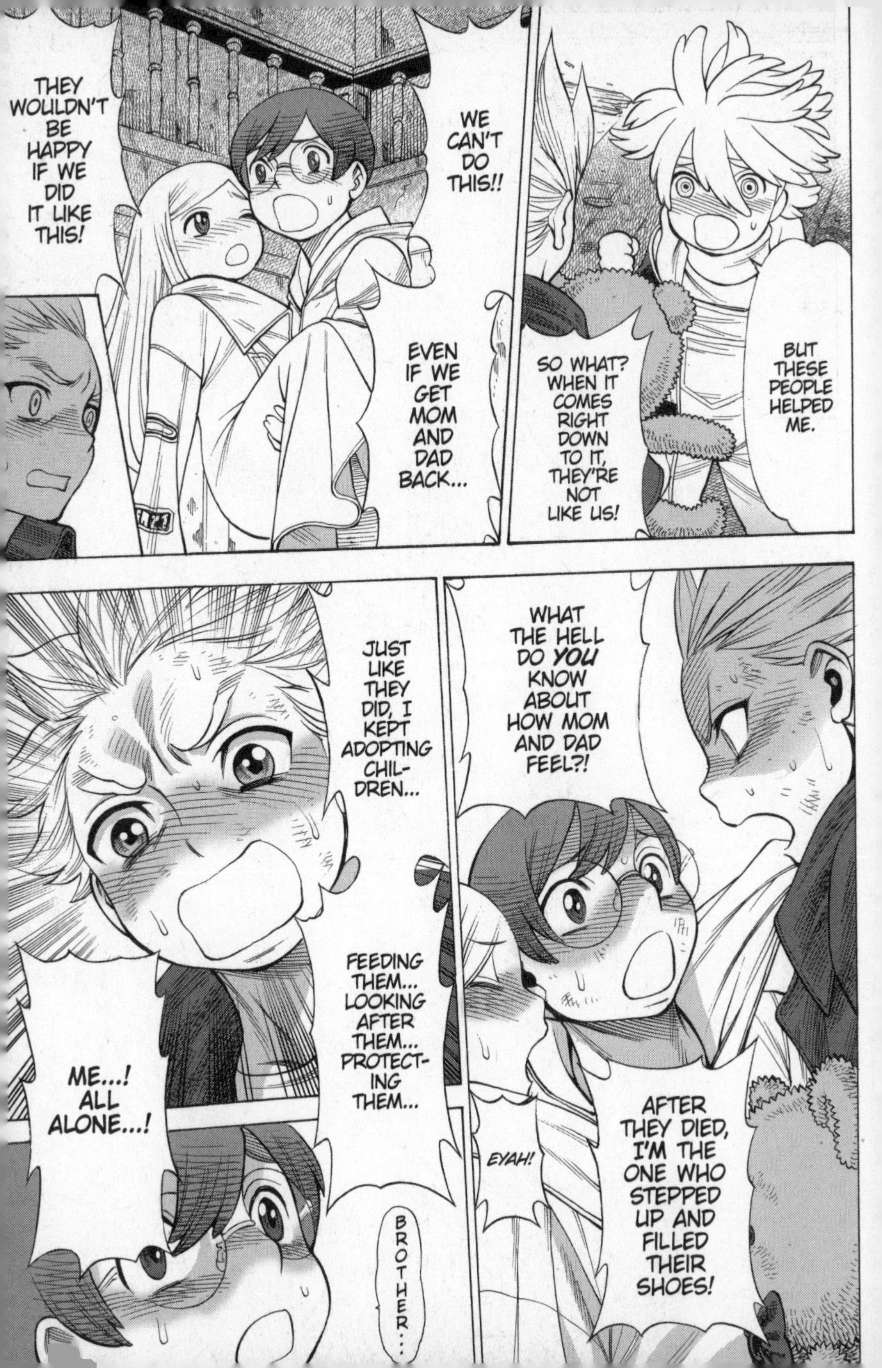
BUT THESE PEOPLE HELPED ME.
SO WHAT? WHEN IT COMES RIGHT DOWN TO IT, THEY'RE NOT LIKE US!
WE CAN'T DO THIS!!
EVEN IF WE GET MOM AND DAD BACK...
THEY WOULDN'T BE HAPPY IF WE DID IT LIKE THIS!
WHAT THE HELL DO *YOU* KNOW ABOUT HOW MOM AND DAD FEEL?!
AFTER THEY DIED, I'M THE ONE WHO STEPPED UP AND FILLED THEIR SHOES!
EYAH!
JUST LIKE THEY DID, I KEPT ADOPTING CHIL- DREN...
FEEDING THEM... LOOKING AFTER THEM... PROTECT- ING THEM...
ME...! ALL ALONE...!
BROTHER...

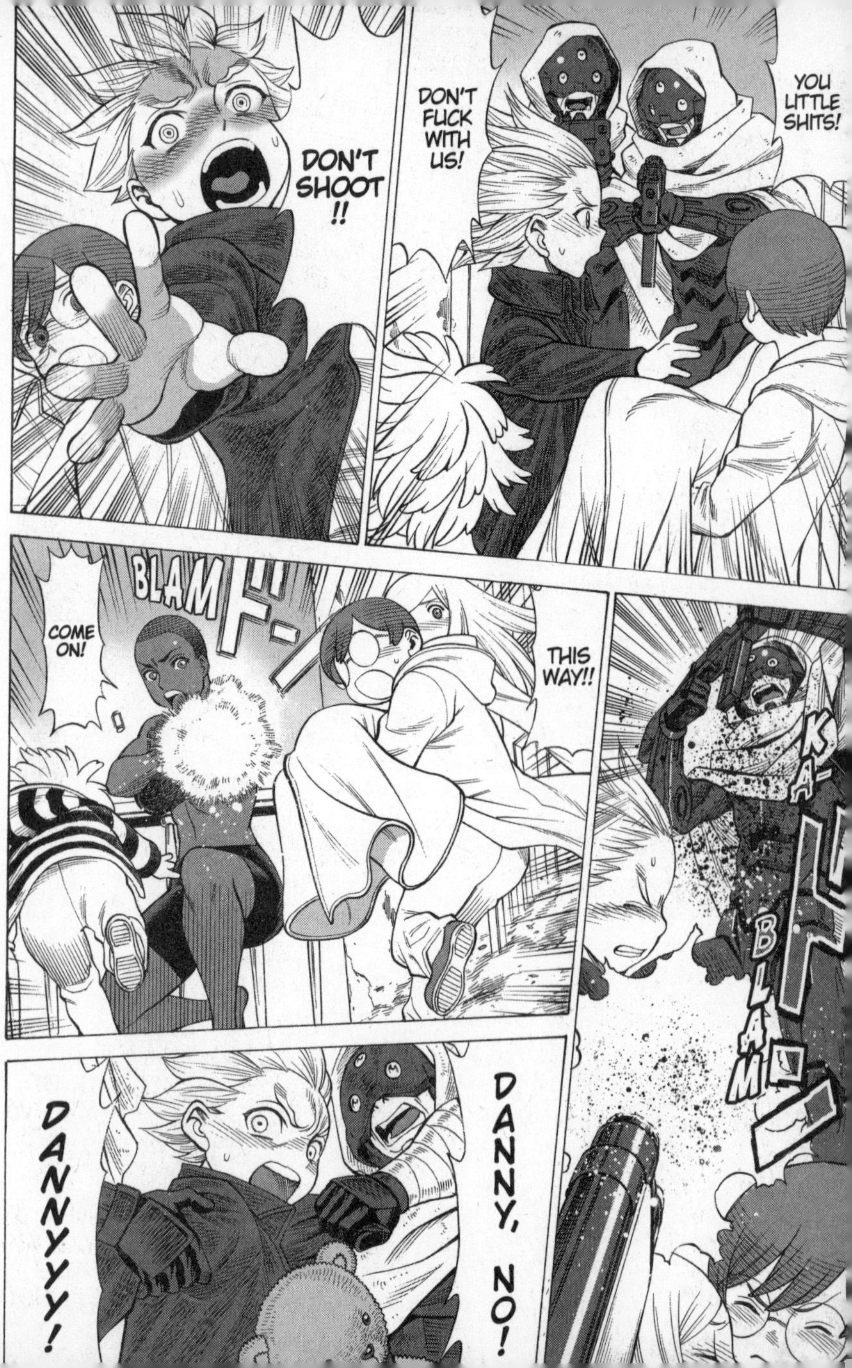
YOU LITTLE SHITS!
DON'T FUCK WITH US!
DON'T SHOOT !!
KA-
BLAM
THIS WAY!!
BLAM
COME ON!
DANNY, NO!
DANNYYY!

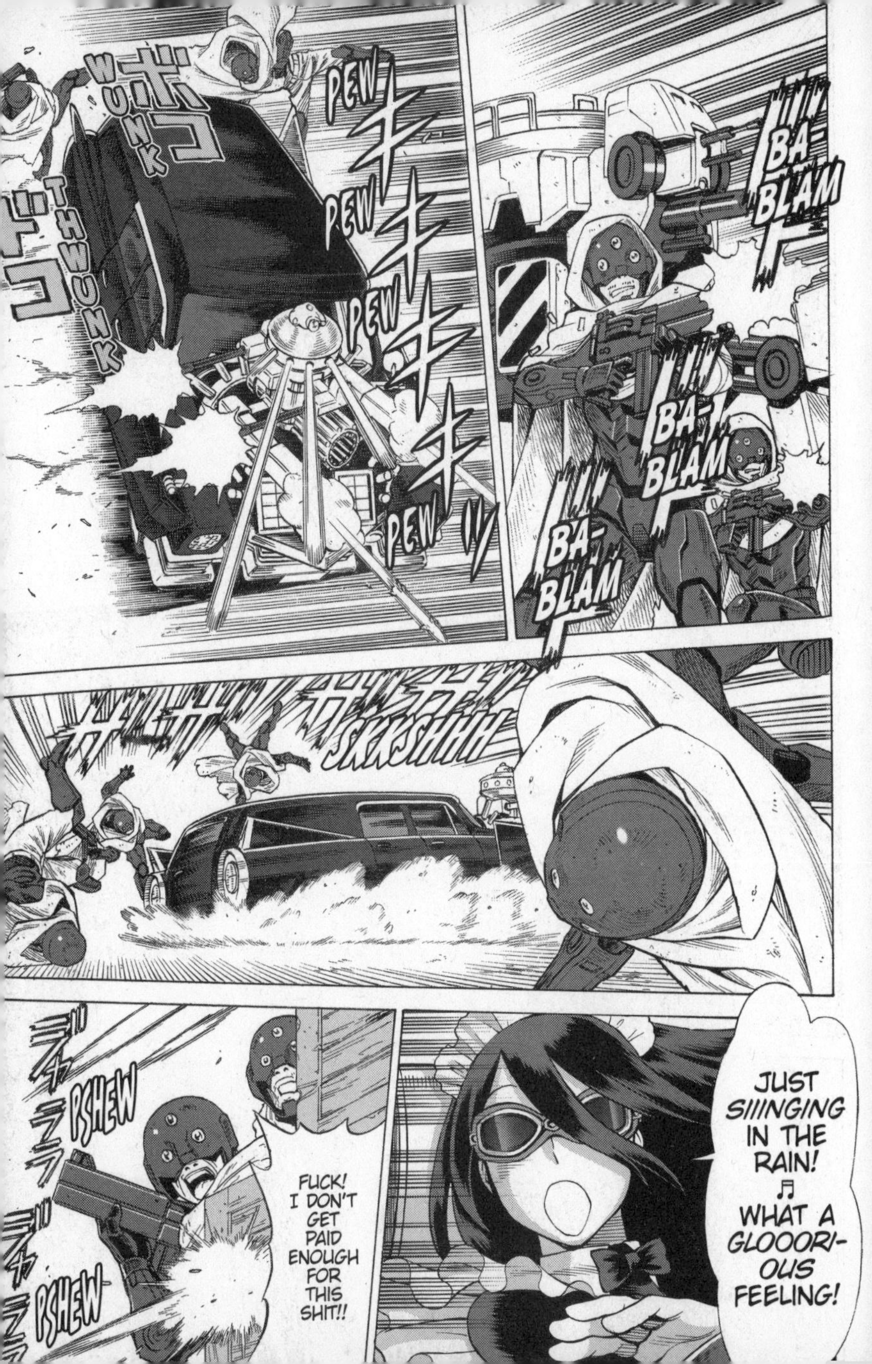
BA-BLAM
BA-BLAM
BA-BLAM
PEW
PEW
PEW
PEW
WUNK
THWUNK
SKRKSHHH
JUST SIIINGING IN THE RAIN! ♫ WHAT A GLOOORI-OUS FEELING!
FUCK! I DON'T GET PAID ENOUGH FOR THIS SHIT!!
PSHEW
PSHEW

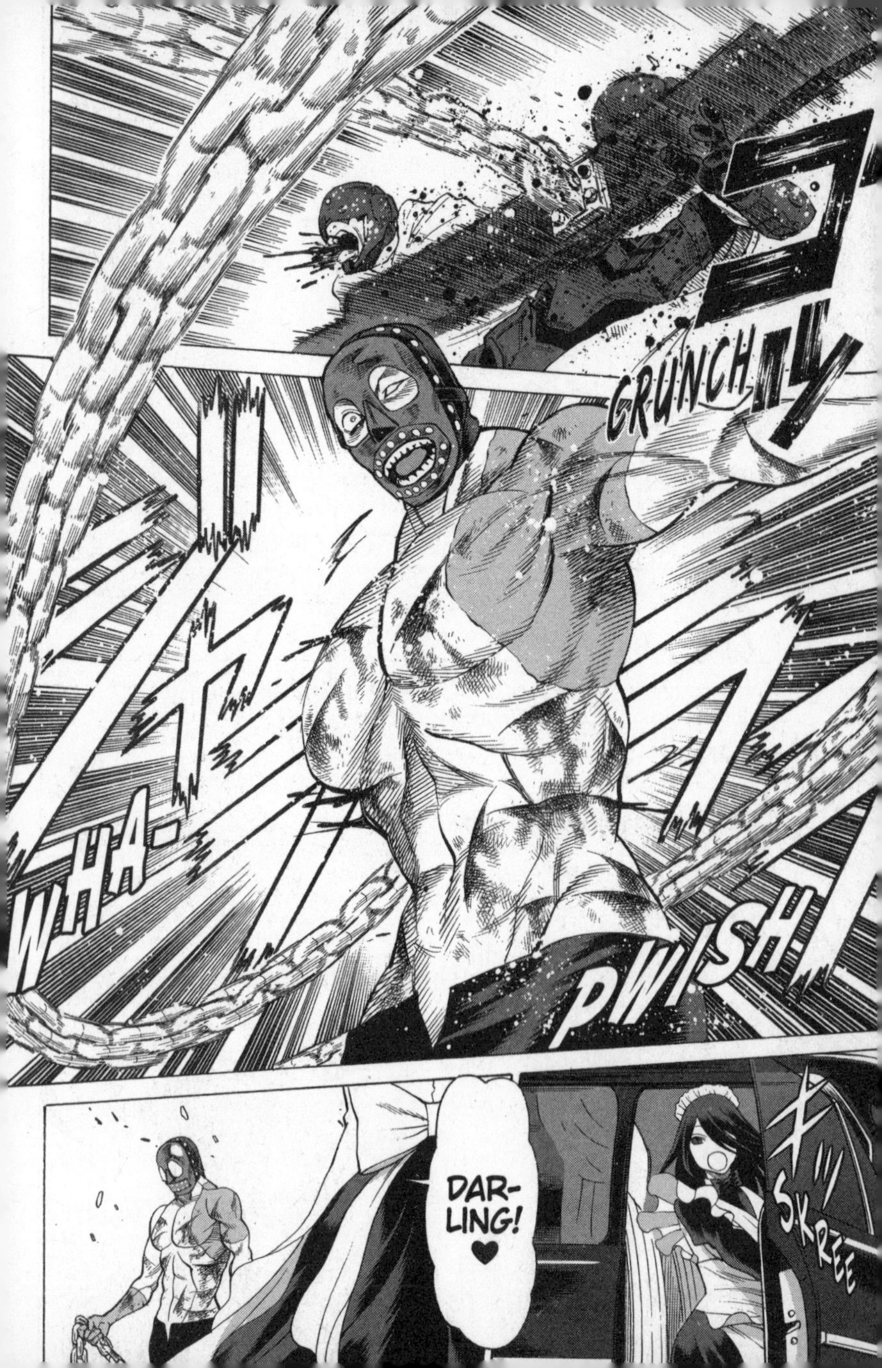

CRUNCH
WHA-
PWISH
SKREE
DAR-
LING!
♥

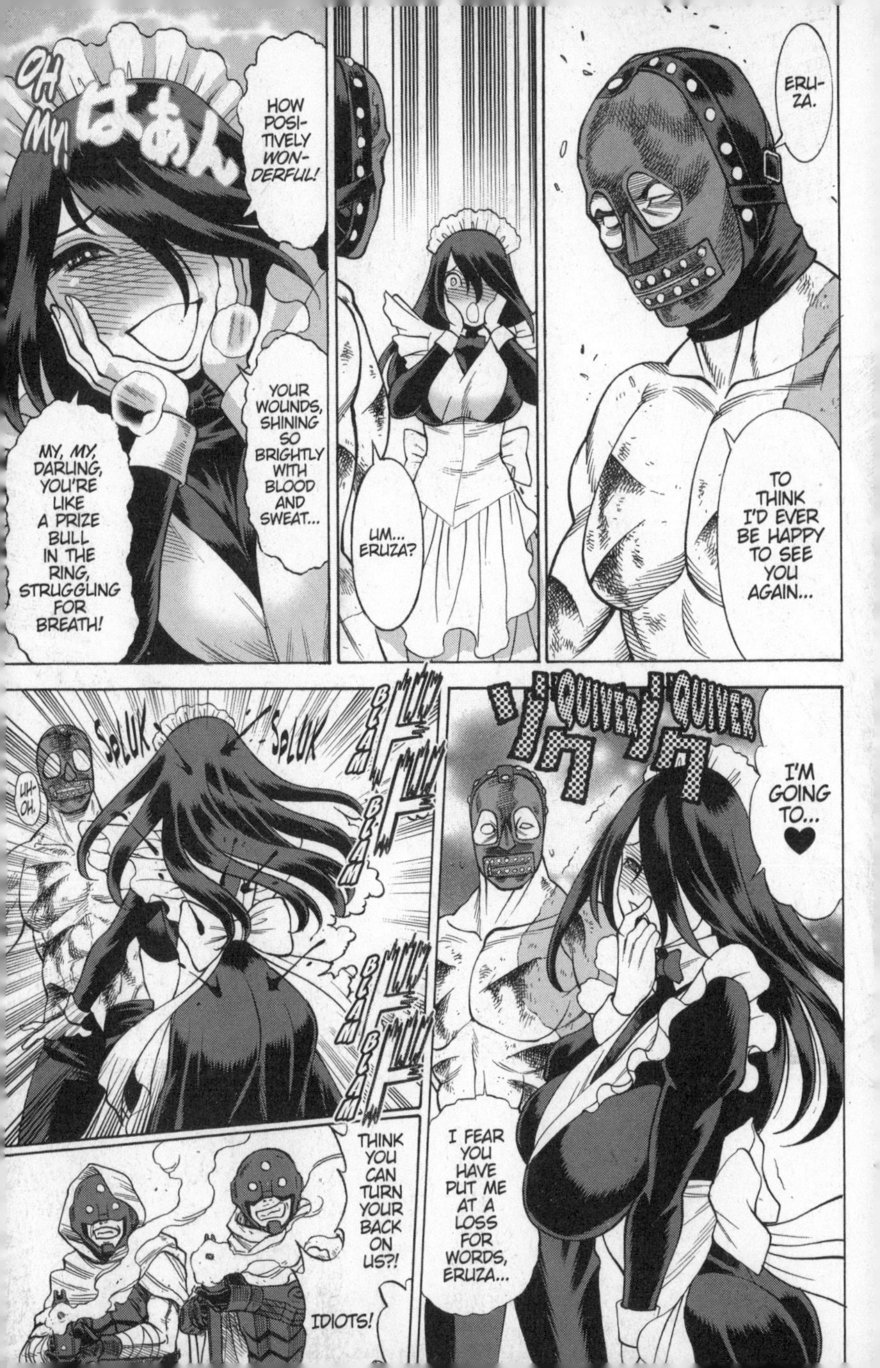
ERU-ZA.
TO THINK I'D EVER BE HAPPY TO SEE YOU AGAIN...
UM... ERUZA?
OH MY!
はあん
HOW POSITIVELY WONDERFUL!
YOUR WOUNDS, SHINING SO BRIGHTLY WITH BLOOD AND SWEAT...
MY, MY, DARLING, YOU'RE LIKE A PRIZE BULL IN THE RING, STRUGGLING FOR BREATH!
QUIVER QUIVER
I'M GOING TO... ♥
I FEAR YOU HAVE PUT ME AT A LOSS FOR WORDS, ERUZA...
BLAM BLAM
BLAM BLAM BLAM
SPLUK
SPLUK
UH-OH.
THINK YOU CAN TURN YOUR BACK ON US?!
IDIOTS!

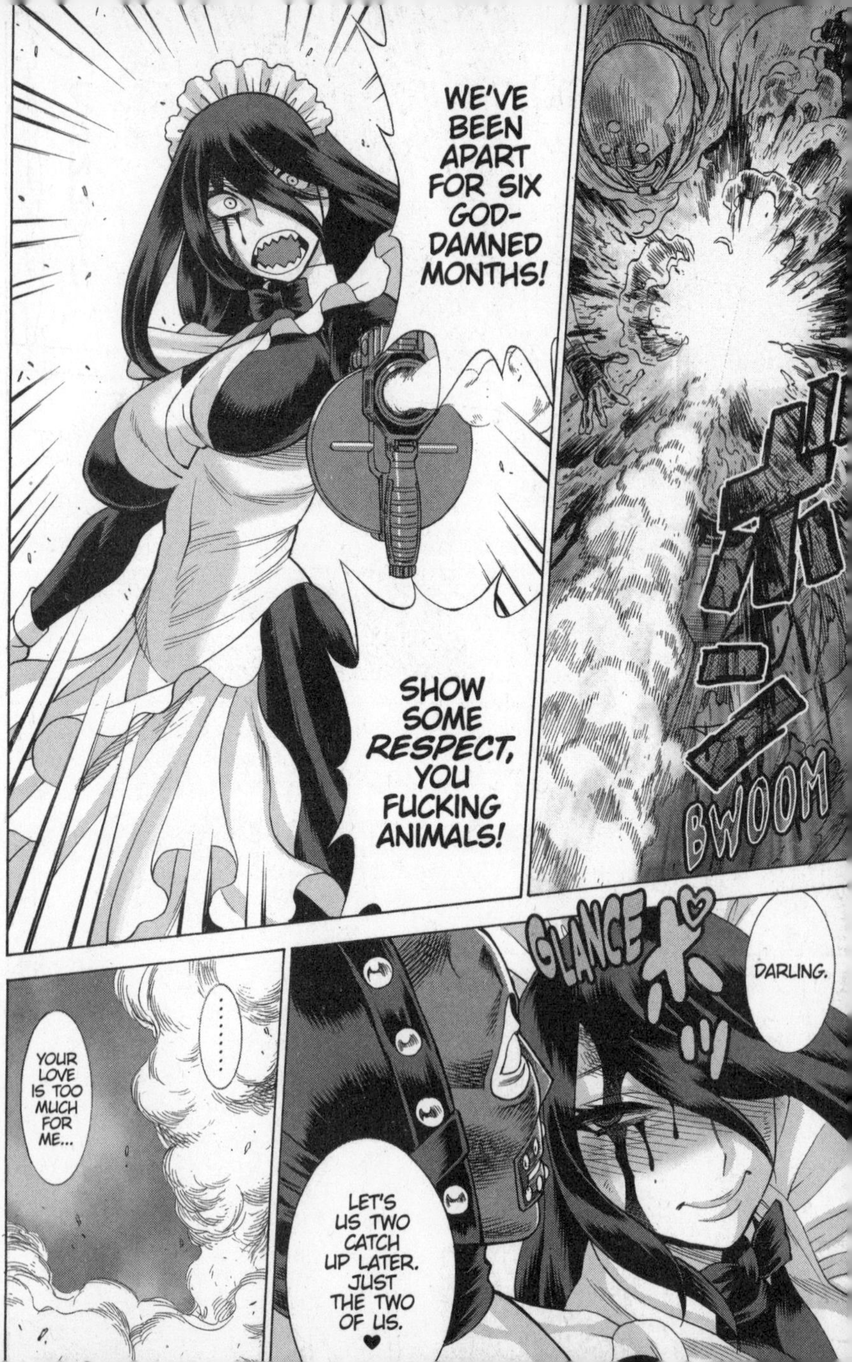
BWOOM
WE'VE BEEN APART FOR SIX GOD-DAMNED MONTHS!
SHOW SOME *RESPECT*, YOU FUCKING ANIMALS!
GLANCE
DARLING.
LET'S US TWO CATCH UP LATER. JUST THE TWO OF US. ♥
......
YOUR LOVE IS TOO MUCH FOR ME...

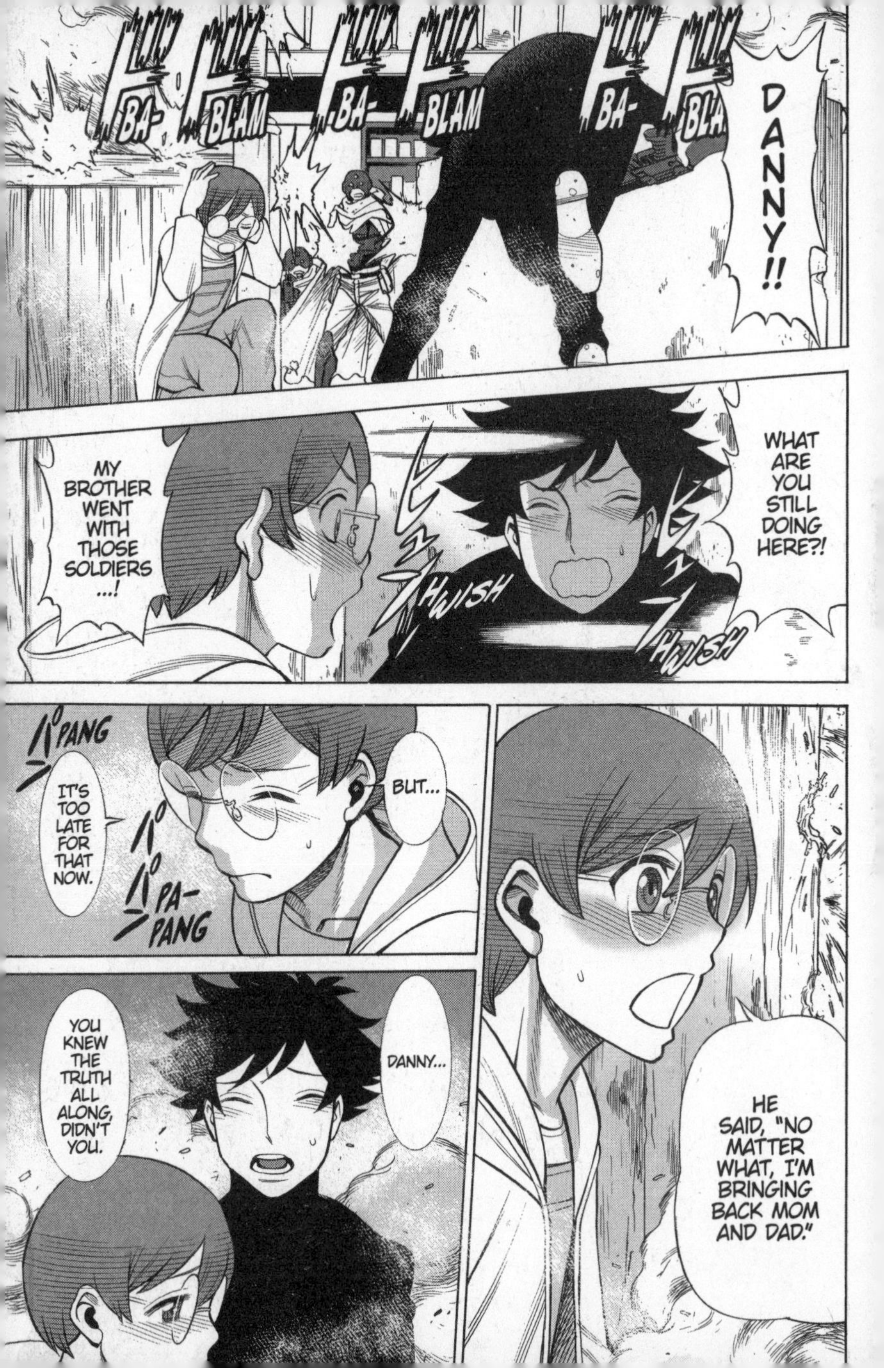
DANNY!!
BA-BLAM
BA-BLAM
BA-BLAM
WHAT ARE YOU STILL DOING HERE?!
HWISH
HWISH
MY BROTHER WENT WITH THOSE SOLDIERS ...!
HE SAID, "NO MATTER WHAT, I'M BRINGING BACK MOM AND DAD."
BUT...
PANG
IT'S TOO LATE FOR THAT NOW.
PA-PANG
DANNY...
YOU KNEW THE TRUTH ALL ALONG, DIDN'T YOU.

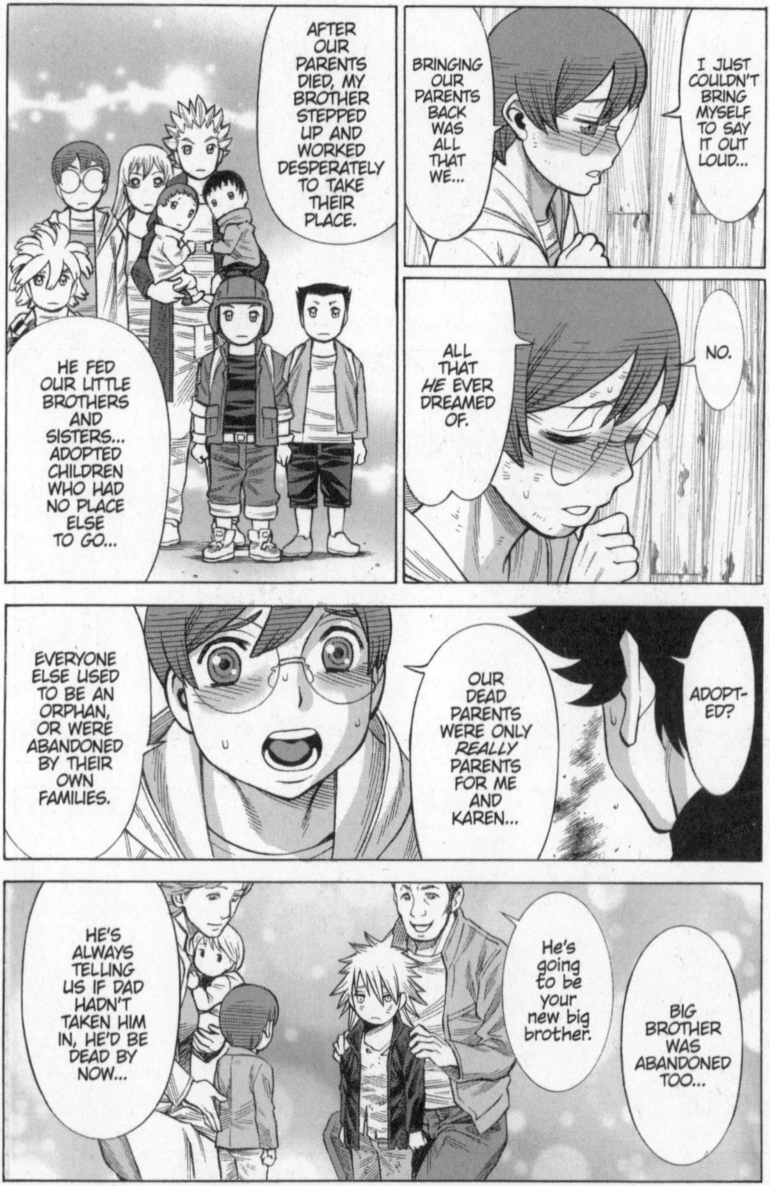
I JUST COULDN'T BRING MYSELF TO SAY IT OUT LOUD...
BRINGING OUR PARENTS BACK WAS ALL THAT WE...
NO.
ALL THAT *HE* EVER DREAMED OF.
AFTER OUR PARENTS DIED, MY BROTHER STEPPED UP AND WORKED DESPERATELY TO TAKE THEIR PLACE.
HE FED OUR LITTLE BROTHERS AND SISTERS... ADOPTED CHILDREN WHO HAD NO PLACE ELSE TO GO...
ADOPT-ED?
OUR DEAD PARENTS WERE ONLY *REALLY* PARENTS FOR ME AND KAREN...
EVERYONE ELSE USED TO BE AN ORPHAN, OR WERE ABANDONED BY THEIR OWN FAMILIES.
BIG BROTHER WAS ABANDONED TOO...
He's going to be your new big brother.
HE'S ALWAYS TELLING US IF DAD HADN'T TAKEN HIM IN, HE'D BE DEAD BY NOW...

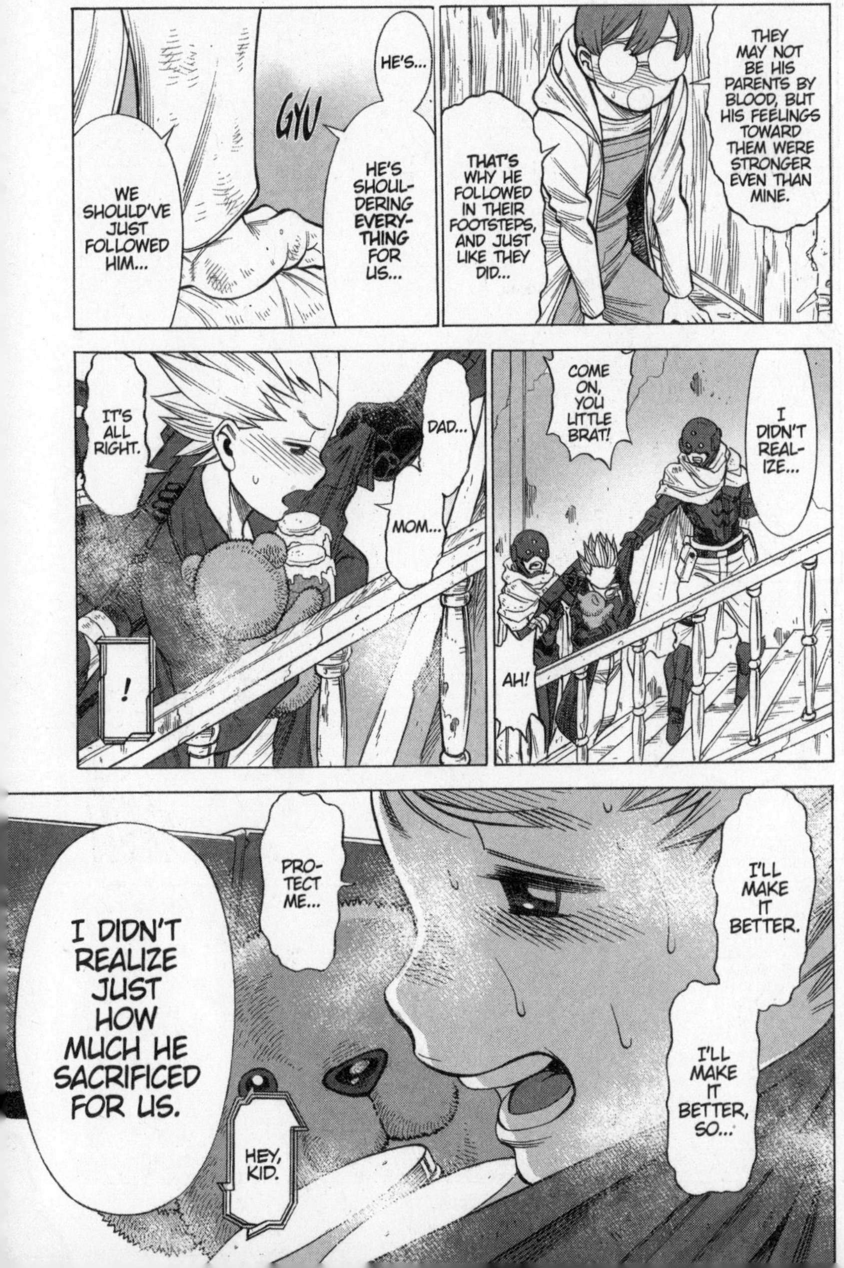
THEY MAY NOT BE HIS PARENTS BY BLOOD, BUT HIS FEELINGS TOWARD THEM WERE STRONGER EVEN THAN MINE.
THAT'S WHY HE FOLLOWED IN THEIR FOOTSTEPS, AND JUST LIKE THEY DID...
HE'S...
GYU
HE'S SHOULDERING EVERYTHING FOR US...
WE SHOULD'VE JUST FOLLOWED HIM...
I DIDN'T REALIZE...
COME ON, YOU LITTLE BRAT!
AH!
DAD...
MOM...
IT'S ALL RIGHT.
!
I'LL MAKE IT BETTER.
I'LL MAKE IT BETTER, SO...
PROTECT ME...
HEY, KID.
I DIDN'T REALIZE JUST HOW MUCH HE SACRIFICED FOR US.

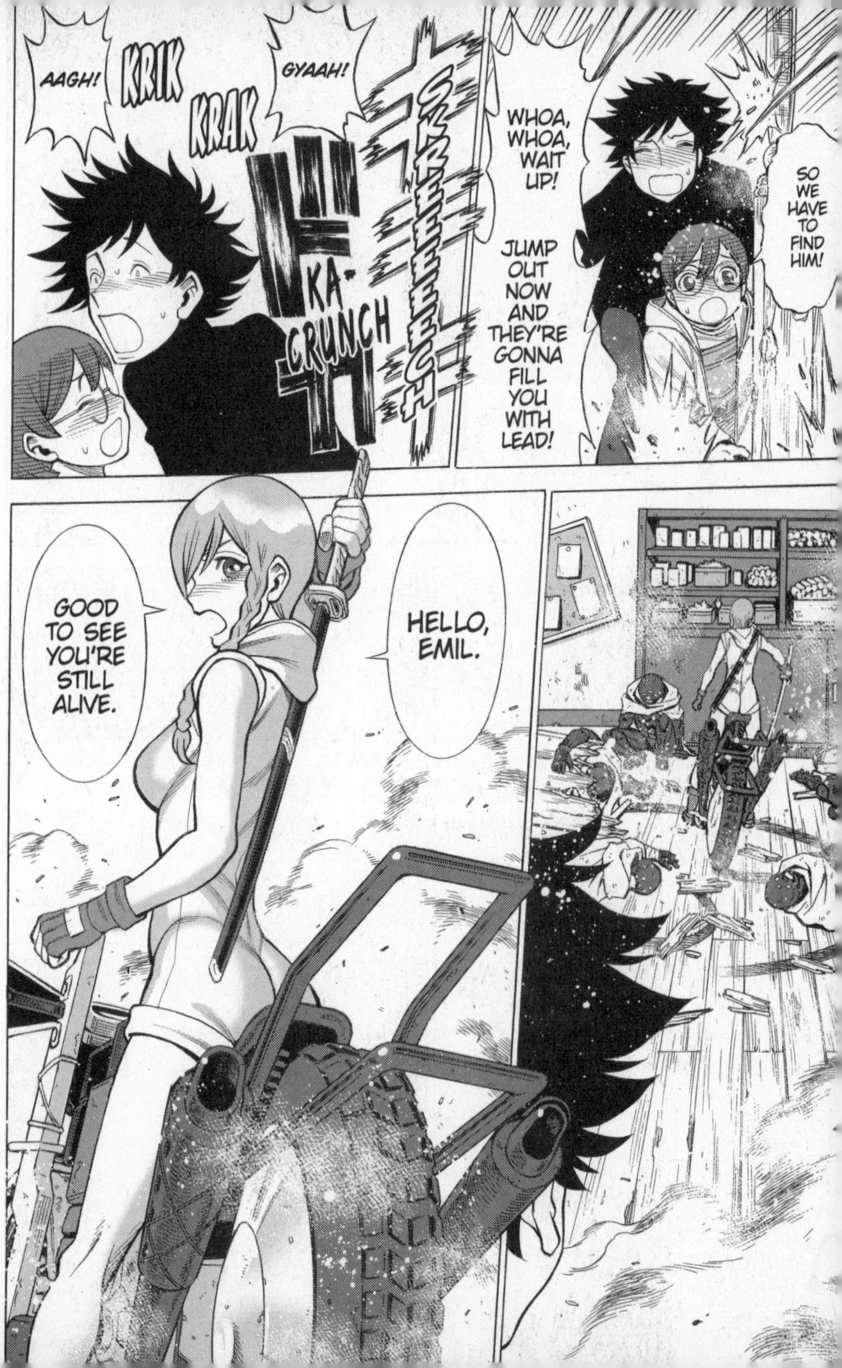
SO WE HAVE TO FIND HIM!
WHOA, WHOA, WAIT UP!
JUMP OUT NOW AND THEY'RE GONNA FILL YOU WITH LEAD!
SKREEEEECH
GYAAH!
KA-CRUNCH
KRIK
KRAK
AAGH!
HELLO, EMIL.
GOOD TO SEE YOU'RE STILL ALIVE.

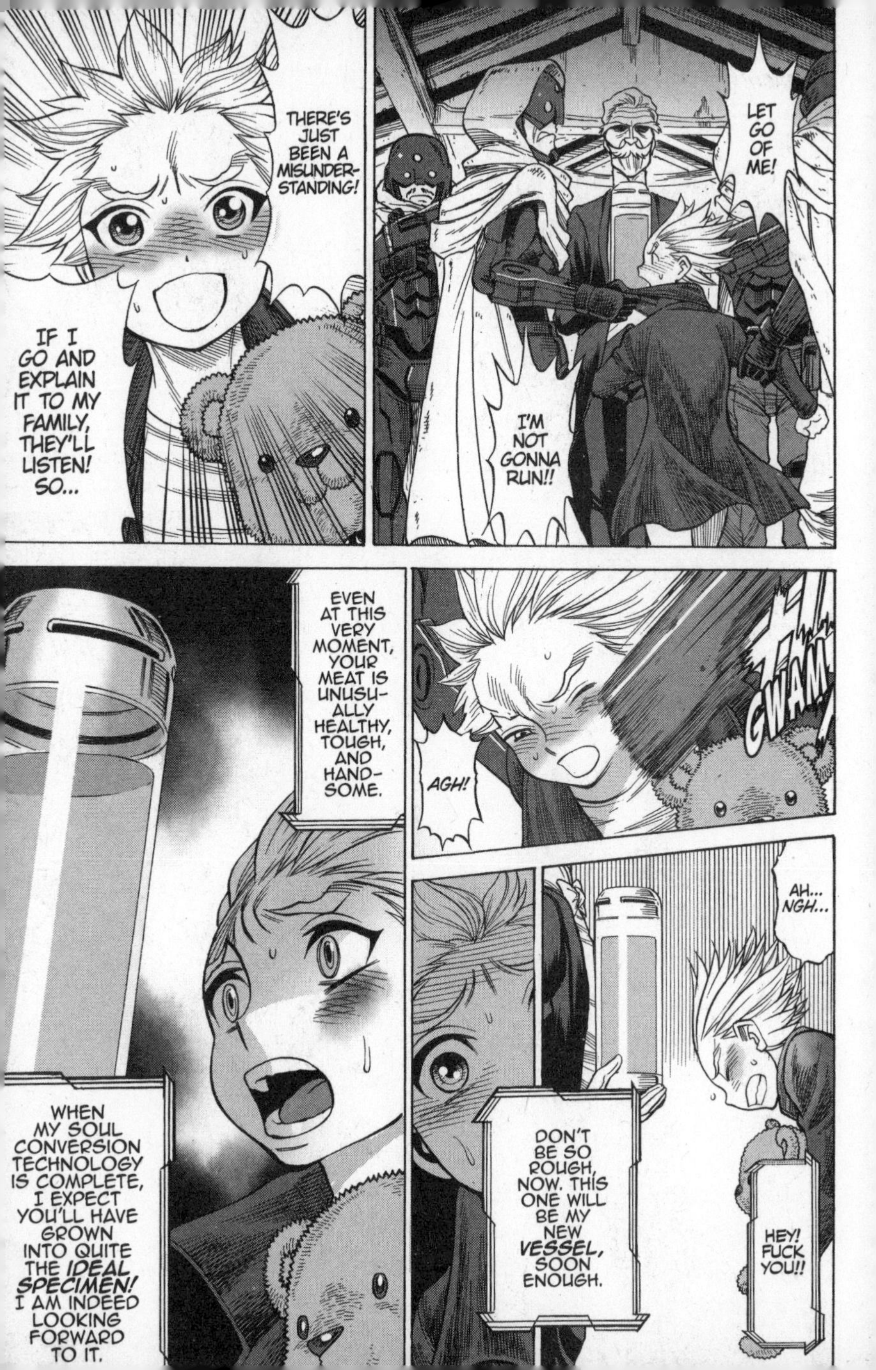
LET GO OF ME!
I'M NOT GONNA RUN!!
THERE'S JUST BEEN A MISUNDERSTANDING!
IF I GO AND EXPLAIN IT TO MY FAMILY, THEY'LL LISTEN! SO...
CWAM
AGH!
AH... NGH...
HEY! FUCK YOU!!
DON'T BE SO ROUGH, NOW. THIS ONE WILL BE MY NEW *VESSEL,* SOON ENOUGH.
EVEN AT THIS VERY MOMENT, YOUR MEAT IS UNUSUALLY HEALTHY, TOUGH, AND HANDSOME.
WHEN MY SOUL CONVERSION TECHNOLOGY IS COMPLETE, I EXPECT YOU'LL HAVE GROWN INTO QUITE THE *IDEAL SPECIMEN!* I AM INDEED LOOKING FORWARD TO IT.

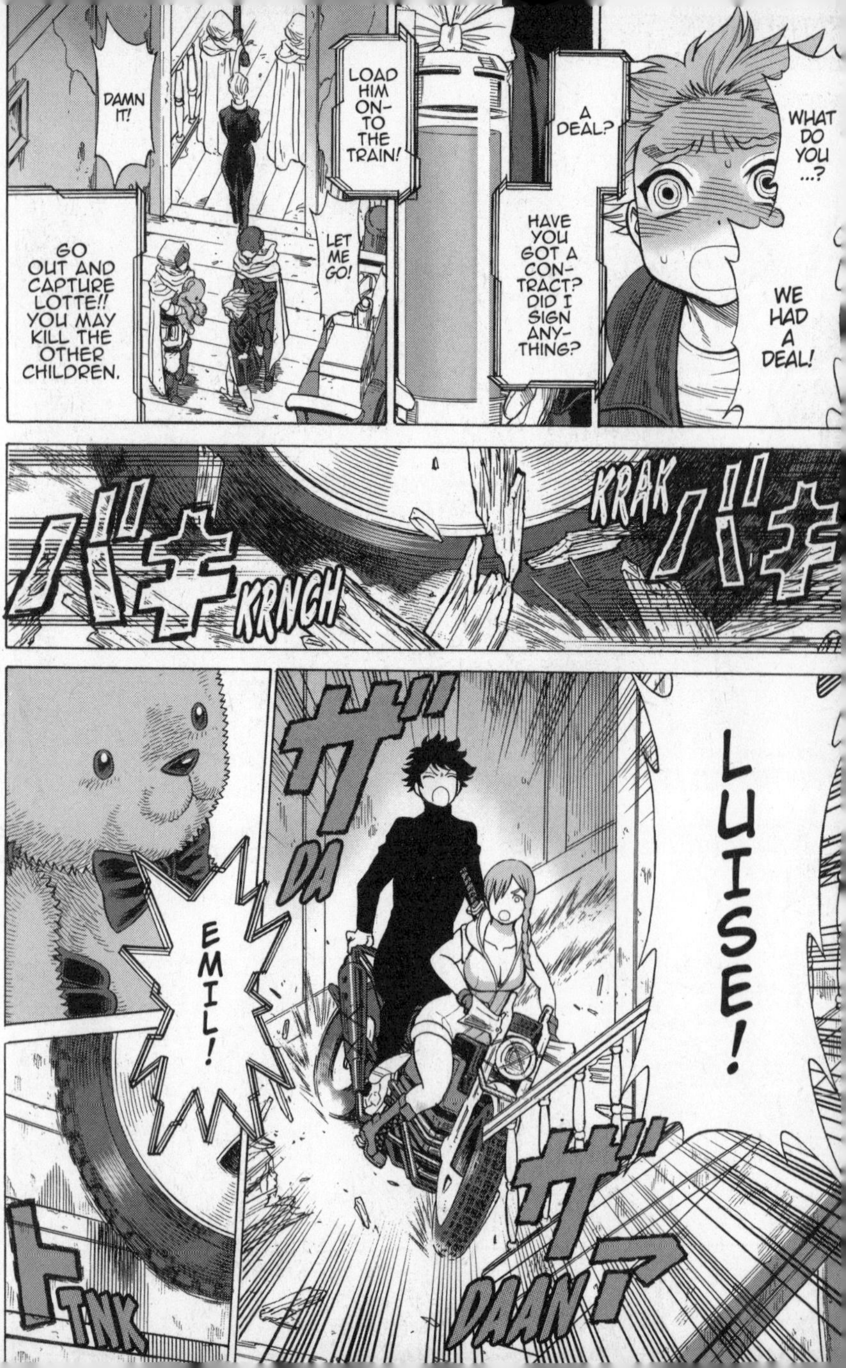
WHAT DO YOU ...?
WE HAD A DEAL!
A DEAL?
HAVE YOU GOT A CONTRACT? DID I SIGN ANYTHING?
LOAD HIM ON-TO THE TRAIN!
LET ME GO!
DAMN IT!
GO OUT AND CAPTURE LOTTE!! YOU MAY KILL THE OTHER CHILDREN.
パキ
KRAK
パキ
KRNCH
LUISE!
ザッ
DA
EMIL!
ザッ
DAAN
ト
TINK

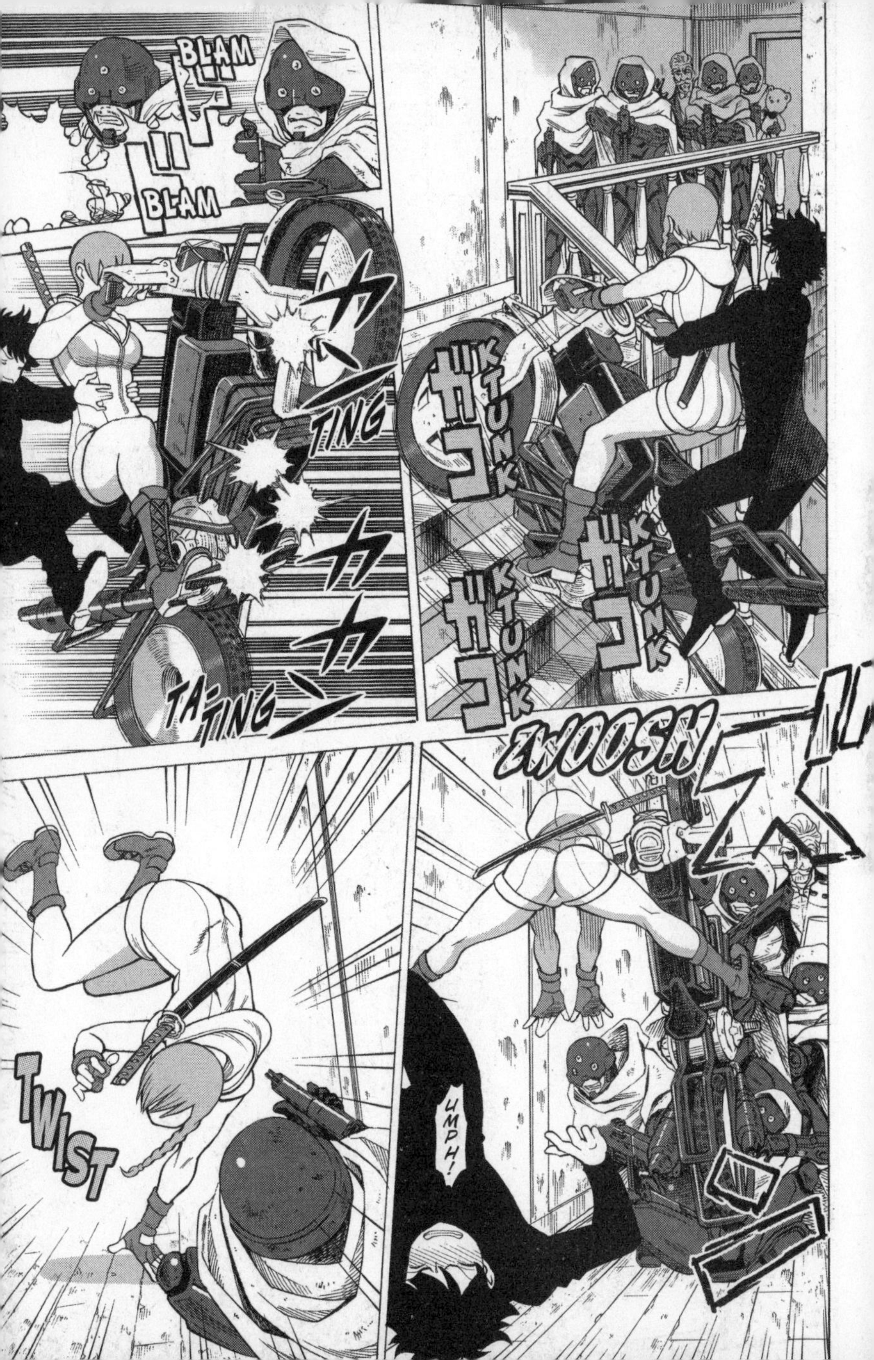
KTUNK
KTUNK
KTUNK
BLAM
BLAM
TING
TA-TING
ZWOOSH
UMPH!
TWIST

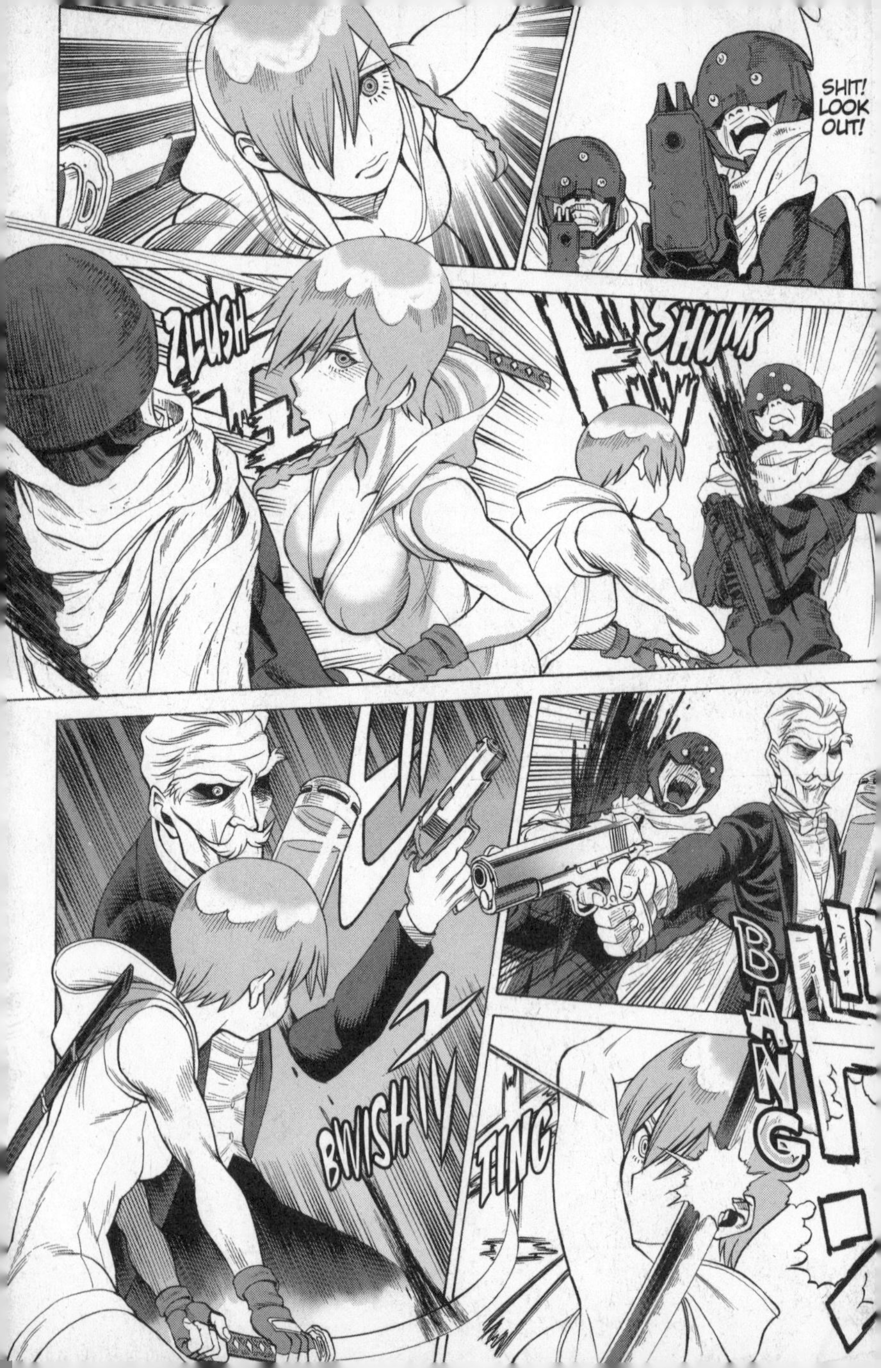
SHIT! LOOK OUT!
SHUNK
ZLUSH
BANG
TING
BWISH

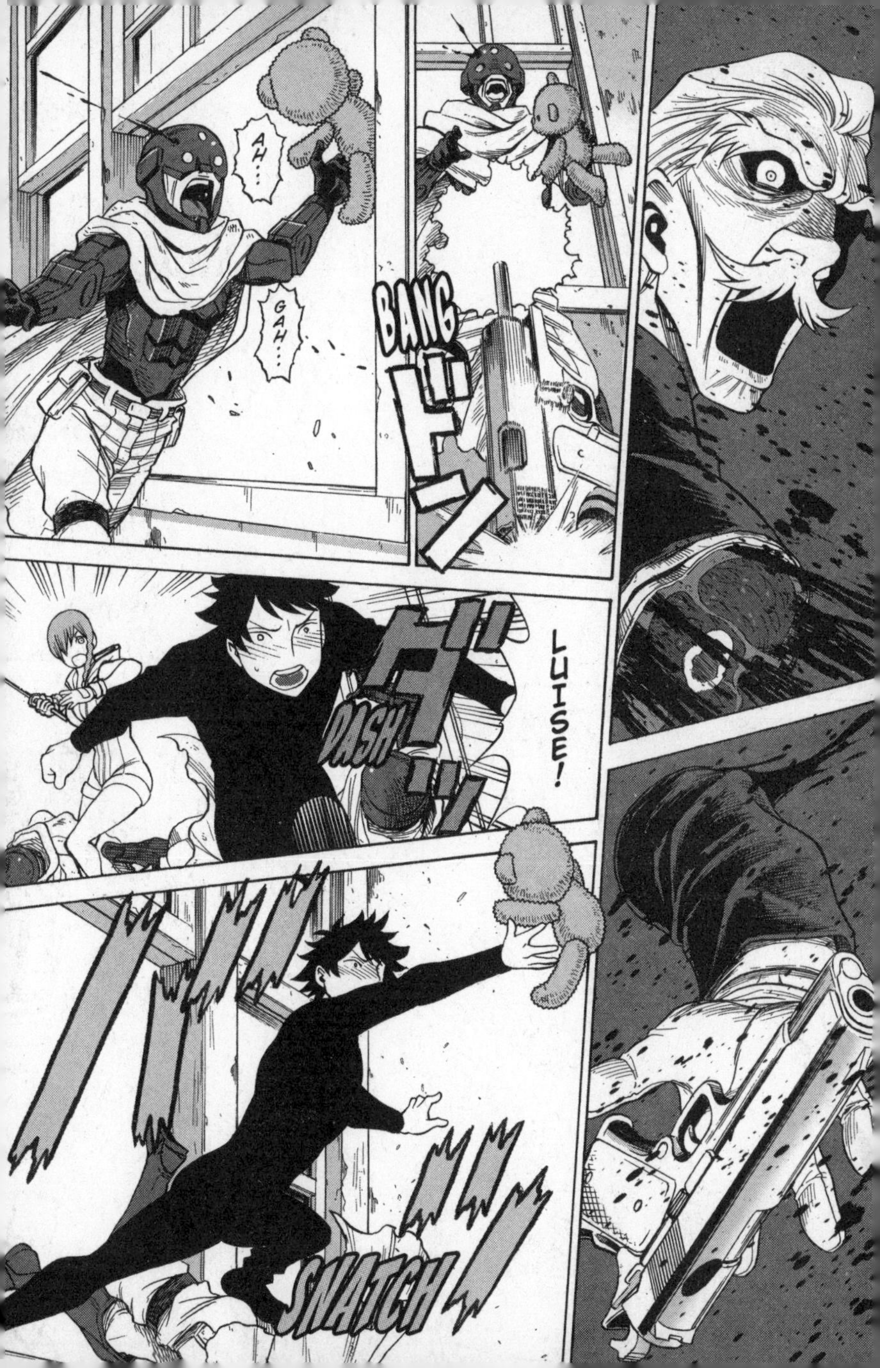

BANG
AH...
GAH...
LUISE!
DASH
SNATCH

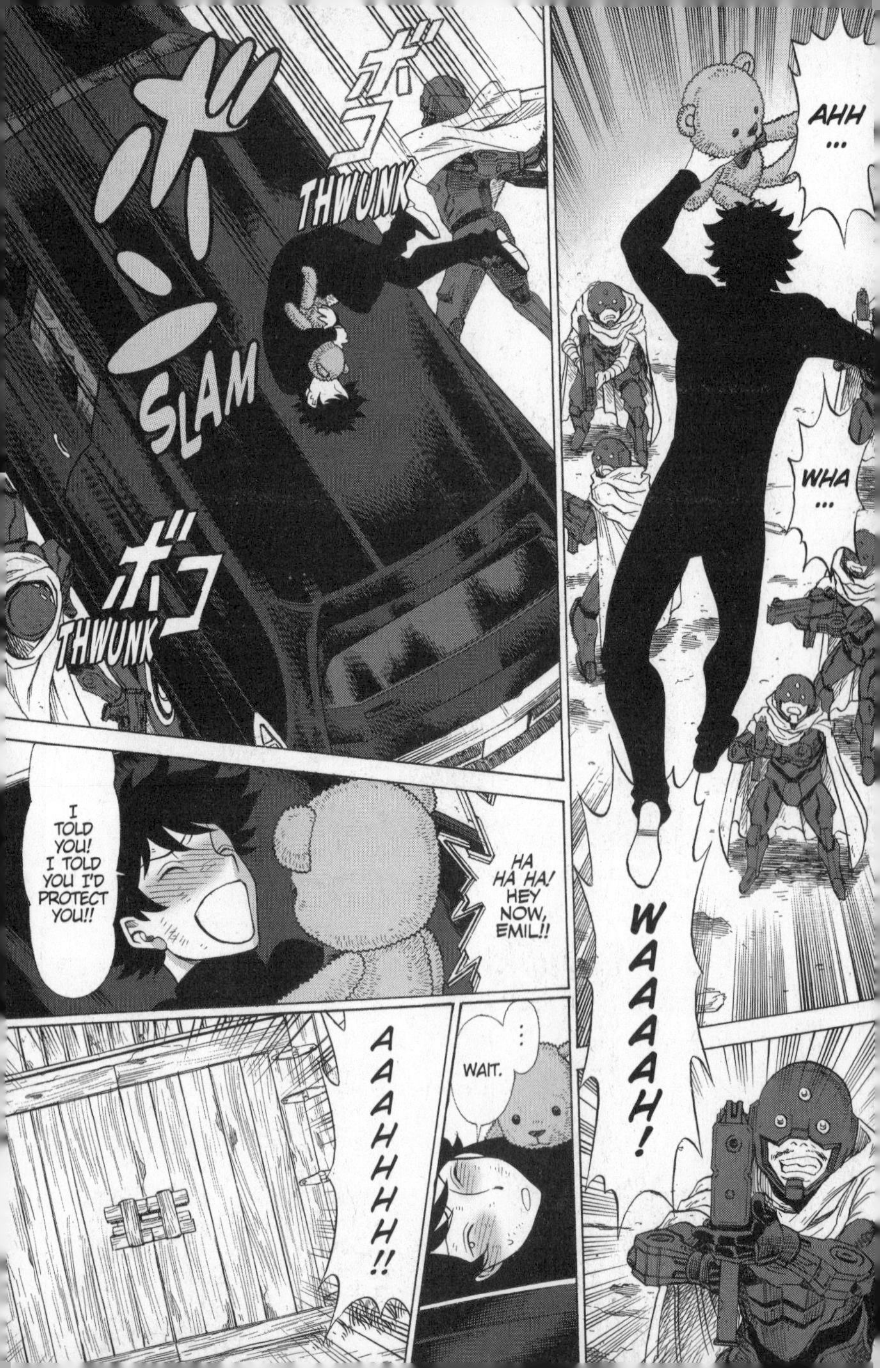

AHH ...
WHA ...
WAAAAAH!
ボコ
THWUNK
SLAM
ボコ
THWUNK
HA HA HA! HEY NOW, EMIL!!
I TOLD YOU! I TOLD YOU I'D PROTECT YOU!!
... WAIT.
AAAAHHHHH!!

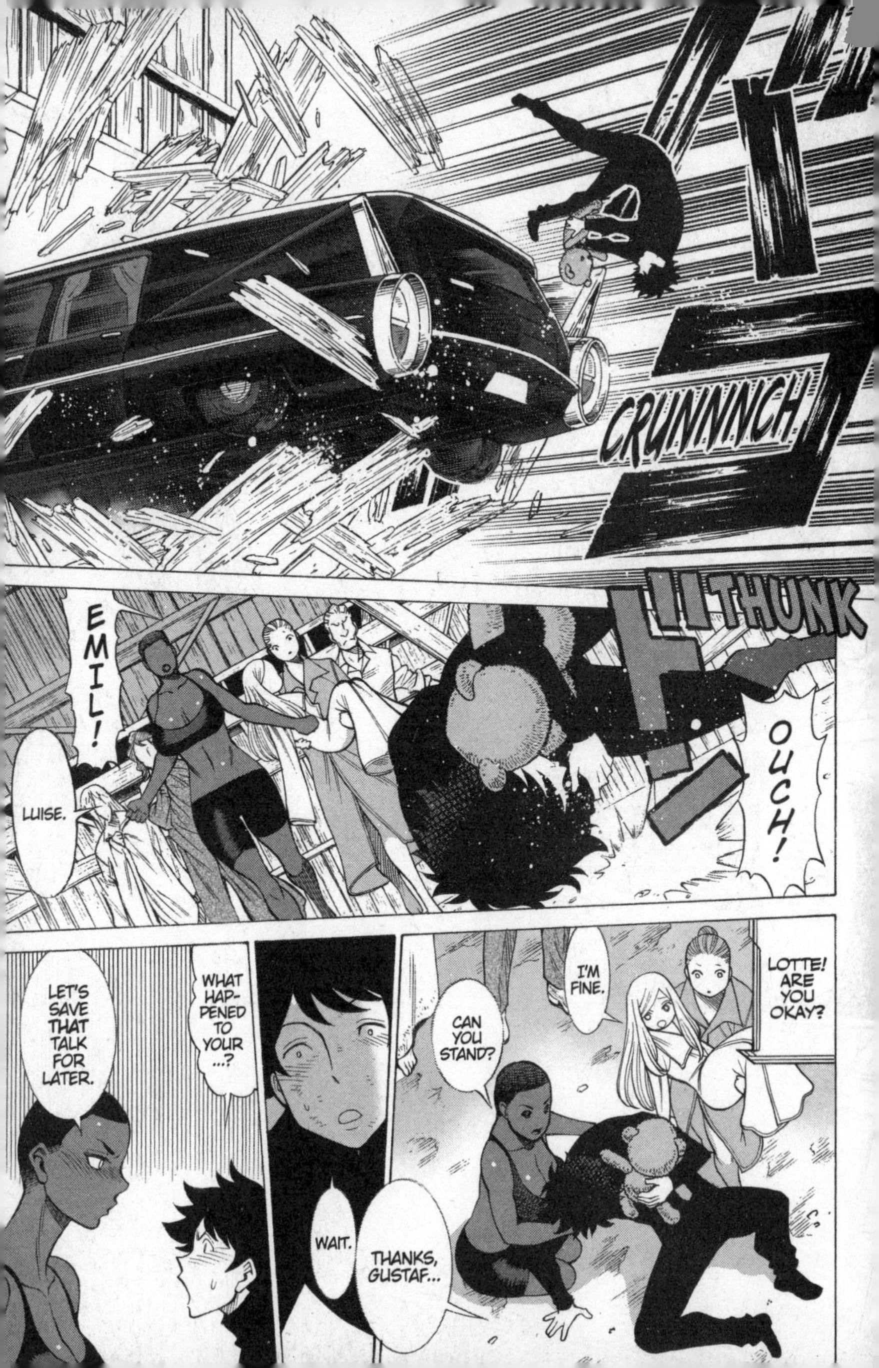
CRUNNNCH
THUNK
OUCH!
EMIL!
LUISE.
LOTTE! ARE YOU OKAY?
I'M FINE.
CAN YOU STAND?
THANKS, GUSTAF...
WAIT.
WHAT HAP-PENED TO YOUR ...?
LET'S SAVE THAT TALK FOR LATER.

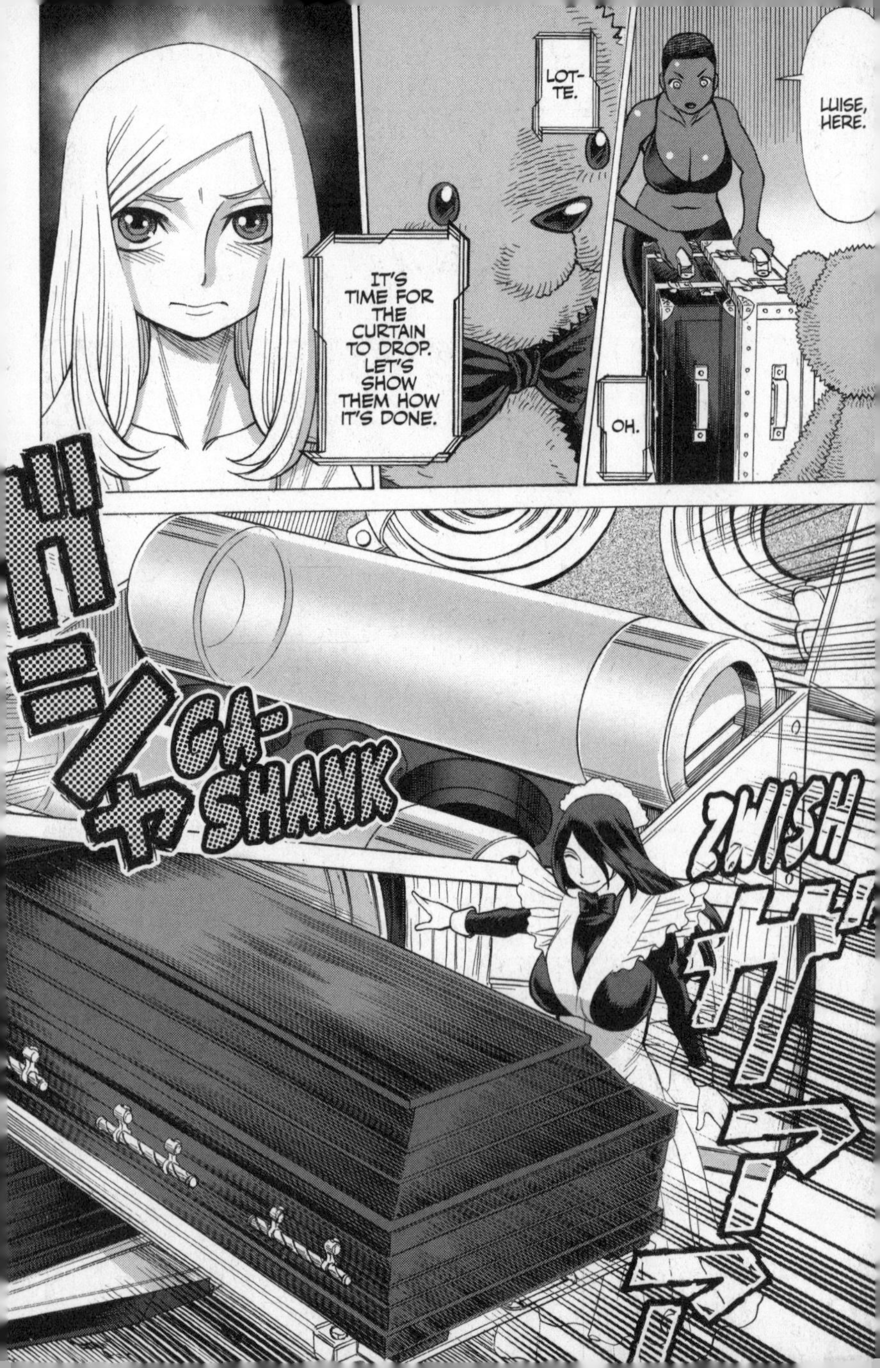
LUISE, HERE.
OH.
LOT-TE.
IT'S TIME FOR THE CURTAIN TO DROP. LET'S SHOW THEM HOW IT'S DONE.
ZWISH
CA-SHANK

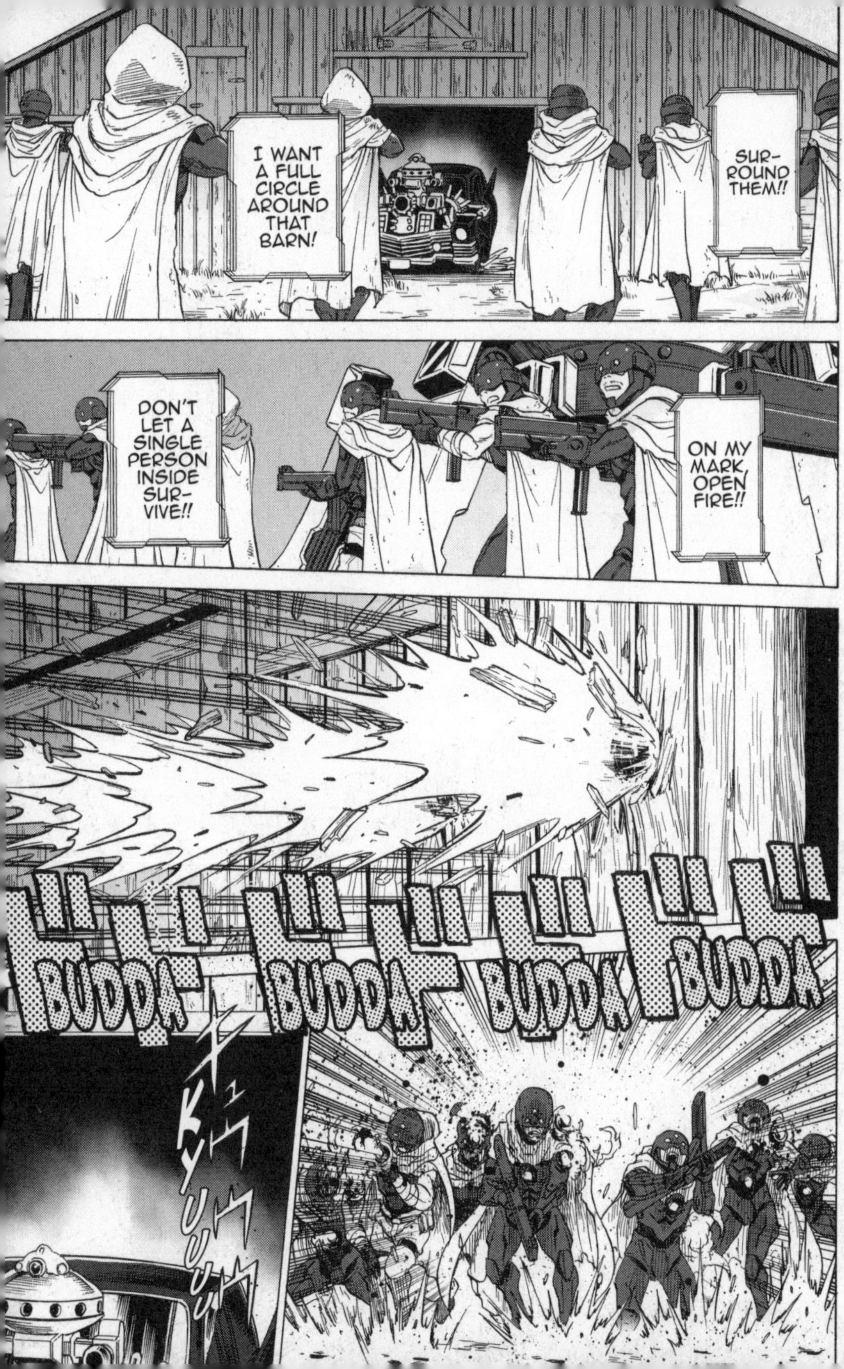
SUR-ROUND THEM!!
I WANT A FULL CIRCLE AROUND THAT BARN!
ON MY MARK, OPEN FIRE!!
DON'T LET A SINGLE PERSON INSIDE SUR-VIVE!!
BUDDA BUDDA BUDDA BUDDA
KYUUUU

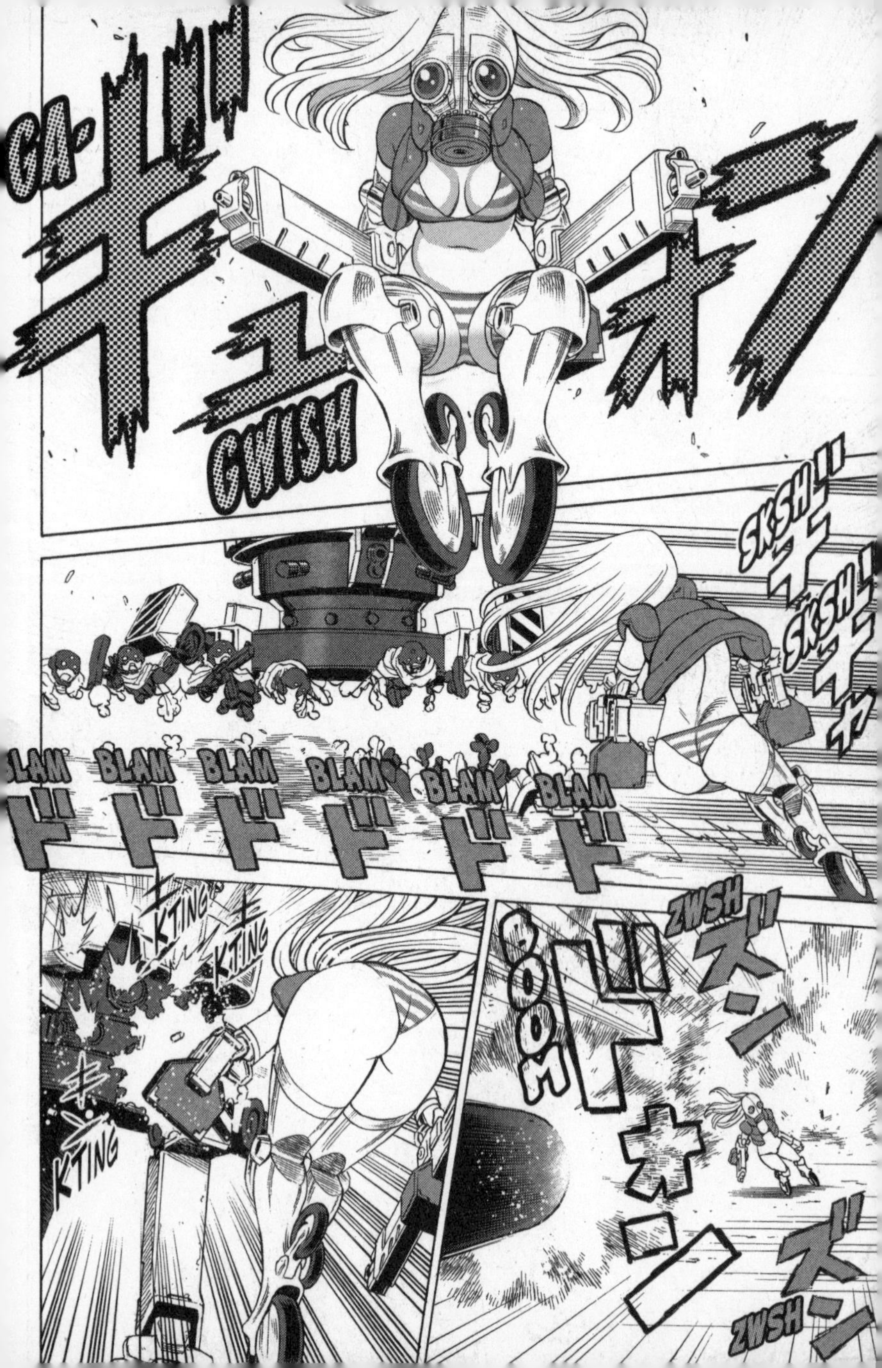
CA-
CWISH
SKSH!!
SKSH!!
BLAM
BLAM
BLAM
BLAM
BLAM
BLAM
ZWSH
BOOM
ZWSH
KTING
KTING
KTING

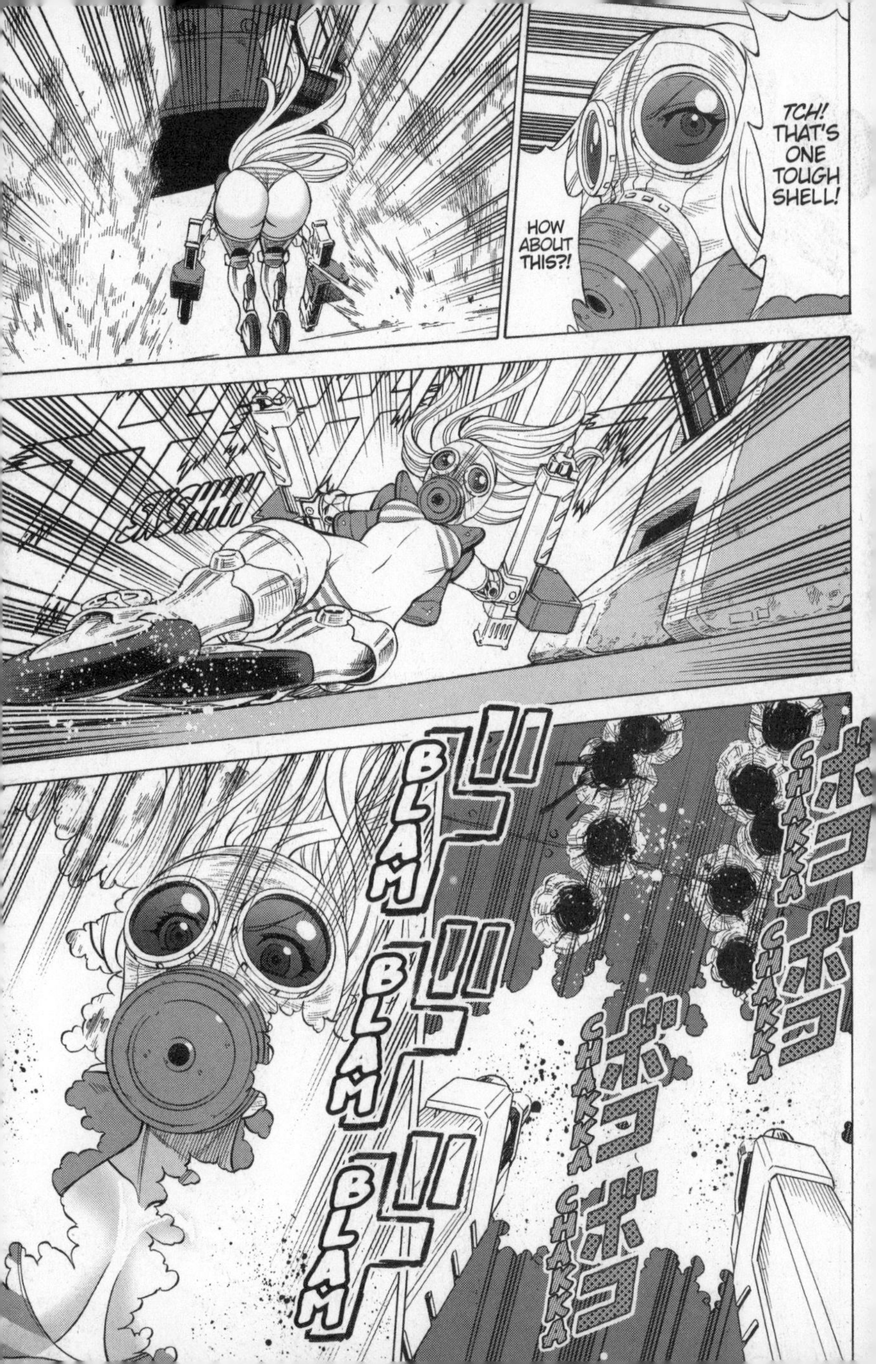
TCH! THAT'S ONE TOUGH SHELL!
HOW ABOUT THIS?!
ボコボコ
CHAKKA CHAKKA
ボコボコ
CHAKKA CHAKKA
BLAM BLAM BLAM

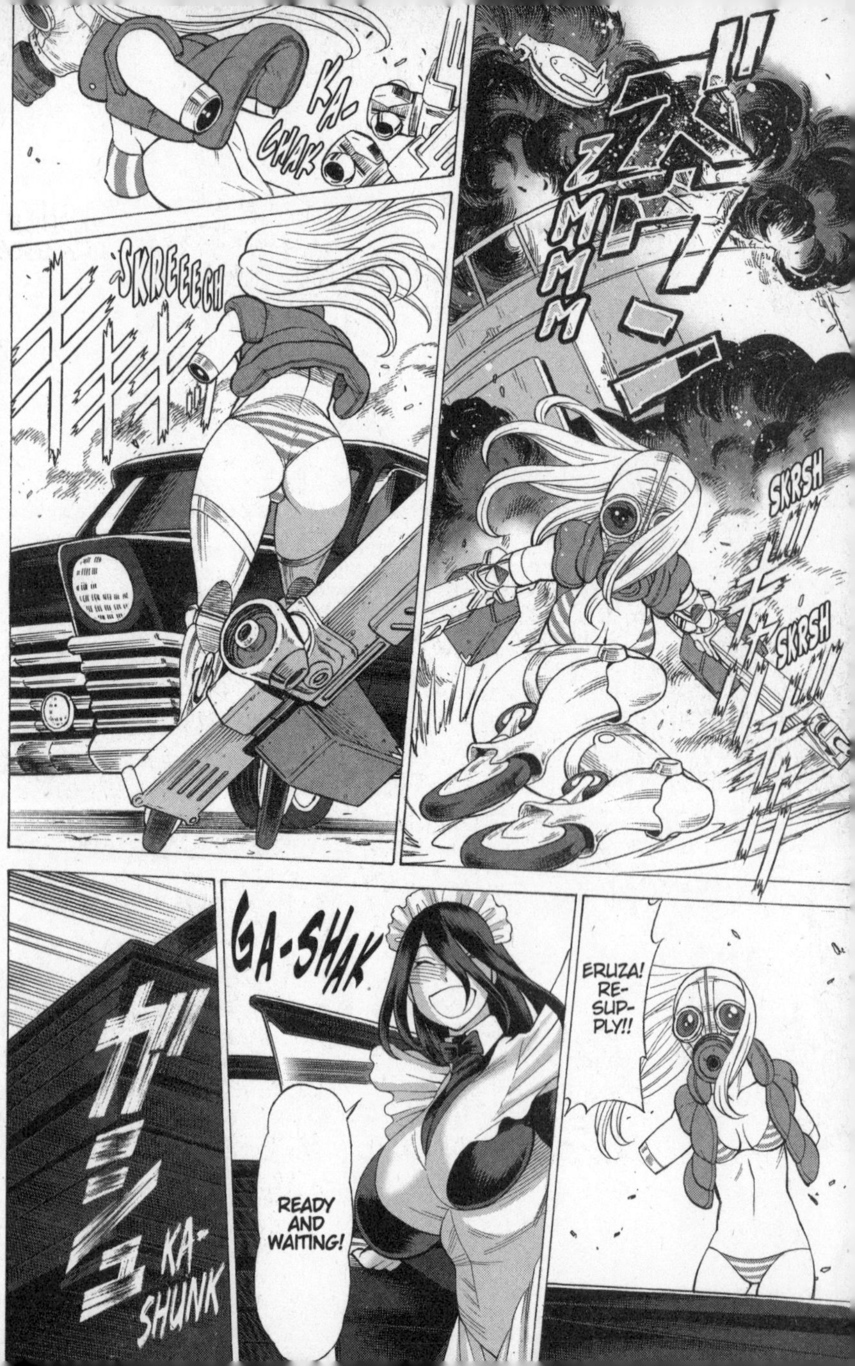
ZMMM
SKRSH
SKRSH
KA-CHAK
SKREEECH
ERUZA! RE-SUP-PLY!!
GA-SHAK
READY AND WAITING!
KA-SHUNK

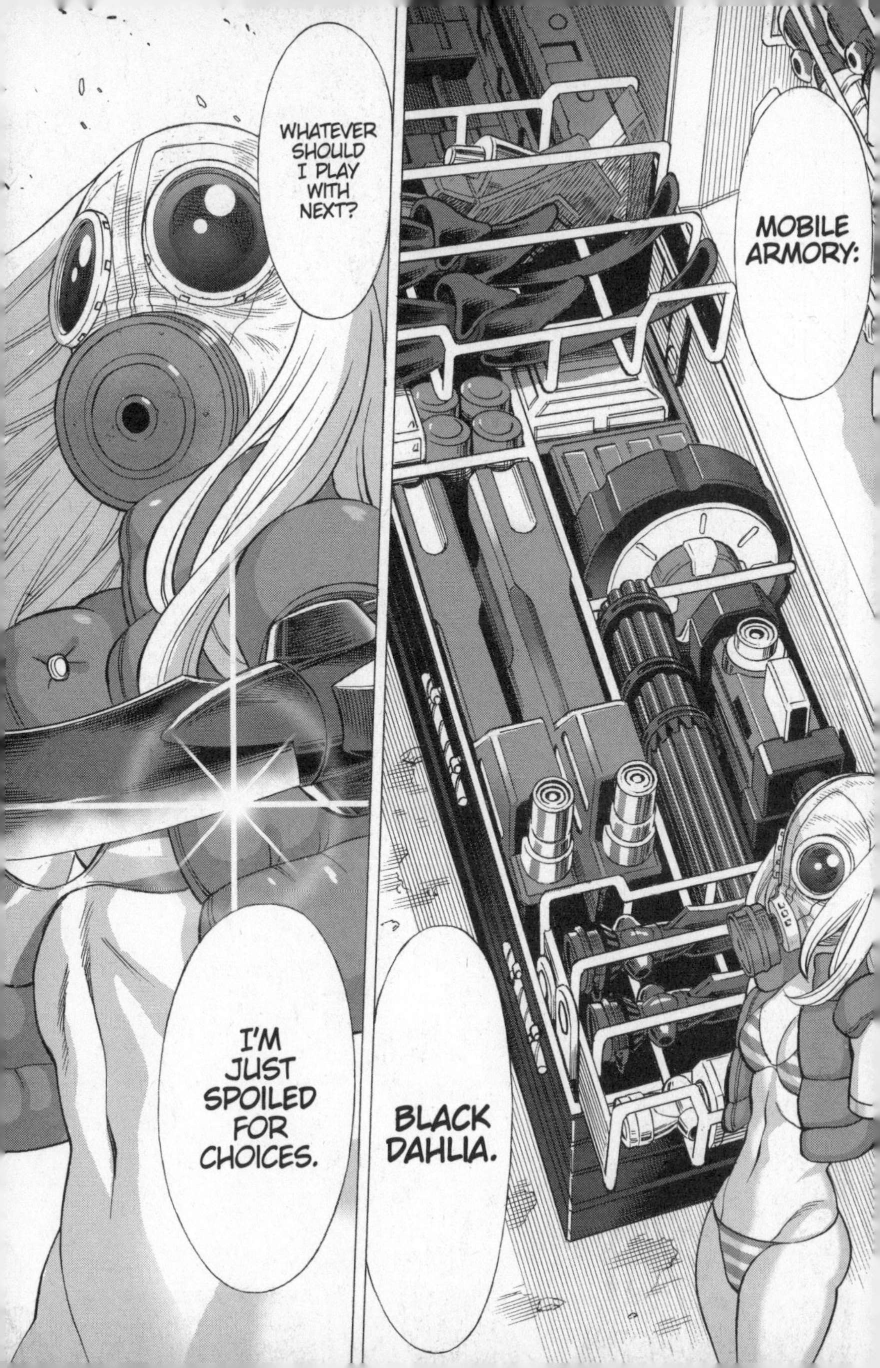
MOBILE ARMORY:
BLACK DAHLIA.
WHATEVER SHOULD I PLAY WITH NEXT?
I'M JUST SPOILED FOR CHOICES.

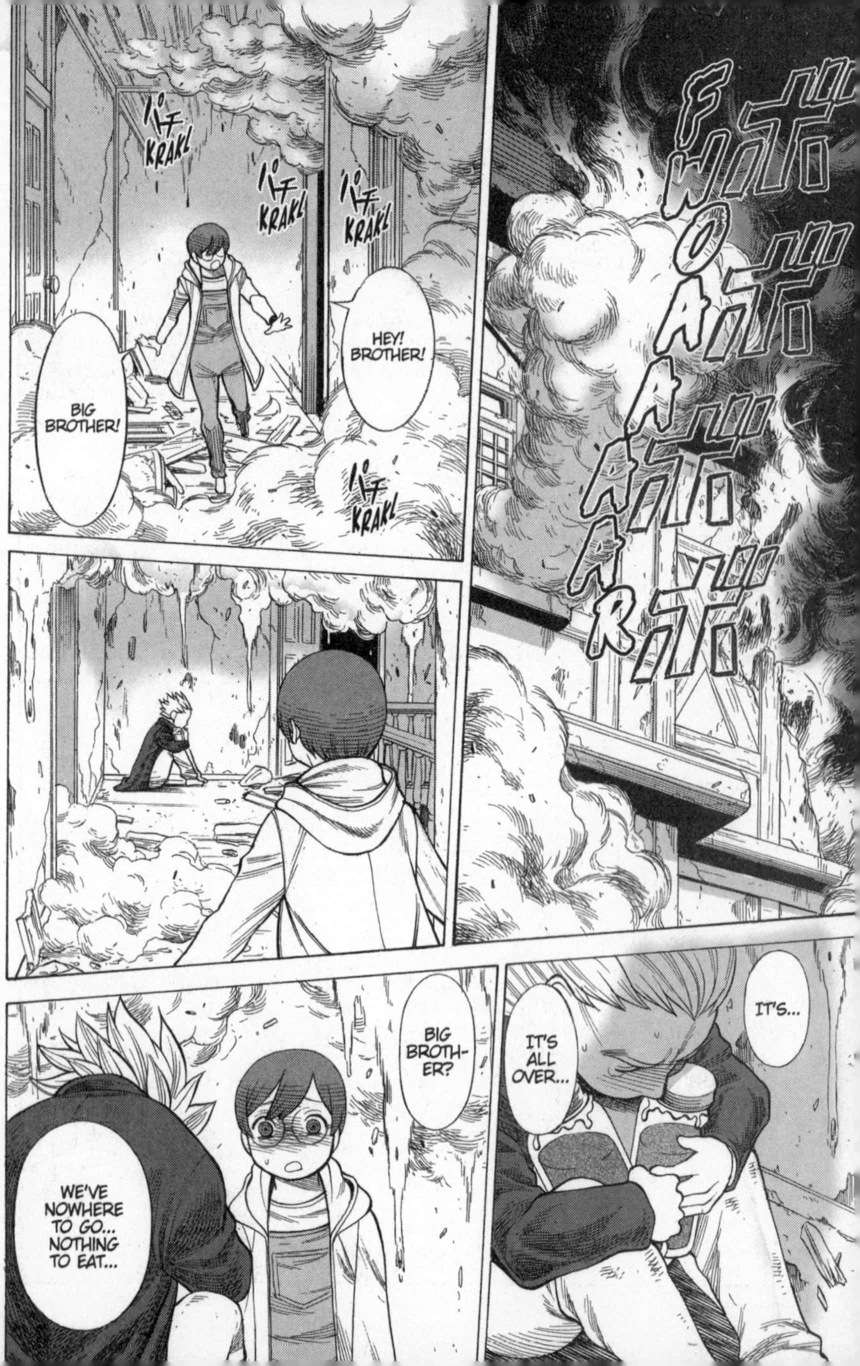
FWOAAAR
HEY! BROTHER!
KRAKL
KRAKL
KRAKL
BIG BROTHER!
KRAKL
IT'S...
IT'S ALL OVER...
BIG BROTH-ER?
WE'VE NOWHERE TO GO... NOTHING TO EAT...

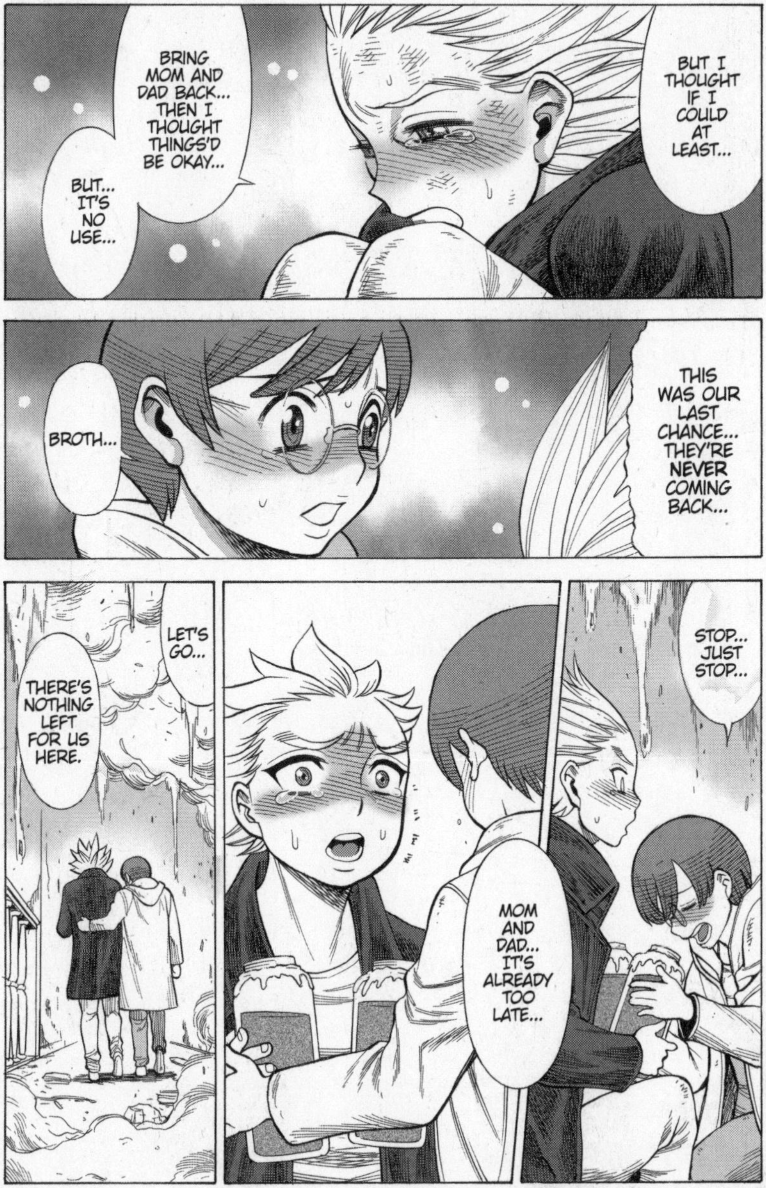
BUT I THOUGHT IF I COULD AT LEAST...
BRING MOM AND DAD BACK... THEN I THOUGHT THINGS'D BE OKAY...
BUT... IT'S NO USE...
THIS WAS OUR LAST CHANCE... THEY'RE NEVER COMING BACK...
BROTH...
STOP... JUST STOP...
MOM AND DAD... IT'S ALREADY TOO LATE...
LET'S GO...
THERE'S NOTHING LEFT FOR US HERE.

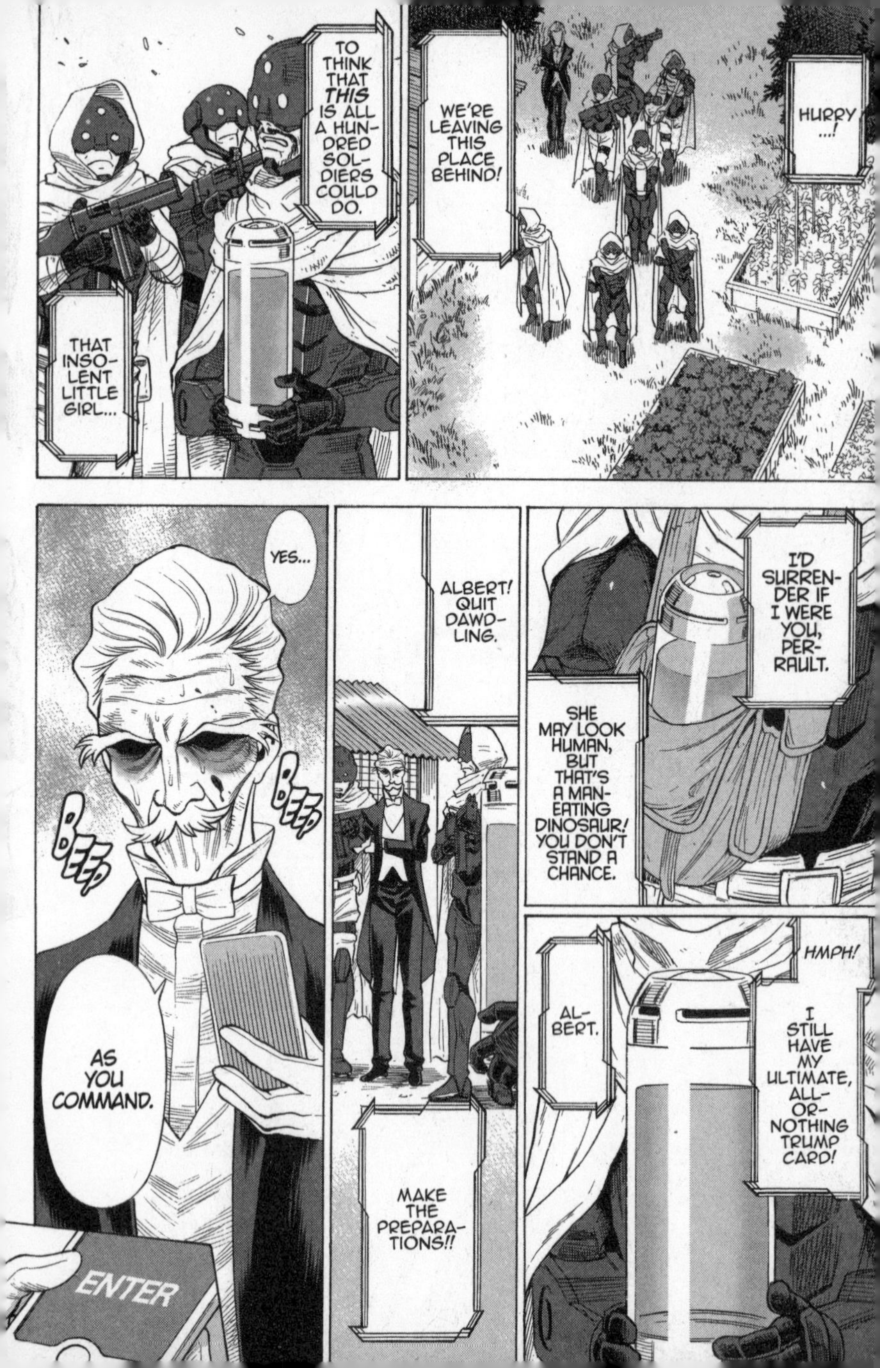
HURRY ...!
WE'RE LEAVING THIS PLACE BEHIND!
TO THINK THAT THIS IS ALL A HUNDRED SOLDIERS COULD DO.
THAT INSOLENT LITTLE GIRL...
I'D SURRENDER IF I WERE YOU, PERRAULT.
SHE MAY LOOK HUMAN, BUT THAT'S A MAN-EATING DINOSAUR! YOU DON'T STAND A CHANCE.
HMPH!
I STILL HAVE MY ULTIMATE, ALL-OR-NOTHING TRUMP CARD!
ALBERT.
ALBERT! QUIT DAWDLING.
MAKE THE PREPARATIONS!!
YES...
BEEP
BEEP
AS YOU COMMAND.
ENTER

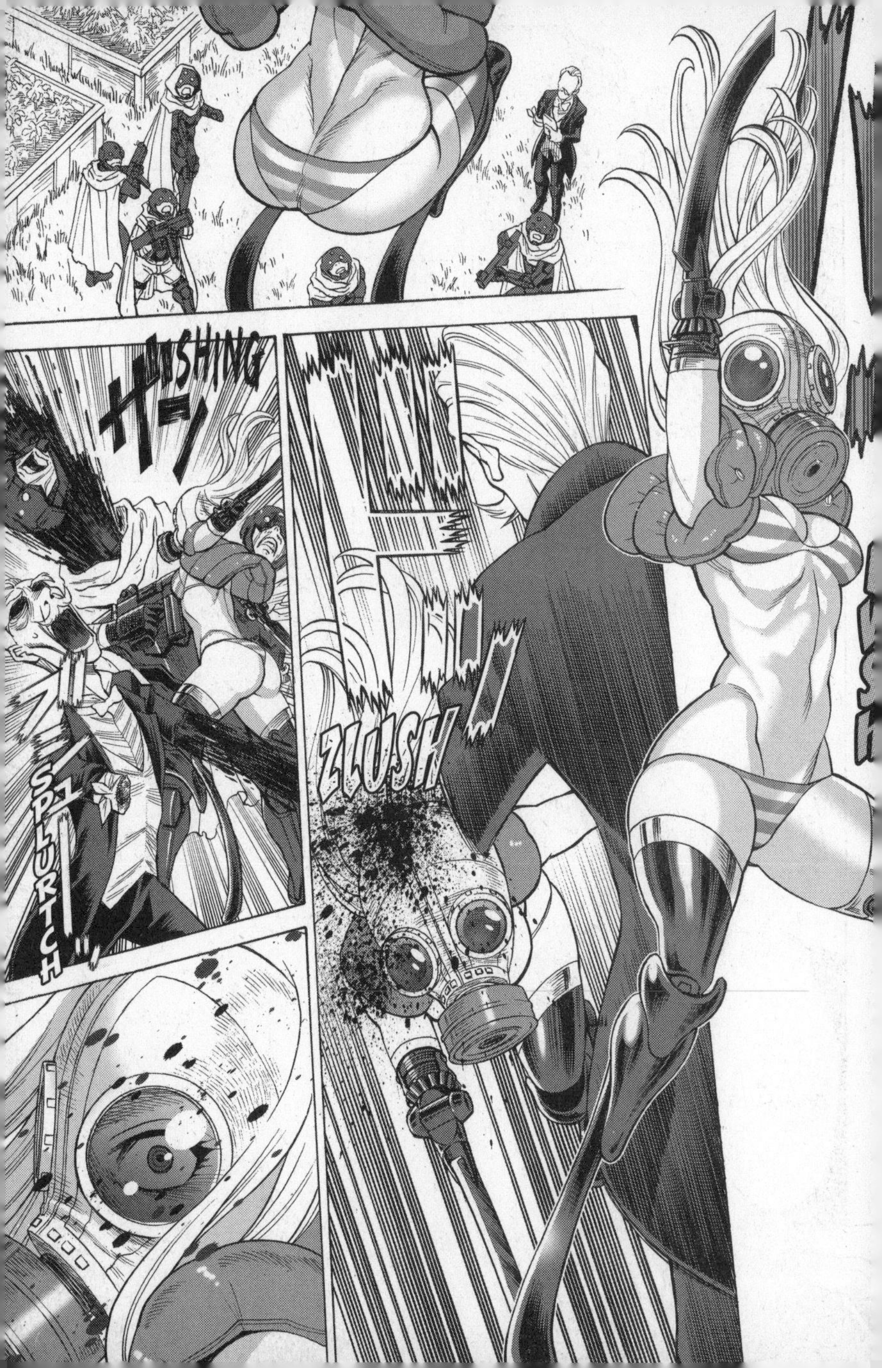
ZLUSH
SHING
SPLURTCH

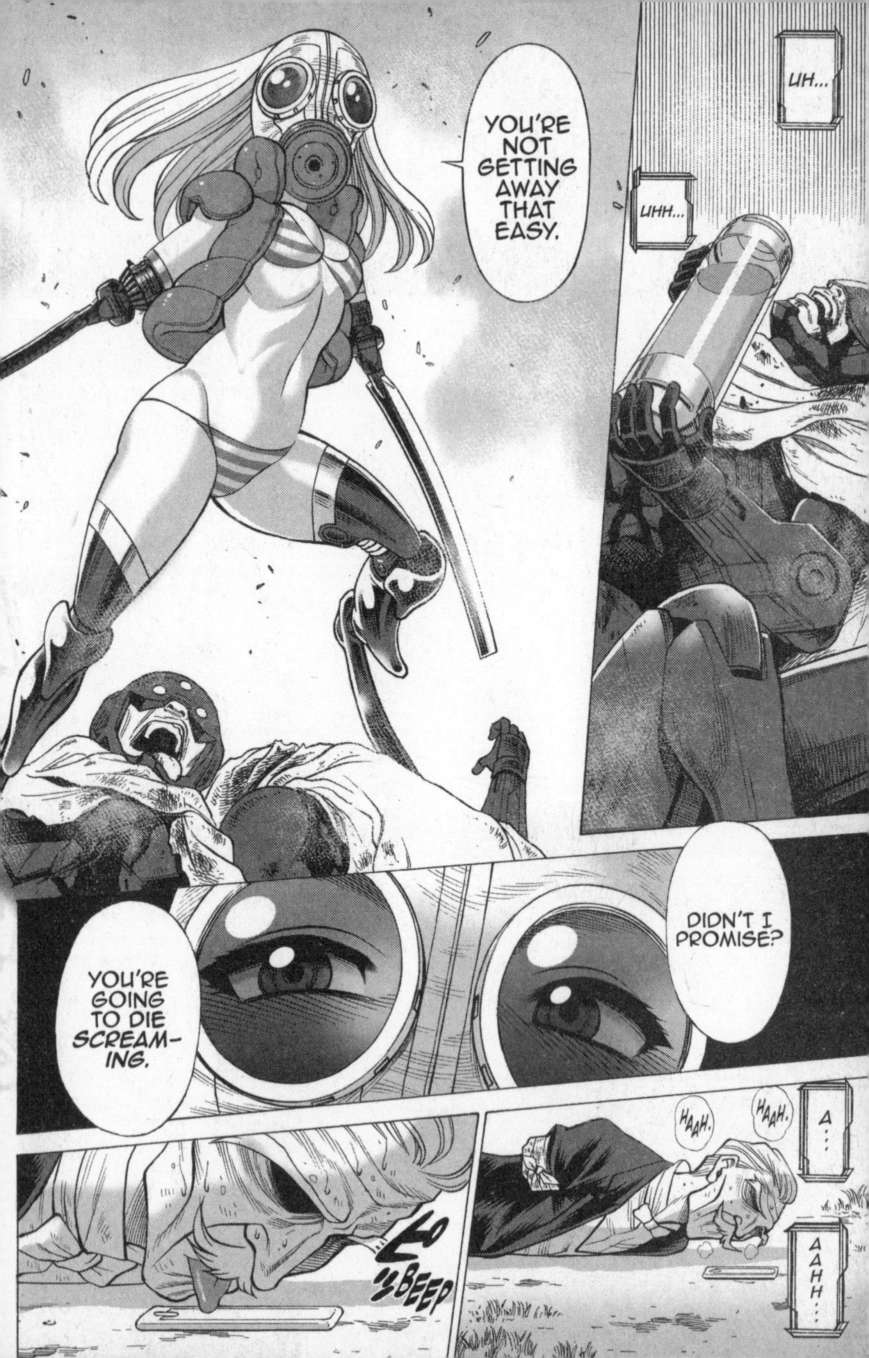
UH...
UHH...
YOU'RE NOT GETTING AWAY THAT EASY.
DIDN'T I PROMISE?
YOU'RE GOING TO DIE SCREAMING.
HAAH.
HAAH.
A...
AAHH...
BEEP

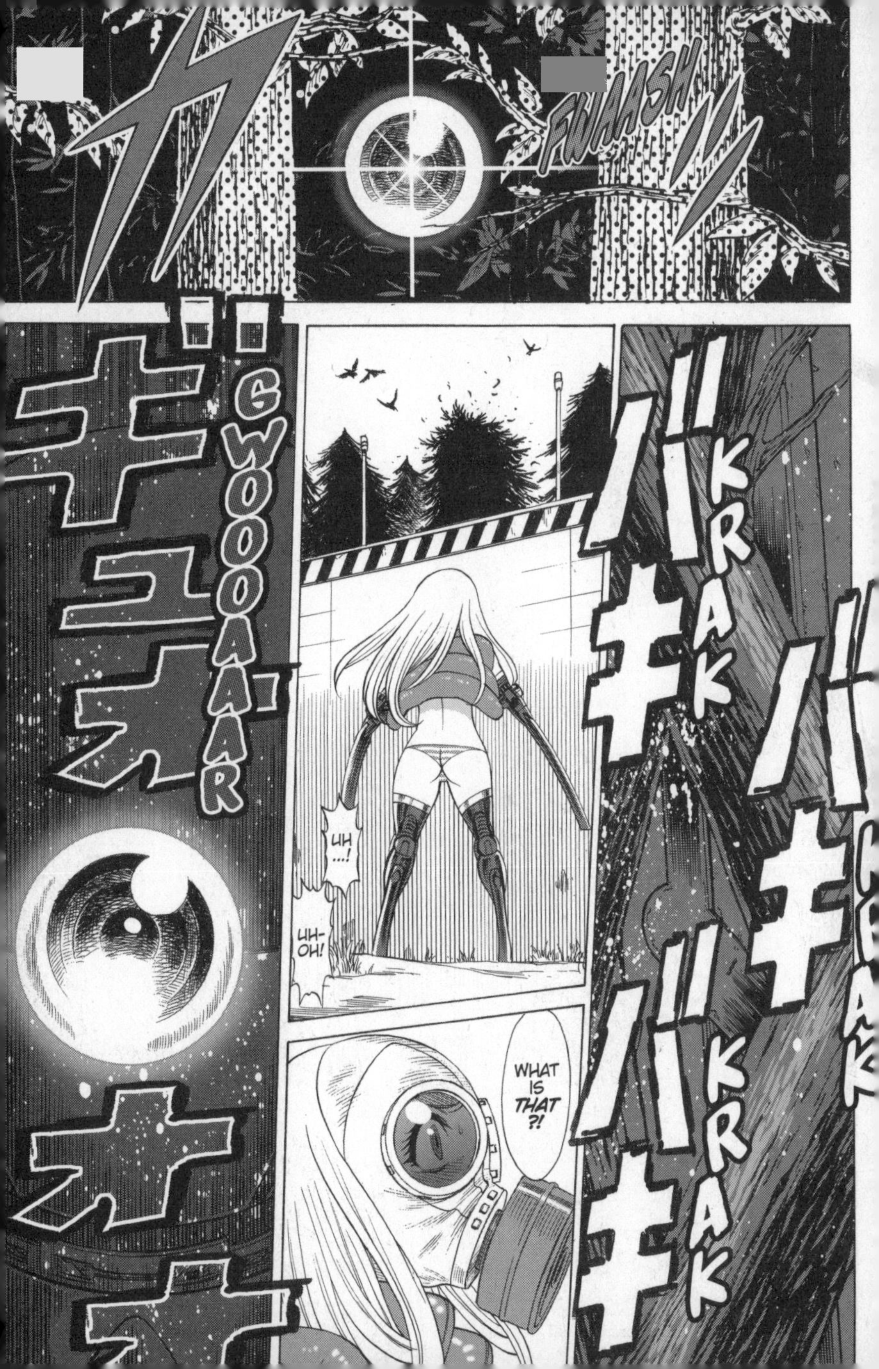
FWAASH
KRAK
KRAK
UH ...!
UH-OH!
WHAT IS THAT?!
GWOOOAAAR

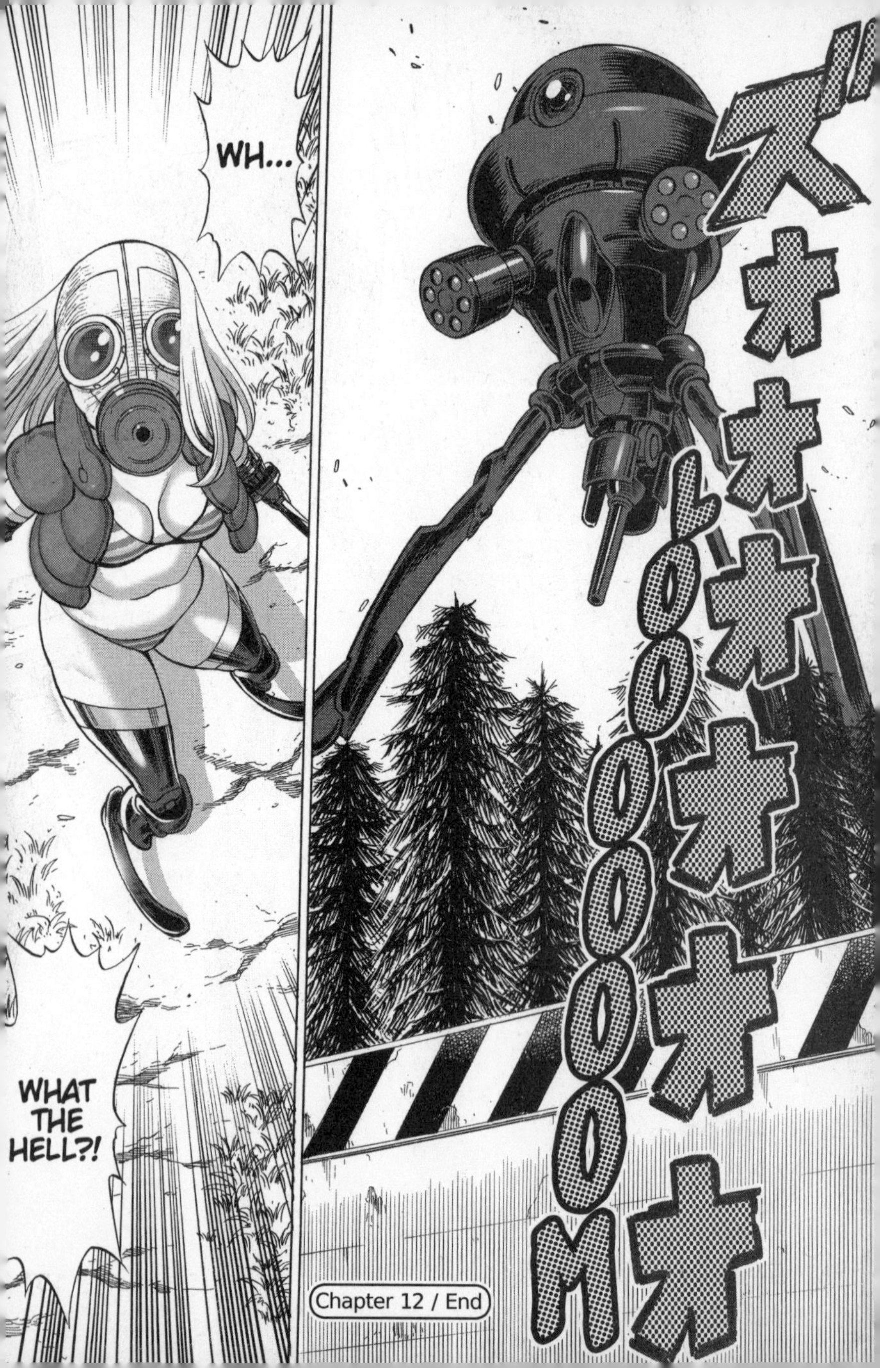
ズオオオオオオ
Chapter 12 / End
WH...
WHAT THE HELL?!

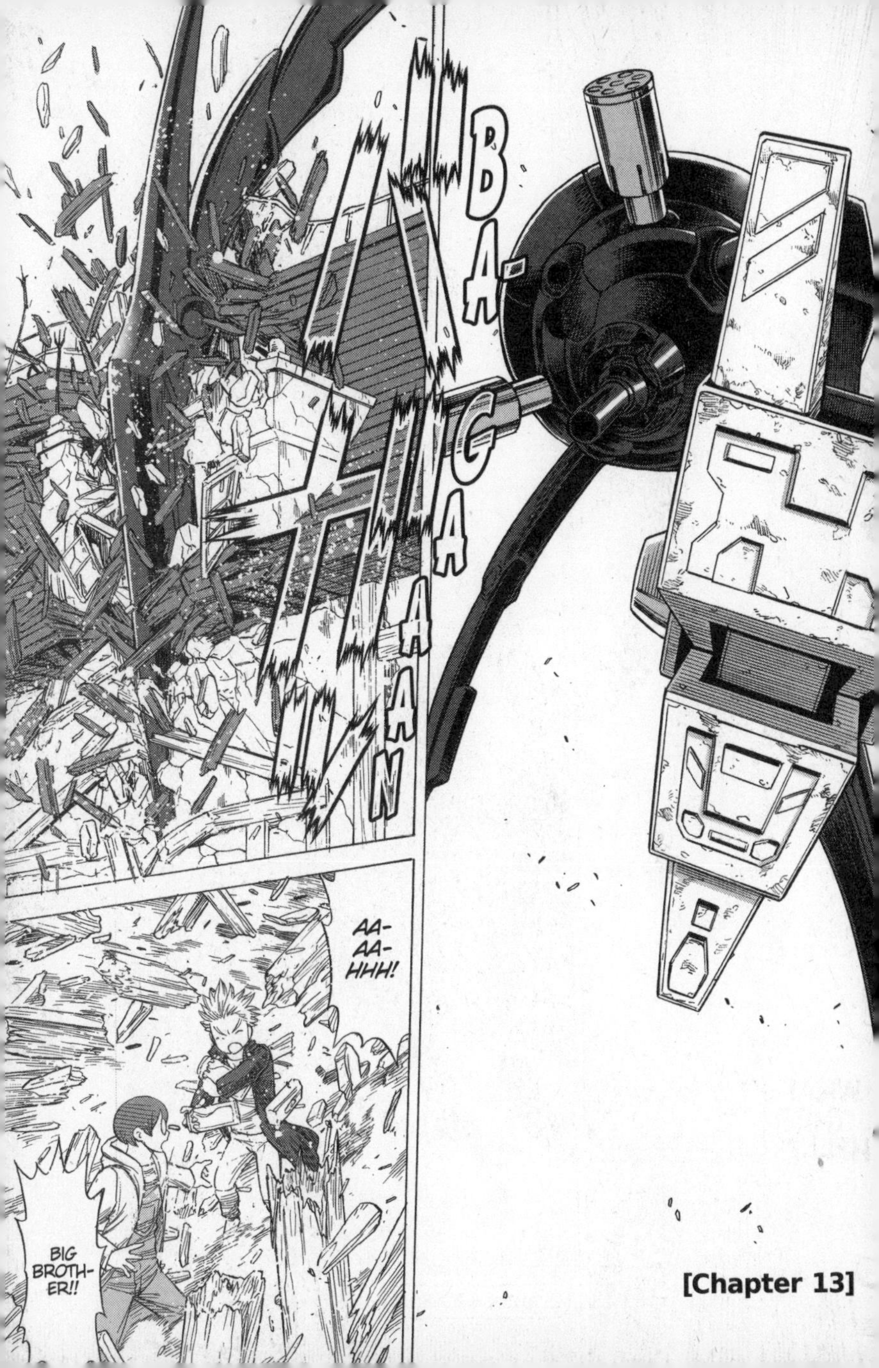
BA-GAAAAN
AA-AA-HHH!
BIG BROTHER!!
[Chapter 13]

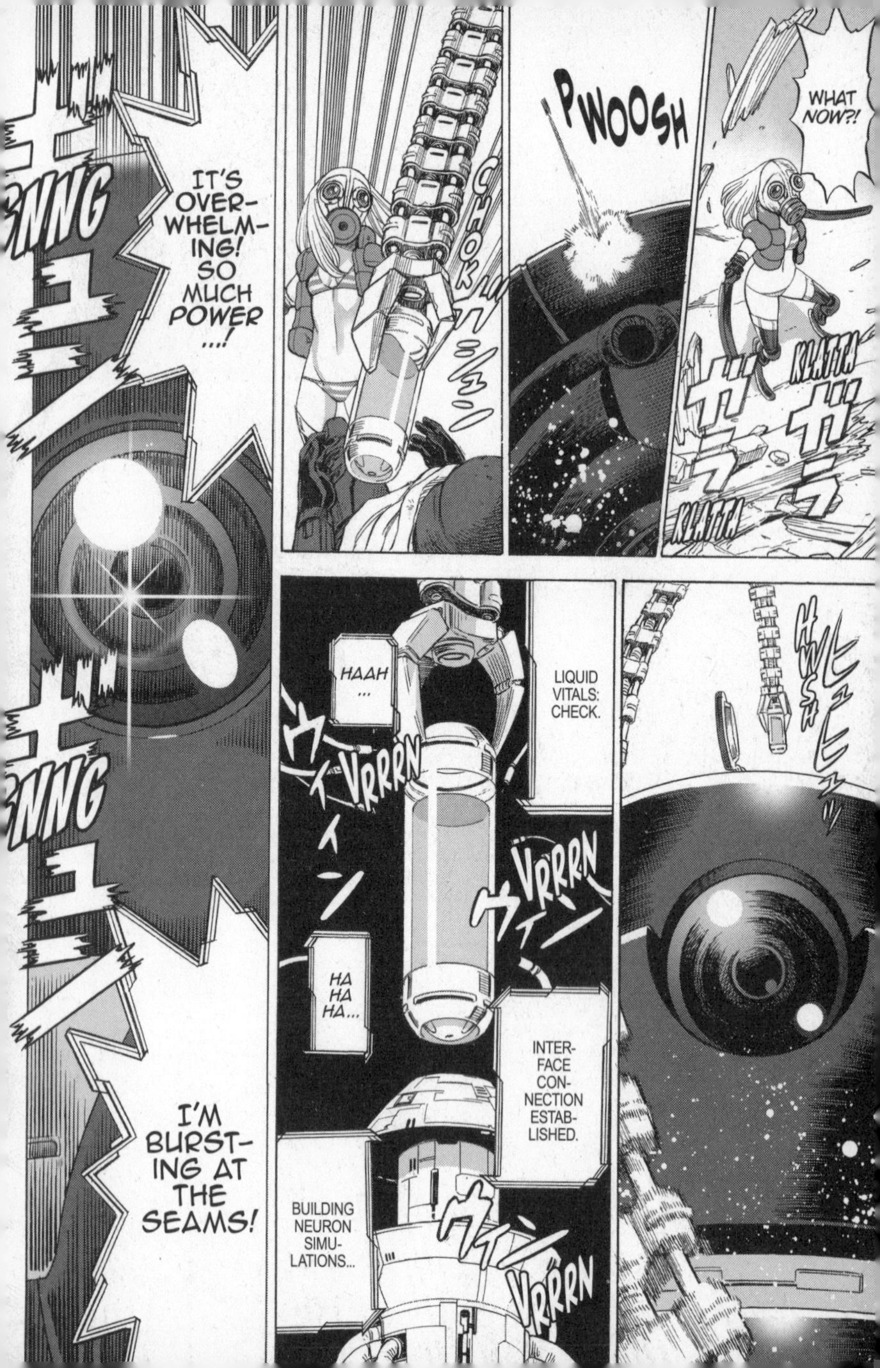
WHAT NOW?!
KLATTA
KLATTA
PWOOSH
CHOK
HWSH
LIQUID VITALS: CHECK.
HAAH...
VRRRN
VRRRN
HA HA HA...
INTERFACE CONNECTION ESTABLISHED.
BUILDING NEURON SIMULATIONS...
VRRRN
IT'S OVERWHELMING! SO MUCH POWER...!
I'M BURSTING AT THE SEAMS!

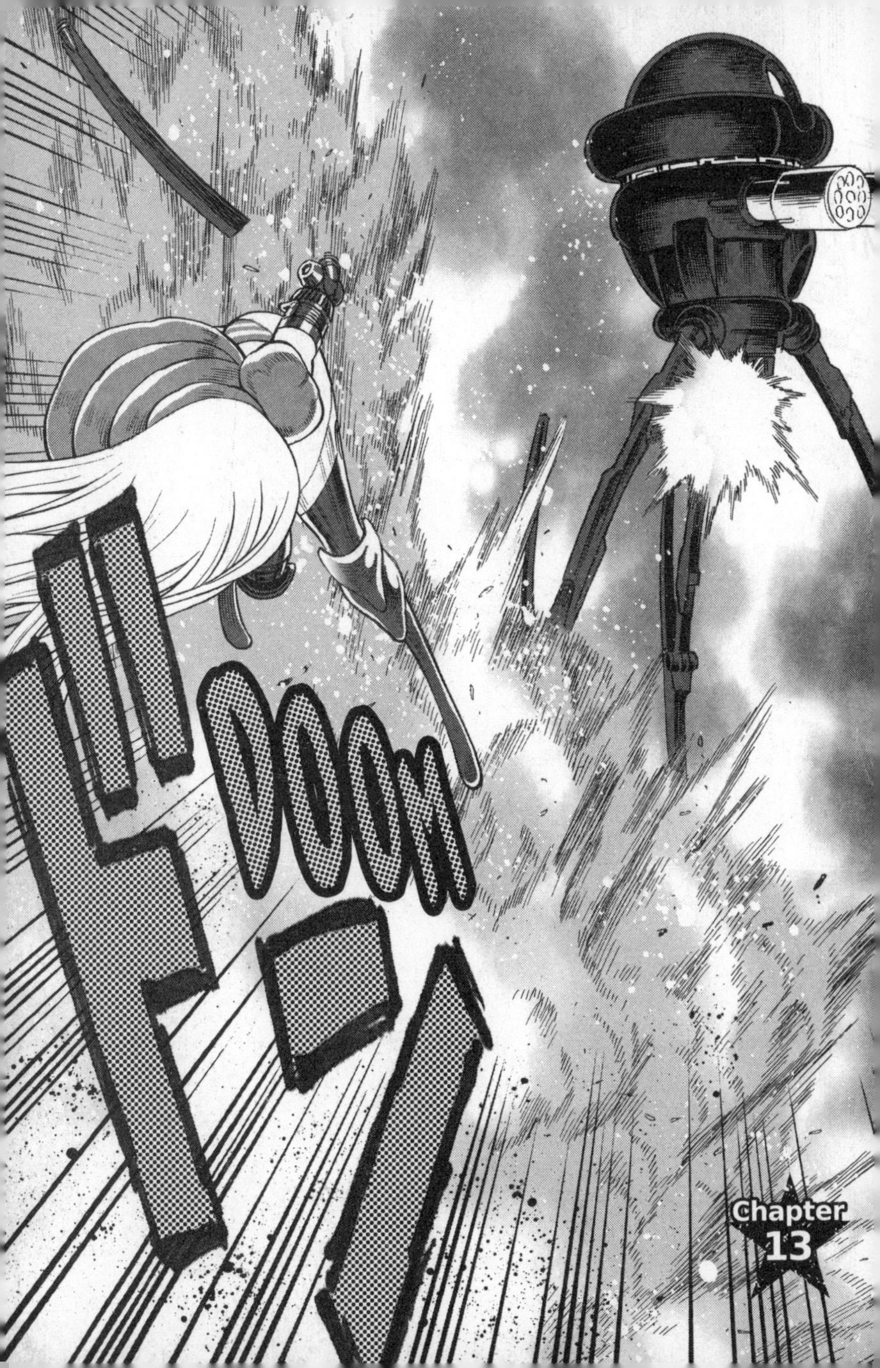
DOOM
Chapter 13

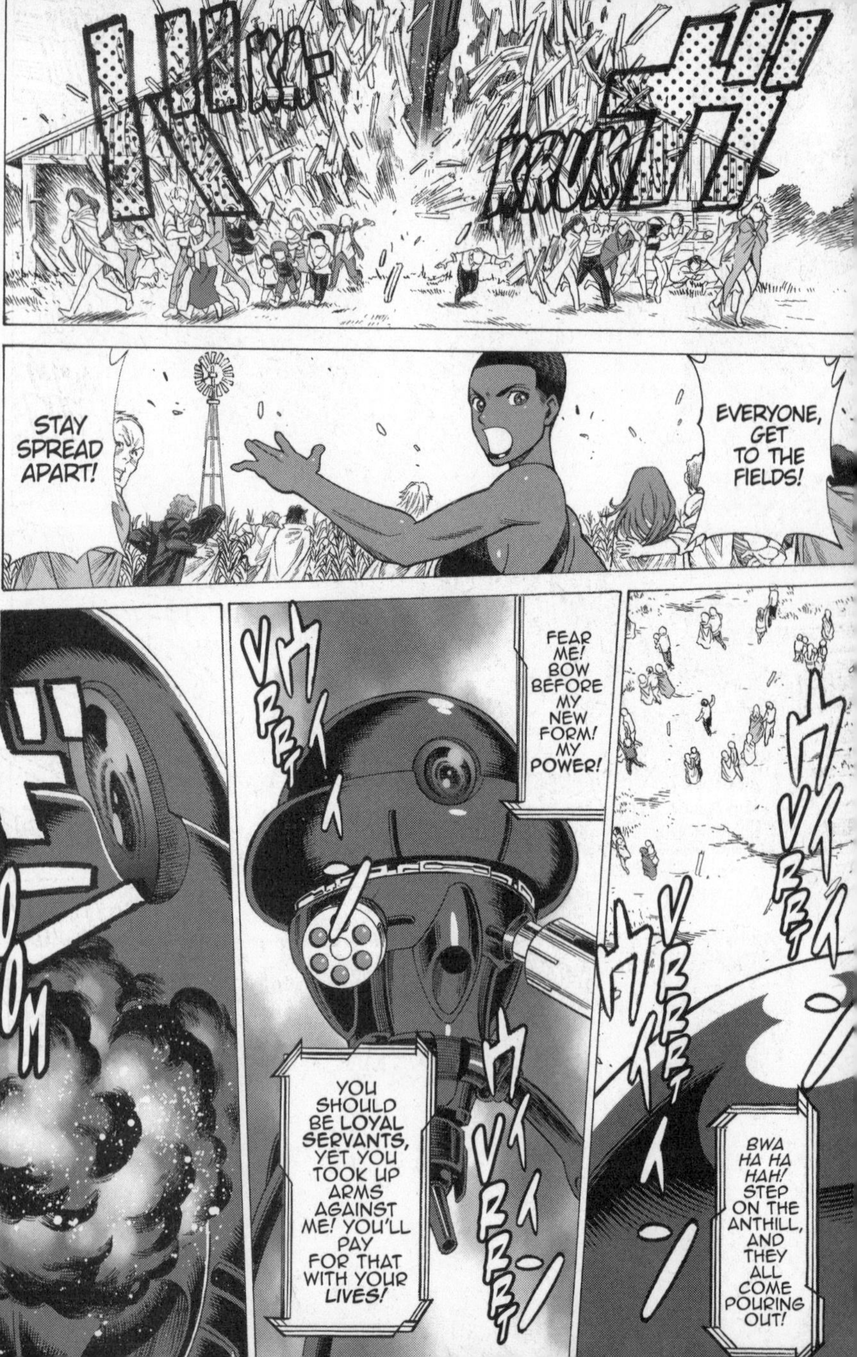
KA-
KRUSH
EVERYONE, GET TO THE FIELDS!
STAY SPREAD APART!
VRRRT
VRRRT
BWA HA HA HAH! STEP ON THE ANTHILL, AND THEY ALL COME POURING OUT!
FEAR ME! BOW BEFORE MY NEW FORM! MY POWER!
VRRT
VRRRT
YOU SHOULD BE LOYAL SERVANTS, YET YOU TOOK UP ARMS AGAINST ME! YOU'LL PAY FOR THAT WITH YOUR LIVES!
BOOOM

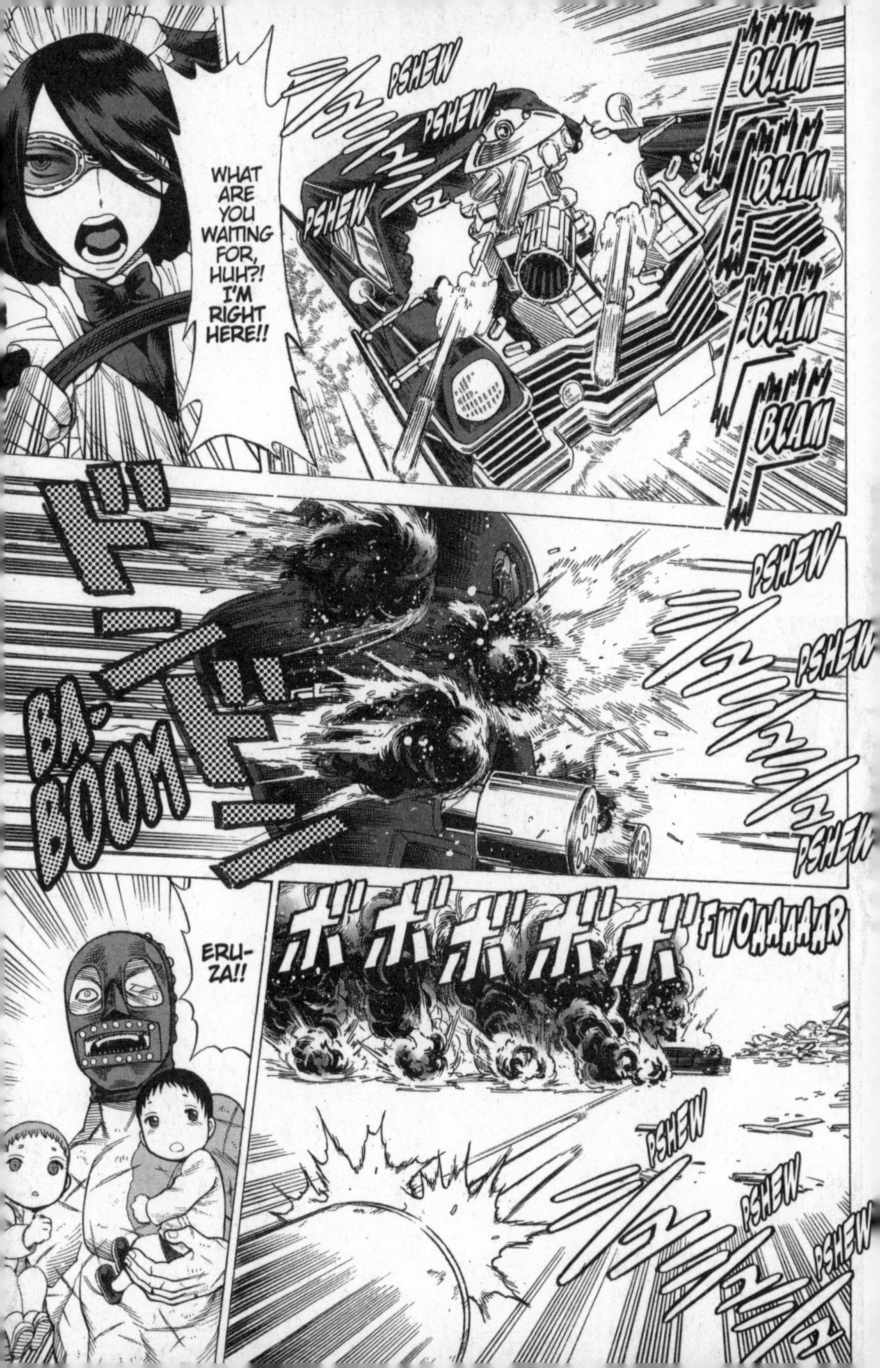
BLAM
BLAM
BLAM
BLAM
PSHEW
PSHEW
PSHEW
WHAT ARE YOU WAITING FOR, HUH?! I'M RIGHT HERE!!
PSHEW
PSHEW
PSHEW
BA-BOOM
ドドド
ボボボボボ
FWOAAAAR
PSHEW
PSHEW
PSHEW
ERU-ZA!!

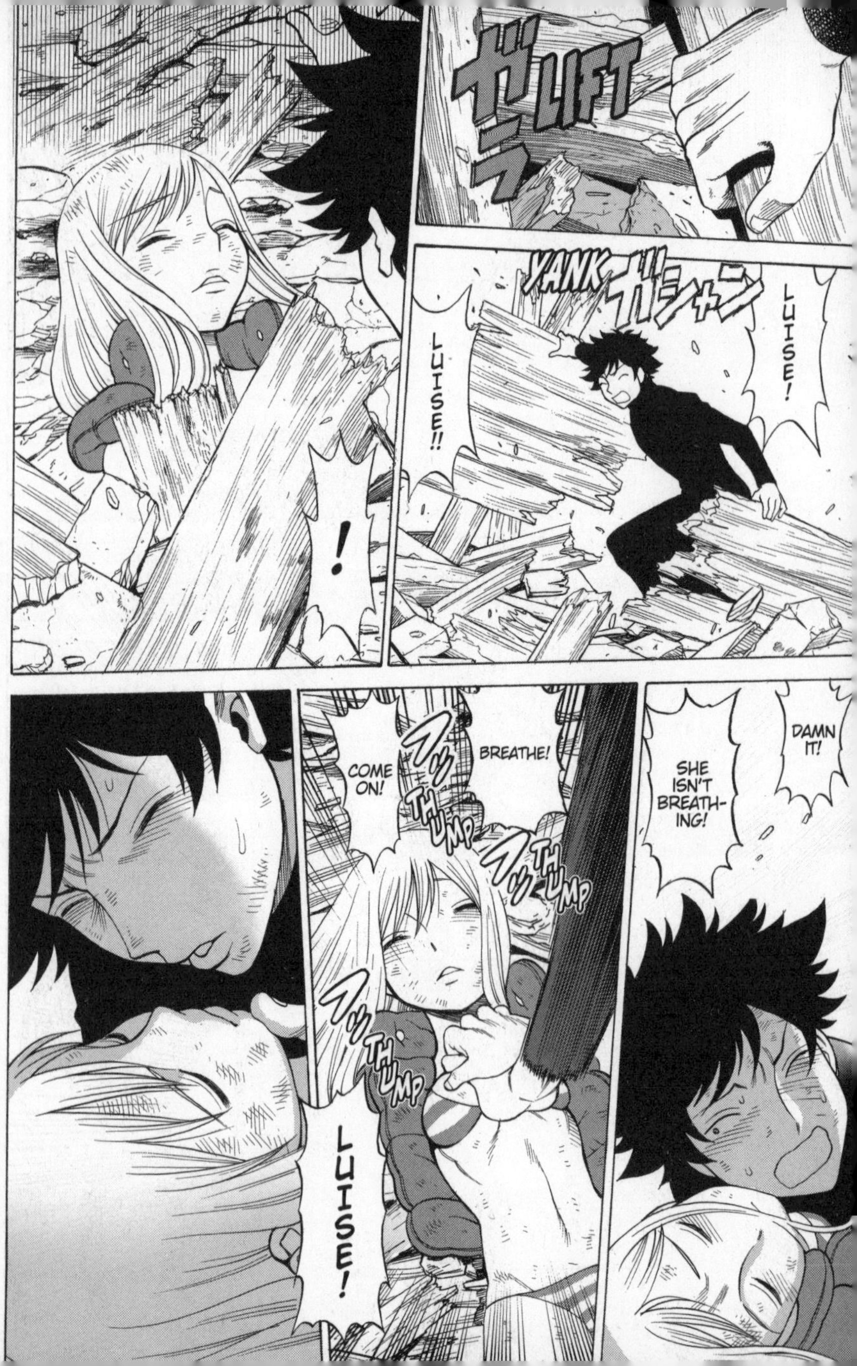
LIFT
LUISE!
YANK
ガシャン
LUISE!!
!
DAMN IT!
SHE ISN'T BREATH-ING!
BREATHE!
COME ON!
THUMP
THUMP
THUMP
LUISE!

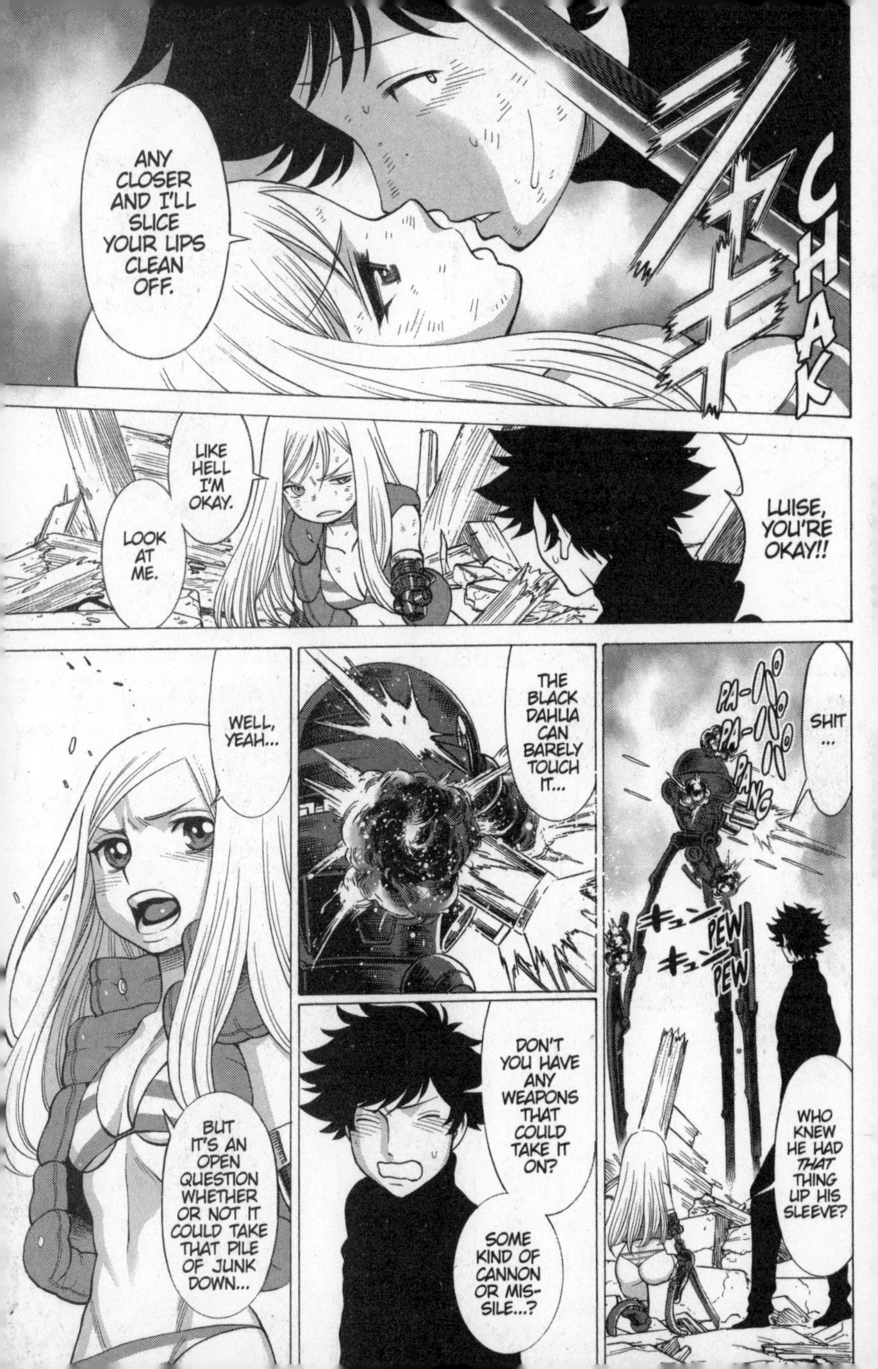
CHAK
ANY CLOSER AND I'LL SLICE YOUR LIPS CLEAN OFF.
LUISE, YOU'RE OKAY!!
LIKE HELL I'M OKAY.
LOOK AT ME.
SHIT...
PA-PA-PANG
PEW PEW
WHO KNEW HE HAD *THAT* THING UP HIS SLEEVE?
THE BLACK DAHLIA CAN BARELY TOUCH IT...
DON'T YOU HAVE ANY WEAPONS THAT COULD TAKE IT ON?
SOME KIND OF CANNON OR MIS-SILE...?
WELL, YEAH...
BUT IT'S AN OPEN QUESTION WHETHER OR NOT IT COULD TAKE THAT PILE OF JUNK DOWN...

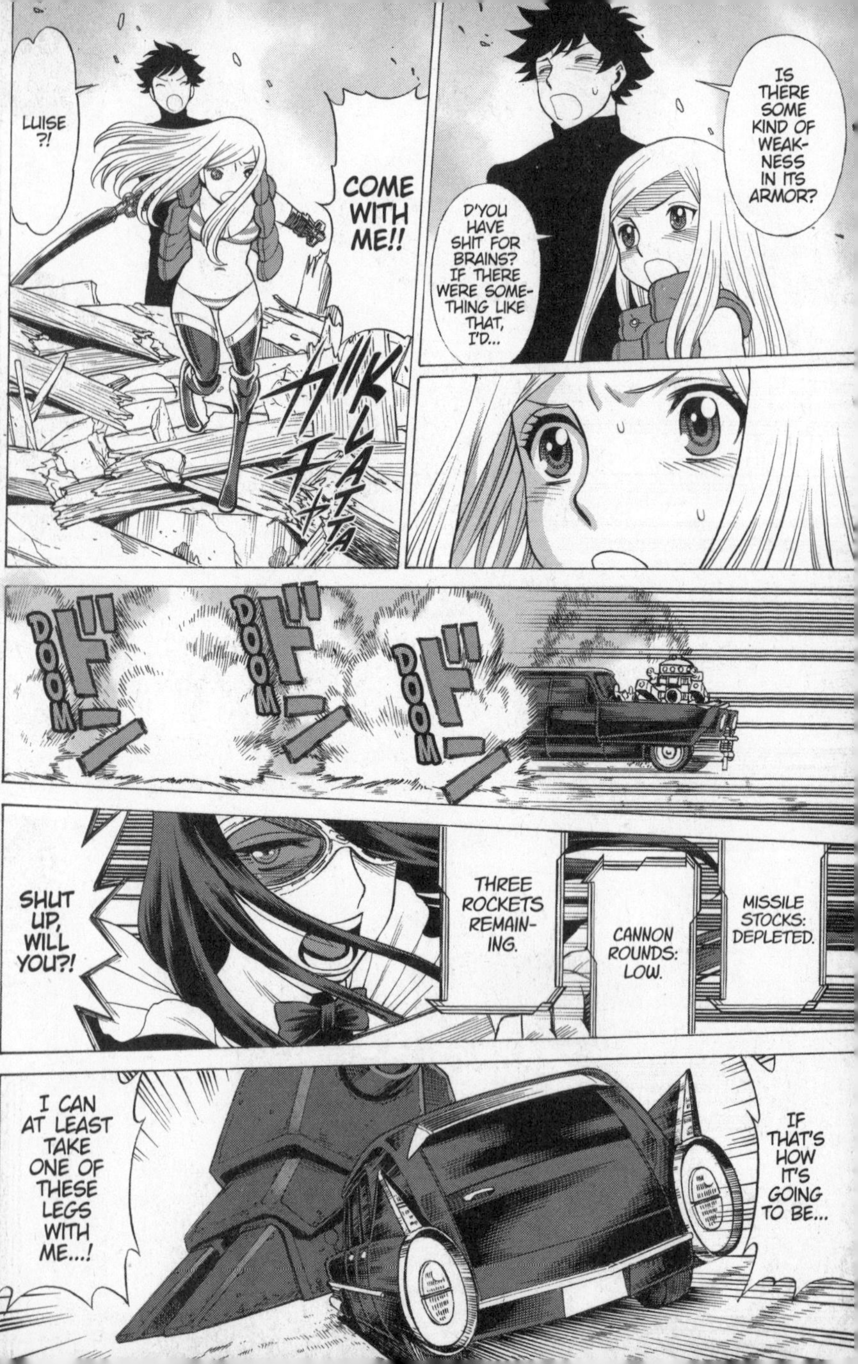
IS THERE SOME KIND OF WEAK-NESS IN ITS ARMOR?
D'YOU HAVE SHIT FOR BRAINS? IF THERE WERE SOME-THING LIKE THAT, I'D...
COME WITH ME!!
LUISE ?!
KLATTA
DOOM
DOOM
DOOM
MISSILE STOCKS: DEPLETED.
CANNON ROUNDS: LOW.
THREE ROCKETS REMAIN-ING.
SHUT UP, WILL YOU?!
IF THAT'S HOW IT'S GOING TO BE...
I CAN AT LEAST TAKE ONE OF THESE LEGS WITH ME...!

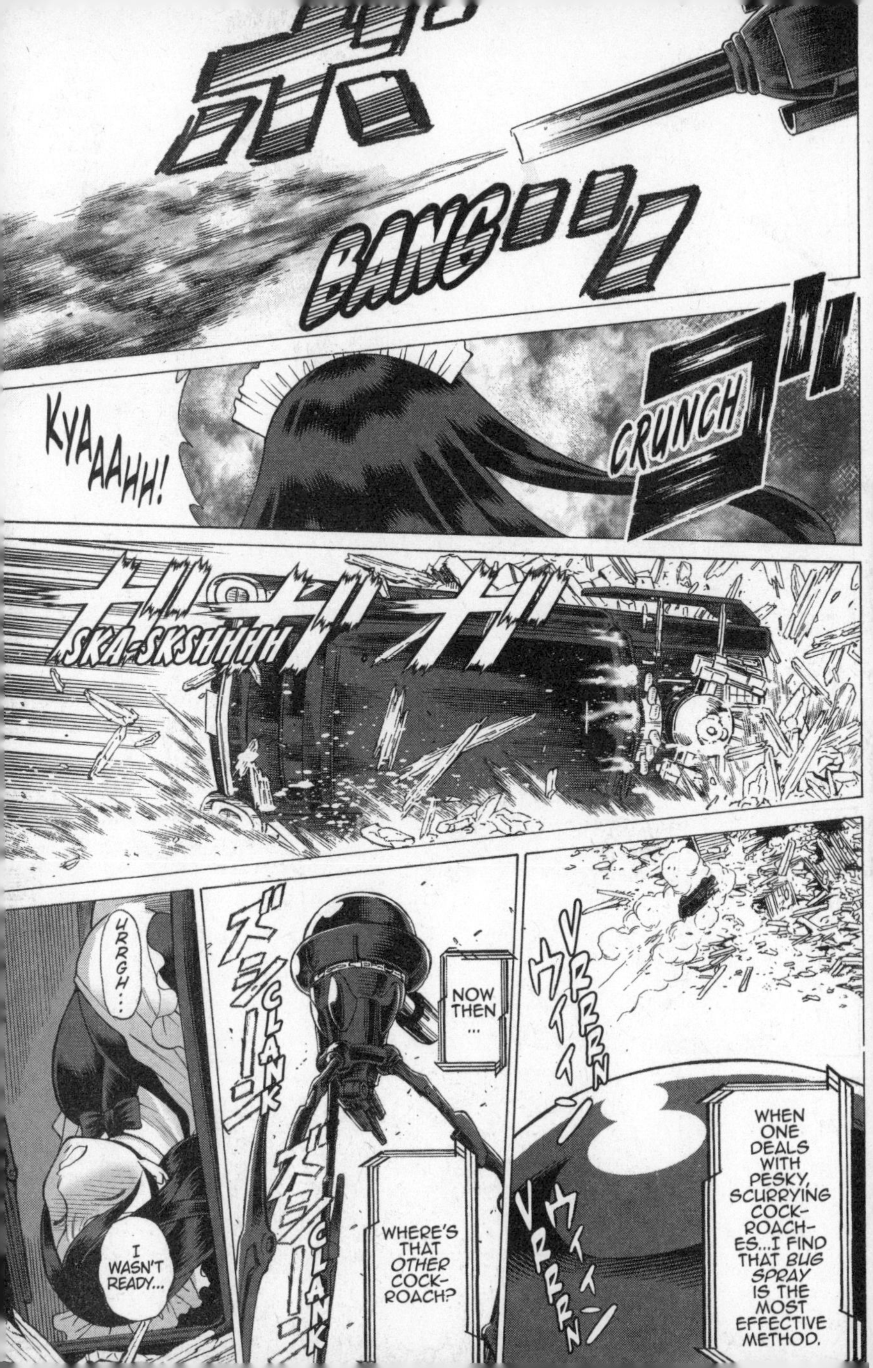
BANG
CRUNCH
KYAAAHH!
SKA-SKSHHHH
VRRRRN
WHEN ONE DEALS WITH PESKY, SCURRYING COCK-ROACH-ES...I FIND THAT *BUG SPRAY* IS THE MOST EFFECTIVE METHOD.
VRRRRN
NOW THEN ...
CLANK
CLANK
WHERE'S THAT *OTHER* COCK-ROACH?
URRGH...
I WASN'T READY...

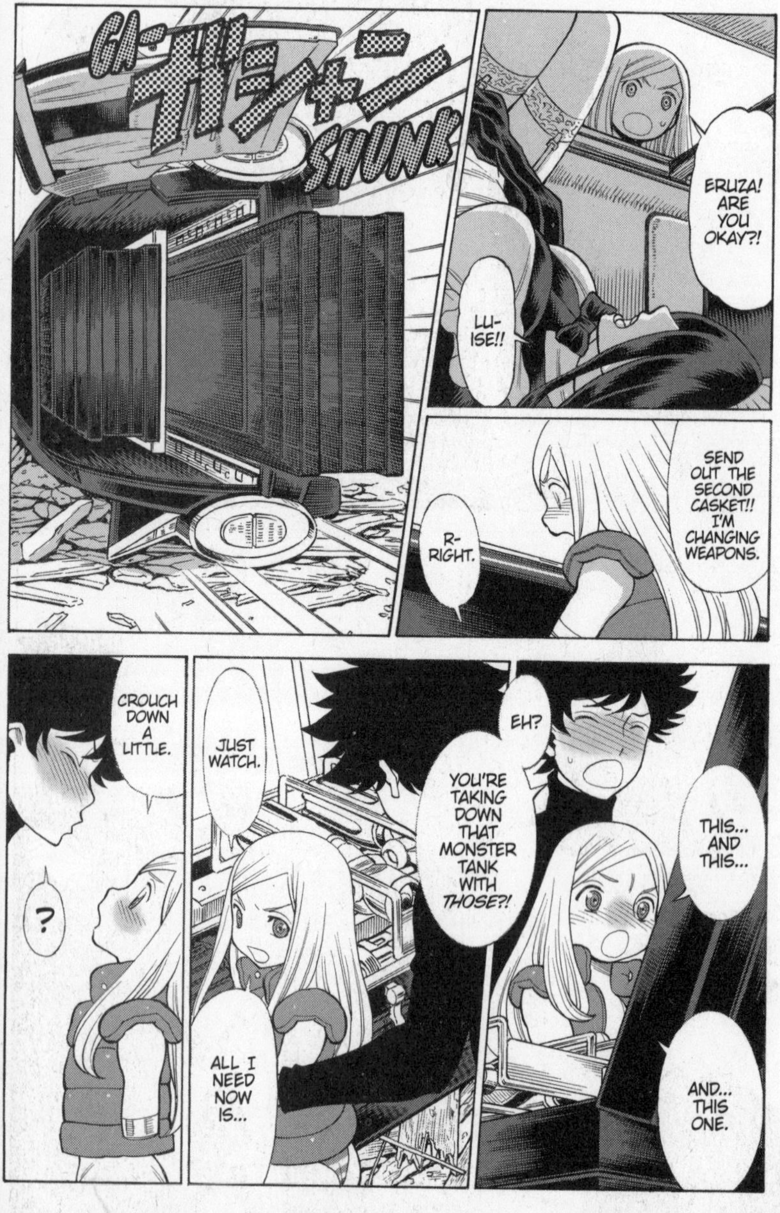
ERUZA! ARE YOU OKAY?!
LU-ISE!!
SEND OUT THE SECOND CASKET!! I'M CHANGING WEAPONS.
R-RIGHT.
GA-
SHUNK
EH?
THIS... AND THIS...
YOU'RE TAKING DOWN THAT MONSTER TANK WITH *THOSE*?!
AND... THIS ONE.
JUST WATCH.
ALL I NEED NOW IS...
CROUCH DOWN A LITTLE.
?

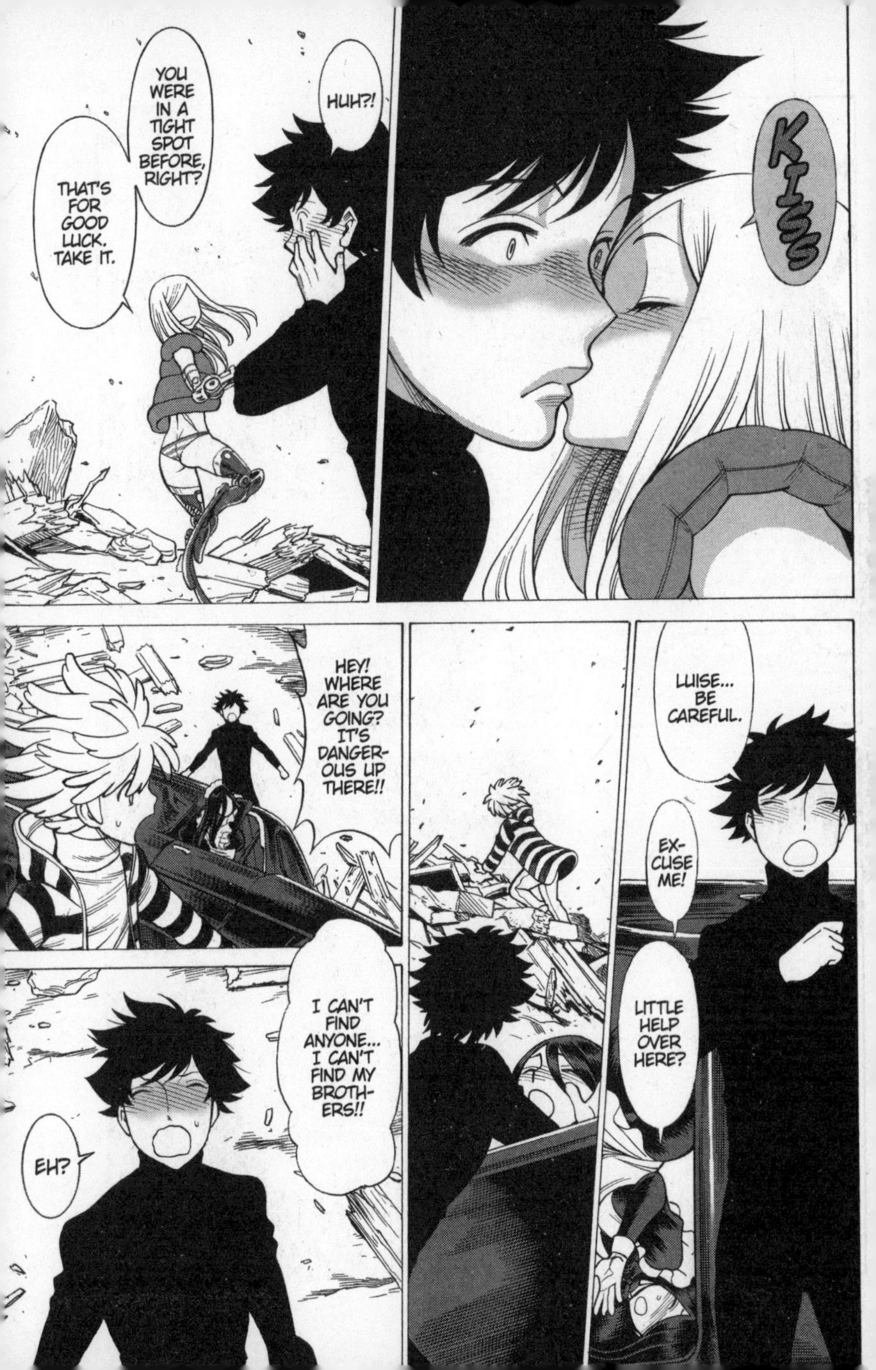
KISS
HUH?!
YOU WERE IN A TIGHT SPOT BEFORE, RIGHT?
THAT'S FOR GOOD LUCK. TAKE IT.
LUISE... BE CAREFUL.
EX-CUSE ME!
LITTLE HELP OVER HERE?
HEY! WHERE ARE YOU GOING? IT'S DANGER-OUS UP THERE!!
I CAN'T FIND ANYONE... I CAN'T FIND MY BROTH-ERS!!
EH?

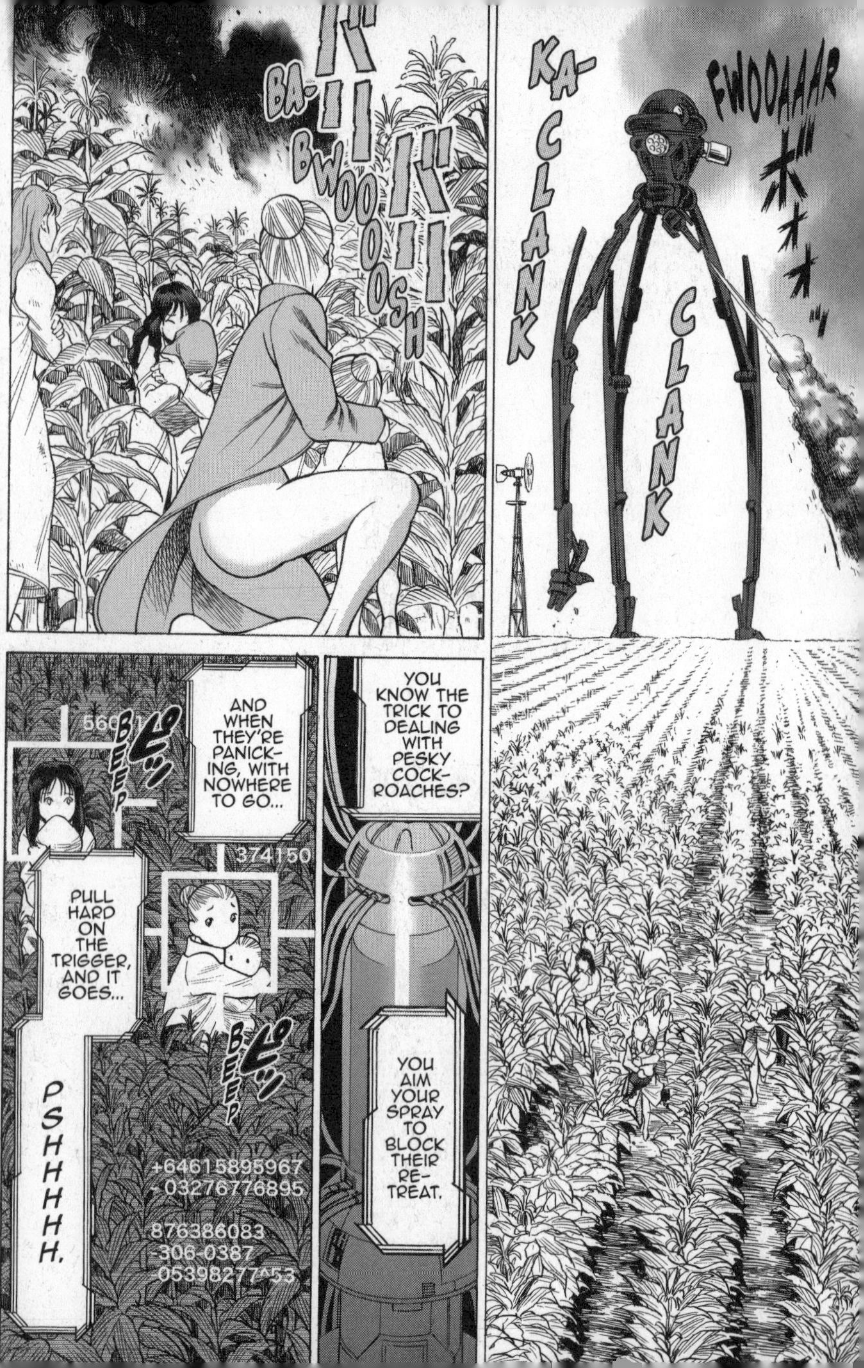
KA-CLANK
FWOOAAAR
CLANK
BA-BWOOOOOSH
YOU KNOW THE TRICK TO DEALING WITH PESKY COCK-ROACHES?
YOU AIM YOUR SPRAY TO BLOCK THEIR RE-TREAT.
AND WHEN THEY'RE PANICK-ING, WITH NOWHERE TO GO...
BEEP
374150
PULL HARD ON THE TRIGGER, AND IT GOES...
BEEP
+64615895967
- 03276776895
876386083
-306-0387
-05398277^53
PSHHHHHH.

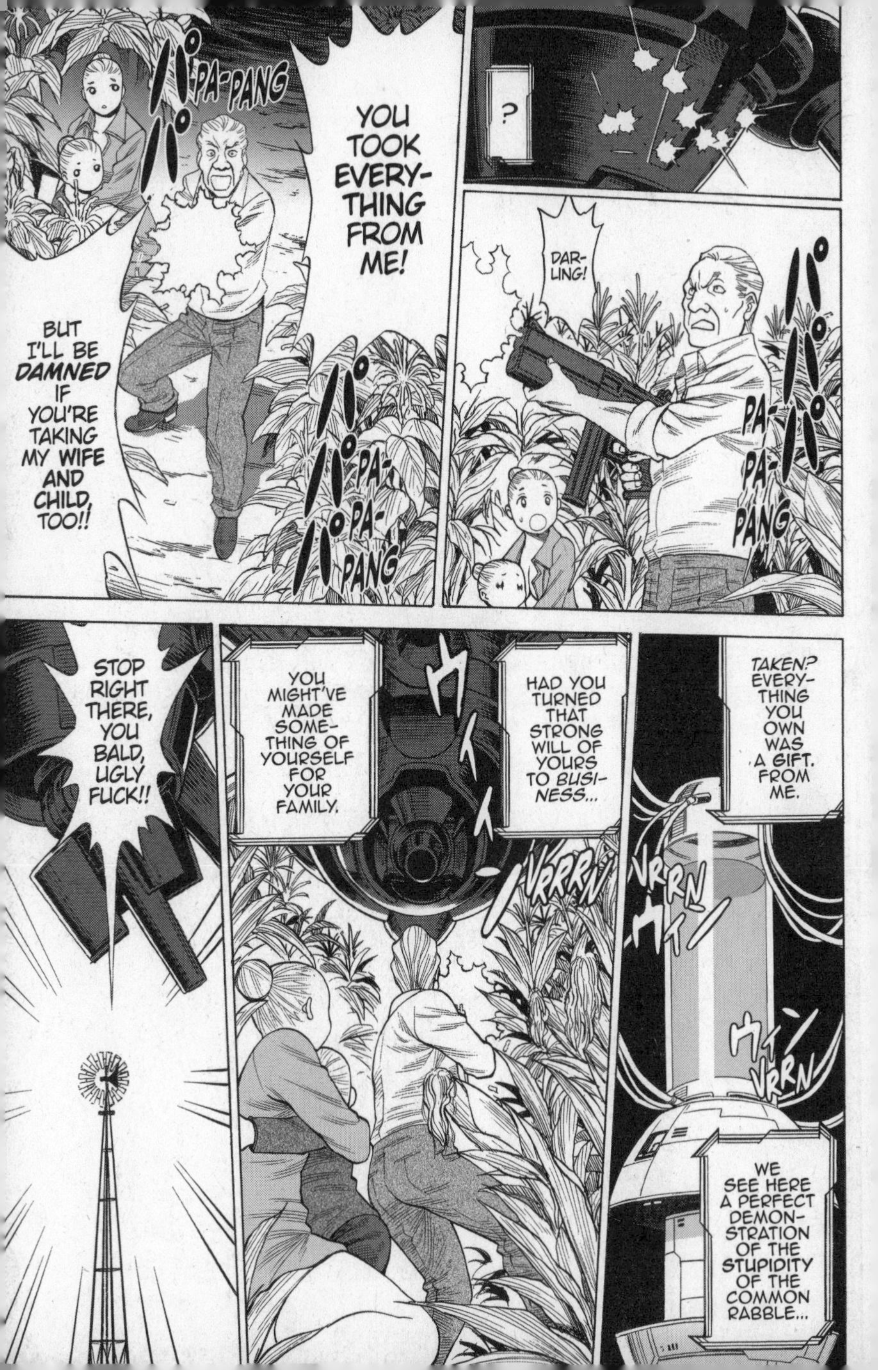
?
DARLING!
PA-PA-PANG
YOU TOOK EVERYTHING FROM ME!
PA-PANG
BUT I'LL BE ***DAMNED*** IF YOU'RE TAKING MY WIFE AND CHILD, TOO!!
PA-PA-PANG
TAKEN? EVERYTHING YOU OWN WAS A GIFT. FROM ME.
VRRN
VRRN
WE SEE HERE A PERFECT DEMONSTRATION OF THE STUPIDITY OF THE COMMON RABBLE...
HAD YOU TURNED THAT STRONG WILL OF YOURS TO *BUSINESS*...
YOU MIGHT'VE MADE SOMETHING OF YOURSELF FOR YOUR FAMILY.
VRRRN
STOP RIGHT THERE, YOU BALD, UGLY FUCK!!

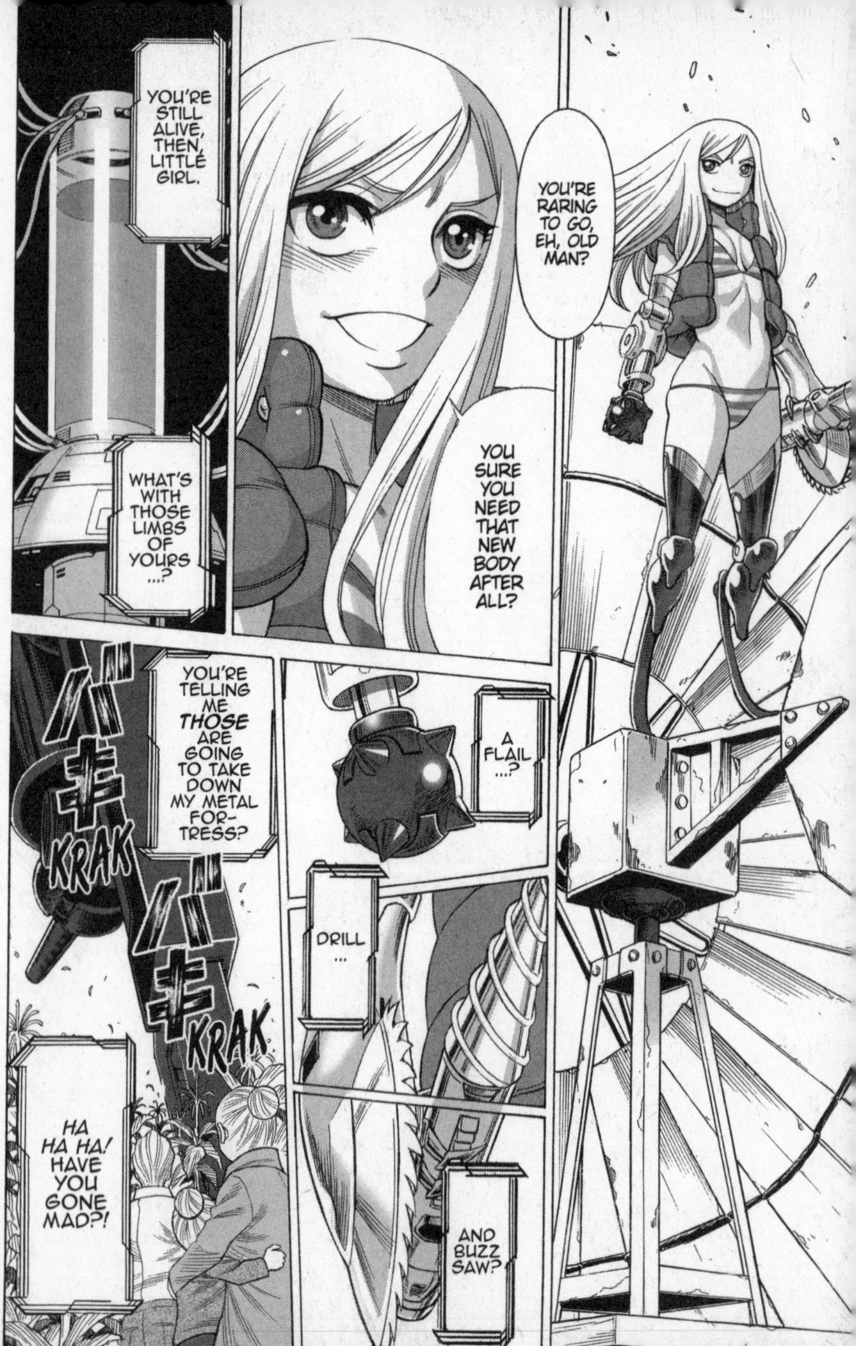
YOU'RE RARING TO GO, EH, OLD MAN?
YOU SURE YOU NEED THAT NEW BODY AFTER ALL?
YOU'RE STILL ALIVE, THEN, LITTLE GIRL.
WHAT'S WITH THOSE LIMBS OF YOURS ...?
A FLAIL ...?
DRILL ...
AND BUZZ SAW?
YOU'RE TELLING ME *THOSE* ARE GOING TO TAKE DOWN MY METAL FOR-TRESS?
KRAK
KRAK
HA HA HA! HAVE YOU GONE MAD?!

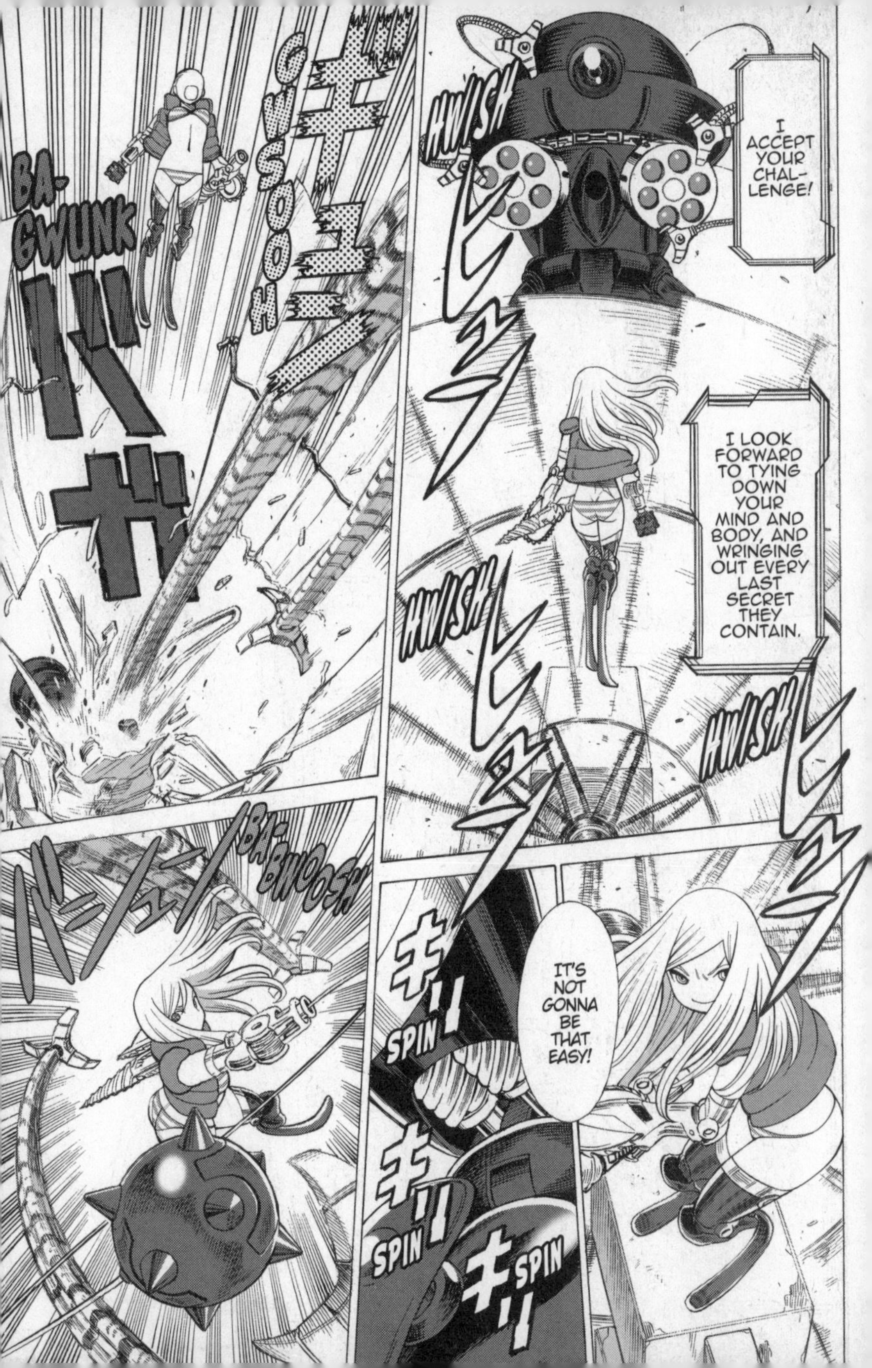
HWISH
I ACCEPT YOUR CHAL-LENGE!
I LOOK FORWARD TO TYING DOWN YOUR MIND AND BODY, AND WRINGING OUT EVERY LAST SECRET THEY CONTAIN.
HWISH
HWISH
BA-GWUNK
WHOOSH
SPIN
IT'S NOT GONNA BE THAT EASY!
SPIN
SPIN
BA-BWOOSH!

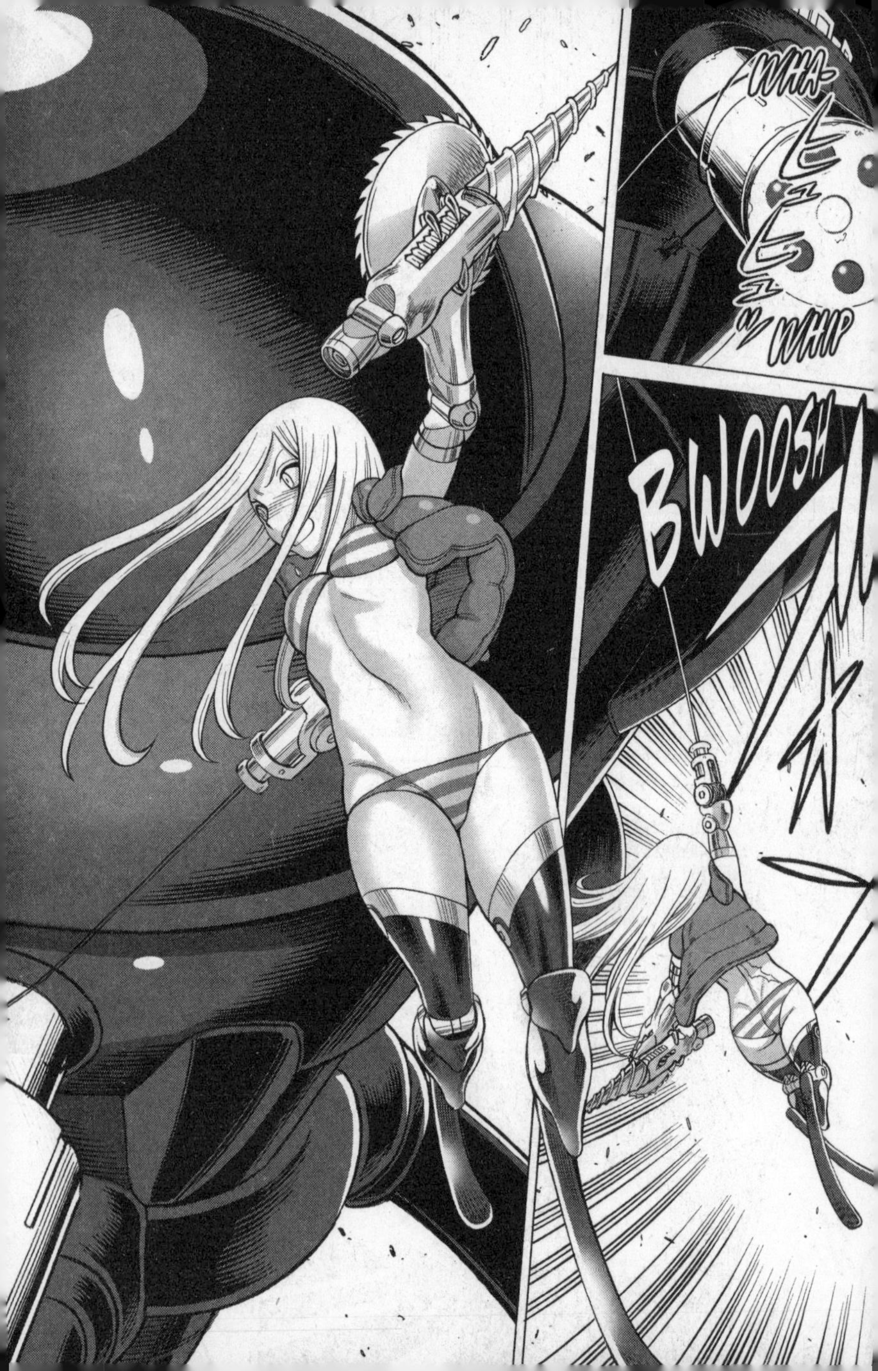
WHA
WHIP
BWOOSH

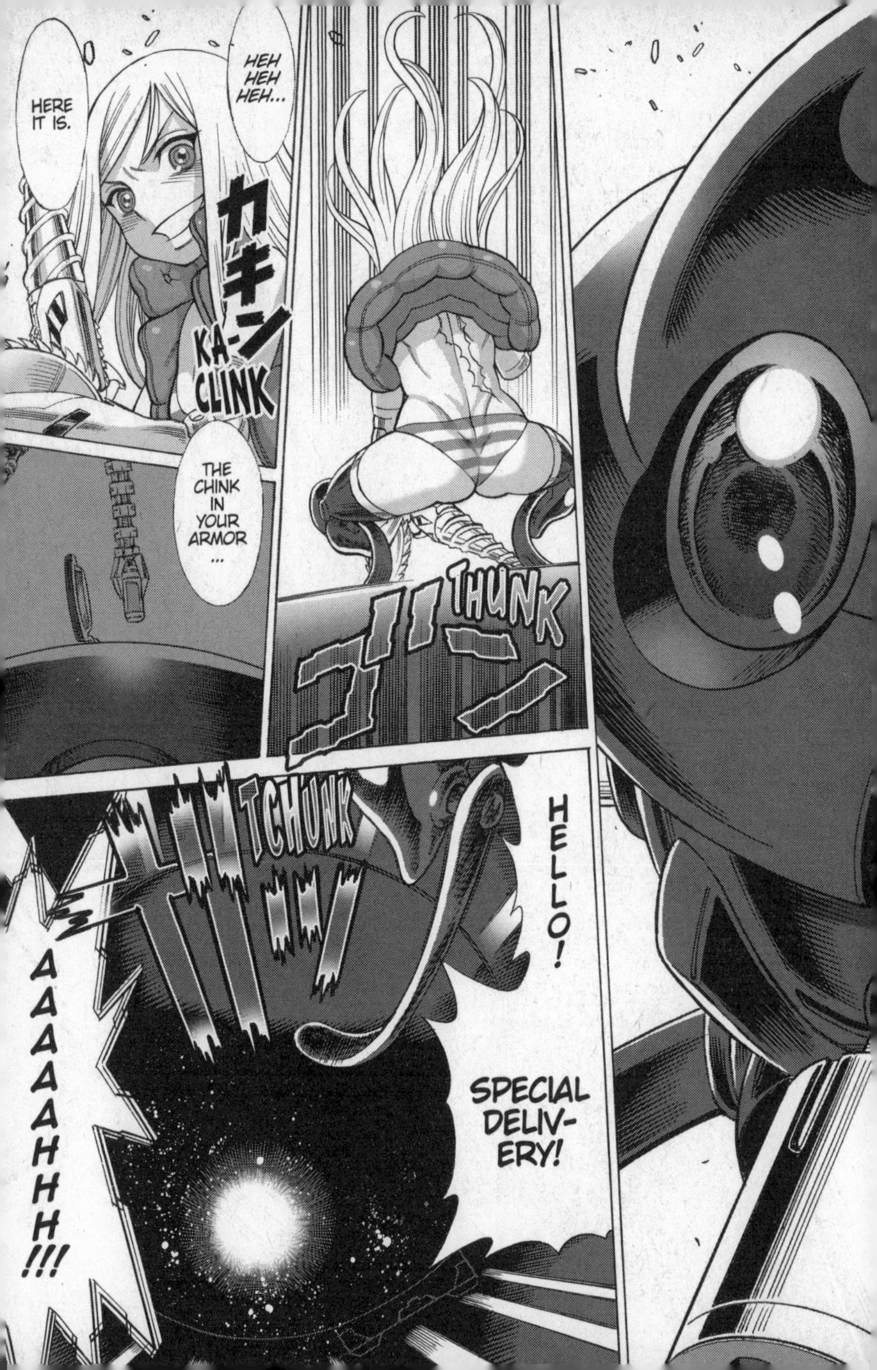
THUNK
HEH HEH HEH...
HERE IT IS.
カキーン
KA-CLINK
THE CHINK IN YOUR ARMOR ...
HELLO!
SPECIAL DELIVERY!
TCHUNK
AAAAAAHHHH!!!

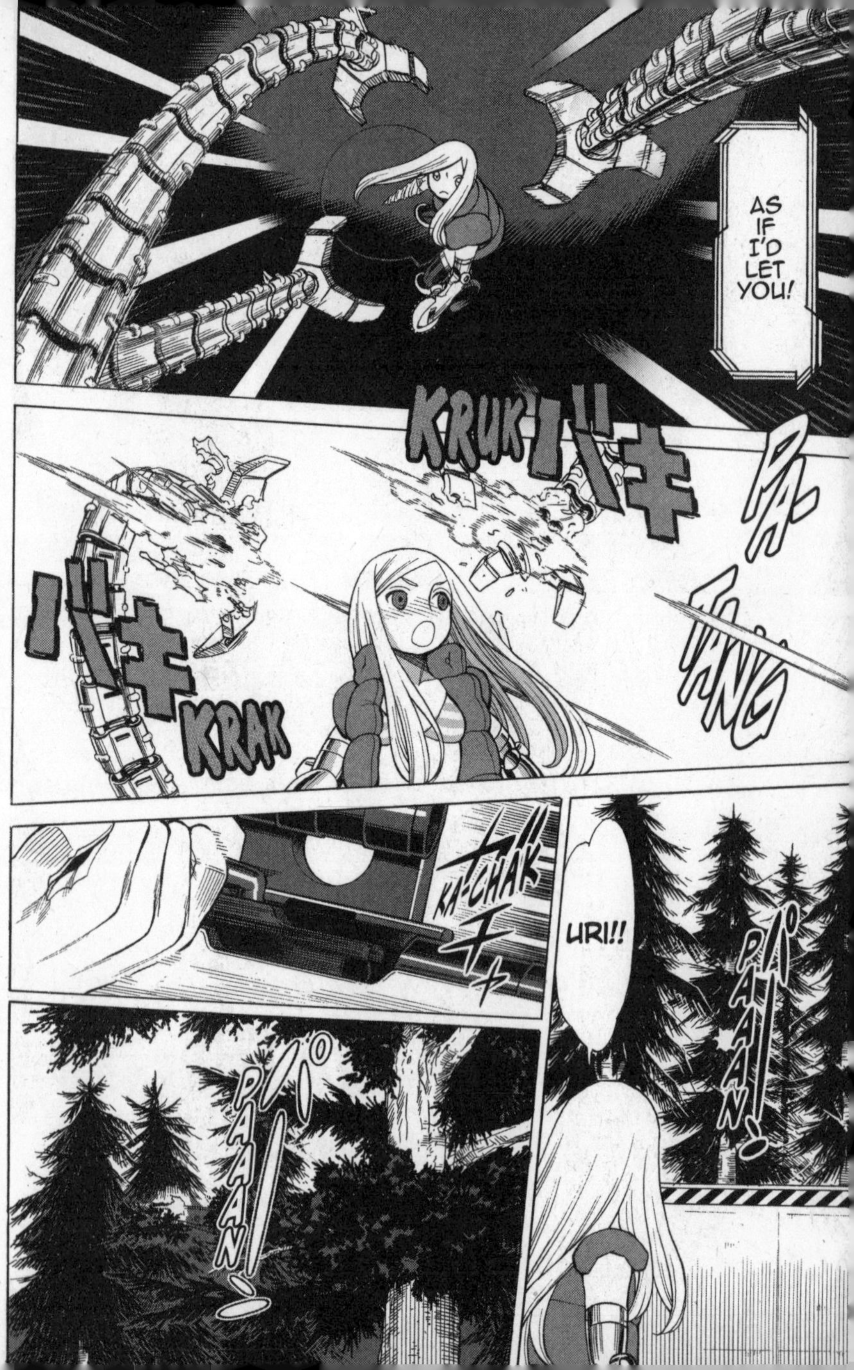
AS IF I'D LET YOU!
PA
TANG
KRUK
KRAK
URI!!
PAAAAN!
KA-CHAK
PAAAAN!

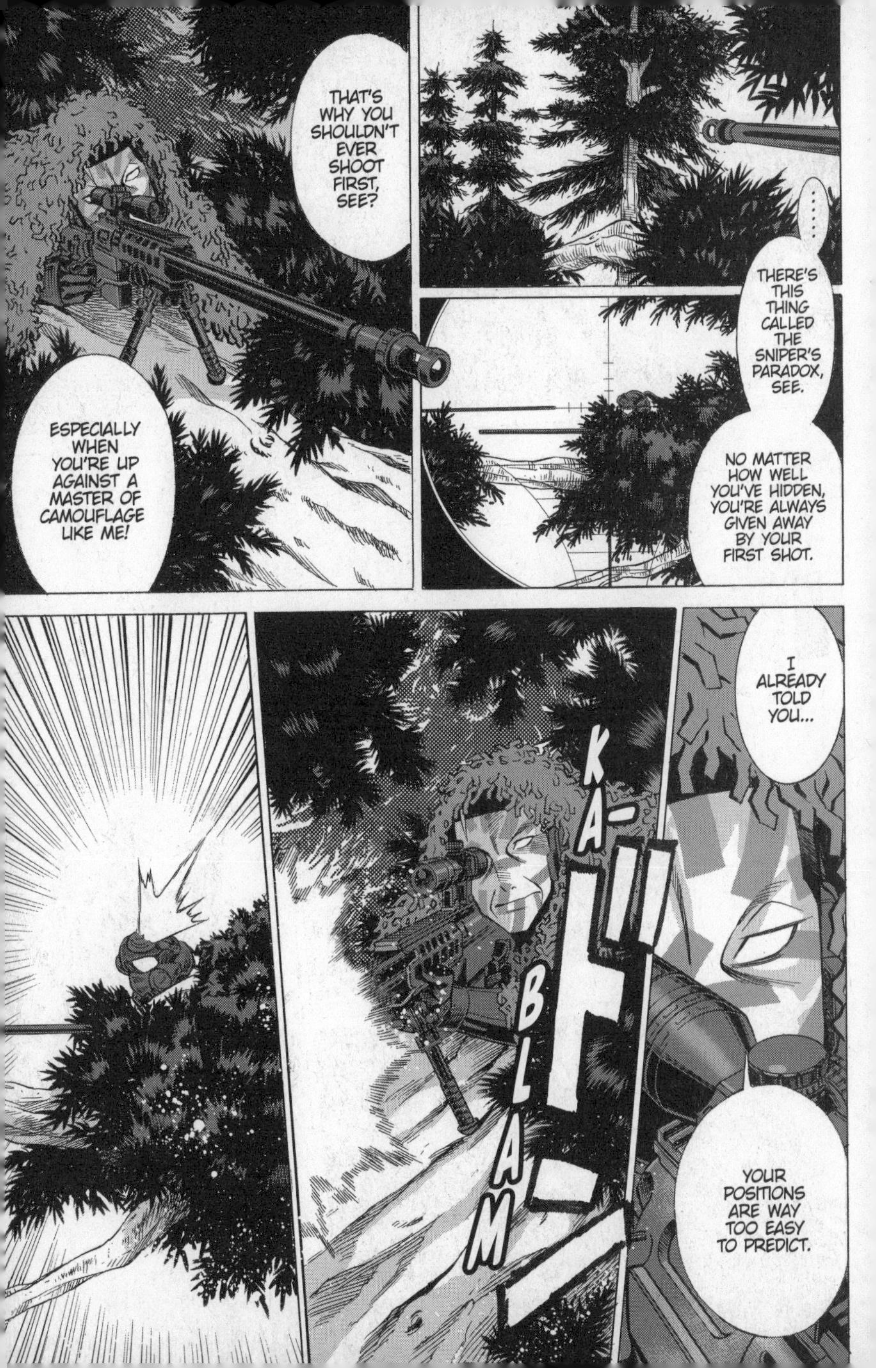

......
THERE'S THIS THING CALLED THE SNIPER'S PARADOX, SEE.
NO MATTER HOW WELL YOU'VE HIDDEN, YOU'RE ALWAYS GIVEN AWAY BY YOUR FIRST SHOT.
THAT'S WHY YOU SHOULDN'T EVER SHOOT FIRST, SEE?
ESPECIALLY WHEN YOU'RE UP AGAINST A MASTER OF CAMOUFLAGE LIKE ME!
I ALREADY TOLD YOU...
YOUR POSITIONS ARE WAY TOO EASY TO PREDICT.
KA-BLAM

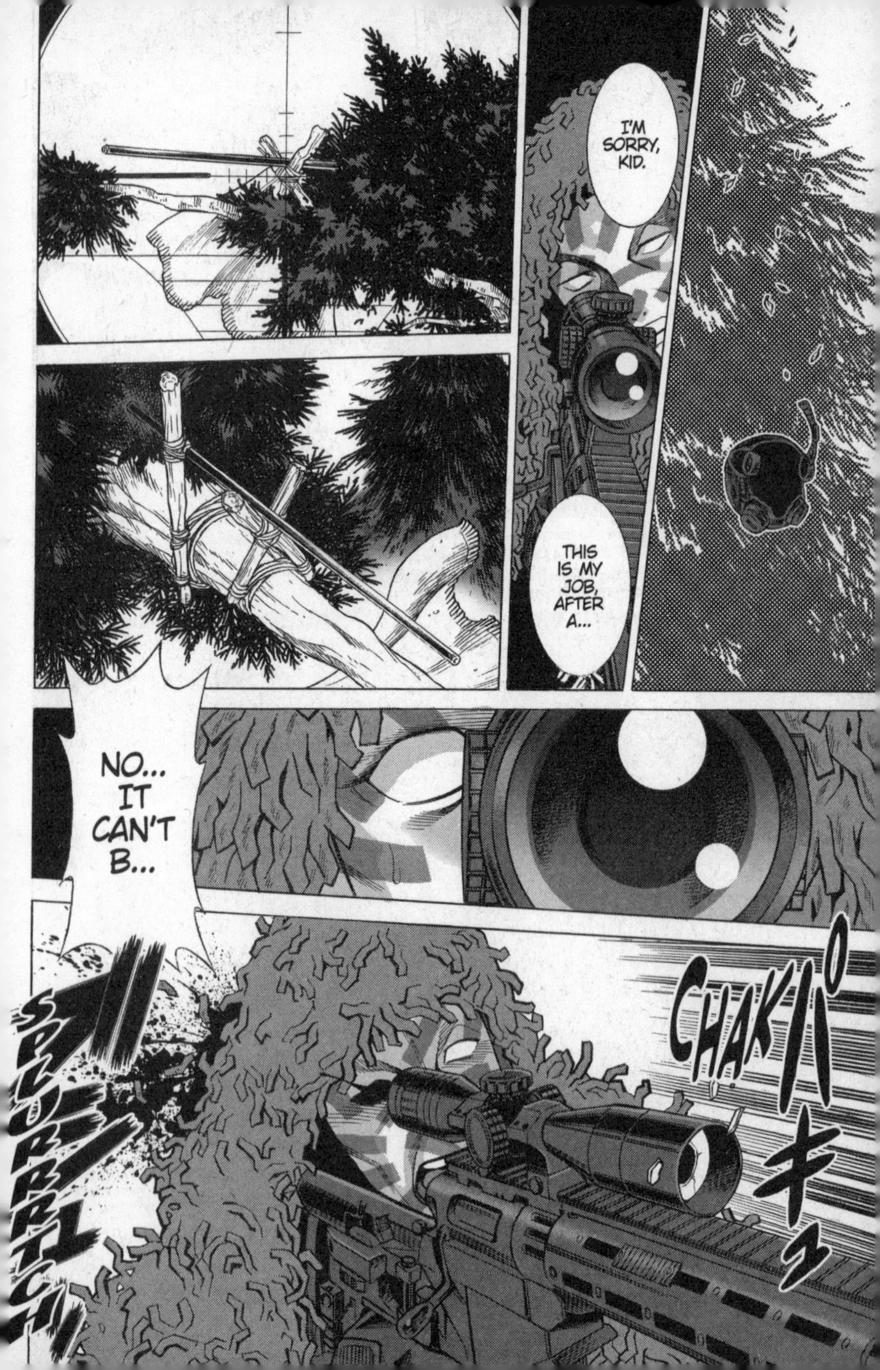
I'M SORRY, KID.
THIS IS MY JOB, AFTER A...
NO... IT CAN'T B...
CHAK
パキン

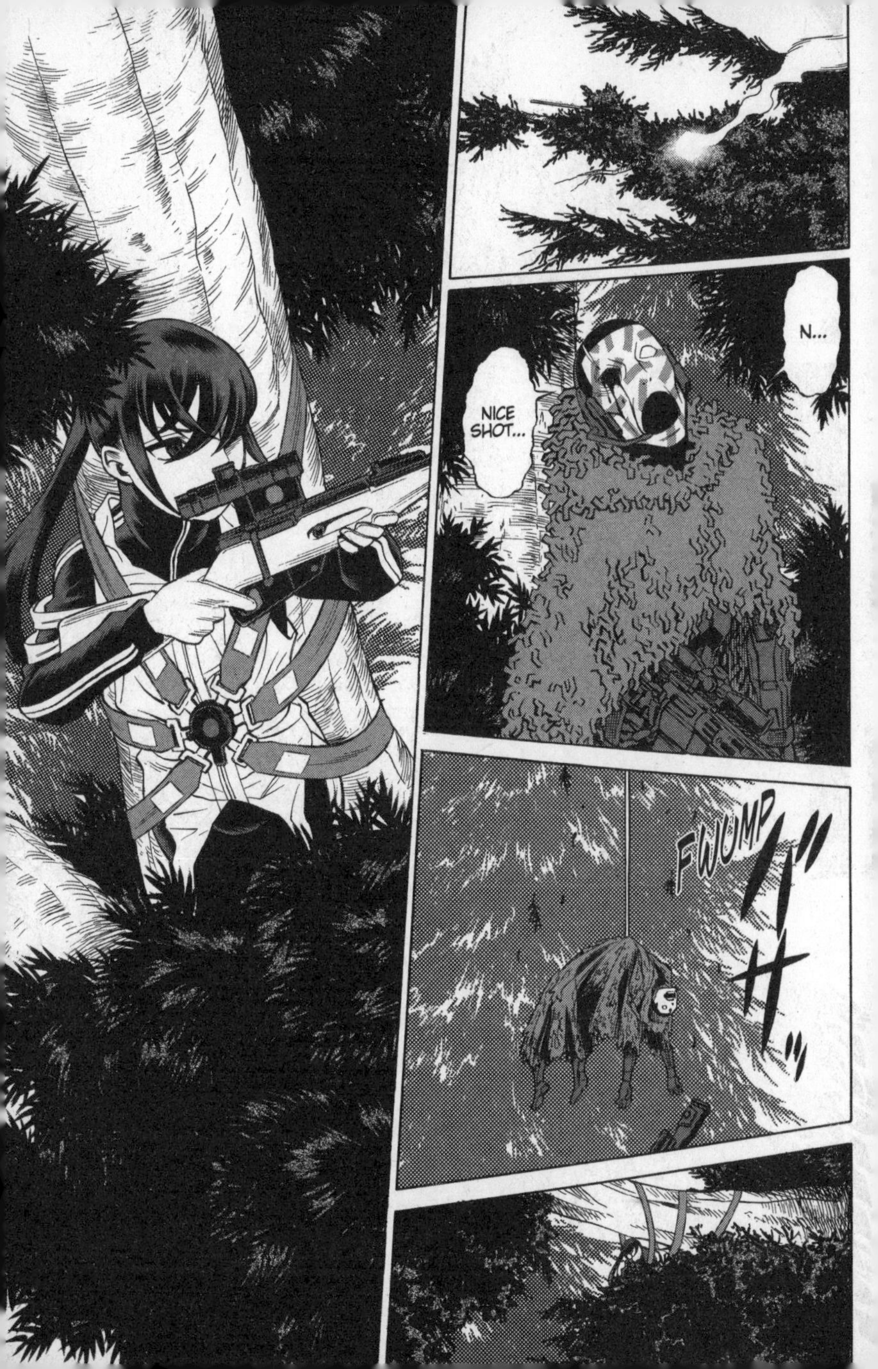
N...
NICE SHOT...
FWUMP

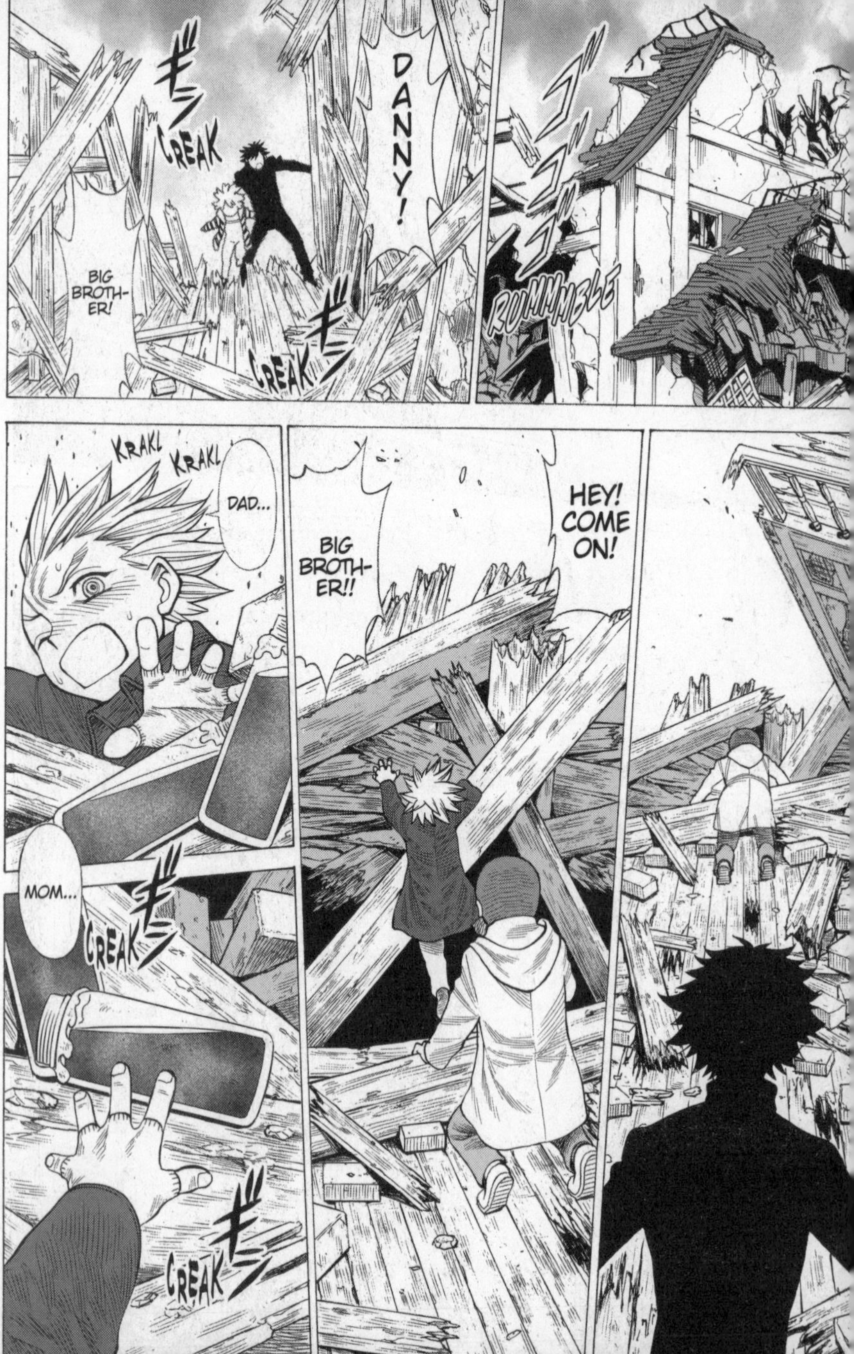
RUMMMBLE
DANNY!
CREAK
CREAK
BIG BROTHER-ER!
HEY! COME ON!
BIG BROTHER-ER!!
KRAKL
KRAKL
DAD...
MOM...
CREAK
CREAK

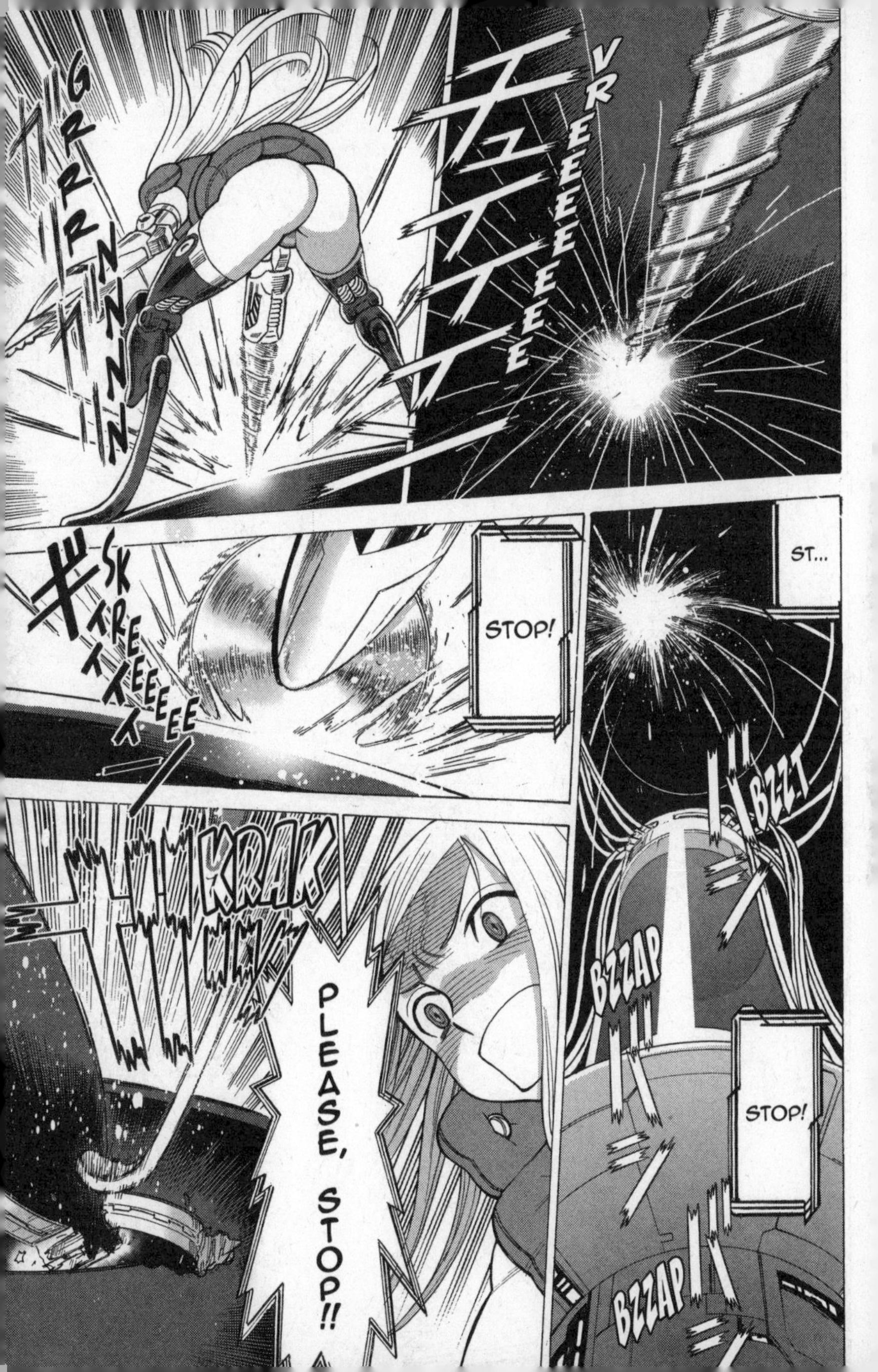
VREEEEEEEEE
GRRRNNNNNN
ST...
BZZT
BZZAP
STOP!
BZZAP
STOP!
SKREEEEEEE
KRAK
PLEASE, STOP!!

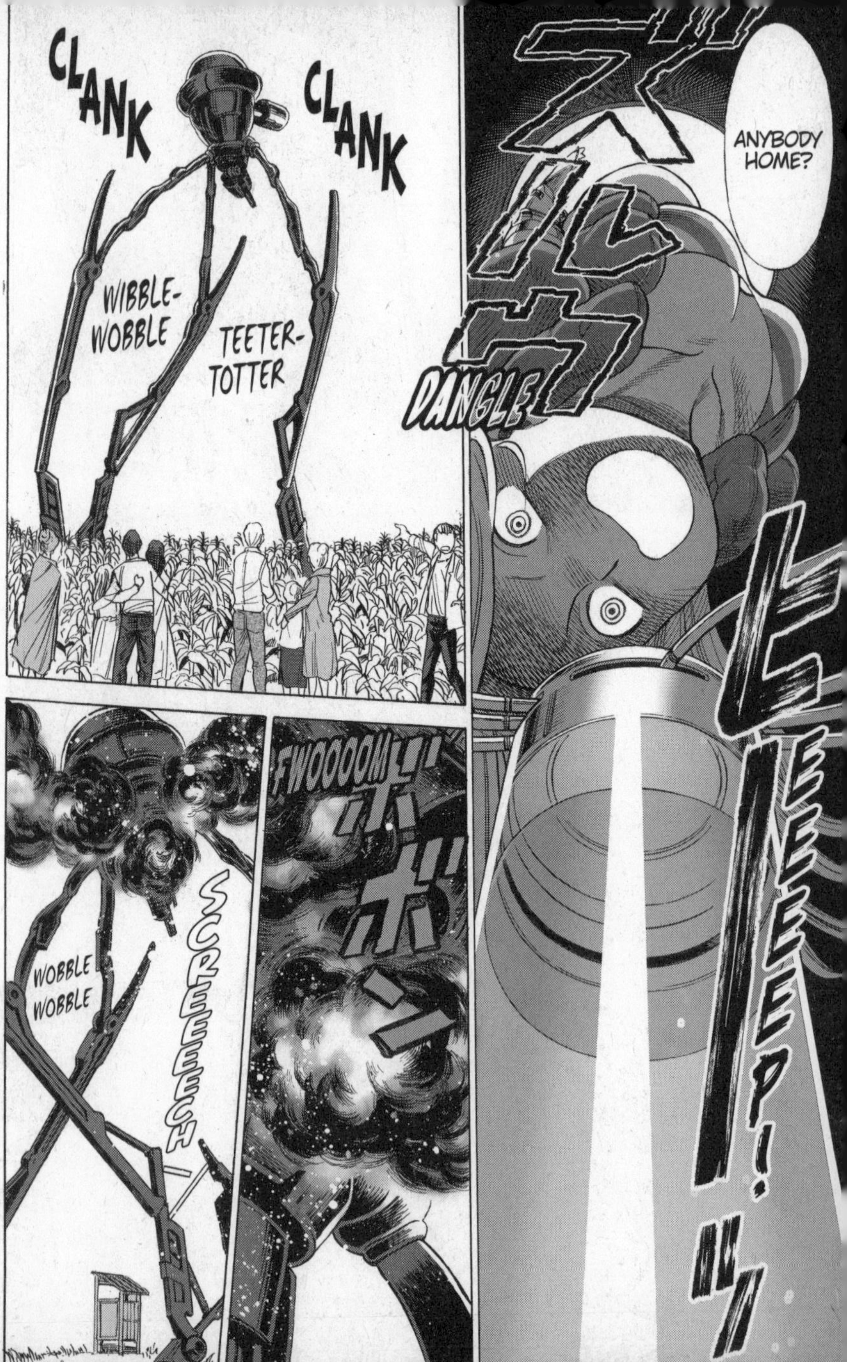
ANYBODY HOME?
DANGLE
EEEEEEEP!
CLANK
CLANK
WIBBLE-WOBBLE
TEETER-TOTTER
FWOOOOM!!
SCREEEECH
WOBBLE WOBBLE

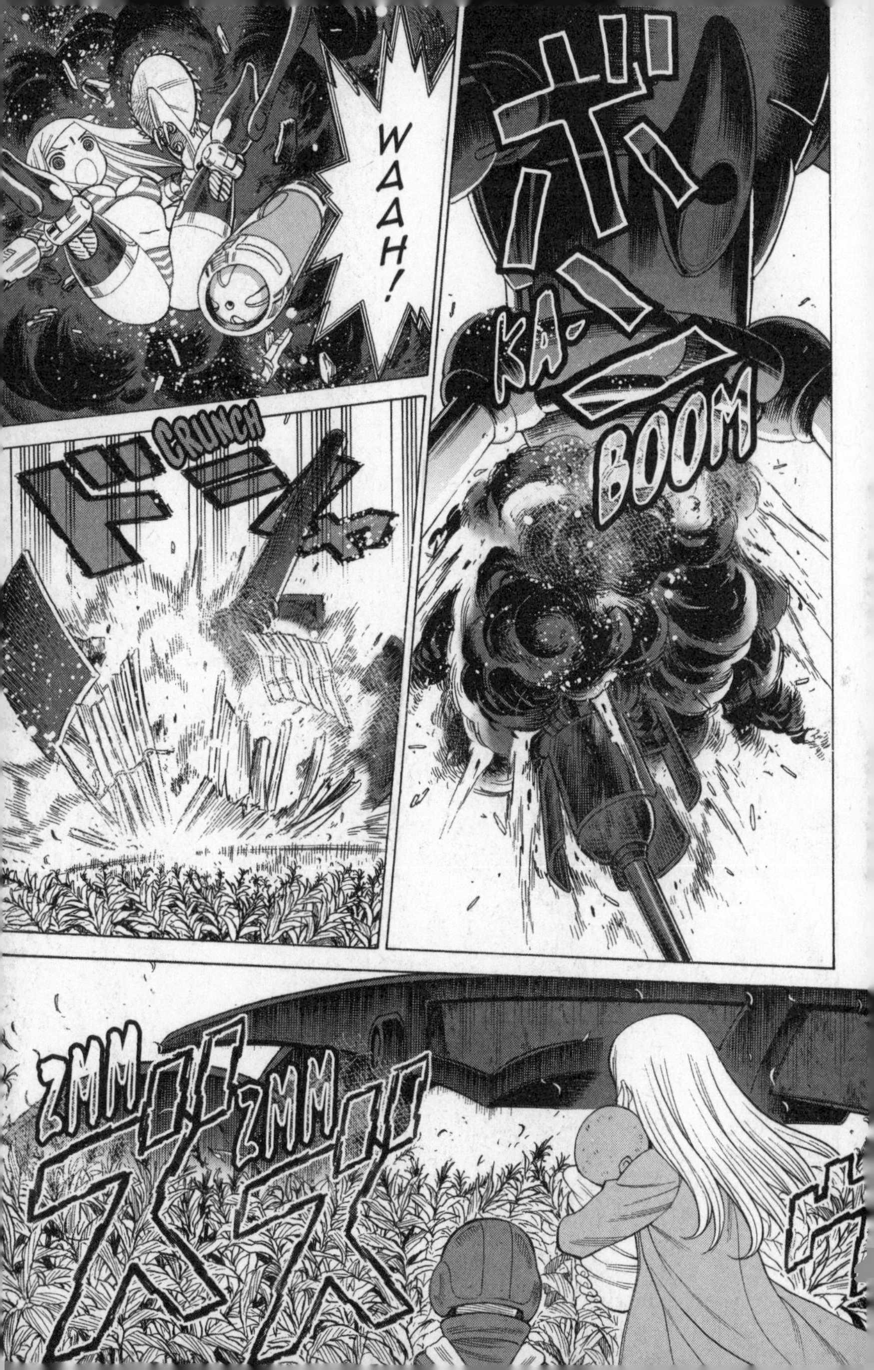
KA-BOOM
WAAAH!
CRUNCH
ZMM ZMM

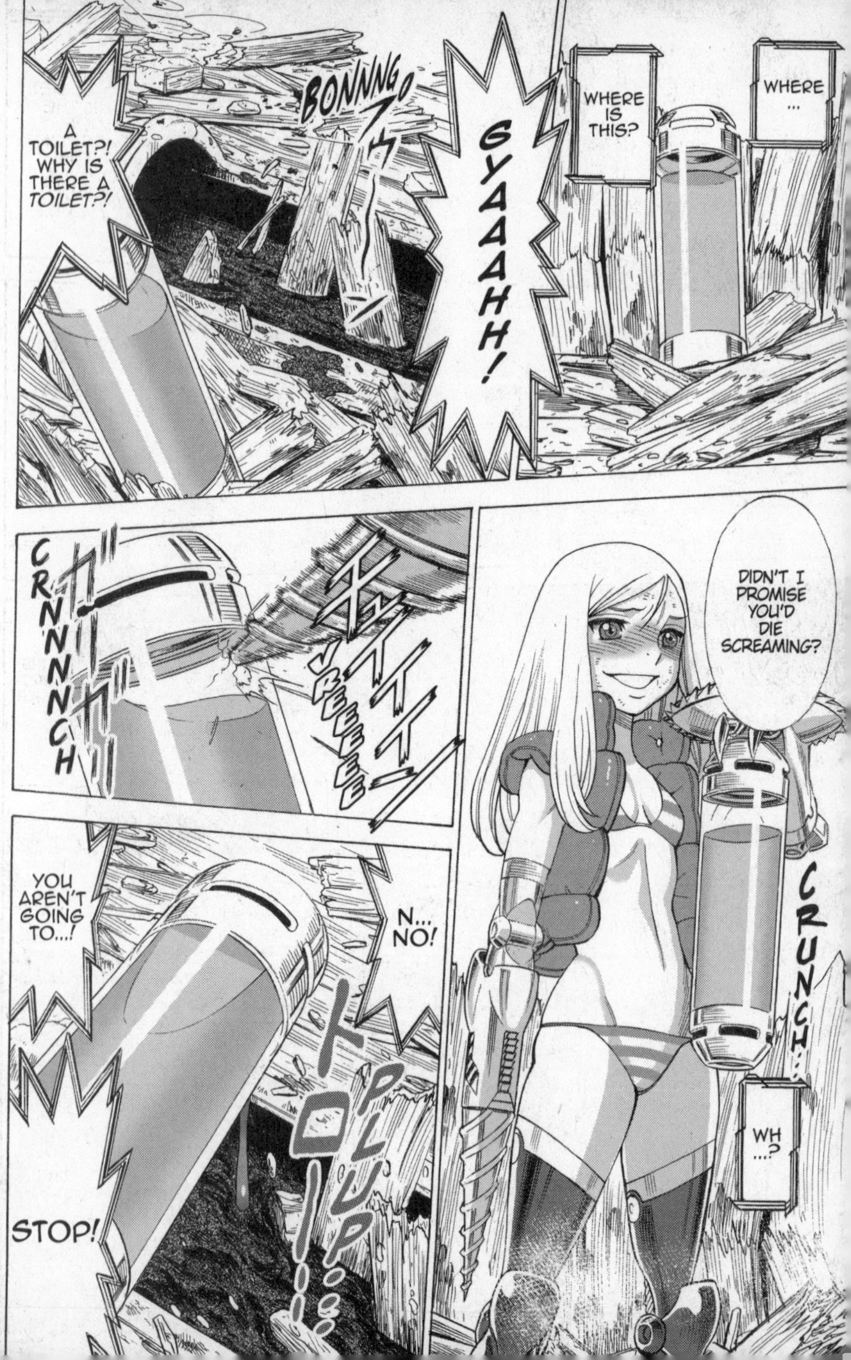
WHERE ...
WHERE IS THIS?
GYAAAHH!
BONNNG
A TOILET?! WHY IS THERE A TOILET?!
DIDN'T I PROMISE YOU'D DIE SCREAMING?
CRUNCH...
WH ...?
CRNNNNNCH
N... NO!
YOU AREN'T GOING TO...!
STOP!

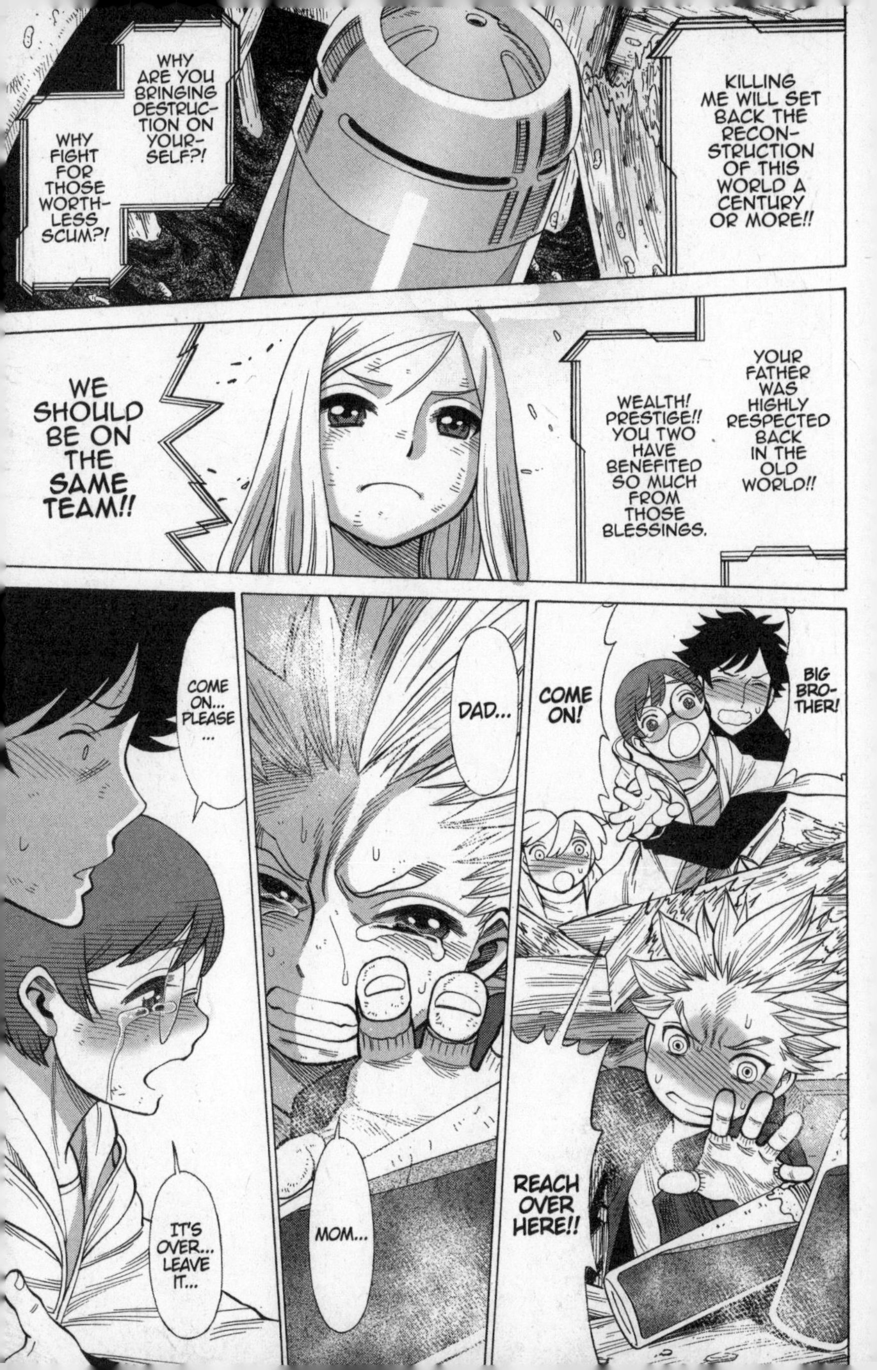
KILLING ME WILL SET BACK THE RECONSTRUCTION OF THIS WORLD A CENTURY OR MORE!!
WHY ARE YOU BRINGING DESTRUCTION ON YOURSELF?!
WHY FIGHT FOR THOSE WORTHLESS SCUM?!
YOUR FATHER WAS HIGHLY RESPECTED BACK IN THE OLD WORLD!!
WEALTH! PRESTIGE!! YOU TWO HAVE BENEFITED SO MUCH FROM THOSE BLESSINGS.
WE SHOULD BE ON THE SAME TEAM!!
BIG BROTHER!
COME ON!
REACH OVER HERE!!
DAD...
MOM...
COME ON... PLEASE...
IT'S OVER... LEAVE IT...

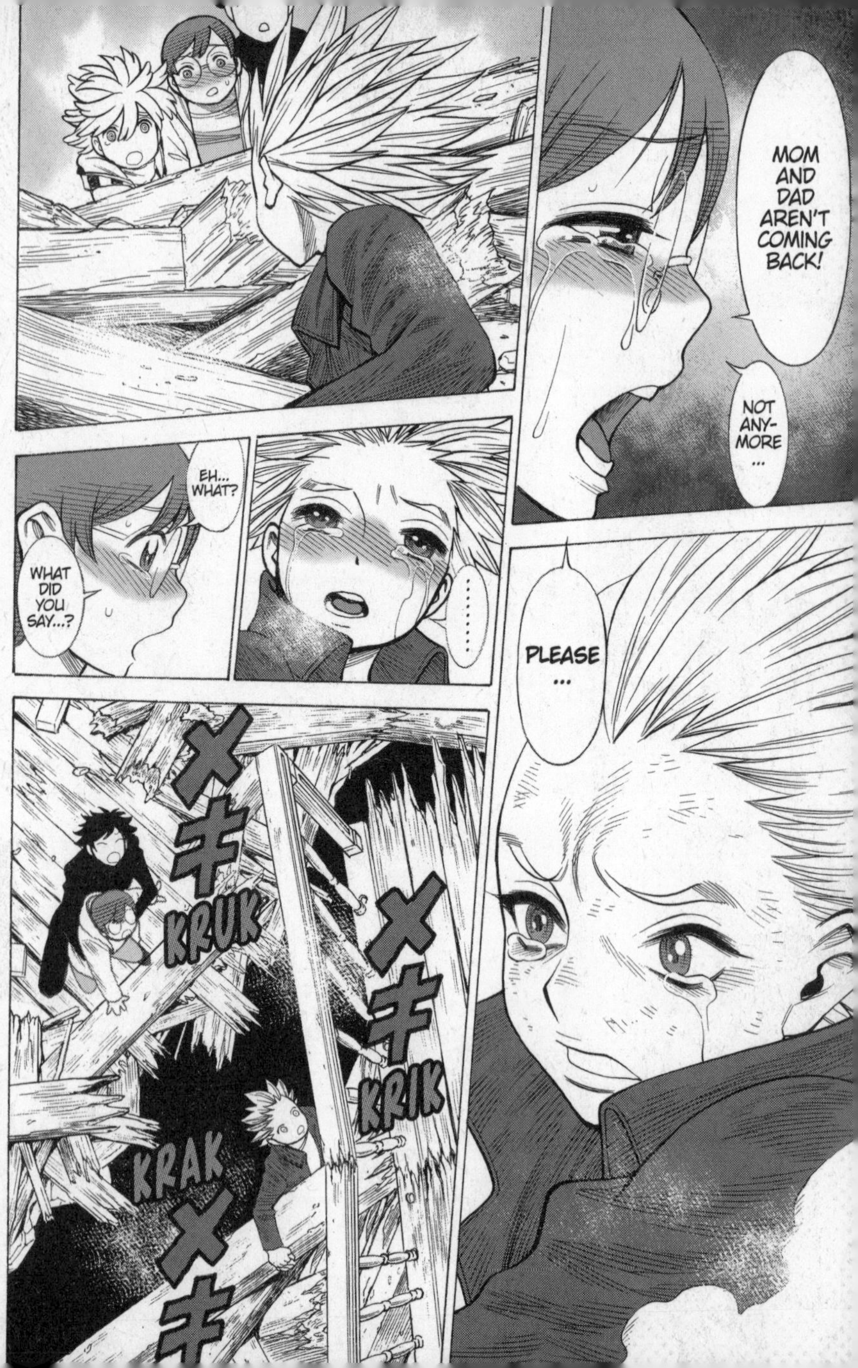
MOM AND DAD AREN'T COMING BACK!
NOT ANYMORE...
PLEASE...
......
EH... WHAT?
WHAT DID YOU SAY...?
KRIK
KRUK
KRAK

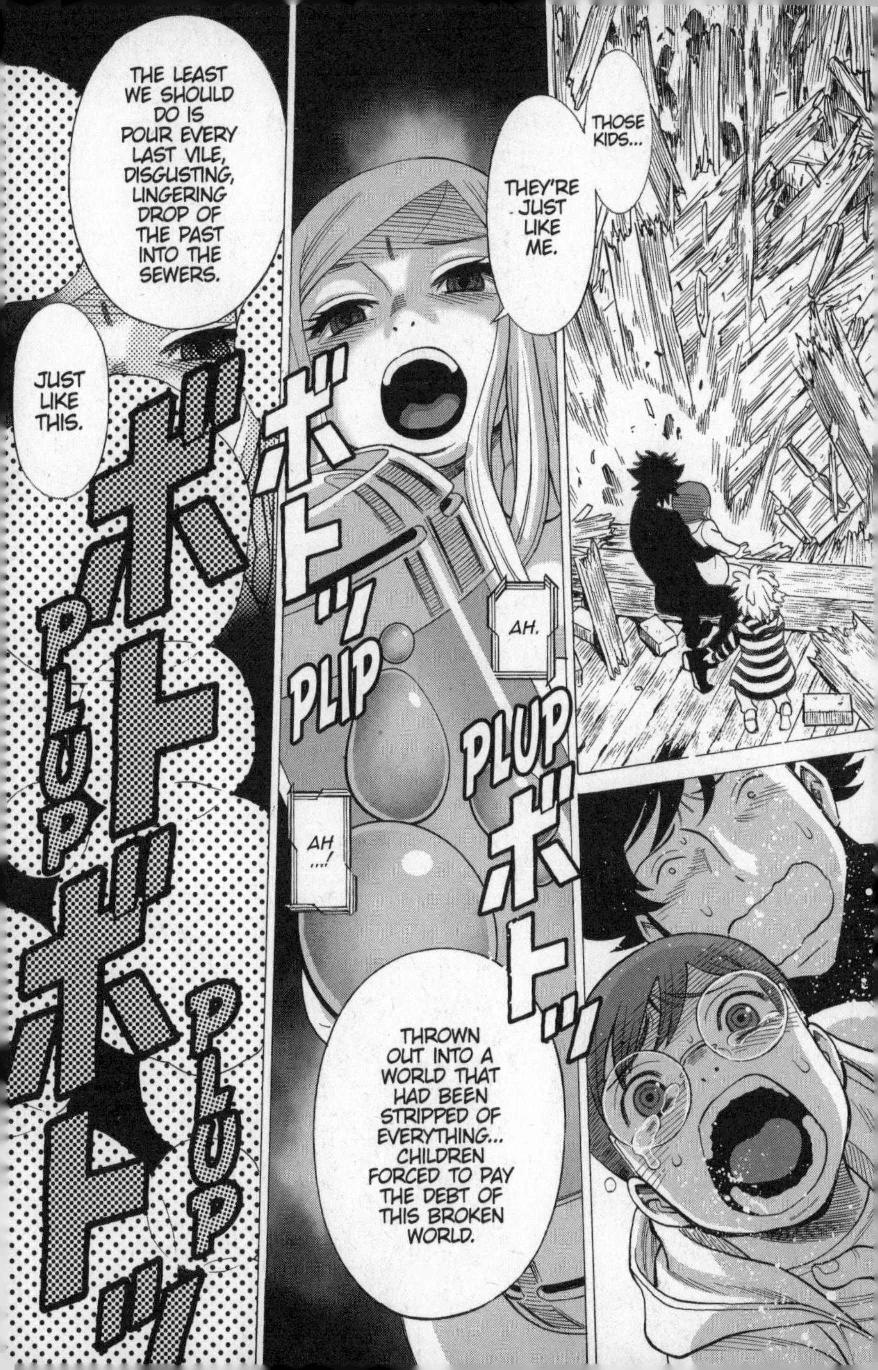
THOSE KIDS...
THEY'RE JUST LIKE ME.
AH.
ボトッ
PLIP
PLUP
ボトッ
AH ...!
THROWN OUT INTO A WORLD THAT HAD BEEN STRIPPED OF EVERYTHING... CHILDREN FORCED TO PAY THE DEBT OF THIS BROKEN WORLD.
THE LEAST WE SHOULD DO IS POUR EVERY LAST VILE, DISGUSTING, LINGERING DROP OF THE PAST INTO THE SEWERS.
JUST LIKE THIS.
ボトッボトッ
PLUP
PLUP

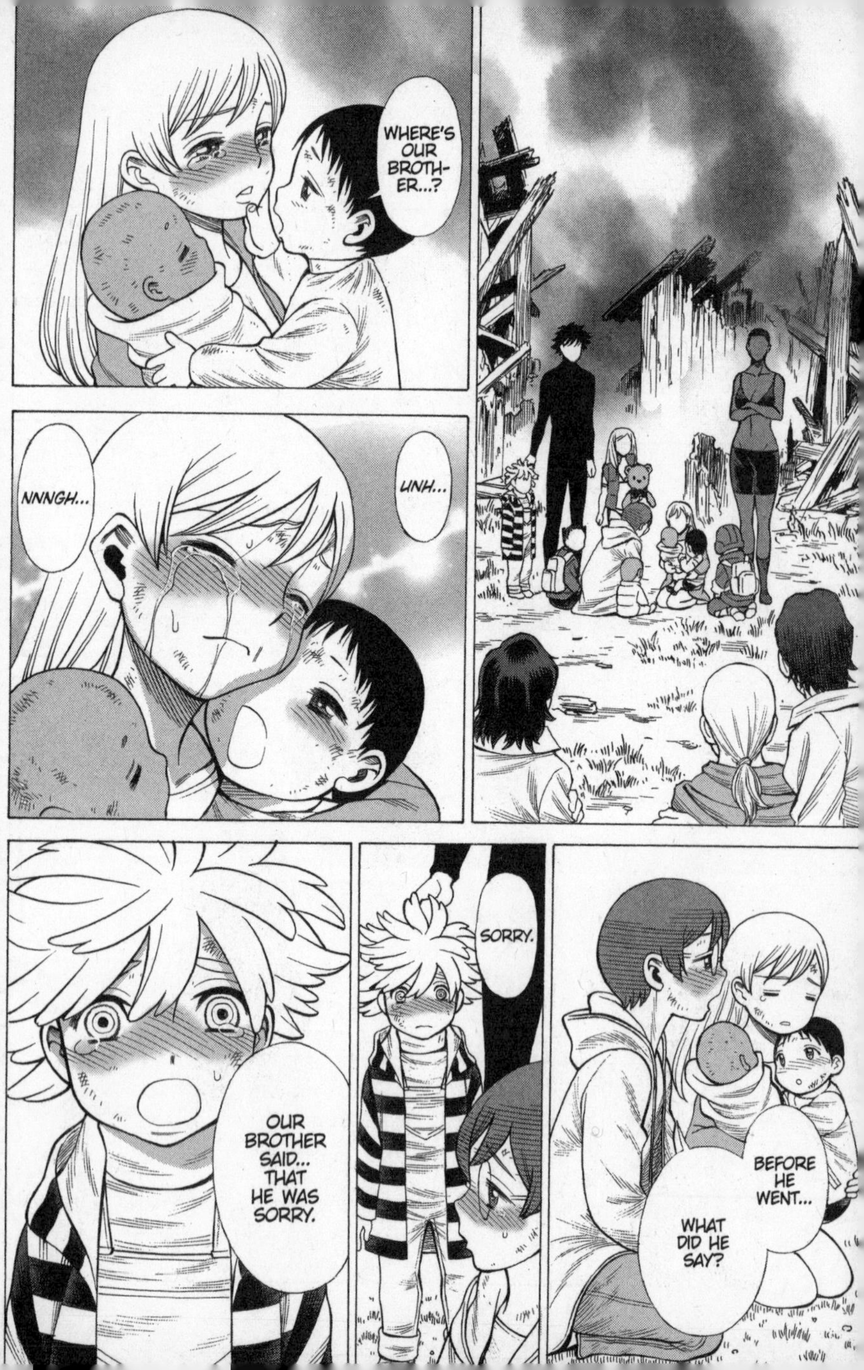
WHERE'S OUR BROTHER...?
UNH...
NNNGH...
BEFORE HE WENT...
WHAT DID HE SAY?
SORRY.
OUR BROTHER SAID... THAT HE WAS SORRY.

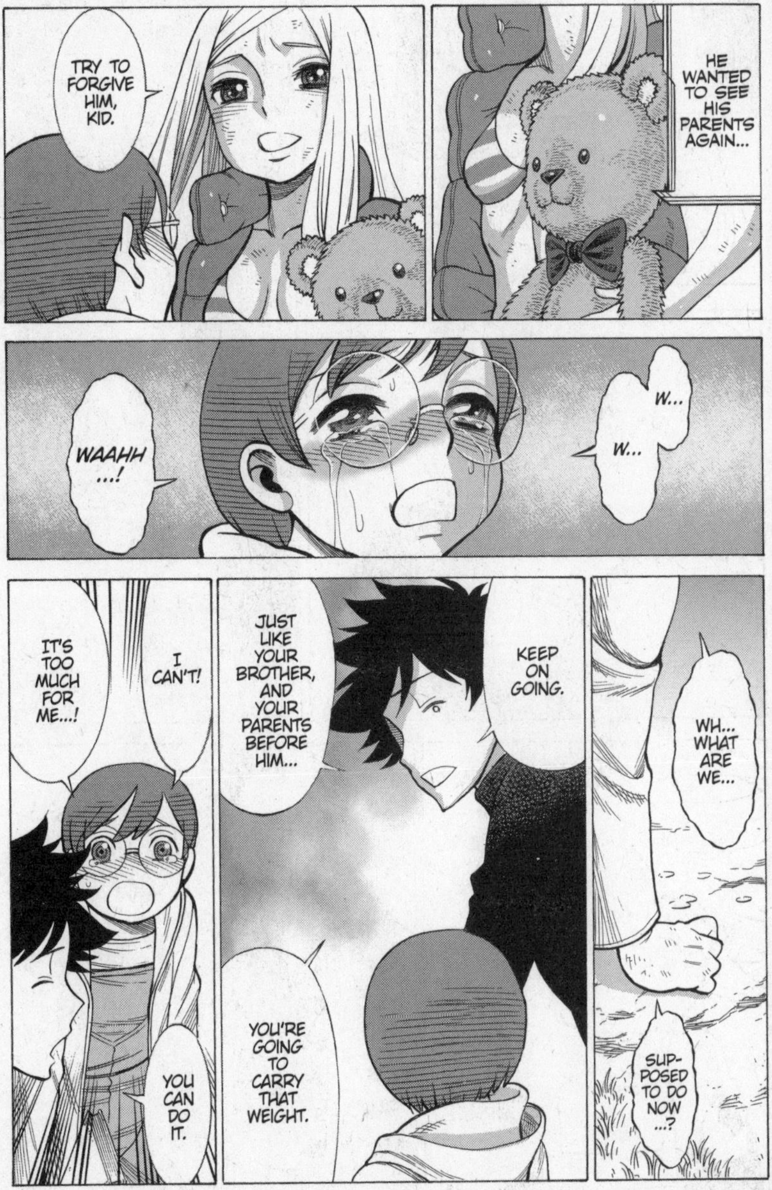
HE WANTED TO SEE HIS PARENTS AGAIN...
TRY TO FORGIVE HIM, KID.
W... W...
WAAHH ...!
WH... WHAT ARE WE...
SUP-POSED TO DO NOW ...?
KEEP ON GOING.
JUST LIKE YOUR BROTHER, AND YOUR PARENTS BEFORE HIM...
YOU'RE GOING TO CARRY THAT WEIGHT.
I CAN'T!
IT'S TOO MUCH FOR ME...!
YOU CAN DO IT.

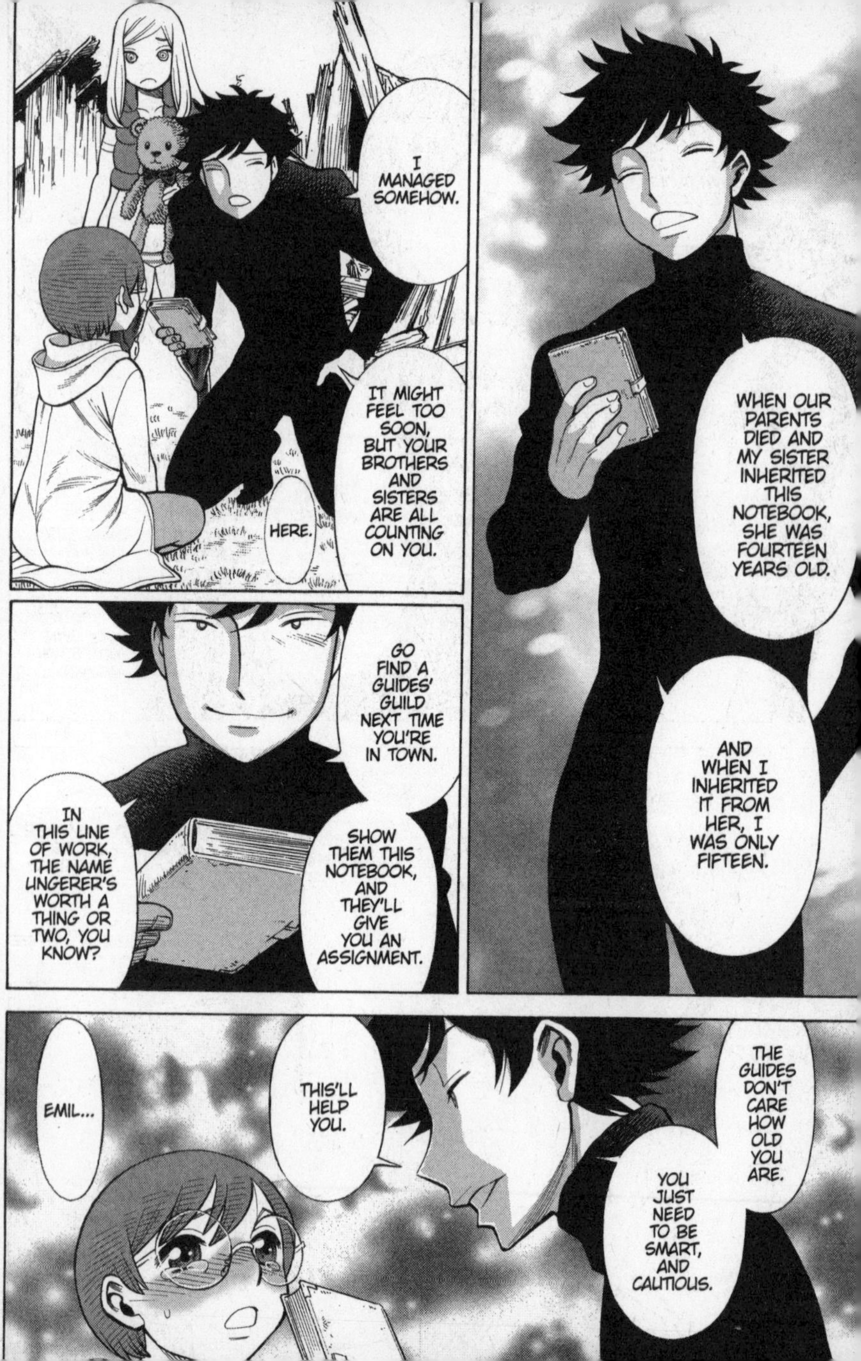

WHEN OUR PARENTS DIED AND MY SISTER INHERITED THIS NOTEBOOK, SHE WAS FOURTEEN YEARS OLD.
AND WHEN I INHERITED IT FROM HER, I WAS ONLY FIFTEEN.
I MANAGED SOMEHOW.
IT MIGHT FEEL TOO SOON, BUT YOUR BROTHERS AND SISTERS ARE ALL COUNTING ON YOU.
HERE.
GO FIND A GUIDES' GUILD NEXT TIME YOU'RE IN TOWN.
SHOW THEM THIS NOTEBOOK, AND THEY'LL GIVE YOU AN ASSIGNMENT.
IN THIS LINE OF WORK, THE NAME UNGERER'S WORTH A THING OR TWO, YOU KNOW?
THE GUIDES DON'T CARE HOW OLD YOU ARE.
YOU JUST NEED TO BE SMART, AND CAUTIOUS.
THIS'LL HELP YOU.
EMIL...

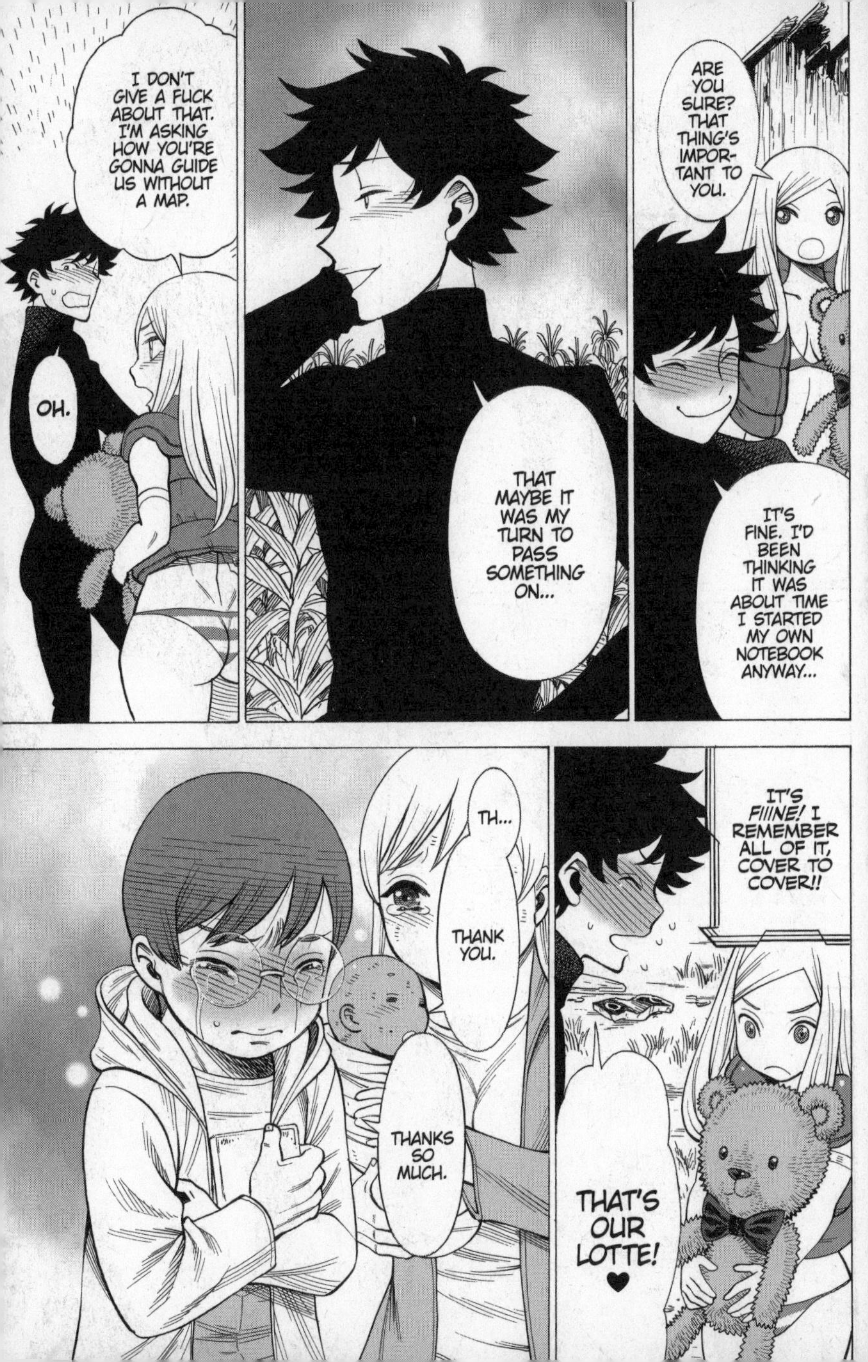
ARE YOU SURE? THAT THING'S IMPOR-TANT TO YOU.
IT'S FINE. I'D BEEN THINKING IT WAS ABOUT TIME I STARTED MY OWN NOTEBOOK ANYWAY...
THAT MAYBE IT WAS MY TURN TO PASS SOMETHING ON...
I DON'T GIVE A FUCK ABOUT THAT. I'M ASKING HOW YOU'RE GONNA GUIDE US WITHOUT A MAP.
OH.
IT'S *FIIINE!* I REMEMBER ALL OF IT, COVER TO COVER!!
THAT'S OUR LOTTE! ♥
TH...
THANK YOU.
THANKS SO MUCH.

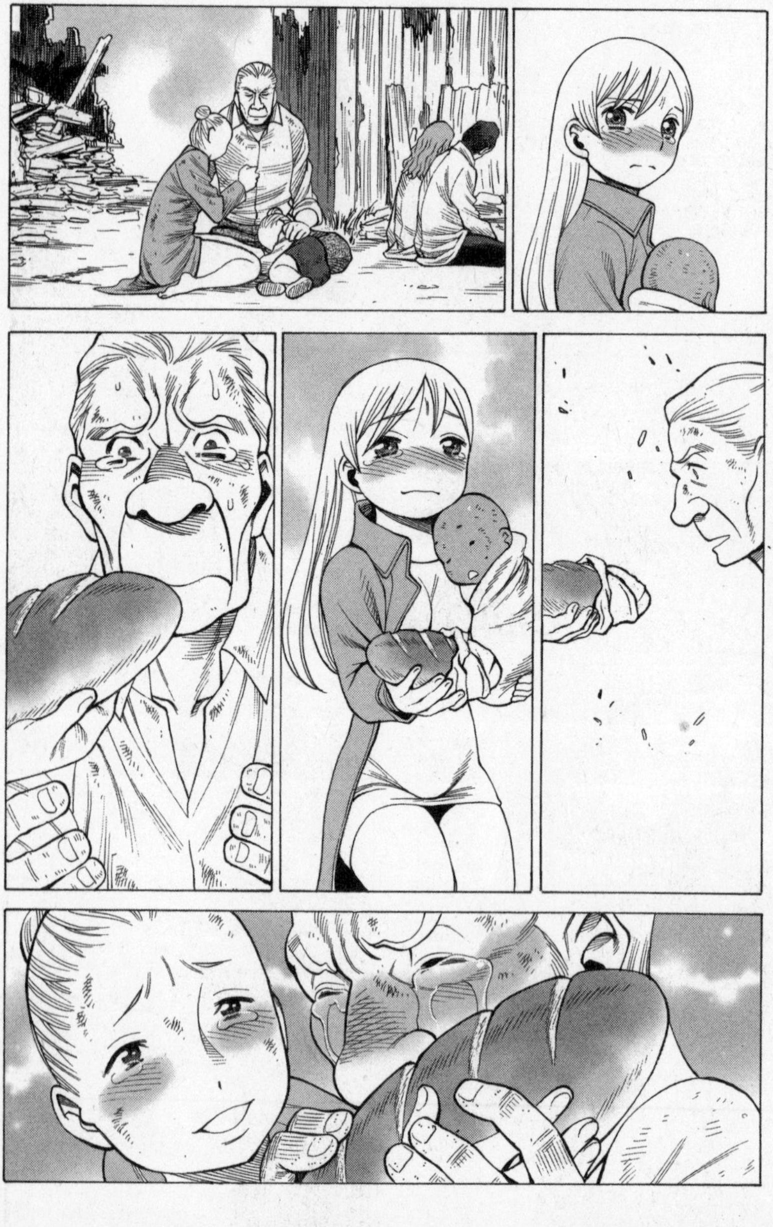

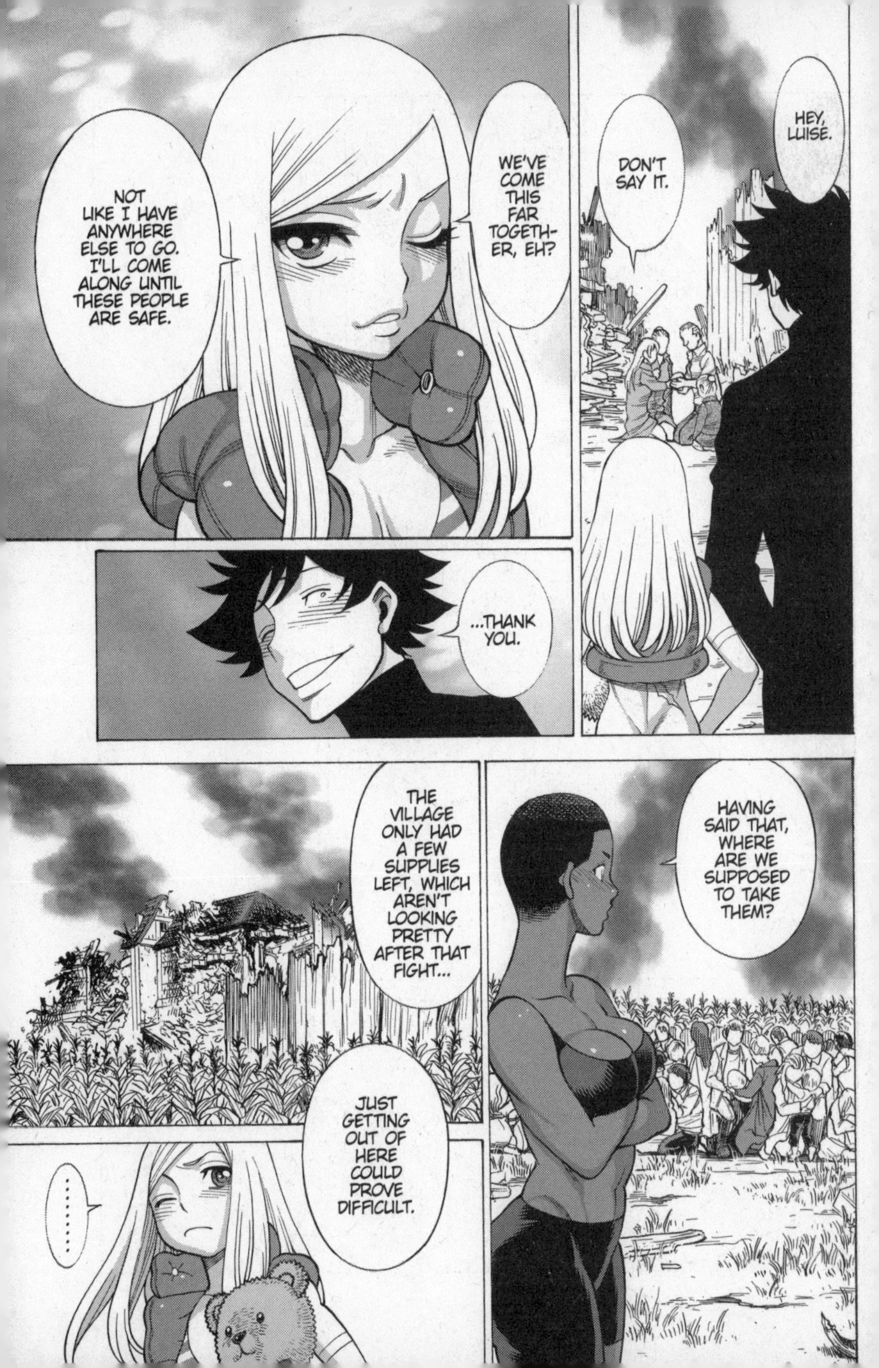
HEY, LUISE.
DON'T SAY IT.
WE'VE COME THIS FAR TOGETHER, EH?
NOT LIKE I HAVE ANYWHERE ELSE TO GO. I'LL COME ALONG UNTIL THESE PEOPLE ARE SAFE.
...THANK YOU.
HAVING SAID THAT, WHERE ARE WE SUPPOSED TO TAKE THEM?
THE VILLAGE ONLY HAD A FEW SUPPLIES LEFT, WHICH AREN'T LOOKING PRETTY AFTER THAT FIGHT...
JUST GETTING OUT OF HERE COULD PROVE DIFFICULT.
....

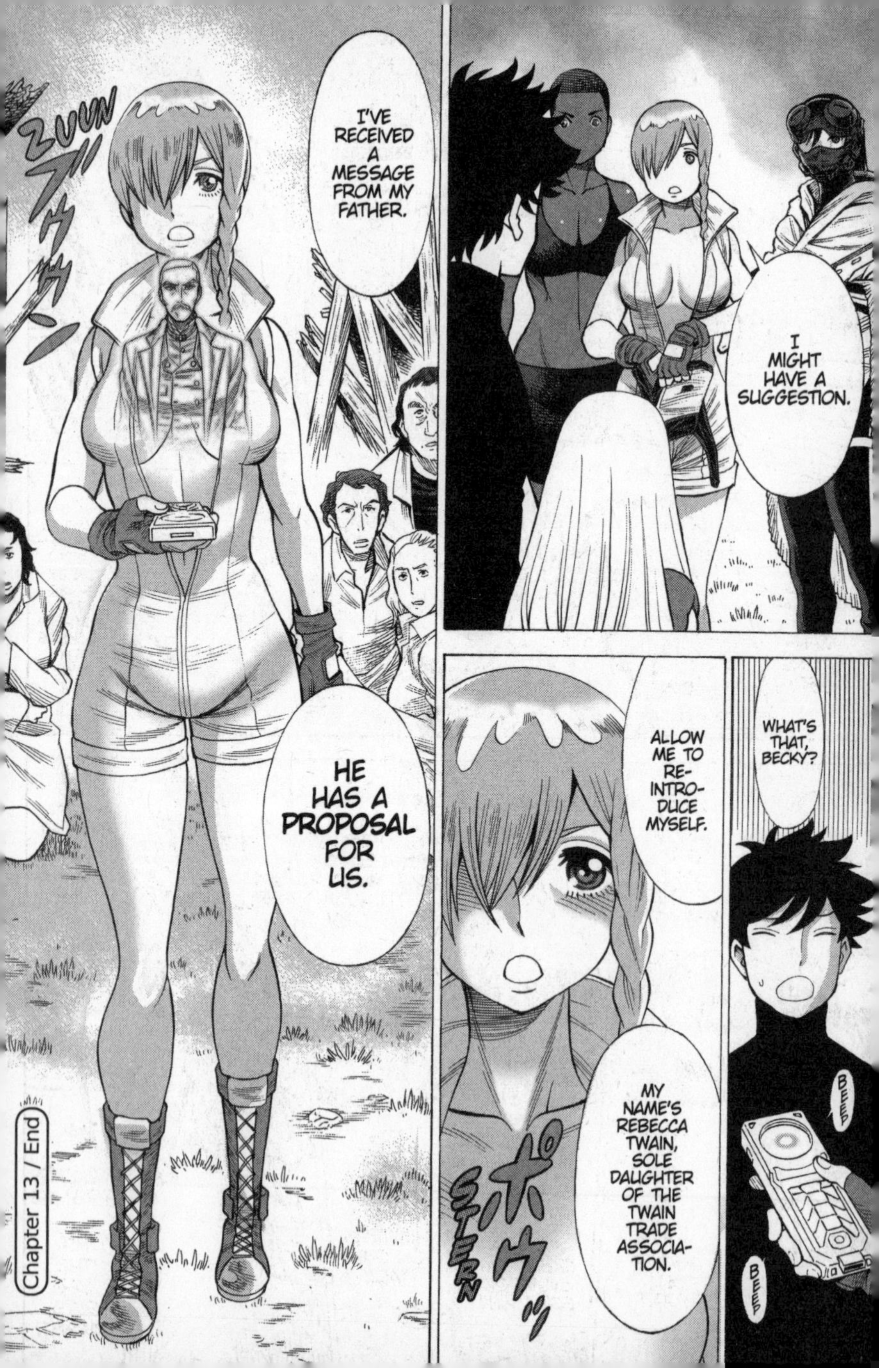
I MIGHT HAVE A SUGGESTION.
WHAT'S THAT, BECKY?
BEEP
BEEP
ALLOW ME TO RE-INTRO-DUCE MYSELF.
MY NAME'S REBECCA TWAIN, SOLE DAUGHTER OF THE TWAIN TRADE ASSOCIA-TION.
STERN
ZUUN
I'VE RECEIVED A MESSAGE FROM MY FATHER.
HE HAS A PROPOSAL FOR US.
Chapter 13 / End

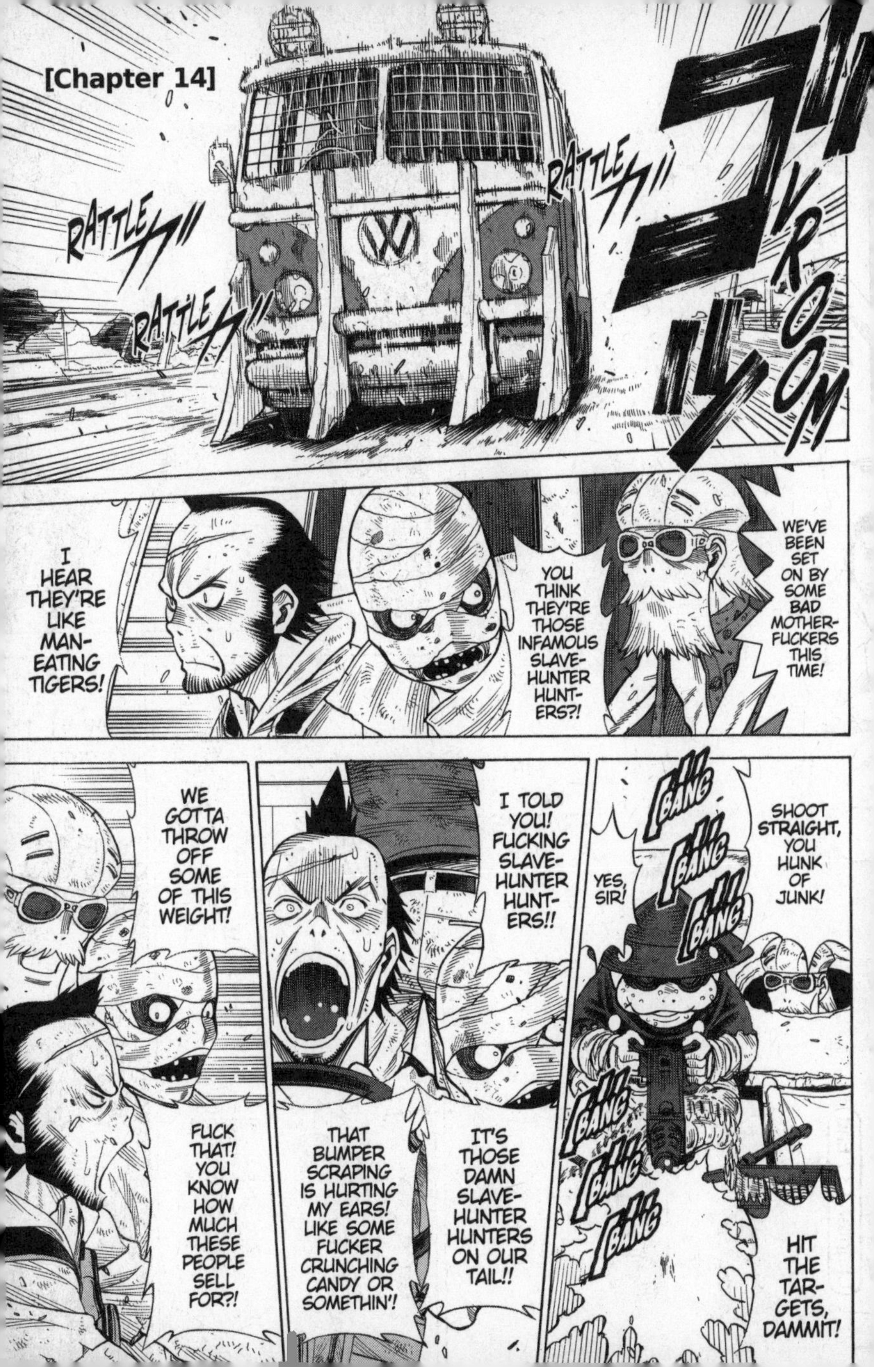
[Chapter 14]
VROOM
RATTLE
RATTLE
RATTLE
WE'VE BEEN SET ON BY SOME BAD MOTHER-FUCKERS THIS TIME!
YOU THINK THEY'RE THOSE INFAMOUS SLAVE-HUNTER HUNTERS?!
I HEAR THEY'RE LIKE MAN-EATING TIGERS!
SHOOT STRAIGHT, YOU HUNK OF JUNK!
BANG BANG BANG
YES, SIR!
BANG BANG BANG
HIT THE TARGETS, DAMMIT!
I TOLD YOU! FUCKING SLAVE-HUNTER HUNTERS!!
IT'S THOSE DAMN SLAVE-HUNTER HUNTERS ON OUR TAIL!!
THAT BUMPER SCRAPING IS HURTING MY EARS! LIKE SOME FUCKER CRUNCHING CANDY OR SOMETHIN'!
WE GOTTA THROW OFF SOME OF THIS WEIGHT!
FUCK THAT! YOU KNOW HOW MUCH THESE PEOPLE SELL FOR?!

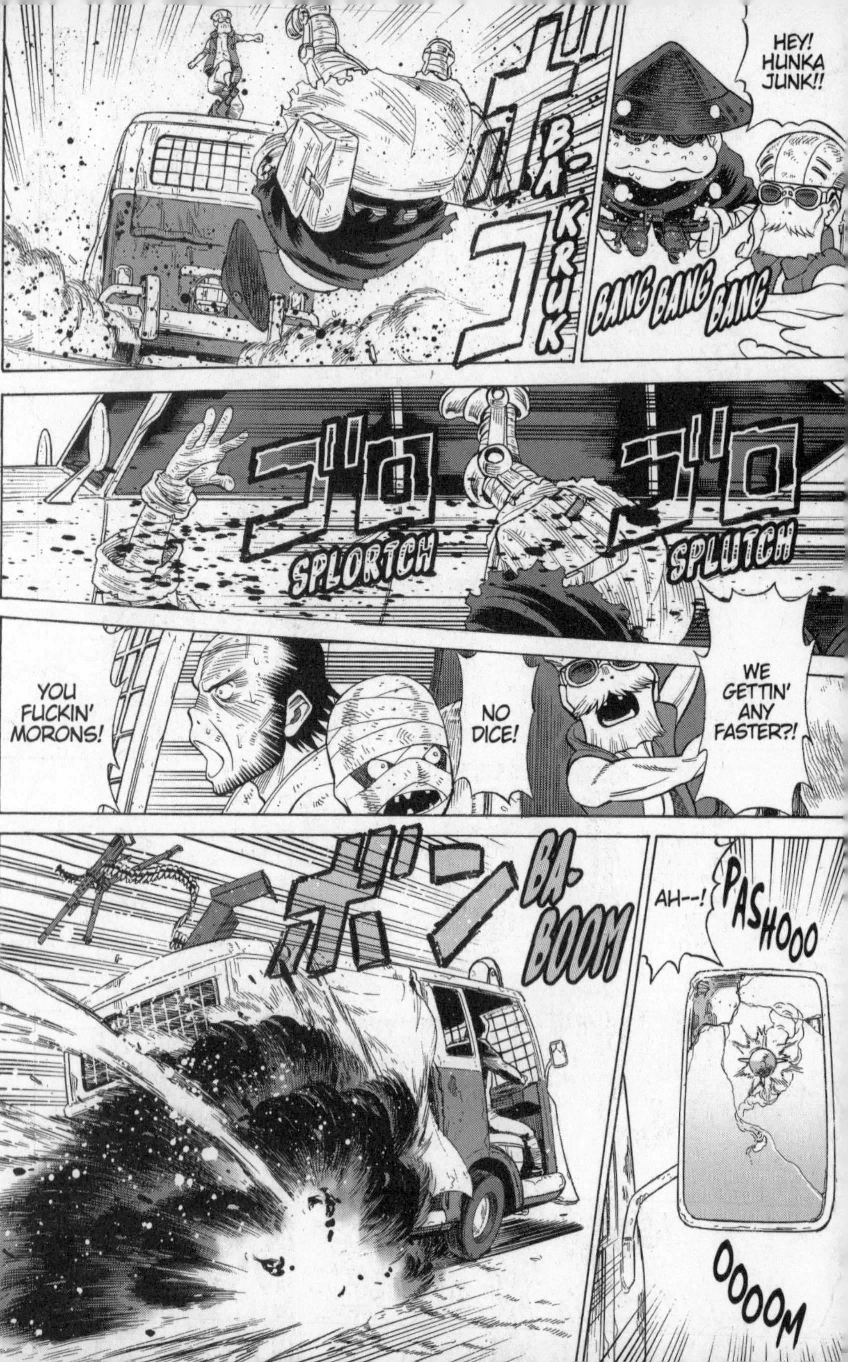
HEY! HUNKA JUNK!!
BANG BANG BANG
BA-KRUK
SPLUTCH
SPLORTCH
WE GETTIN' ANY FASTER?!
NO DICE!
YOU FUCKIN' MORONS!
AH--!
PASHOOO
OOOOM
BA-BOOM

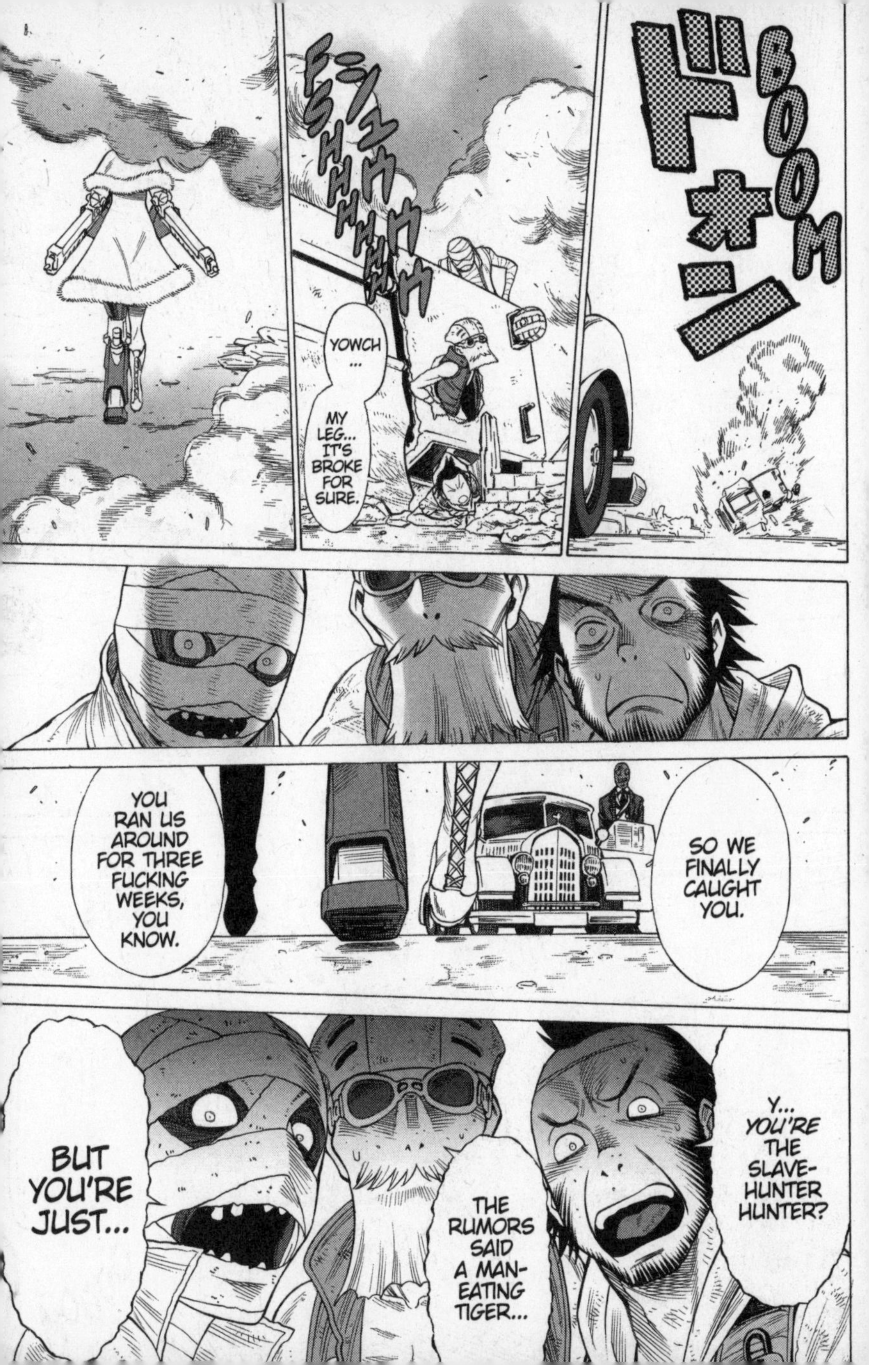
BOOM
FSHHHHHH
YOWCH...
MY LEG... IT'S BROKE FOR SURE.
SO WE FINALLY CAUGHT YOU.
YOU RAN US AROUND FOR THREE FUCKING WEEKS, YOU KNOW.
Y... YOU'RE THE SLAVE-HUNTER HUNTER?
THE RUMORS SAID A MAN-EATING TIGER...
BUT YOU'RE JUST...

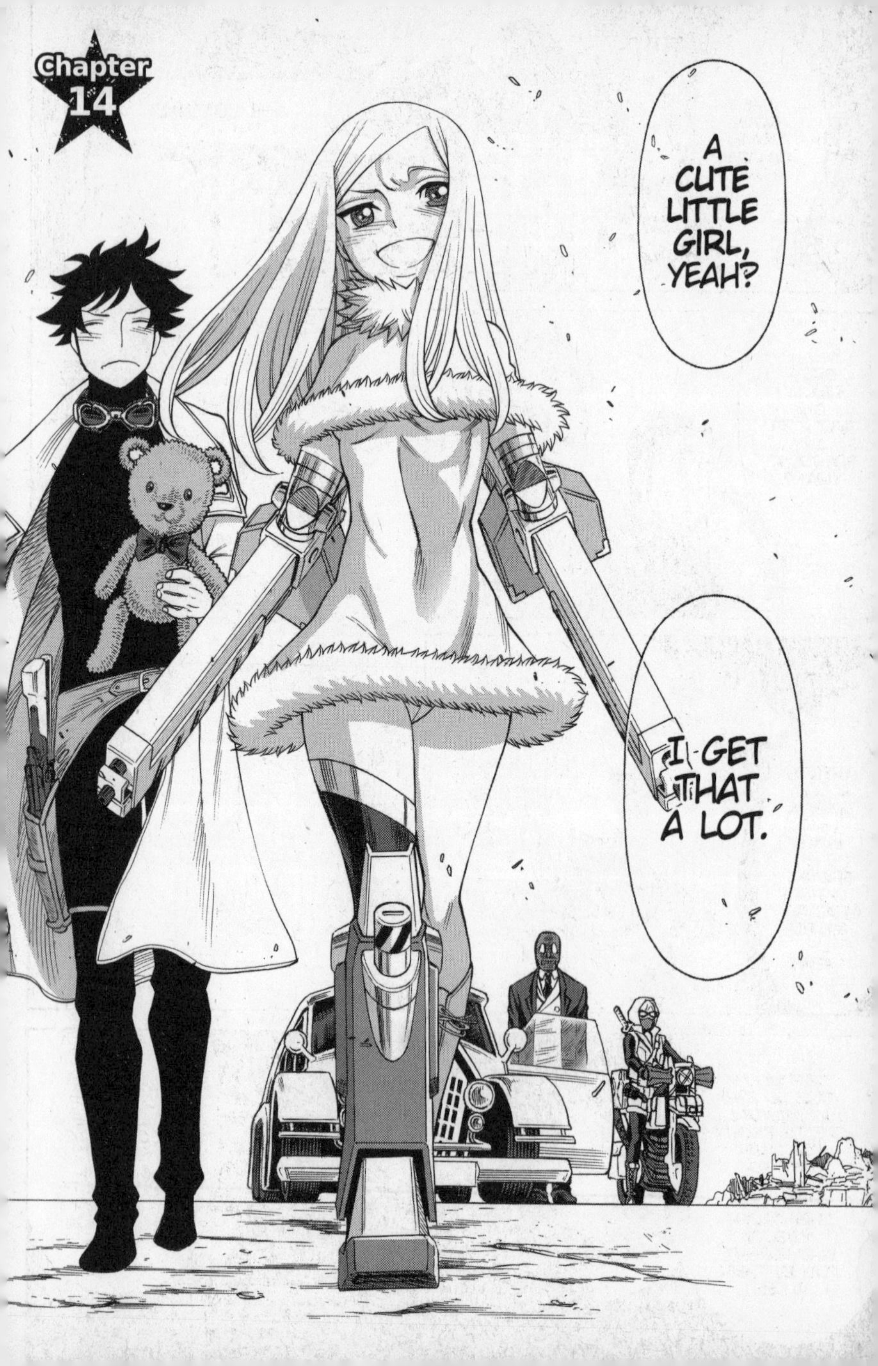
Chapter 14
A CUTE LITTLE GIRL, YEAH?
I GET THAT A LOT.

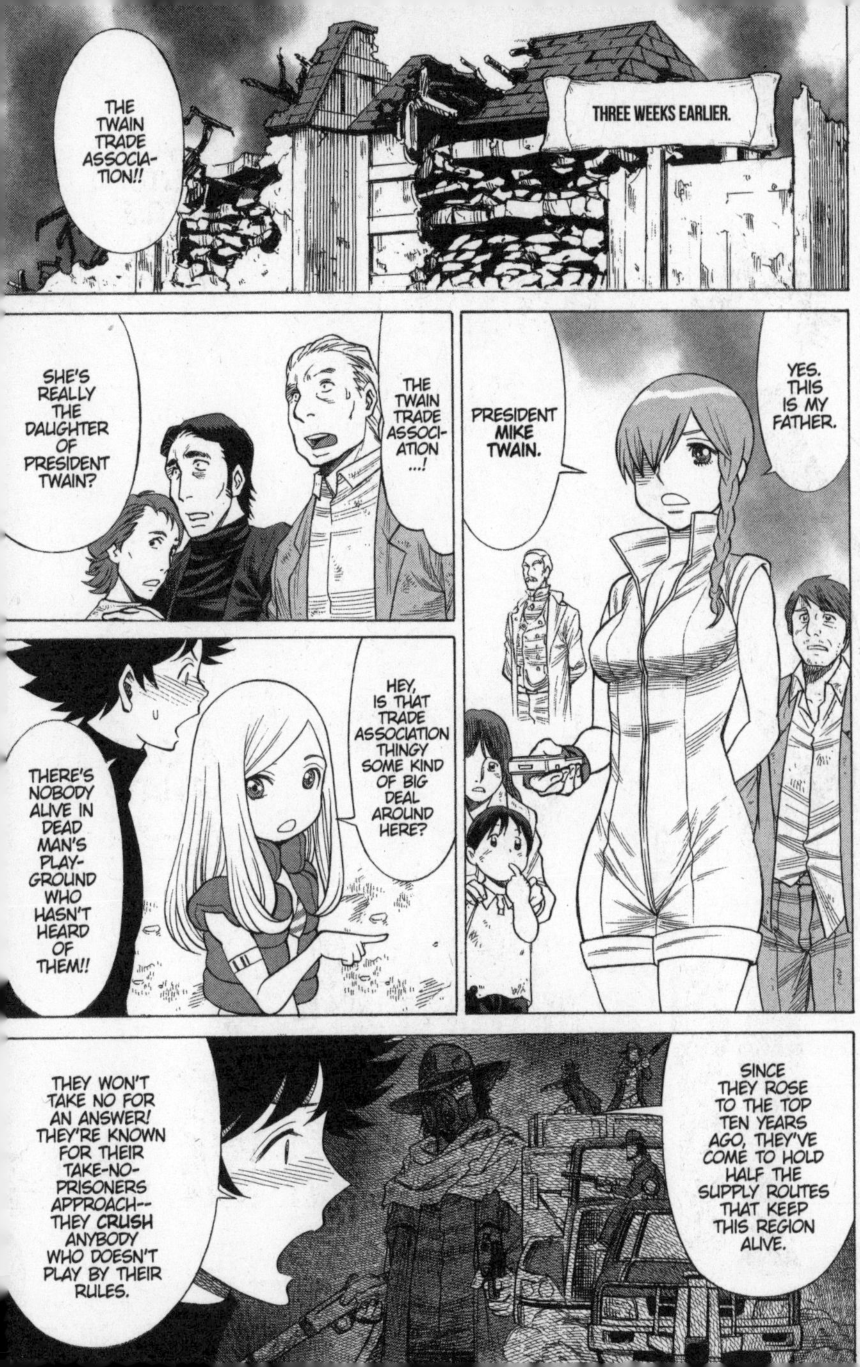
THREE WEEKS EARLIER.
THE TWAIN TRADE ASSOCIATION!!
YES. THIS IS MY FATHER.
PRESIDENT MIKE TWAIN.
THE TWAIN TRADE ASSOCIATION ...!
SHE'S REALLY THE DAUGHTER OF PRESIDENT TWAIN?
HEY, IS THAT TRADE ASSOCIATION THINGY SOME KIND OF BIG DEAL AROUND HERE?
THERE'S NOBODY ALIVE IN DEAD MAN'S PLAYGROUND WHO HASN'T HEARD OF THEM!!
SINCE THEY ROSE TO THE TOP TEN YEARS AGO, THEY'VE COME TO HOLD HALF THE SUPPLY ROUTES THAT KEEP THIS REGION ALIVE.
THEY WON'T TAKE NO FOR AN ANSWER! THEY'RE KNOWN FOR THEIR TAKE-NO-PRISONERS APPROACH-- THEY CRUSH ANYBODY WHO DOESN'T PLAY BY THEIR RULES.

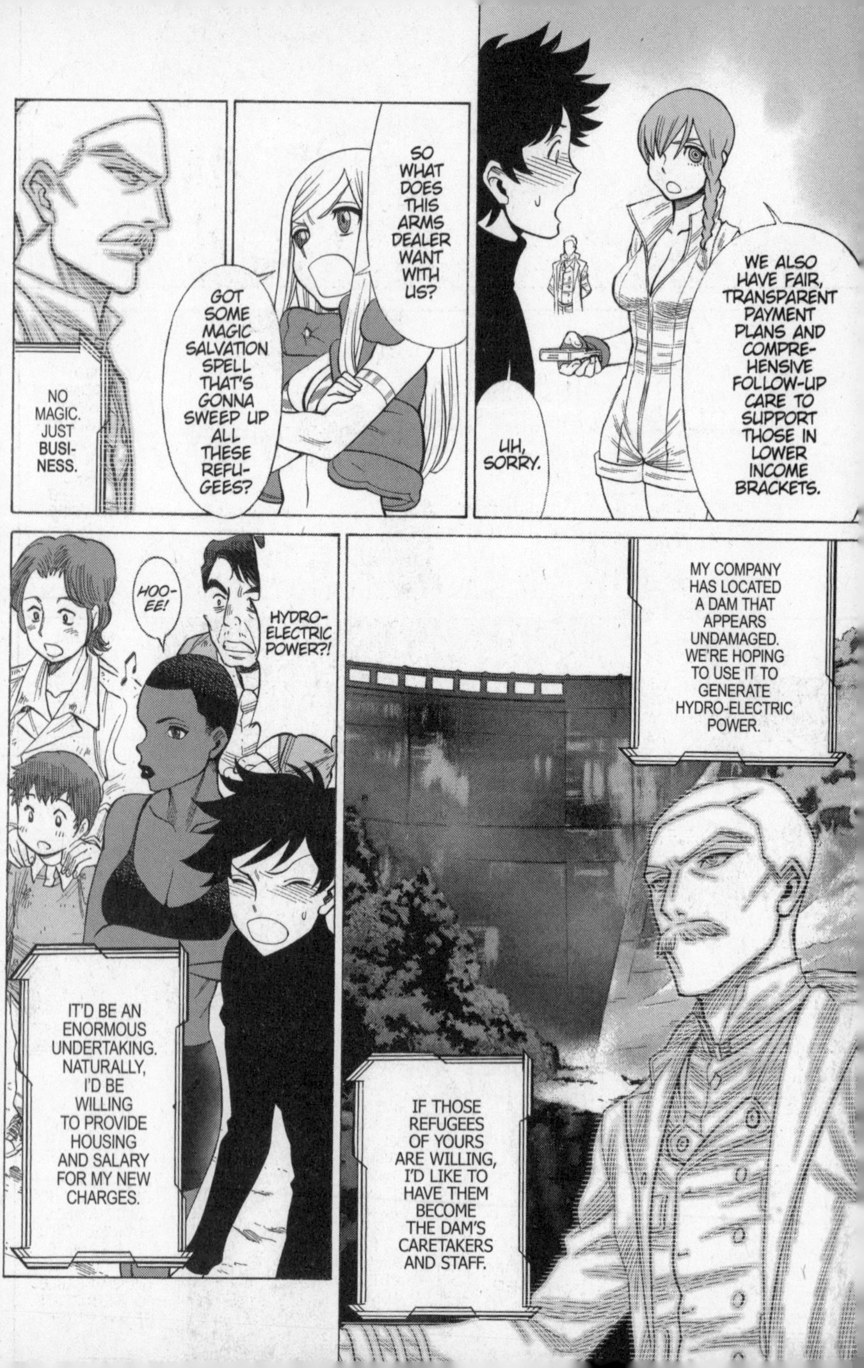
WE ALSO HAVE FAIR, TRANSPARENT PAYMENT PLANS AND COMPREHENSIVE FOLLOW-UP CARE TO SUPPORT THOSE IN LOWER INCOME BRACKETS.
UH, SORRY.
SO WHAT DOES THIS ARMS DEALER WANT WITH US?
GOT SOME MAGIC SALVATION SPELL THAT'S GONNA SWEEP UP ALL THESE REFUGEES?
NO MAGIC. JUST BUSINESS.
MY COMPANY HAS LOCATED A DAM THAT APPEARS UNDAMAGED. WE'RE HOPING TO USE IT TO GENERATE HYDRO-ELECTRIC POWER.
IF THOSE REFUGEES OF YOURS ARE WILLING, I'D LIKE TO HAVE THEM BECOME THE DAM'S CARETAKERS AND STAFF.
HYDRO-ELECTRIC POWER?!
HOO-EE!
IT'D BE AN ENORMOUS UNDERTAKING. NATURALLY, I'D BE WILLING TO PROVIDE HOUSING AND SALARY FOR MY NEW CHARGES.

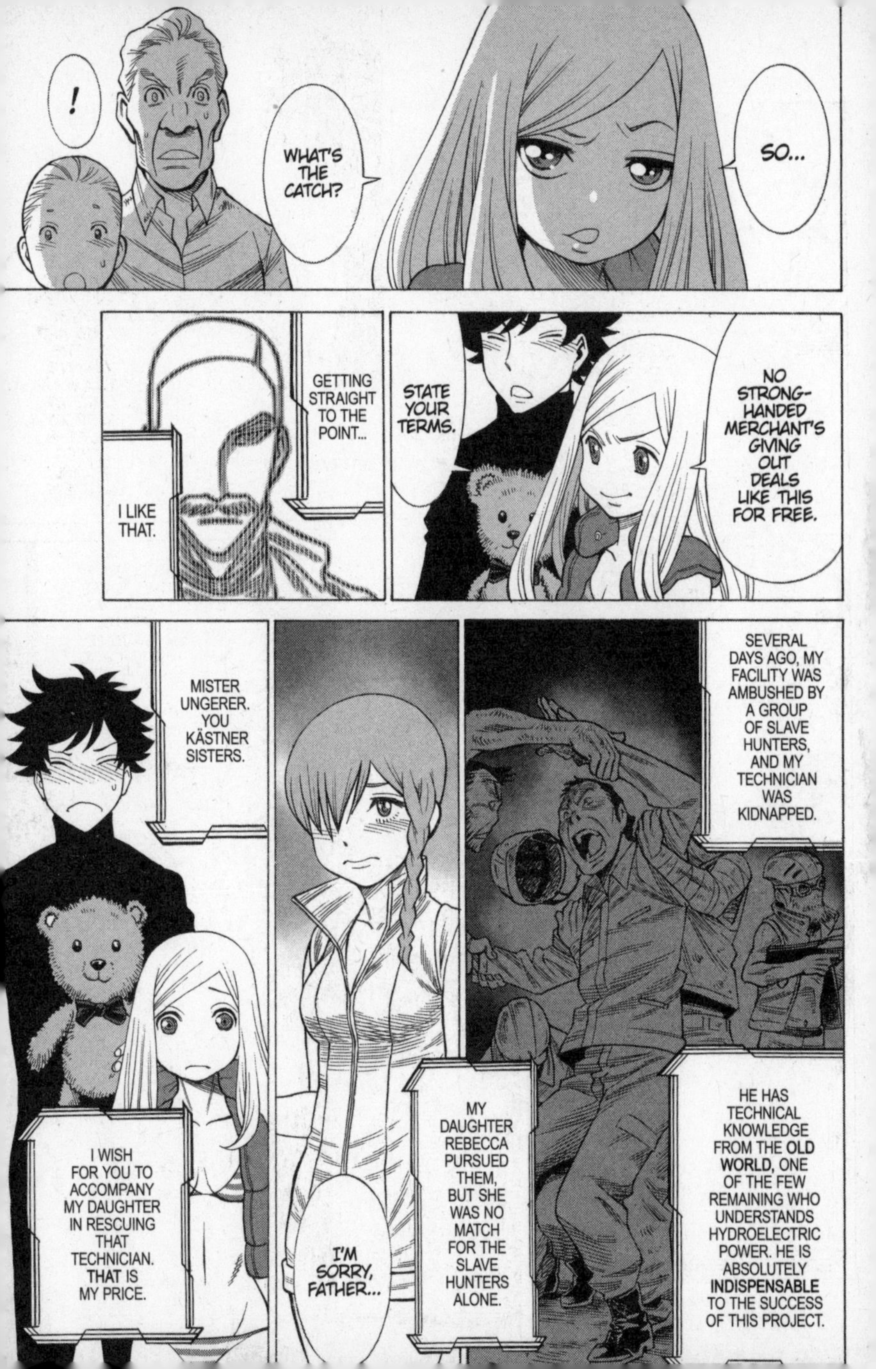
SO...
WHAT'S THE CATCH?
!
NO STRONG-HANDED MERCHANT'S GIVING OUT DEALS LIKE THIS FOR FREE.
STATE YOUR TERMS.
GETTING STRAIGHT TO THE POINT...
I LIKE THAT.
SEVERAL DAYS AGO, MY FACILITY WAS AMBUSHED BY A GROUP OF SLAVE HUNTERS, AND MY TECHNICIAN WAS KIDNAPPED.
HE HAS TECHNICAL KNOWLEDGE FROM THE OLD WORLD, ONE OF THE FEW REMAINING WHO UNDERSTANDS HYDROELECTRIC POWER. HE IS ABSOLUTELY INDISPENSABLE TO THE SUCCESS OF THIS PROJECT.
MY DAUGHTER REBECCA PURSUED THEM, BUT SHE WAS NO MATCH FOR THE SLAVE HUNTERS ALONE.
I'M SORRY, FATHER...
MISTER UNGERER. YOU KÄSTNER SISTERS.
I WISH FOR YOU TO ACCOMPANY MY DAUGHTER IN RESCUING THAT TECHNICIAN. THAT IS MY PRICE.

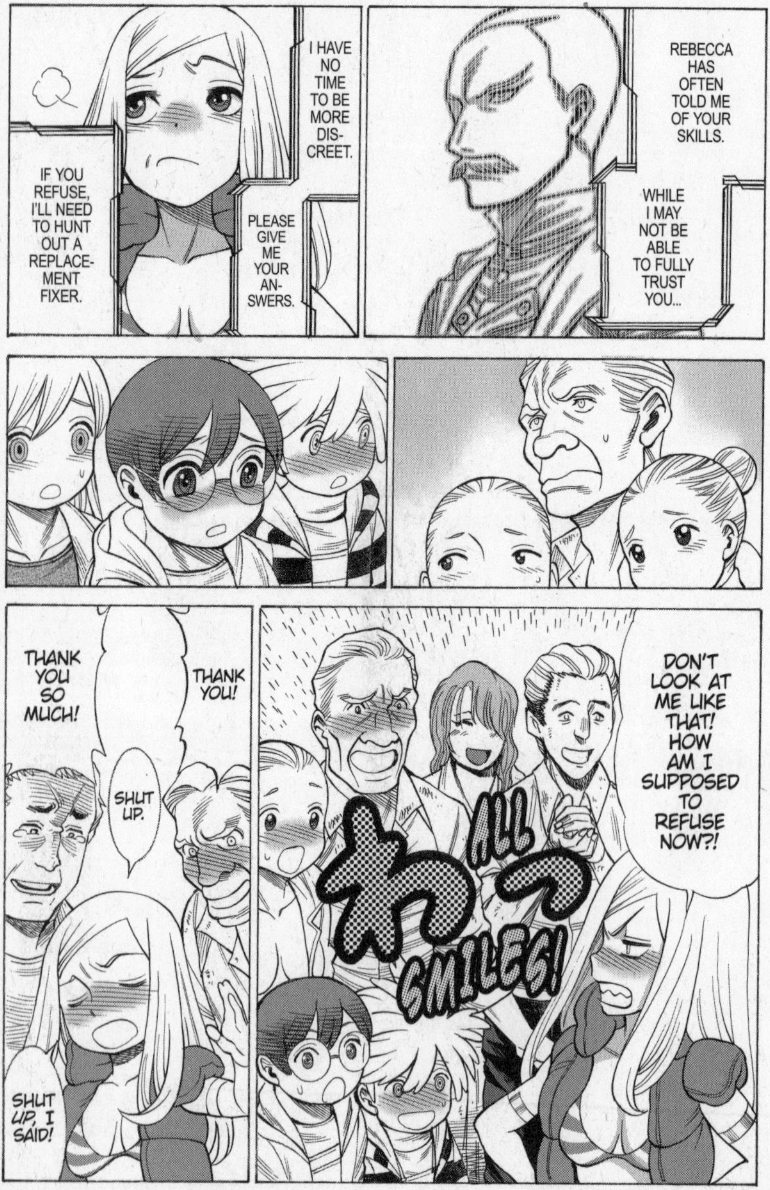
REBECCA HAS OFTEN TOLD ME OF YOUR SKILLS.
WHILE I MAY NOT BE ABLE TO FULLY TRUST YOU...
I HAVE NO TIME TO BE MORE DIS-CREET.
PLEASE GIVE ME YOUR AN-SWERS.
IF YOU REFUSE, I'LL NEED TO HUNT OUT A REPLACE-MENT FIXER.
DON'T LOOK AT ME LIKE THAT! HOW AM I SUPPOSED TO REFUSE NOW?!
ALL SMILES!
THANK YOU!
THANK YOU SO MUCH!
SHUT UP.
SHUT UP, I SAID!

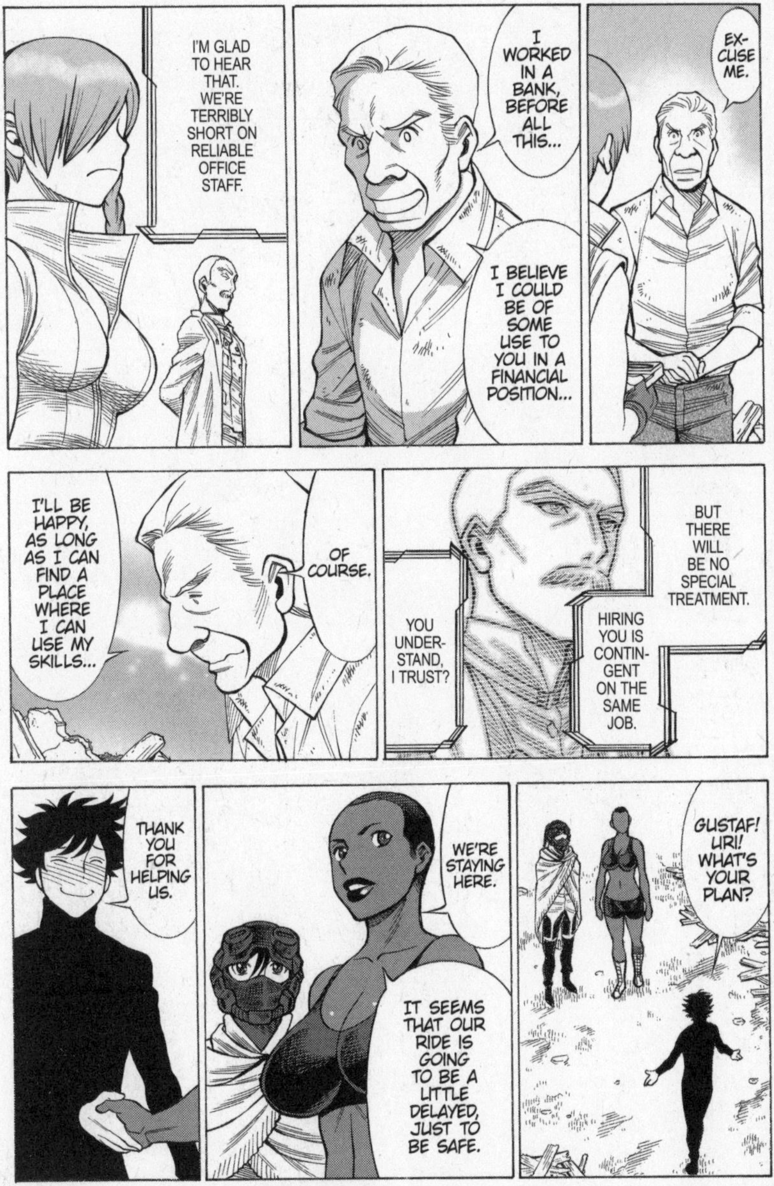
EXCUSE ME.
I WORKED IN A BANK, BEFORE ALL THIS...
I BELIEVE I COULD BE OF SOME USE TO YOU IN A FINANCIAL POSITION...
I'M GLAD TO HEAR THAT. WE'RE TERRIBLY SHORT ON RELIABLE OFFICE STAFF.
BUT THERE WILL BE NO SPECIAL TREATMENT.
HIRING YOU IS CONTINGENT ON THE SAME JOB.
YOU UNDERSTAND, I TRUST?
OF COURSE.
I'LL BE HAPPY, AS LONG AS I CAN FIND A PLACE WHERE I CAN USE MY SKILLS...
GUSTAF! URI! WHAT'S YOUR PLAN?
WE'RE STAYING HERE.
IT SEEMS THAT OUR RIDE IS GOING TO BE A LITTLE DELAYED, JUST TO BE SAFE.
THANK YOU FOR HELPING US.

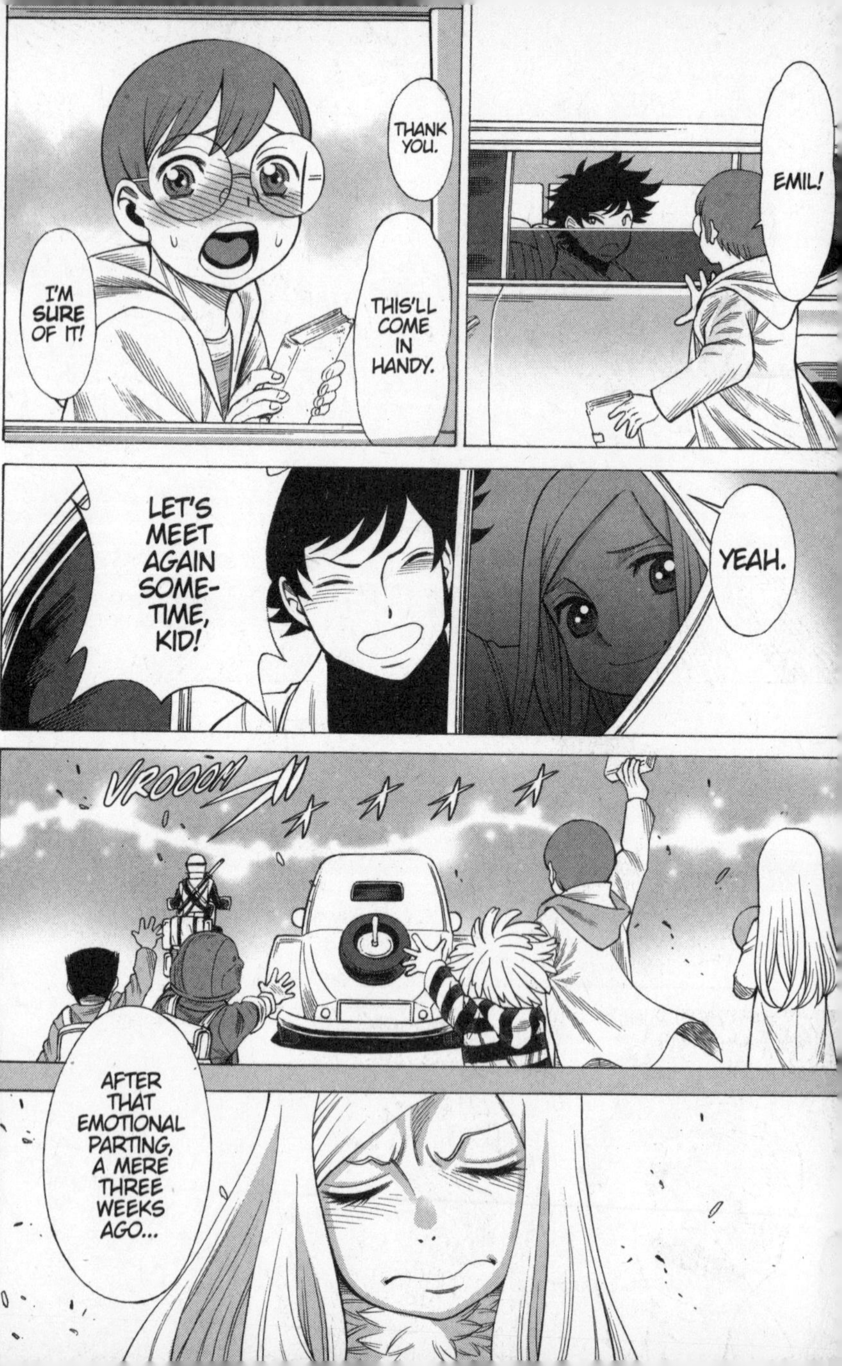
EMIL!
THANK YOU.
THIS'LL COME IN HANDY.
I'M SURE OF IT!
YEAH.
LET'S MEET AGAIN SOME-TIME, KID!
VROOOOM
AFTER THAT EMOTIONAL PARTING, A MERE THREE WEEKS AGO...

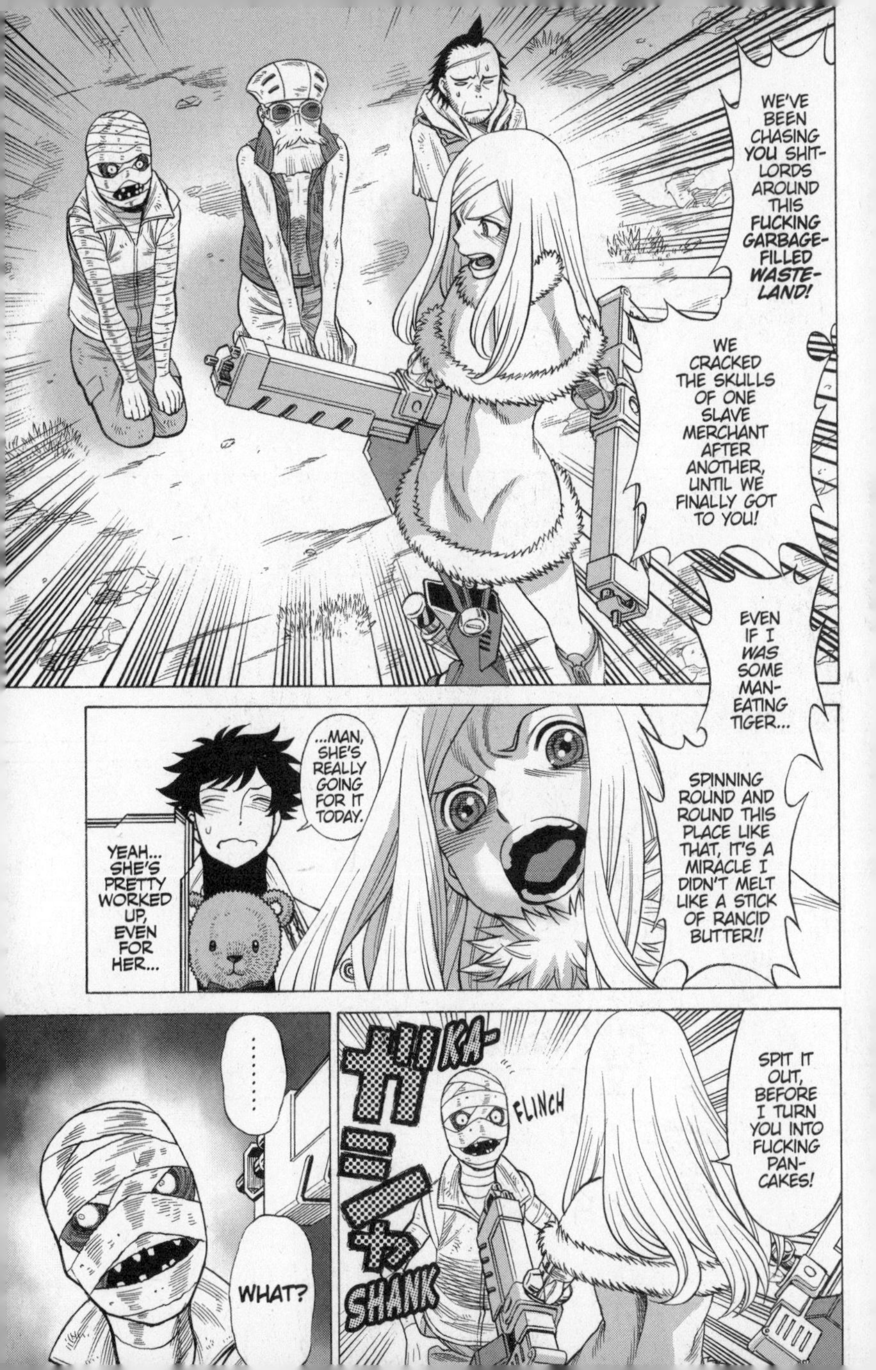
WE'VE BEEN CHASING YOU SHIT-LORDS AROUND THIS FUCKING GARBAGE-FILLED WASTE-LAND!
WE CRACKED THE SKULLS OF ONE SLAVE MERCHANT AFTER ANOTHER, UNTIL WE FINALLY GOT TO YOU!
EVEN IF I WAS SOME MAN-EATING TIGER...
SPINNING ROUND AND ROUND THIS PLACE LIKE THAT, IT'S A MIRACLE I DIDN'T MELT LIKE A STICK OF RANCID BUTTER!!
...MAN, SHE'S REALLY GOING FOR IT TODAY.
YEAH... SHE'S PRETTY WORKED UP, EVEN FOR HER...
SPIT IT OUT, BEFORE I TURN YOU INTO FUCKING PAN-CAKES!
FLINCH
KA-SHANK
......
WHAT?

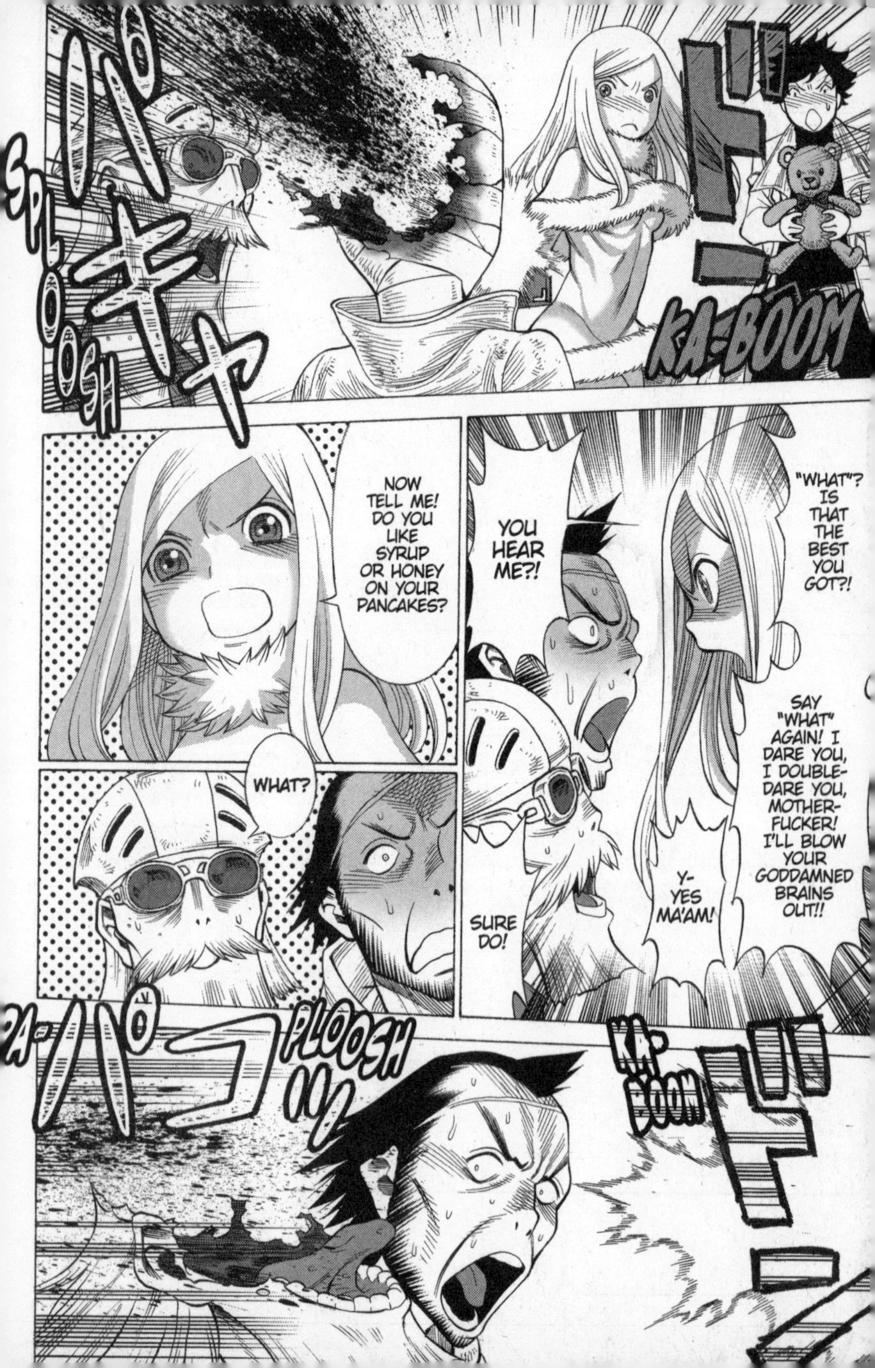
KA-BOOM
SPLOOSH
"WHAT"? IS THAT THE BEST YOU GOT?!
YOU HEAR ME?!
SAY "WHAT" AGAIN! I DARE YOU, I DOUBLE-DARE YOU, MOTHER-FUCKER! I'LL BLOW YOUR GODDAMNED BRAINS OUT!!
Y-YES MA'AM!
SURE DO!
NOW TELL ME! DO YOU LIKE SYRUP OR HONEY ON YOUR PANCAKES?
WHAT?
KA-BOOM
PLOOSH
PA-

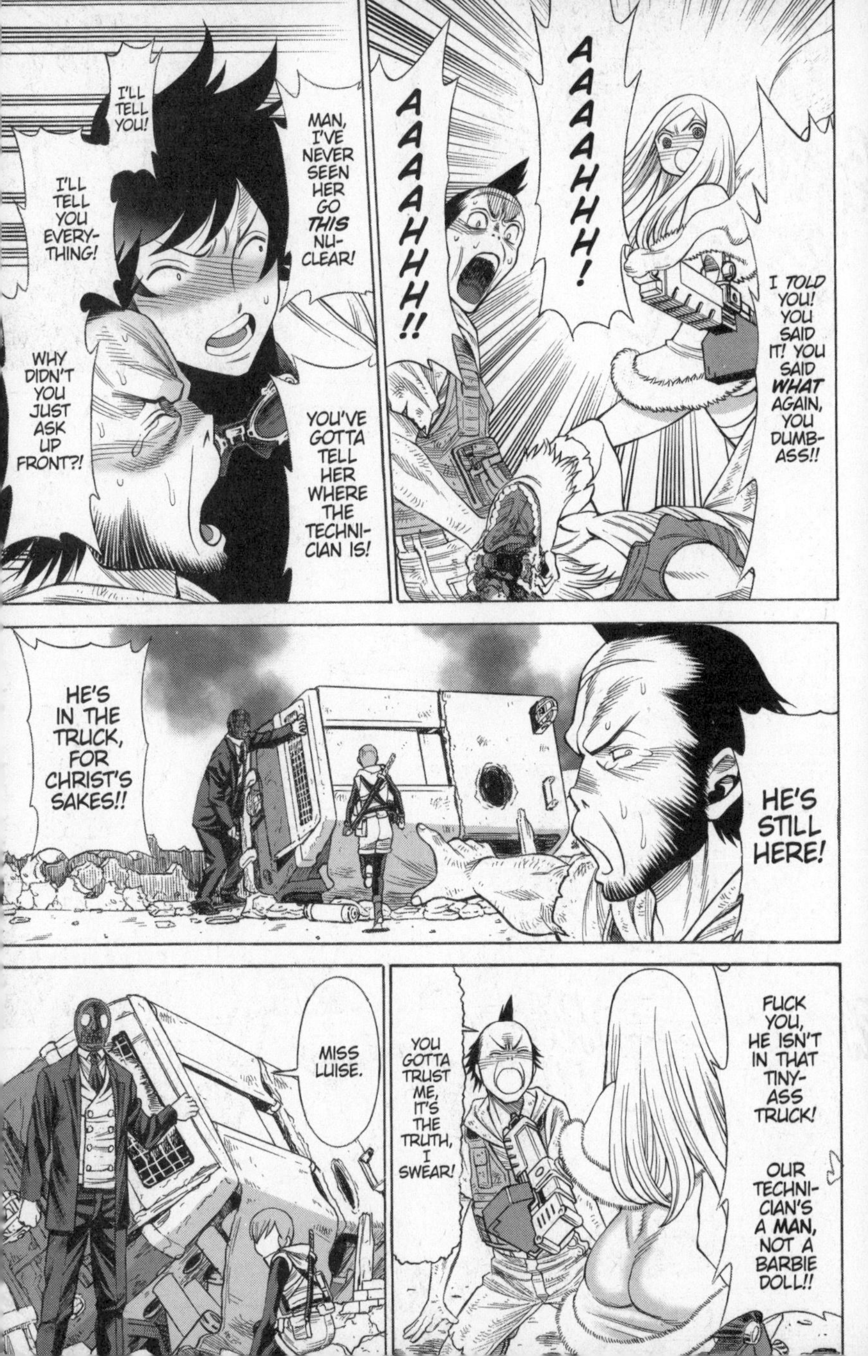
AAAAHHH!
I TOLD YOU! YOU SAID IT! YOU SAID WHAT AGAIN, YOU DUMBASS!!
AAAAHHH!!
MAN, I'VE NEVER SEEN HER GO THIS NUCLEAR!
YOU'VE GOTTA TELL HER WHERE THE TECHNICIAN IS!
I'LL TELL YOU!
I'LL TELL YOU EVERYTHING!
WHY DIDN'T YOU JUST ASK UP FRONT?!
HE'S STILL HERE!
HE'S IN THE TRUCK, FOR CHRIST'S SAKES!!
FUCK YOU, HE ISN'T IN THAT TINY-ASS TRUCK!
OUR TECHNICIAN'S A MAN, NOT A BARBIE DOLL!!
YOU GOTTA TRUST ME, IT'S THE TRUTH, I SWEAR!
MISS LUISE.

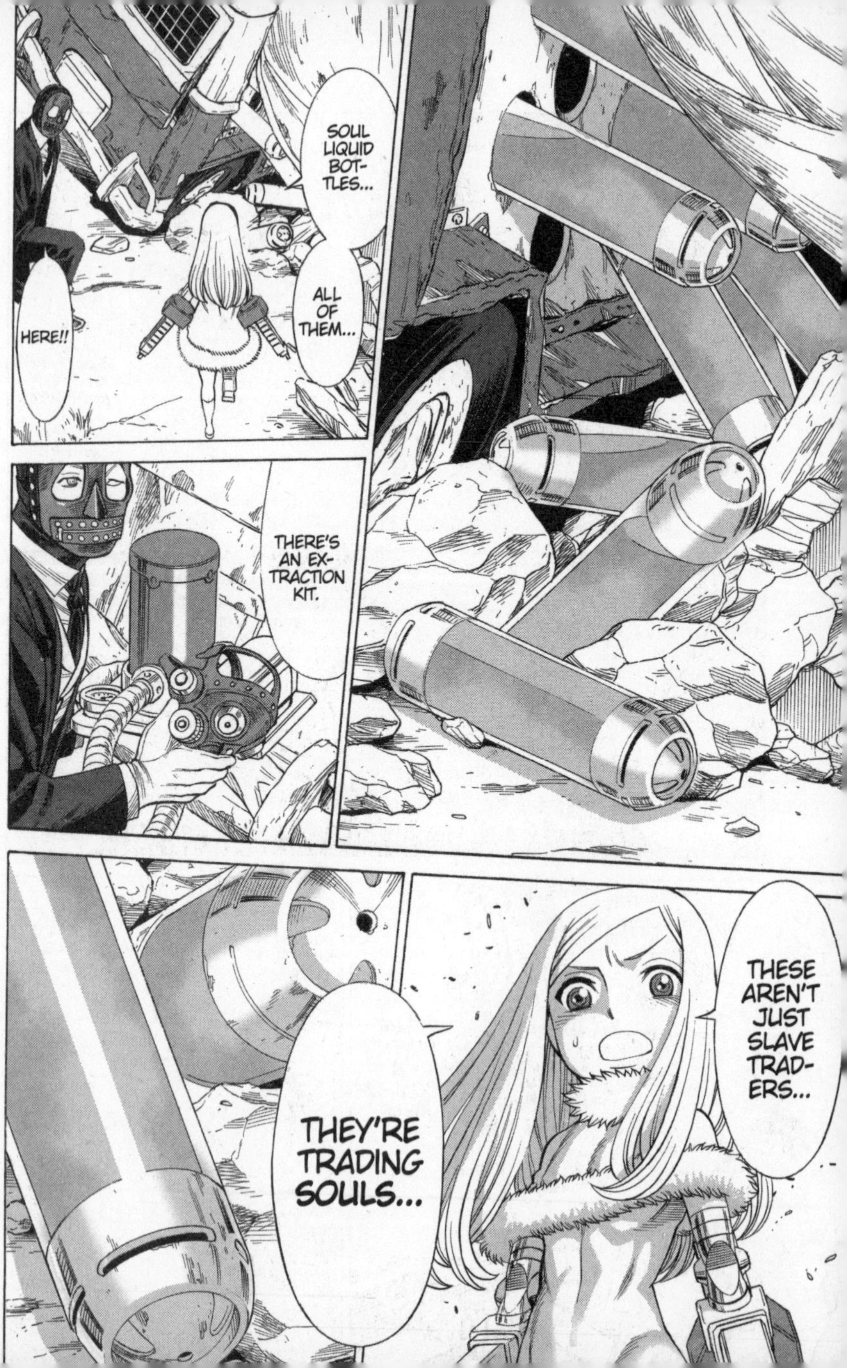
SOUL LIQUID BOT-TLES...
ALL OF THEM...
HERE!!
THERE'S AN EX-TRACTION KIT.
THESE AREN'T JUST SLAVE TRAD-ERS...
THEY'RE TRADING SOULS...

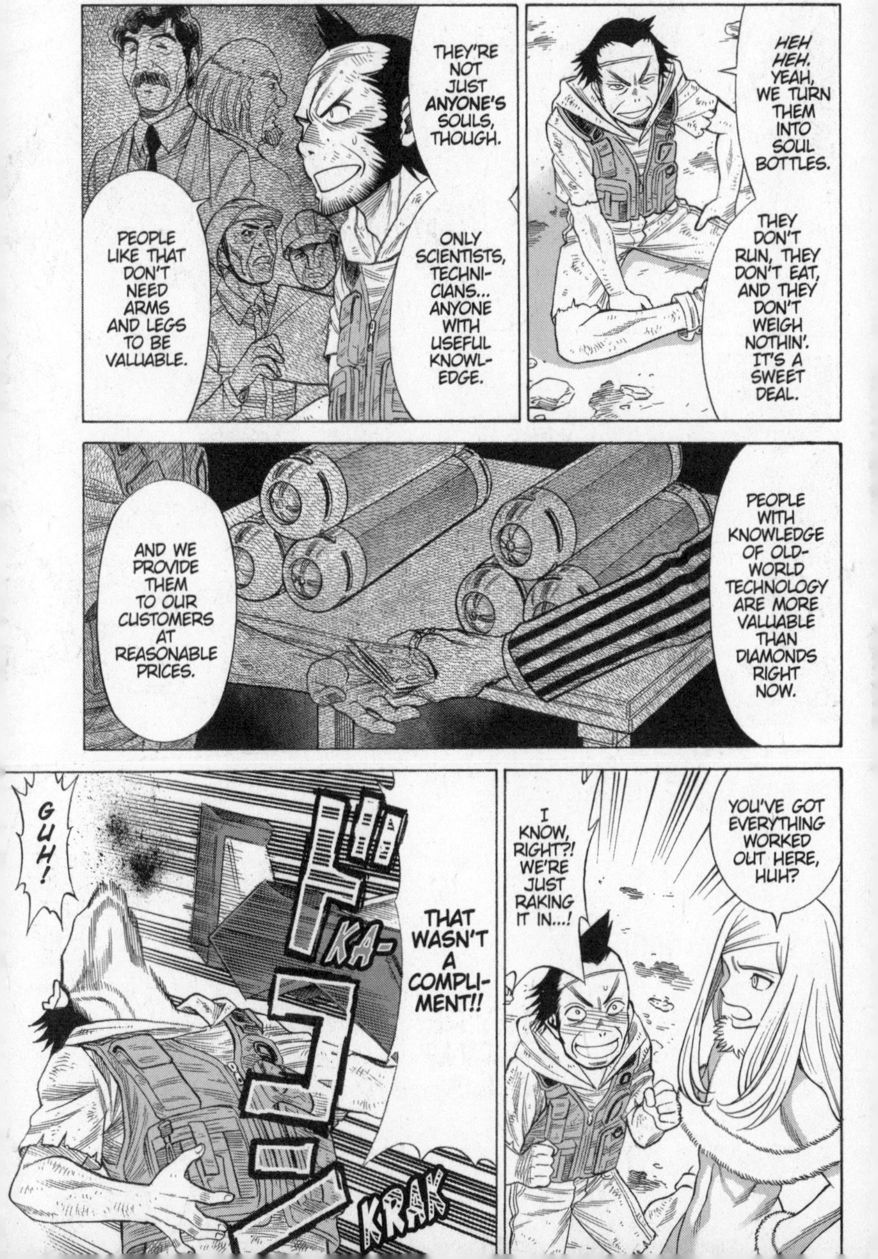
HEH HEH. YEAH, WE TURN THEM INTO SOUL BOTTLES.
THEY DON'T RUN, THEY DON'T EAT, AND THEY DON'T WEIGH NOTHIN'. IT'S A SWEET DEAL.
THEY'RE NOT JUST ANYONE'S SOULS, THOUGH.
ONLY SCIENTISTS, TECHNICIANS... ANYONE WITH USEFUL KNOWLEDGE.
PEOPLE LIKE THAT DON'T NEED ARMS AND LEGS TO BE VALUABLE.
PEOPLE WITH KNOWLEDGE OF OLD-WORLD TECHNOLOGY ARE MORE VALUABLE THAN DIAMONDS RIGHT NOW.
AND WE PROVIDE THEM TO OUR CUSTOMERS AT REASONABLE PRICES.
YOU'VE GOT EVERYTHING WORKED OUT HERE, HUH?
I KNOW, RIGHT?! WE'RE JUST RAKING IT IN...!
THAT WASN'T A COMPLIMENT!!
KA-
KRAK
GUH!

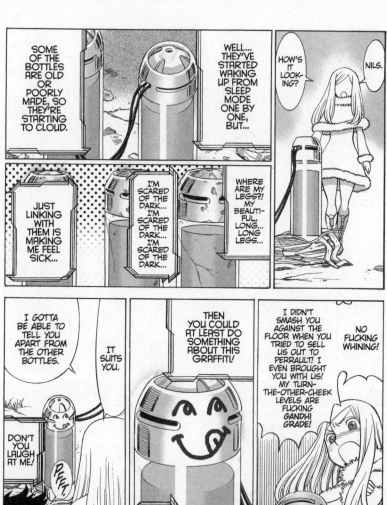

NILS.
HOW'S IT LOOKING?
WELL... THEY'VE STARTED WAKING UP FROM SLEEP MODE ONE BY ONE, BUT...
SOME OF THE BOTTLES ARE OLD OR POORLY MADE, SO THEY'RE STARTING TO CLOUD.
WHERE ARE MY LEGS?! MY BEAUTIFUL, LONG... LONG LEGS...
I'M SCARED OF THE DARK... I'M SCARED OF THE DARK... I'M SCARED OF THE DARK...
JUST LINKING WITH THEM IS MAKING ME FEEL SICK...
NO FUCKING WHINING!
I DIDN'T SMASH YOU AGAINST THE FLOOR WHEN YOU TRIED TO SELL US OUT TO PERRAULT! I EVEN BROUGHT YOU WITH US! MY TURN-THE-OTHER-CHEEK LEVELS ARE FUCKING GANDHI GRADE!
THEN YOU COULD AT LEAST DO SOMETHING ABOUT THIS GRAFFITI!
IT'S REALLY NOT HELPFUL.
IT SUITS YOU.
I GOTTA BE ABLE TO TELL YOU APART FROM THE OTHER BOTTLES.
PFFT.
DON'T YOU LAUGH AT ME!

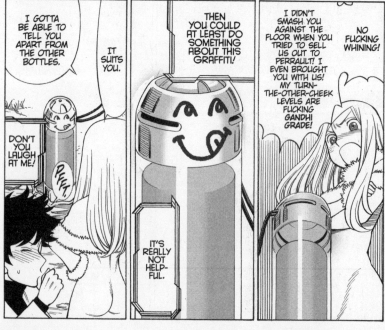

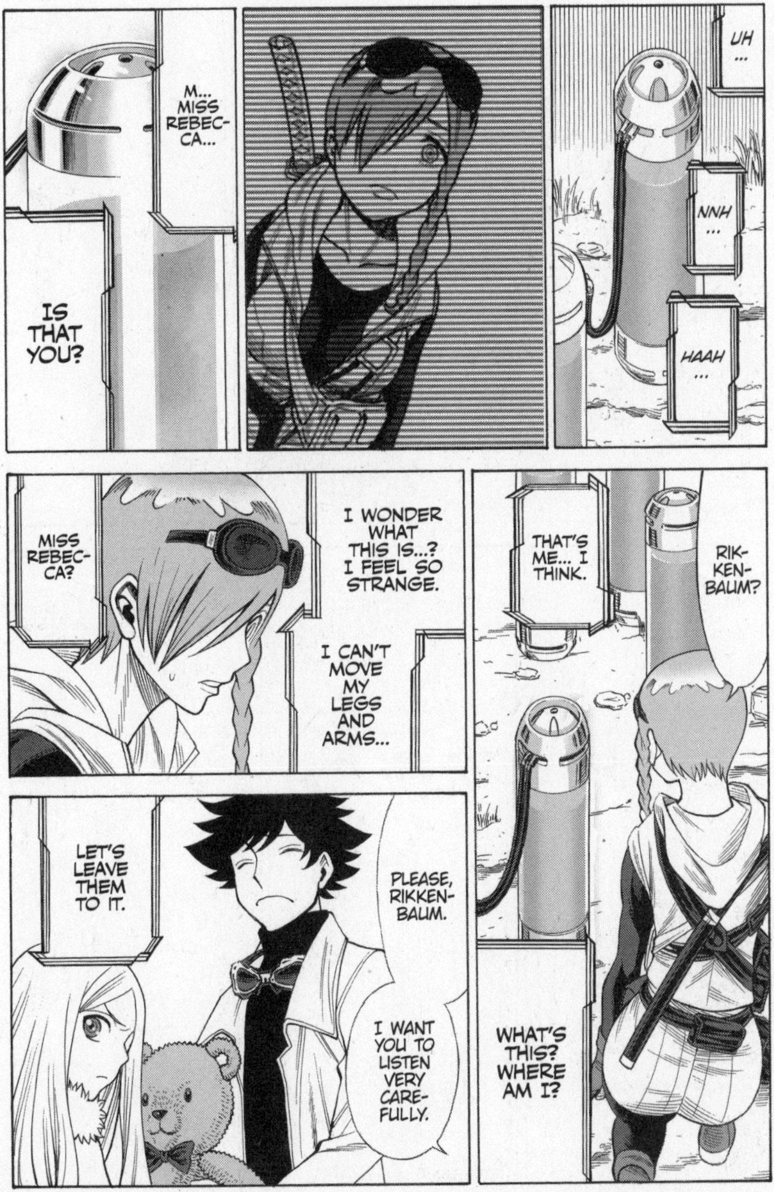
UH...
NNH...
HAAH...
M... MISS REBEC-CA...
IS THAT YOU?
RIK-KEN-BAUM?
THAT'S ME... I THINK.
WHAT'S THIS? WHERE AM I?
I WONDER WHAT THIS IS...? I FEEL SO STRANGE.
I CAN'T MOVE MY LEGS AND ARMS...
MISS REBEC-CA?
PLEASE, RIKKEN-BAUM.
I WANT YOU TO LISTEN VERY CARE-FULLY.
LET'S LEAVE THEM TO IT.

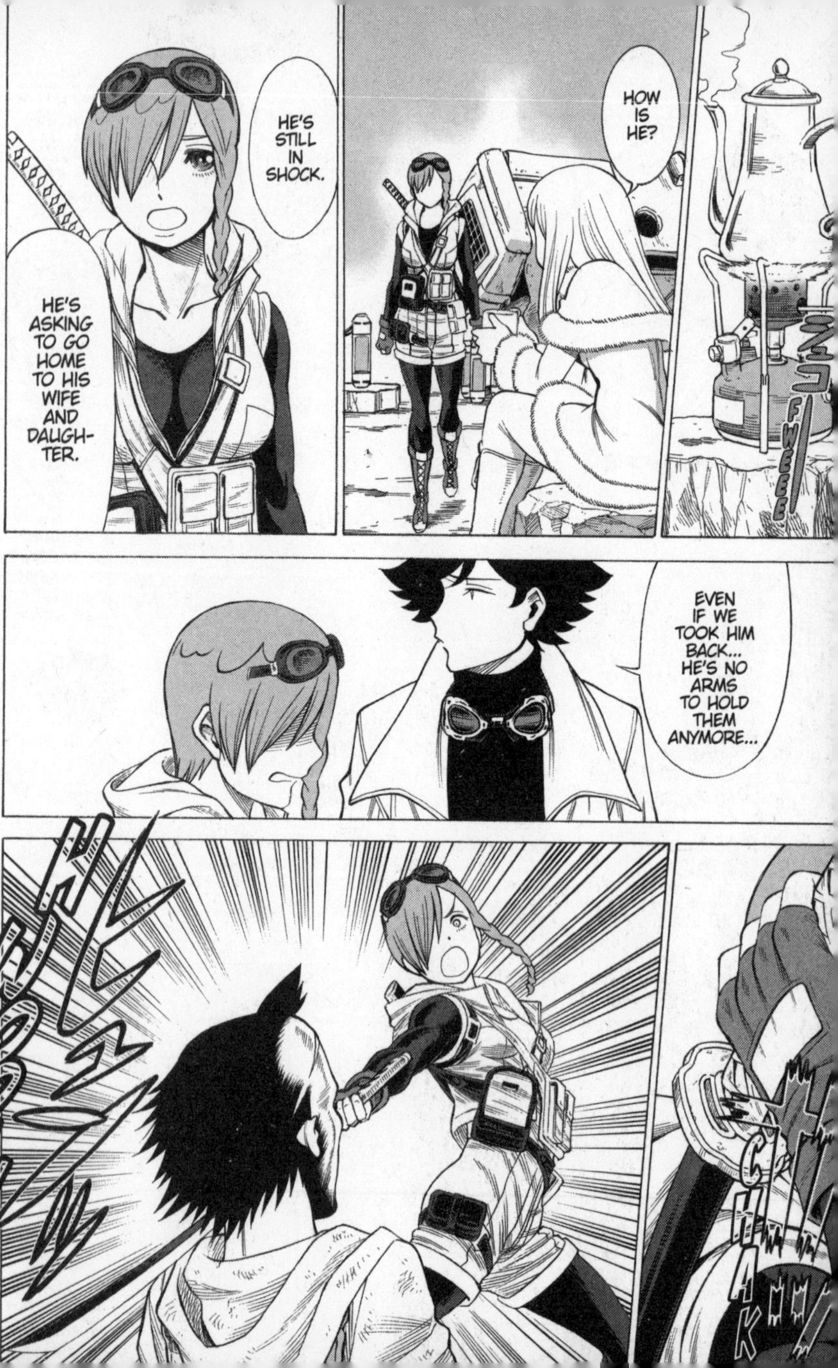
FWEEE
HOW IS HE?
HE'S STILL IN SHOCK.
HE'S ASKING TO GO HOME TO HIS WIFE AND DAUGH-TER.
EVEN IF WE TOOK HIM BACK... HE'S NO ARMS TO HOLD THEM ANYMORE...
CHAK!!
WHOOSH

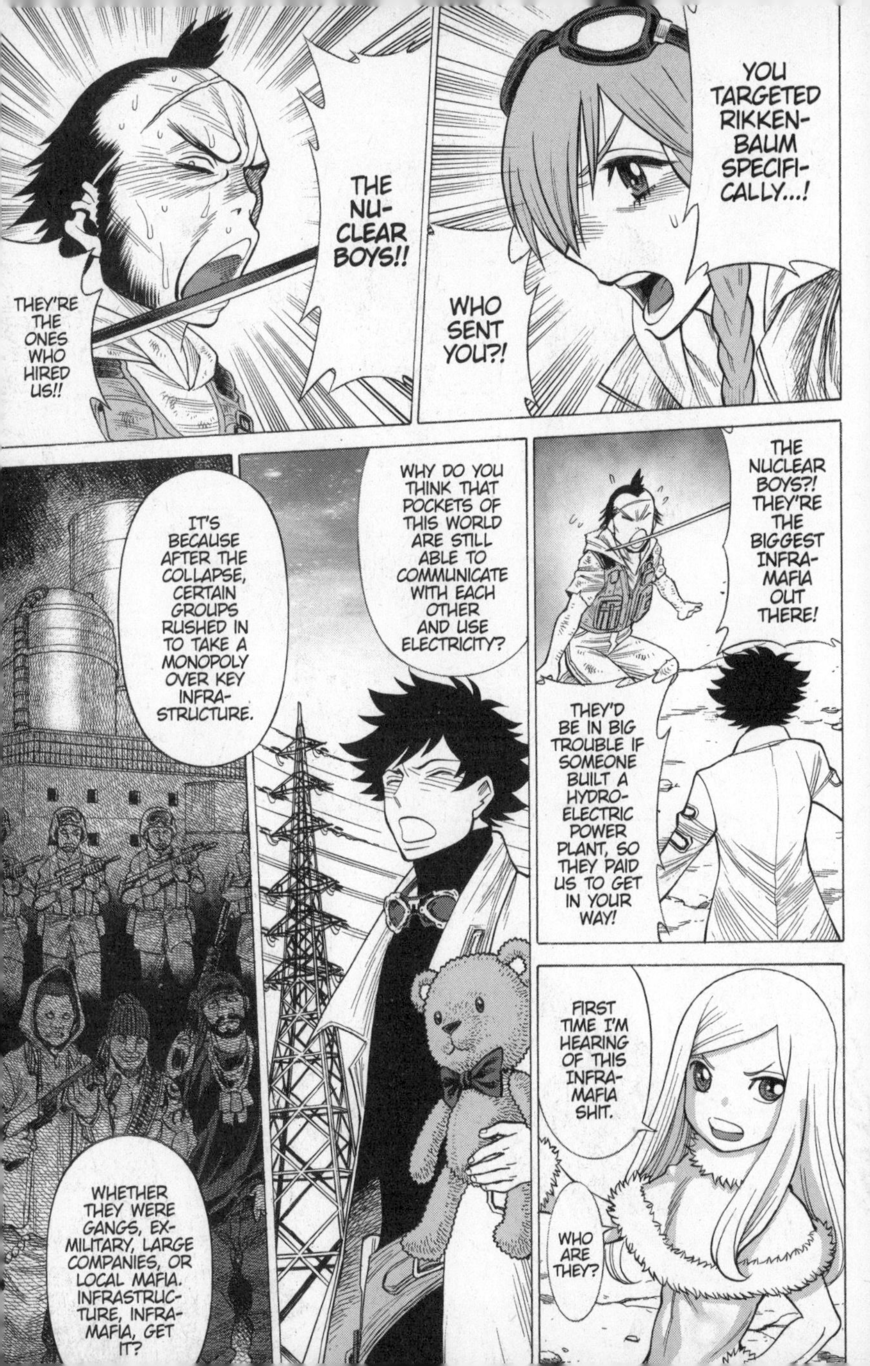
YOU TARGETED RIKKEN-BAUM SPECIFI-CALLY...!
WHO SENT YOU?!
THE NU-CLEAR BOYS!!
THEY'RE THE ONES WHO HIRED US!!
THE NUCLEAR BOYS?! THEY'RE THE BIGGEST INFRA-MAFIA OUT THERE!
THEY'D BE IN BIG TROUBLE IF SOMEONE BUILT A HYDRO-ELECTRIC POWER PLANT, SO THEY PAID US TO GET IN YOUR WAY!
FIRST TIME I'M HEARING OF THIS INFRA-MAFIA SHIT.
WHO ARE THEY?
WHY DO YOU THINK THAT POCKETS OF THIS WORLD ARE STILL ABLE TO COMMUNICATE WITH EACH OTHER AND USE ELECTRICITY?
IT'S BECAUSE AFTER THE COLLAPSE, CERTAIN GROUPS RUSHED IN TO TAKE A MONOPOLY OVER KEY INFRA-STRUCTURE.
WHETHER THEY WERE GANGS, EX-MILITARY, LARGE COMPANIES, OR LOCAL MAFIA. INFRASTRUC-TURE, INFRA-MAFIA, GET IT?

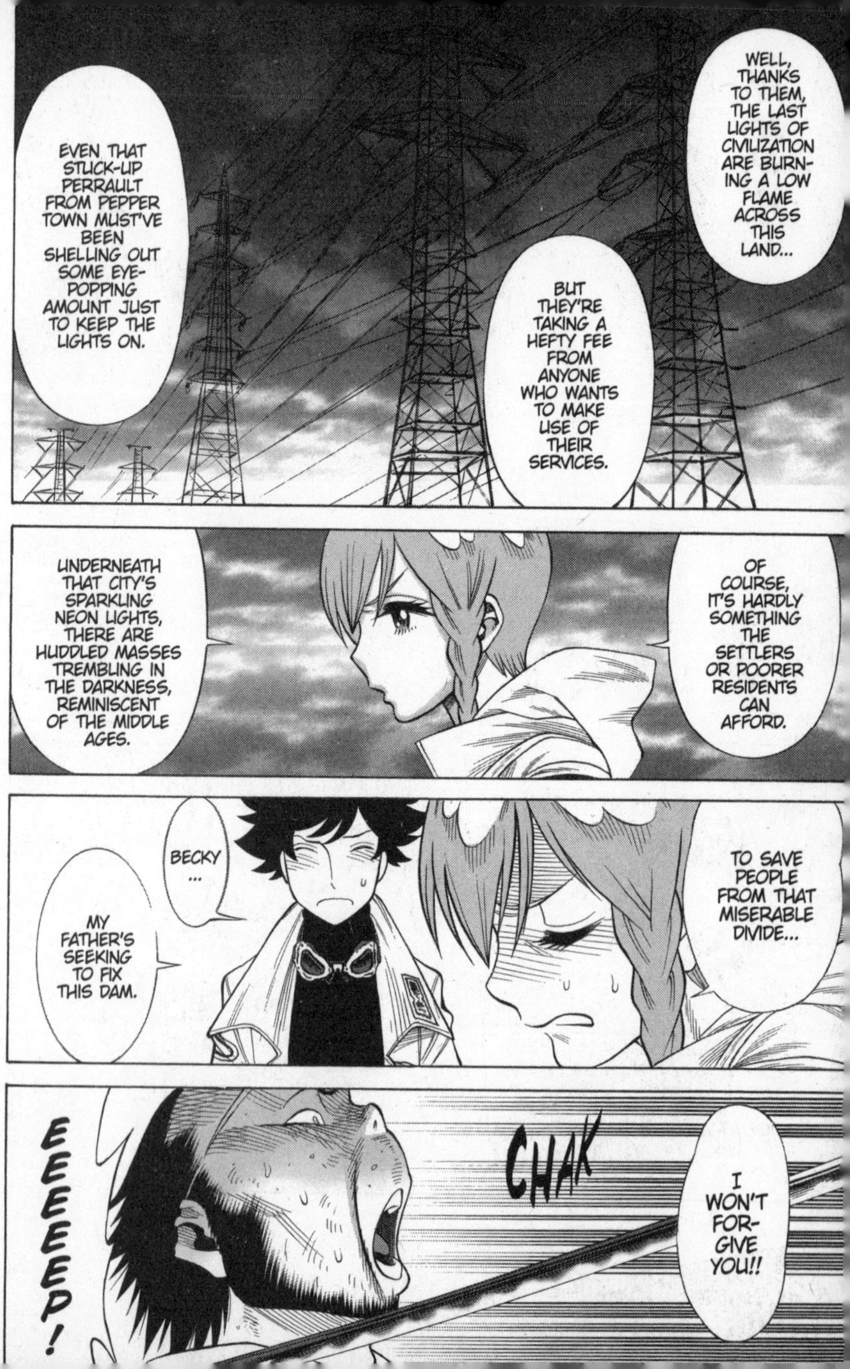
WELL, THANKS TO THEM, THE LAST LIGHTS OF CIVILIZATION ARE BURNING A LOW FLAME ACROSS THIS LAND...
BUT THEY'RE TAKING A HEFTY FEE FROM ANYONE WHO WANTS TO MAKE USE OF THEIR SERVICES.
EVEN THAT STUCK-UP PERRAULT FROM PEPPER TOWN MUST'VE BEEN SHELLING OUT SOME EYE-POPPING AMOUNT JUST TO KEEP THE LIGHTS ON.
OF COURSE, IT'S HARDLY SOMETHING THE SETTLERS OR POORER RESIDENTS CAN AFFORD.
UNDERNEATH THAT CITY'S SPARKLING NEON LIGHTS, THERE ARE HUDDLED MASSES TREMBLING IN THE DARKNESS, REMINISCENT OF THE MIDDLE AGES.
TO SAVE PEOPLE FROM THAT MISERABLE DIVIDE...
BECKY...
MY FATHER'S SEEKING TO FIX THIS DAM.
I WON'T FORGIVE YOU!!
CHAK
EEEEEEEP!

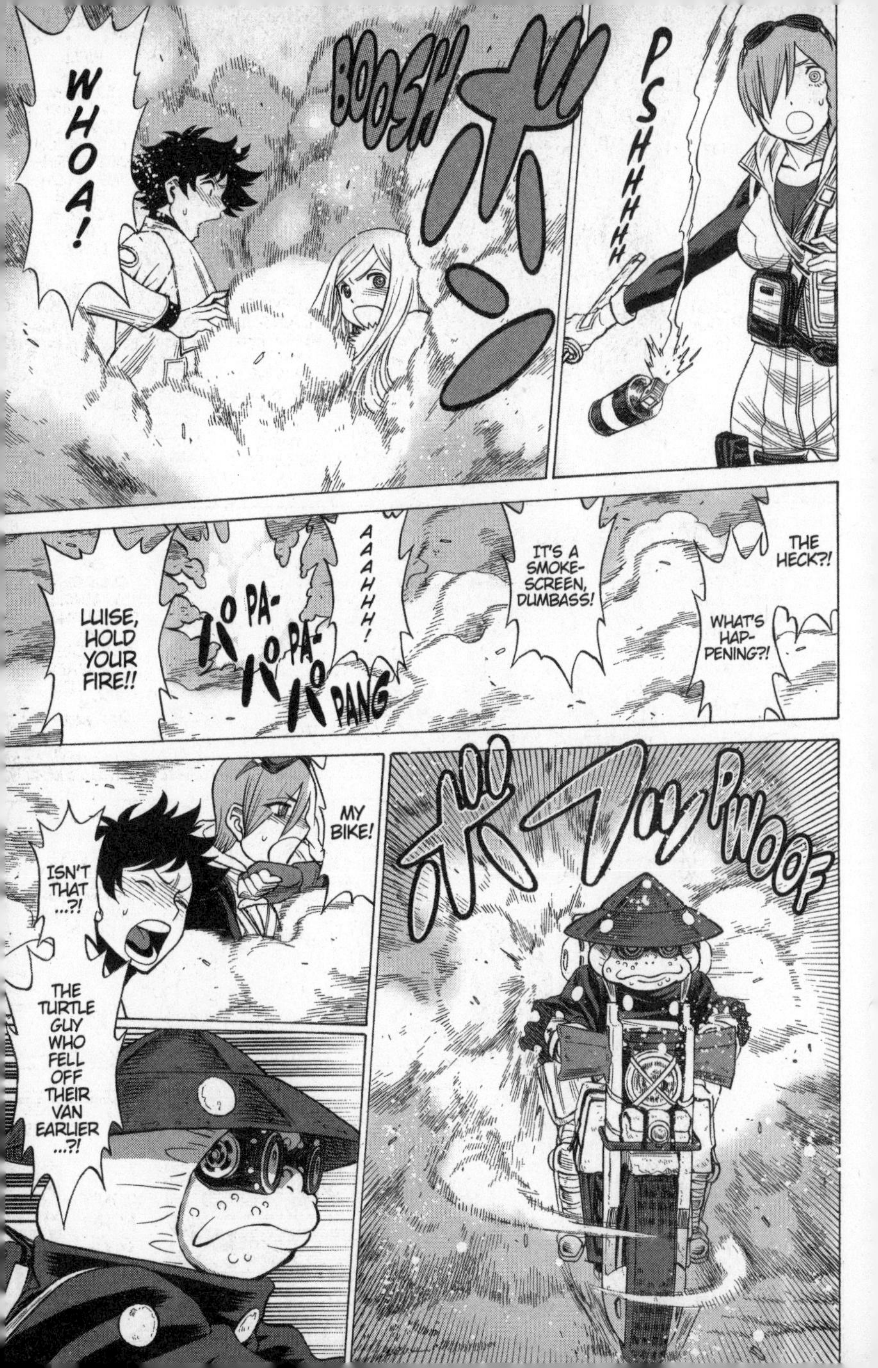
PSHHHHHH
BOOSH
WHOA!
THE HECK?!
WHAT'S HAP-PENING?!
IT'S A SMOKE-SCREEN, DUMBASS!
AAAHHH!
PA-PA-PANG
LUISE, HOLD YOUR FIRE!!
PWOOF
MY BIKE!
ISN'T THAT ...?!
THE TURTLE GUY WHO FELL OFF THEIR VAN EARLIER ...?!

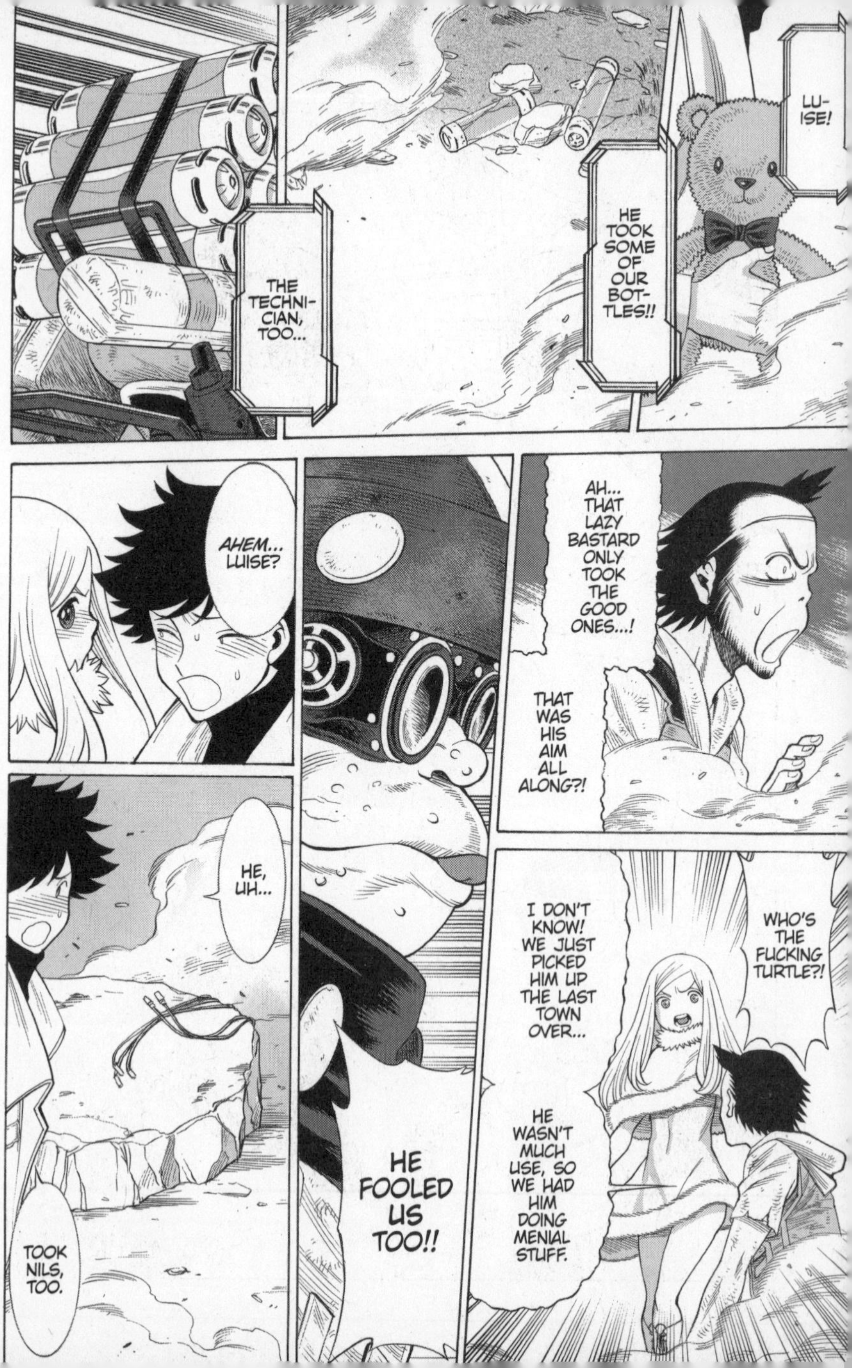
LU-ISE!
HE TOOK SOME OF OUR BOT-TLES!!
THE TECHNI-CIAN, TOO...
AH... THAT LAZY BASTARD ONLY TOOK THE GOOD ONES...!
THAT WAS HIS AIM ALL ALONG?!
WHO'S THE FUCKING TURTLE?!
I DON'T KNOW! WE JUST PICKED HIM UP THE LAST TOWN OVER...
HE WASN'T MUCH USE, SO WE HAD HIM DOING MENIAL STUFF.
HE FOOLED US TOO!!
AHEM... LUISE?
HE, UH...
TOOK NILS, TOO.

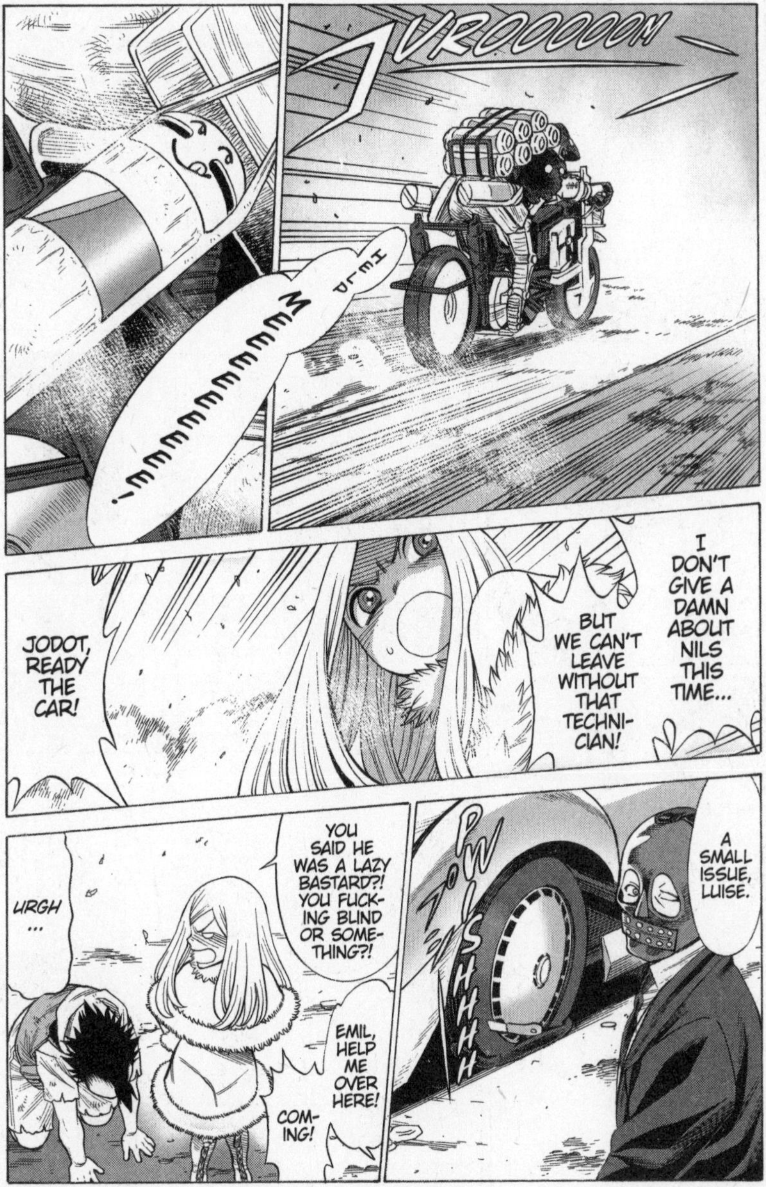
VROOOOON
HELP MEEEEEEEEEE!
I DON'T GIVE A DAMN ABOUT NILS THIS TIME...
BUT WE CAN'T LEAVE WITHOUT THAT TECHNI-CIAN!
JODOT, READY THE CAR!
A SMALL ISSUE, LUISE.
PWISHHHHH
YOU SAID HE WAS A LAZY BASTARD?! YOU FUCK-ING BLIND OR SOME-THING?!
URGH...
EMIL, HELP ME OVER HERE!
COM-ING!

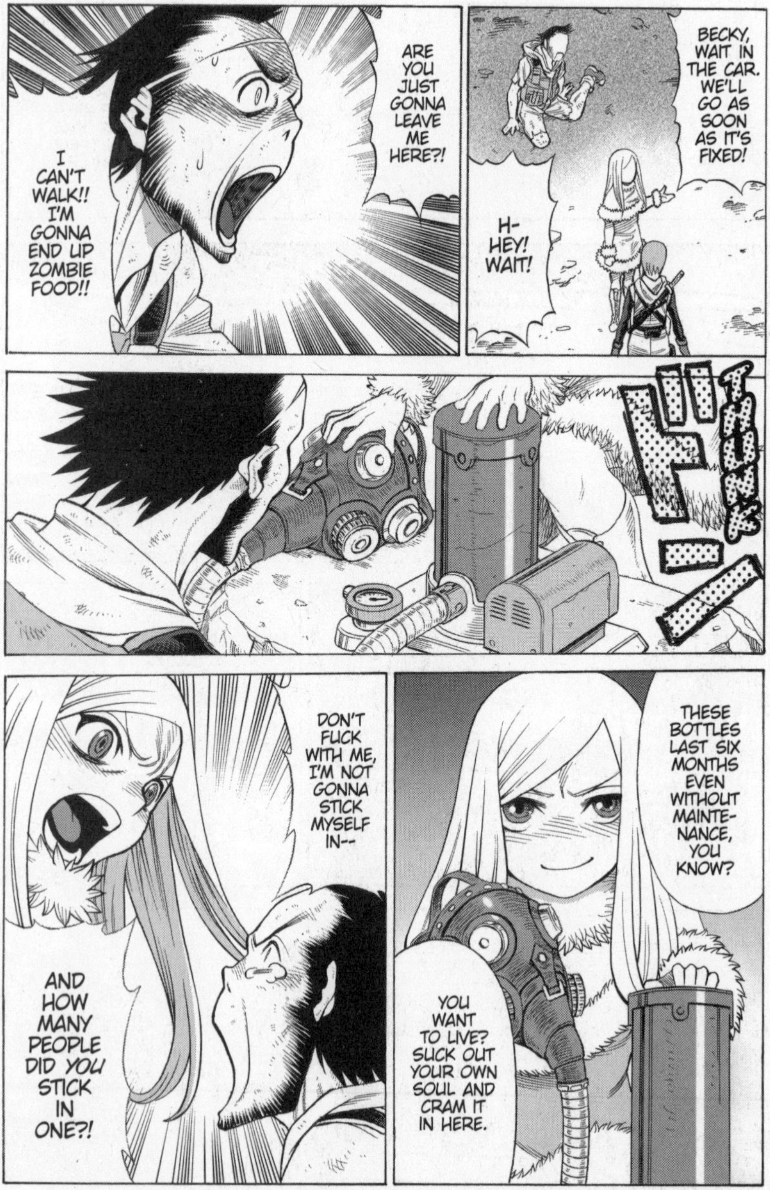
BECKY, WAIT IN THE CAR. WE'LL GO AS SOON AS IT'S FIXED!
H-HEY! WAIT!
ARE YOU JUST GONNA LEAVE ME HERE?!
I CAN'T WALK!! I'M GONNA END UP ZOMBIE FOOD!!
THUNK
THESE BOTTLES LAST SIX MONTHS EVEN WITHOUT MAINTE-NANCE, YOU KNOW?
YOU WANT TO LIVE? SUCK OUT YOUR OWN SOUL AND CRAM IT IN HERE.
DON'T FUCK WITH ME, I'M NOT GONNA STICK MYSELF IN--
AND HOW MANY PEOPLE DID *YOU* STICK IN ONE?!

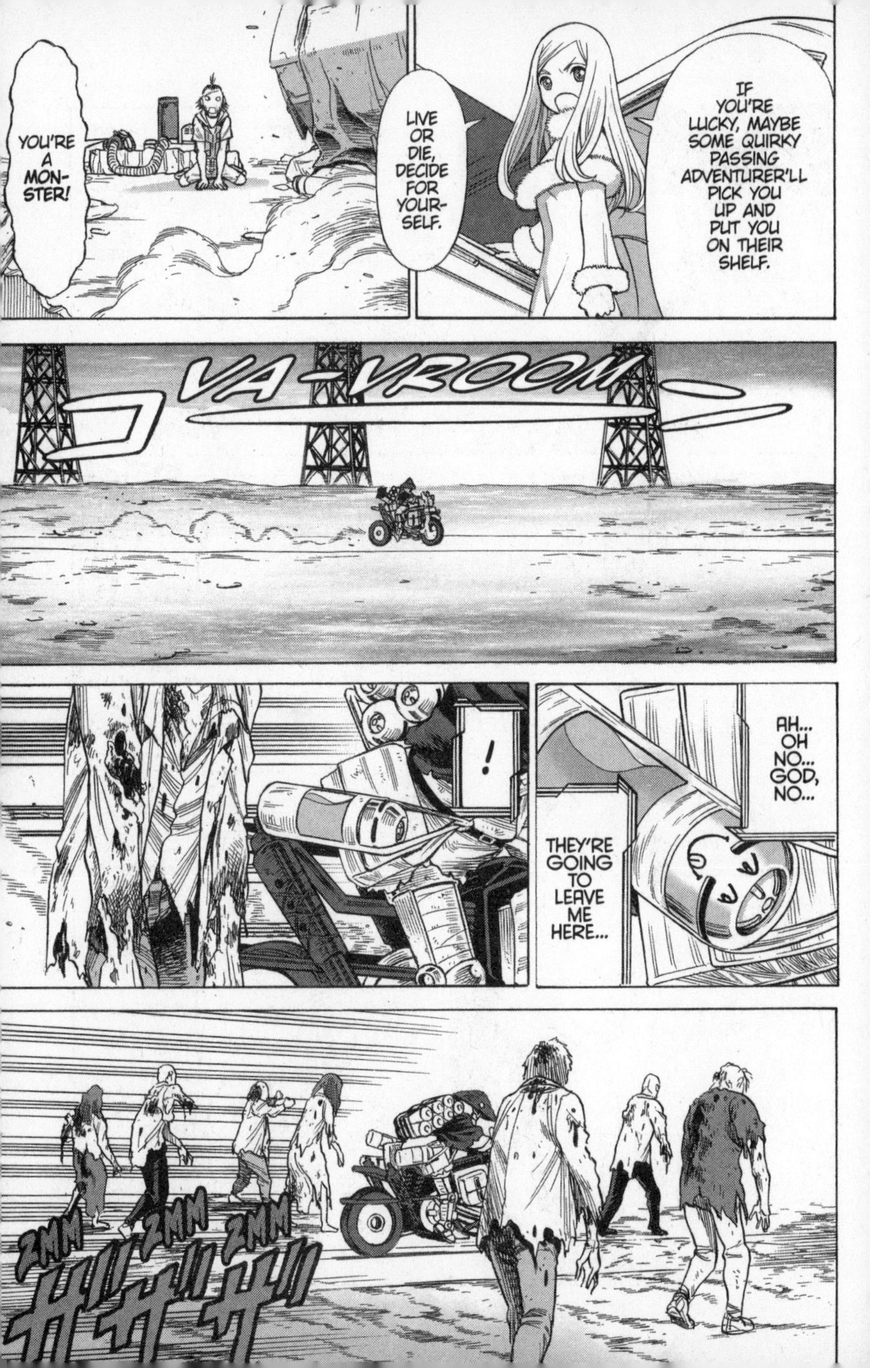
IF YOU'RE LUCKY, MAYBE SOME QUIRKY PASSING ADVENTURER'LL PICK YOU UP AND PUT YOU ON THEIR SHELF.
LIVE OR DIE, DECIDE FOR YOURSELF.
YOU'RE A MONSTER!
VA-VROOM
AH... OH NO... GOD, NO...
THEY'RE GOING TO LEAVE ME HERE...
!
ZMMSH!!
ZMMSH!!
ZMMSH!!

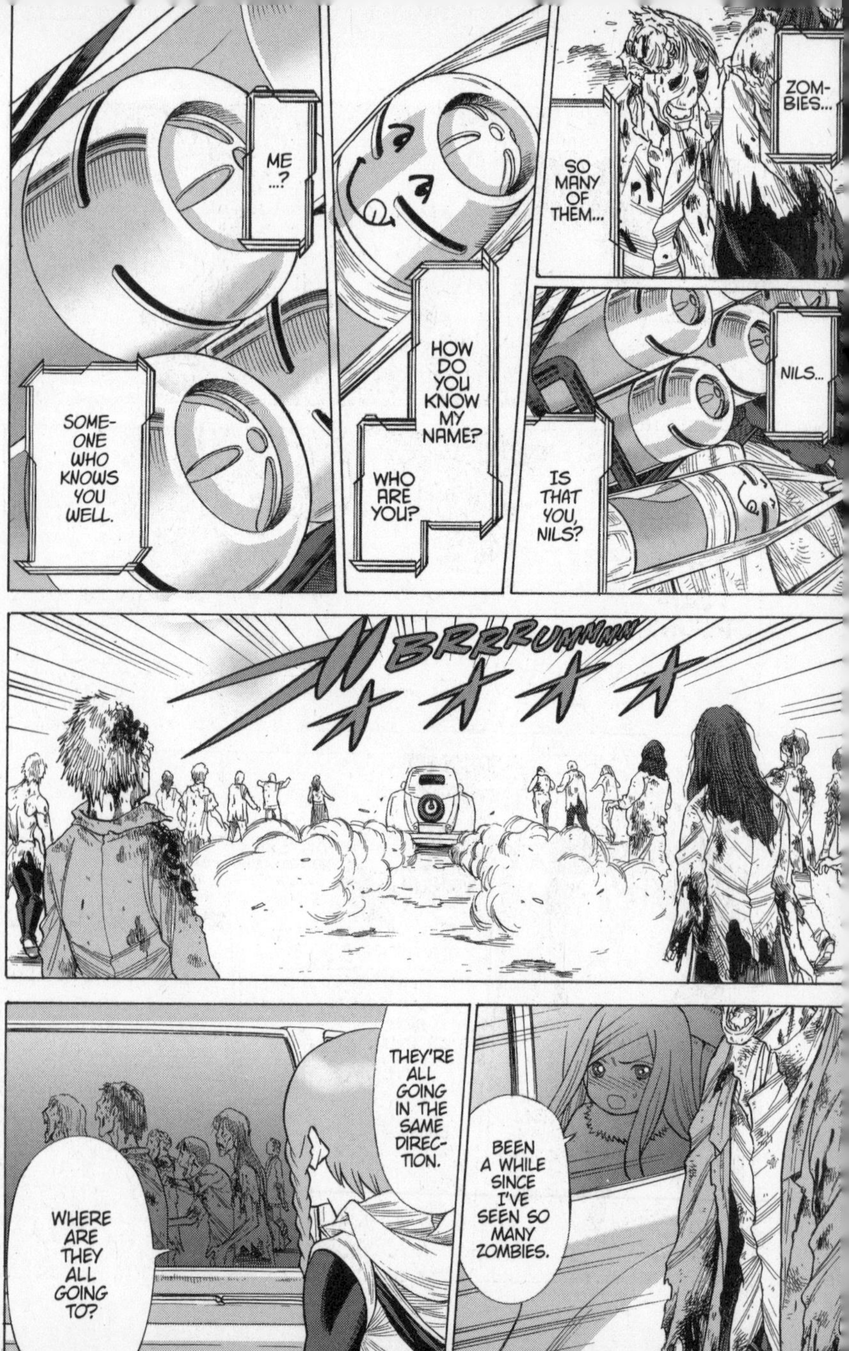
ZOMBIES...
SO MANY OF THEM...
NILS...
IS THAT YOU, NILS?
HOW DO YOU KNOW MY NAME?
WHO ARE YOU?
ME ...?
SOMEONE WHO KNOWS YOU WELL.
BRRRUMMMM
THEY'RE ALL GOING IN THE SAME DIRECTION.
BEEN A WHILE SINCE I'VE SEEN SO MANY ZOMBIES.
WHERE ARE THEY ALL GOING TO?

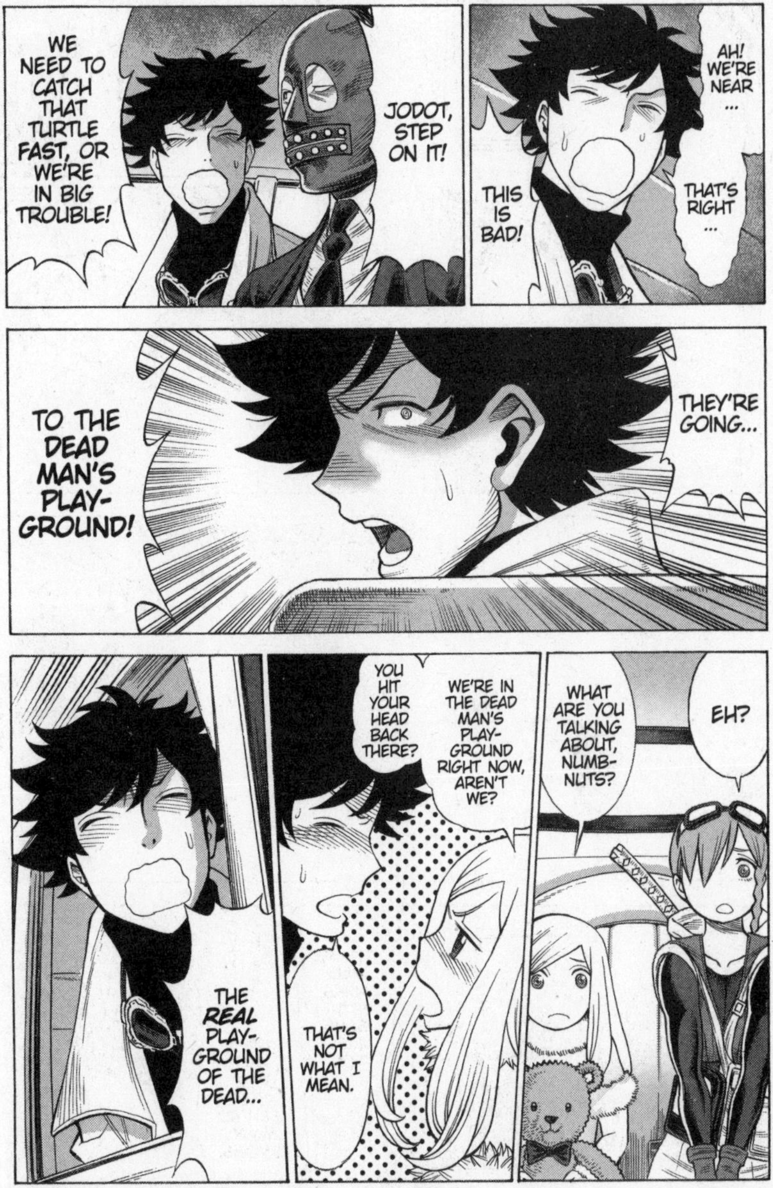
AH! WE'RE NEAR ...
THAT'S RIGHT ...
THIS IS BAD!
WE NEED TO CATCH THAT TURTLE FAST, OR WE'RE IN BIG TROUBLE!
JODOT, STEP ON IT!
THEY'RE GOING...
TO THE DEAD MAN'S PLAY-GROUND!
EH?
WHAT ARE YOU TALKING ABOUT, NUMB-NUTS?
WE'RE IN THE DEAD MAN'S PLAY-GROUND RIGHT NOW, AREN'T WE?
YOU HIT YOUR HEAD BACK THERE?
THAT'S NOT WHAT I MEAN.
THE *REAL* PLAY-GROUND OF THE DEAD...

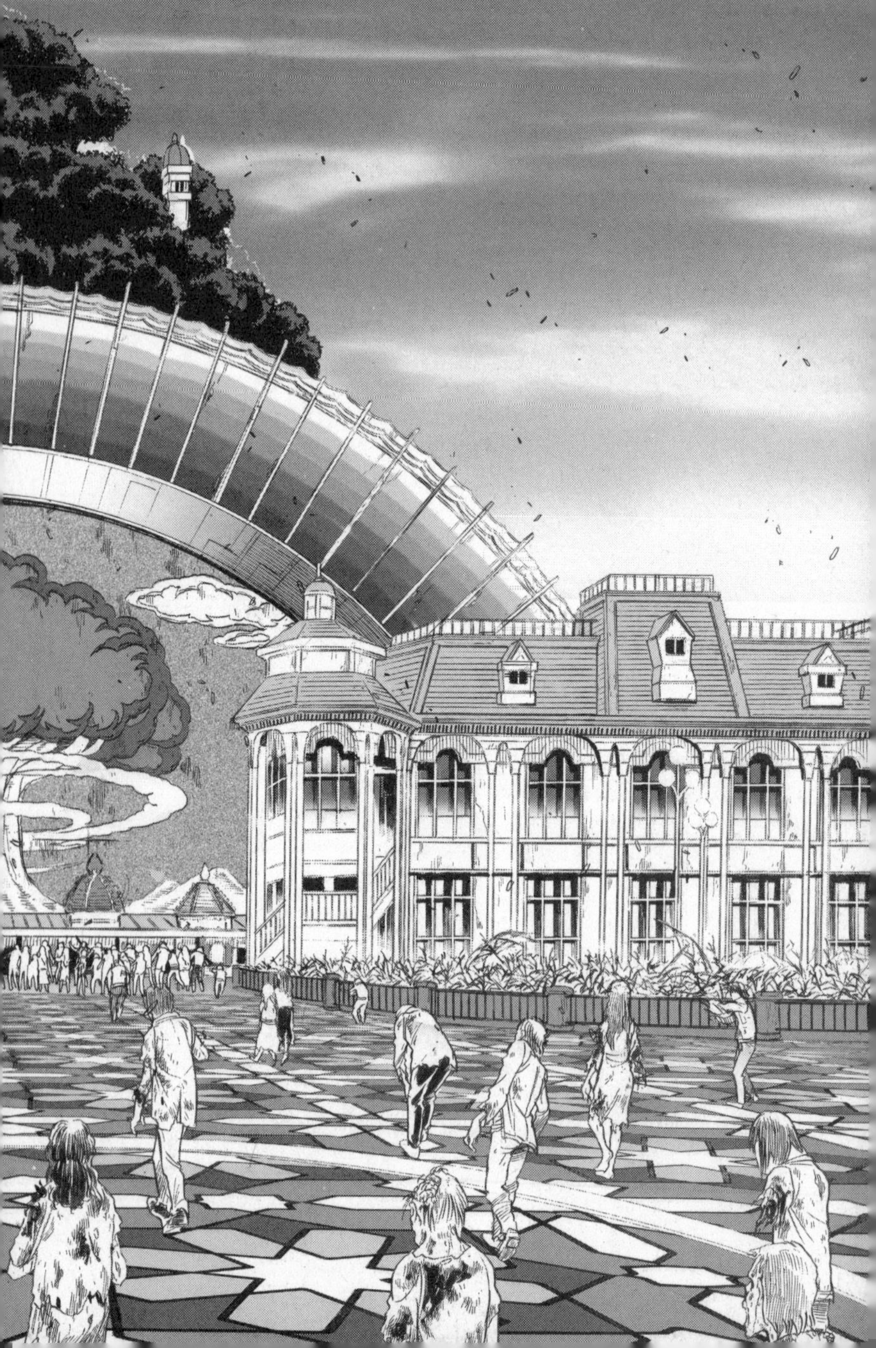

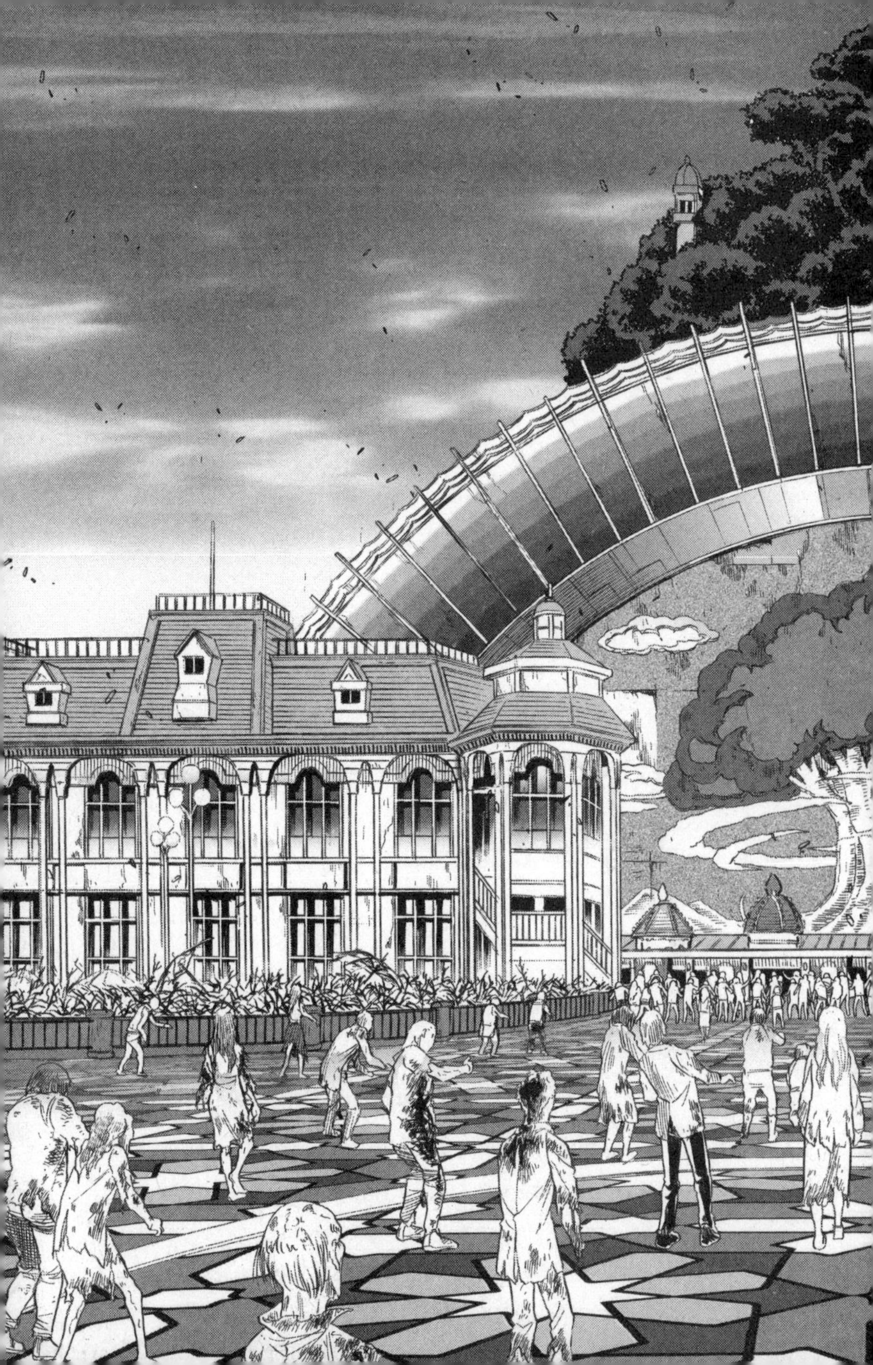

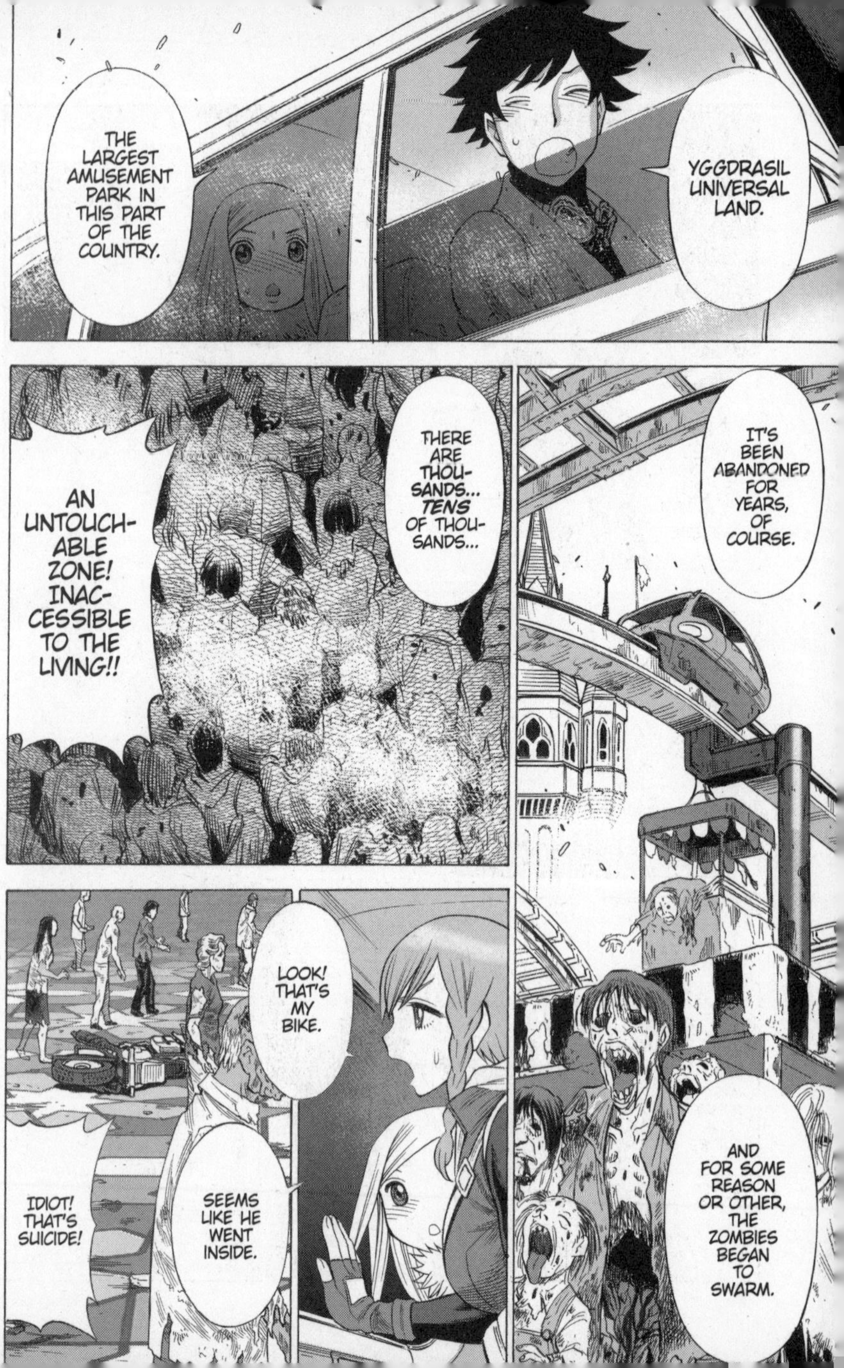
YGGDRASIL UNIVERSAL LAND.
THE LARGEST AMUSEMENT PARK IN THIS PART OF THE COUNTRY.
IT'S BEEN ABANDONED FOR YEARS, OF COURSE.
AND FOR SOME REASON OR OTHER, THE ZOMBIES BEGAN TO SWARM.
THERE ARE THOUSANDS... *TENS* OF THOUSANDS...
AN UNTOUCHABLE ZONE! INACCESSIBLE TO THE LIVING!!
LOOK! THAT'S MY BIKE.
SEEMS LIKE HE WENT INSIDE.
IDIOT! THAT'S SUICIDE!

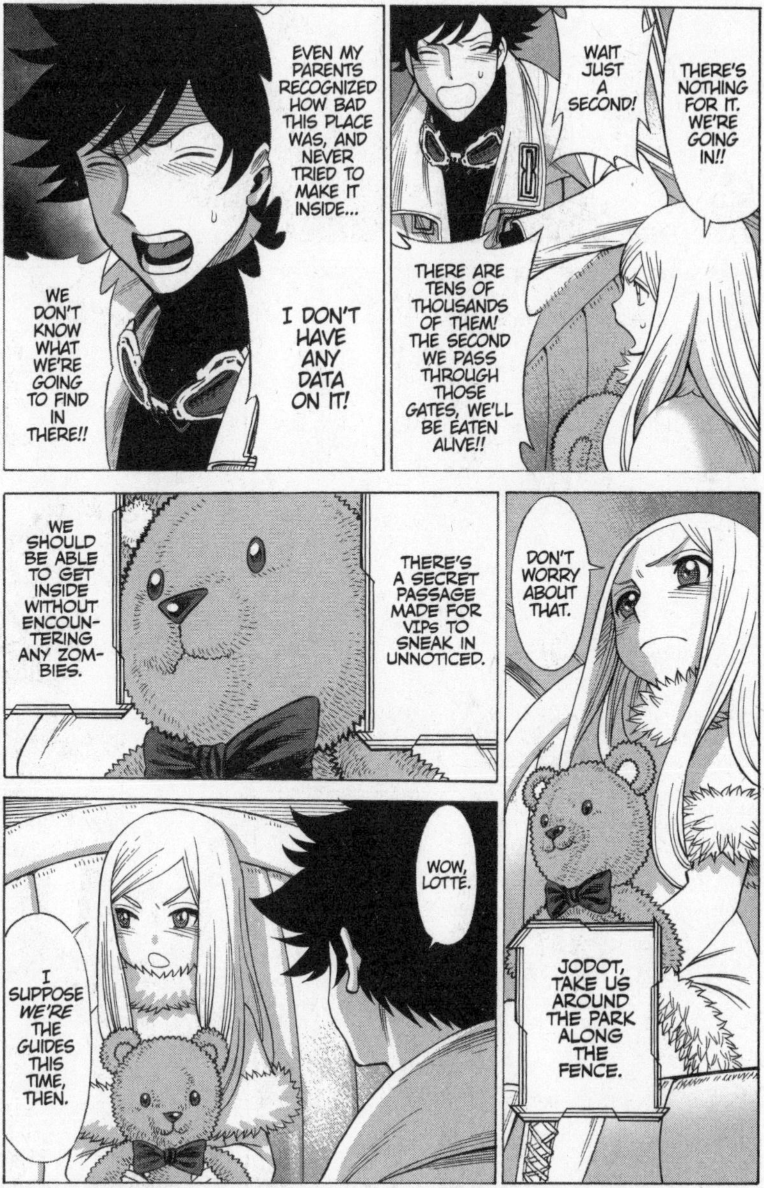
THERE'S NOTHING FOR IT. WE'RE GOING IN!!
WAIT JUST A SECOND!
THERE ARE TENS OF THOUSANDS OF THEM! THE SECOND WE PASS THROUGH THOSE GATES, WE'LL BE EATEN ALIVE!!
EVEN MY PARENTS RECOGNIZED HOW BAD THIS PLACE WAS, AND NEVER TRIED TO MAKE IT INSIDE...
I DON'T HAVE ANY DATA ON IT!
WE DON'T KNOW WHAT WE'RE GOING TO FIND IN THERE!!
DON'T WORRY ABOUT THAT.
JODOT, TAKE US AROUND THE PARK ALONG THE FENCE.
THERE'S A SECRET PASSAGE MADE FOR VIPs TO SNEAK IN UNNOTICED.
WE SHOULD BE ABLE TO GET INSIDE WITHOUT ENCOUNTERING ANY ZOMBIES.
WOW, LOTTE.
I SUPPOSE *WE'RE* THE GUIDES THIS TIME, THEN.

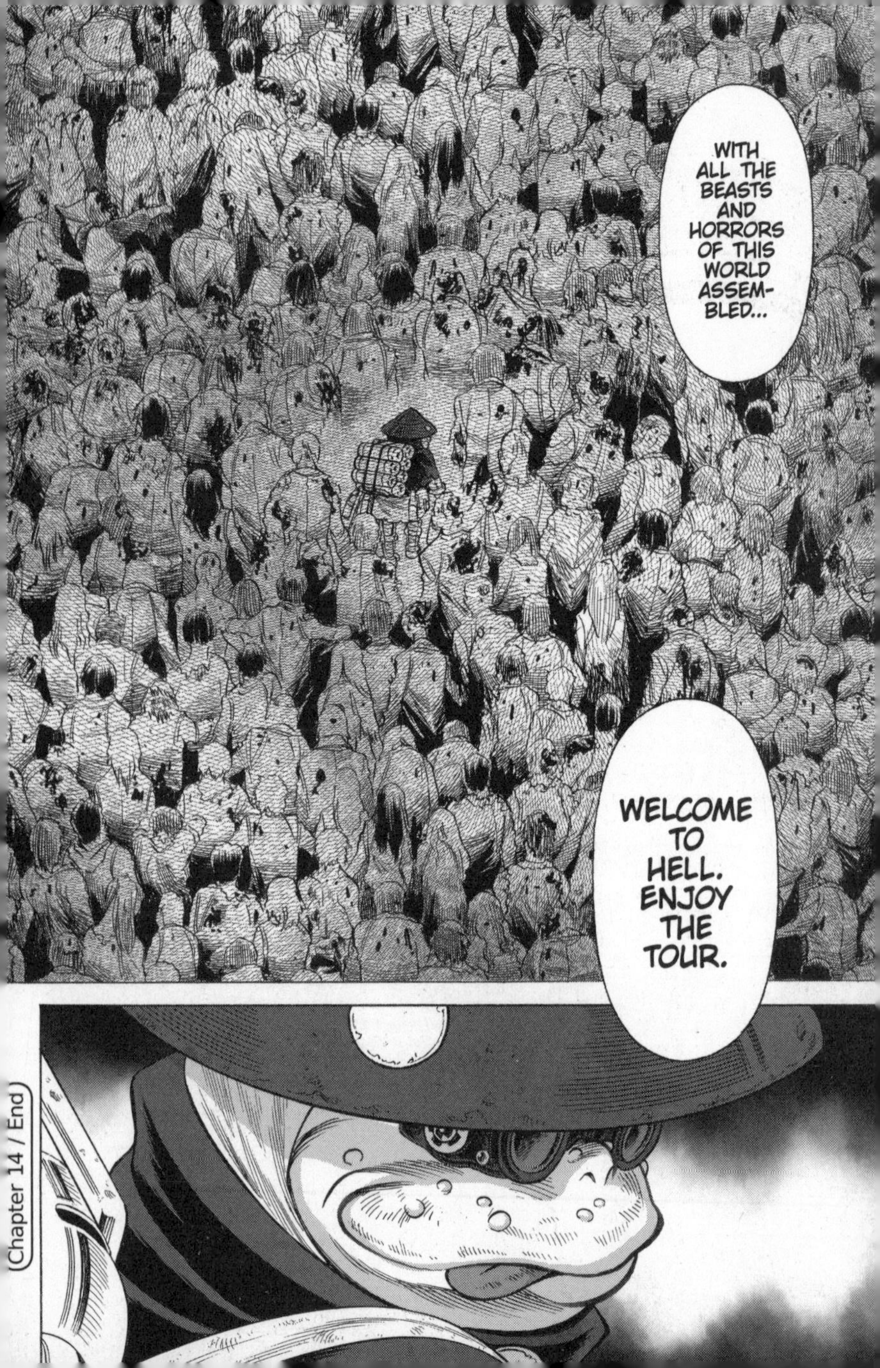
WITH ALL THE BEASTS AND HORRORS OF THIS WORLD ASSEM-BLED...
WELCOME TO HELL. ENJOY THE TOUR.

(Chapter 14 / End)

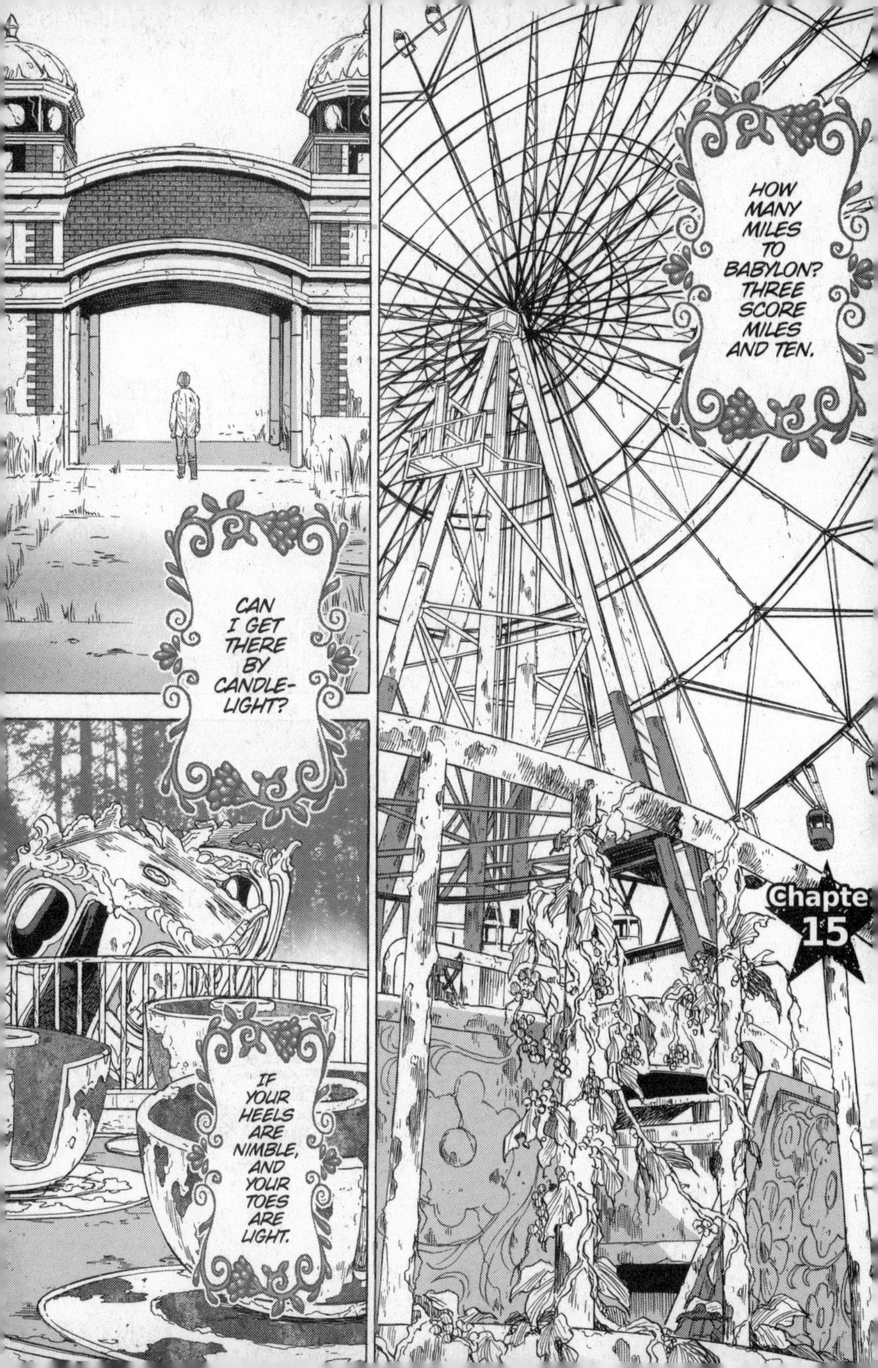
HOW MANY MILES TO BABYLON? THREE SCORE MILES AND TEN.
Chapte
15
CAN I GET THERE BY CANDLE-LIGHT?
IF YOUR HEELS ARE NIMBLE, AND YOUR TOES ARE LIGHT.

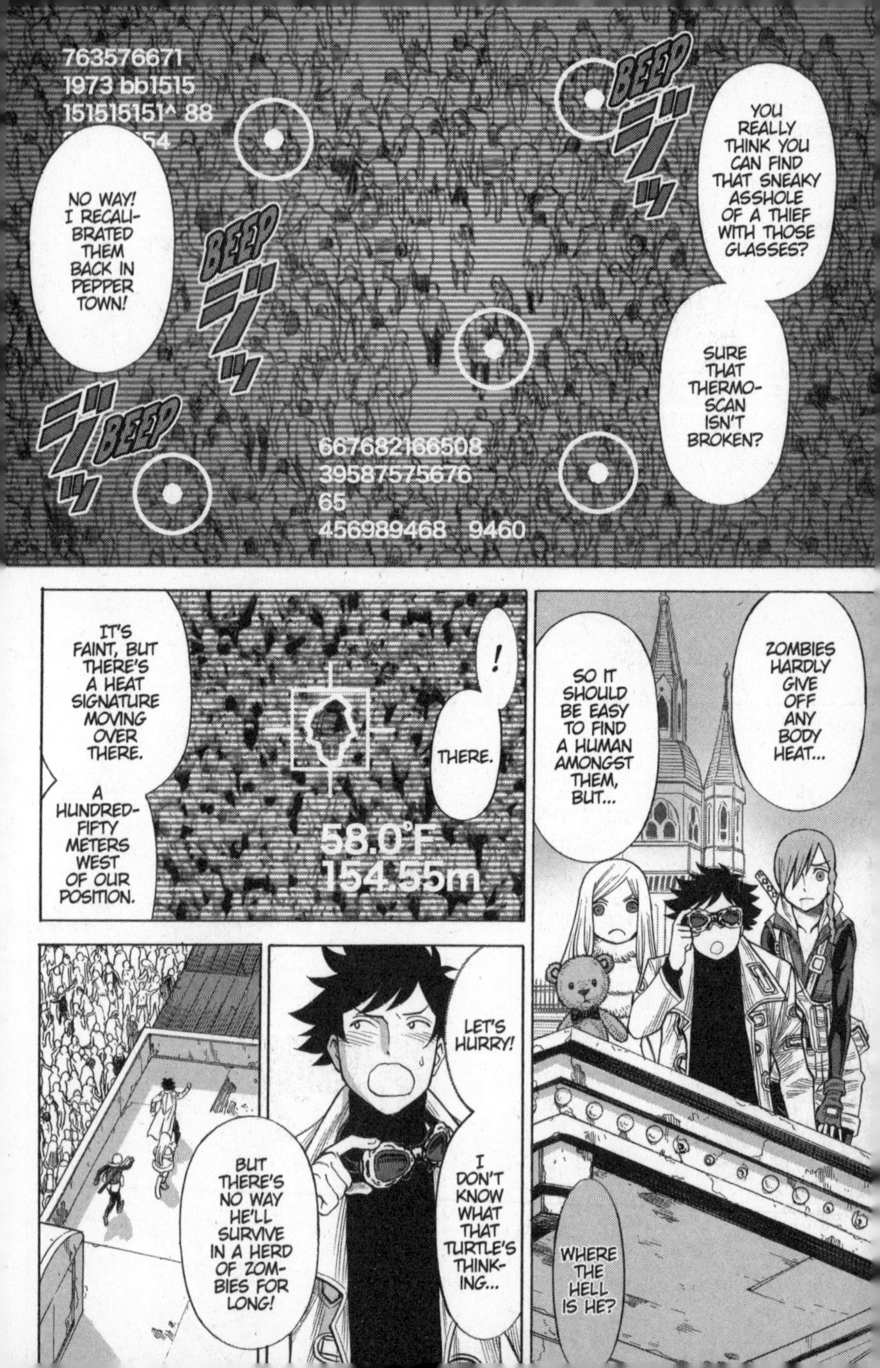
YOU REALLY THINK YOU CAN FIND THAT SNEAKY ASSHOLE OF A THIEF WITH THOSE GLASSES?
SURE THAT THERMO-SCAN ISN'T BROKEN?
BEEP
BEEP
NO WAY! I RECALIBRATED THEM BACK IN PEPPER TOWN!
BEEP
763576671
1973 bb1515
151515151^ 88
667682166508
39587575676
65
456989468 9460
ZOMBIES HARDLY GIVE OFF ANY BODY HEAT...
SO IT SHOULD BE EASY TO FIND A HUMAN AMONGST THEM, BUT...
WHERE THE HELL IS HE?
!
THERE.
58.0°F
154.55m
IT'S FAINT, BUT THERE'S A HEAT SIGNATURE MOVING OVER THERE.
A HUNDRED-FIFTY METERS WEST OF OUR POSITION.
LET'S HURRY!
I DON'T KNOW WHAT THAT TURTLE'S THINKING...
BUT THERE'S NO WAY HE'LL SURVIVE IN A HERD OF ZOMBIES FOR LONG!

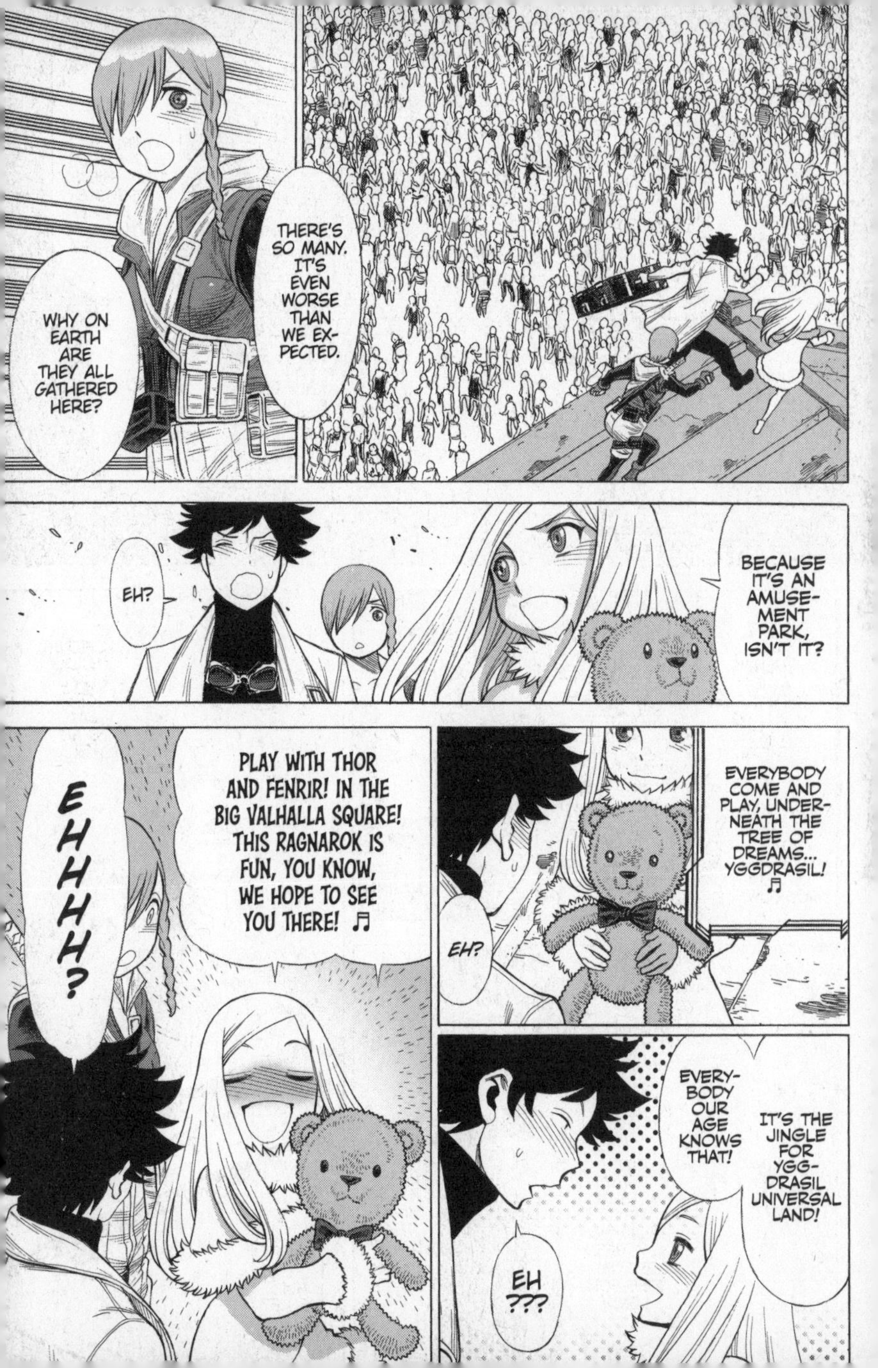
THERE'S SO MANY. IT'S EVEN WORSE THAN WE EX-PECTED.
WHY ON EARTH ARE THEY ALL GATHERED HERE?
BECAUSE IT'S AN AMUSE-MENT PARK, ISN'T IT?
EH?
EVERYBODY COME AND PLAY, UNDER-NEATH THE TREE OF DREAMS... YGGDRASIL! ♫
EH?
IT'S THE JINGLE FOR YGG-DRASIL UNIVERSAL LAND!
EVERY-BODY OUR AGE KNOWS THAT!
EH ???
PLAY WITH THOR AND FENRIR! IN THE BIG VALHALLA SQUARE! THIS RAGNAROK IS FUN, YOU KNOW, WE HOPE TO SEE YOU THERE! ♫
EHHHHH?

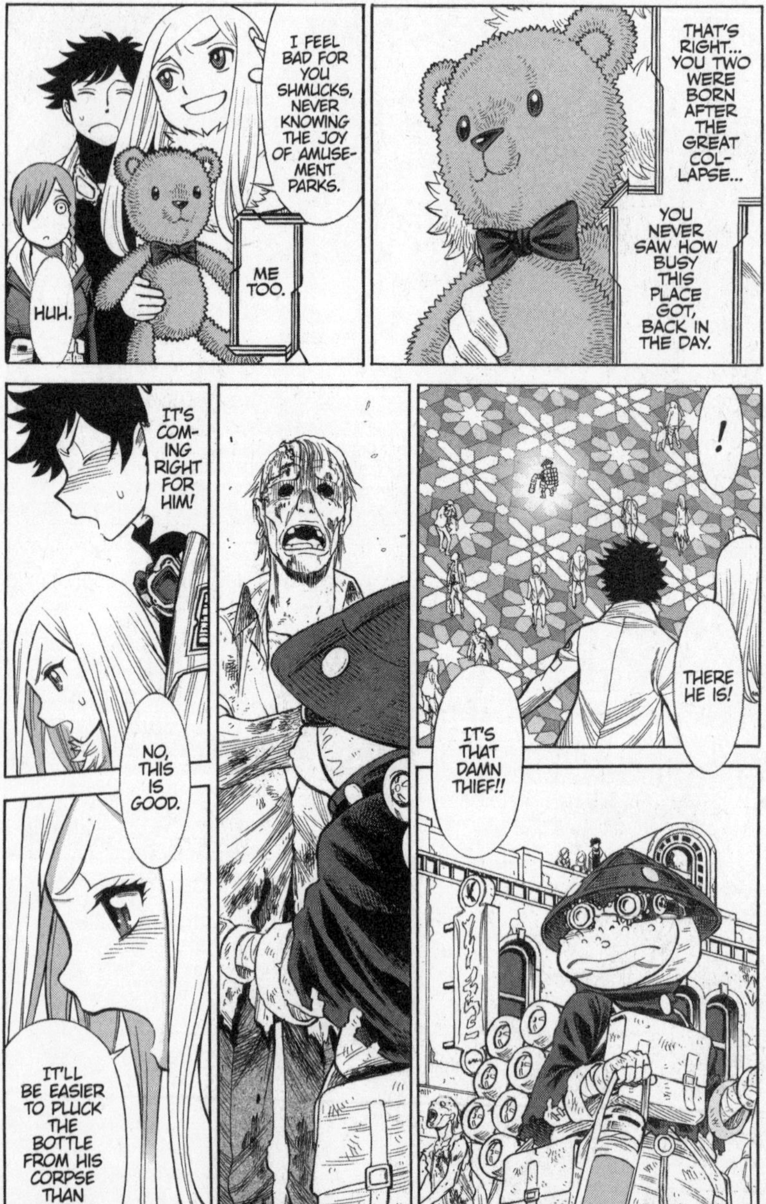
THAT'S RIGHT... YOU TWO WERE BORN AFTER THE GREAT COLLAPSE...
YOU NEVER SAW HOW BUSY THIS PLACE GOT, BACK IN THE DAY.
I FEEL BAD FOR YOU SHMUCKS, NEVER KNOWING THE JOY OF AMUSEMENT PARKS.
ME TOO.
HUH.
!
THERE HE IS!
IT'S THAT DAMN THIEF!!
IT'S COMING RIGHT FOR HIM!
NO, THIS IS GOOD.
IT'LL BE EASIER TO PLUCK THE BOTTLE FROM HIS CORPSE THAN TAKE IT DIRECTLY.

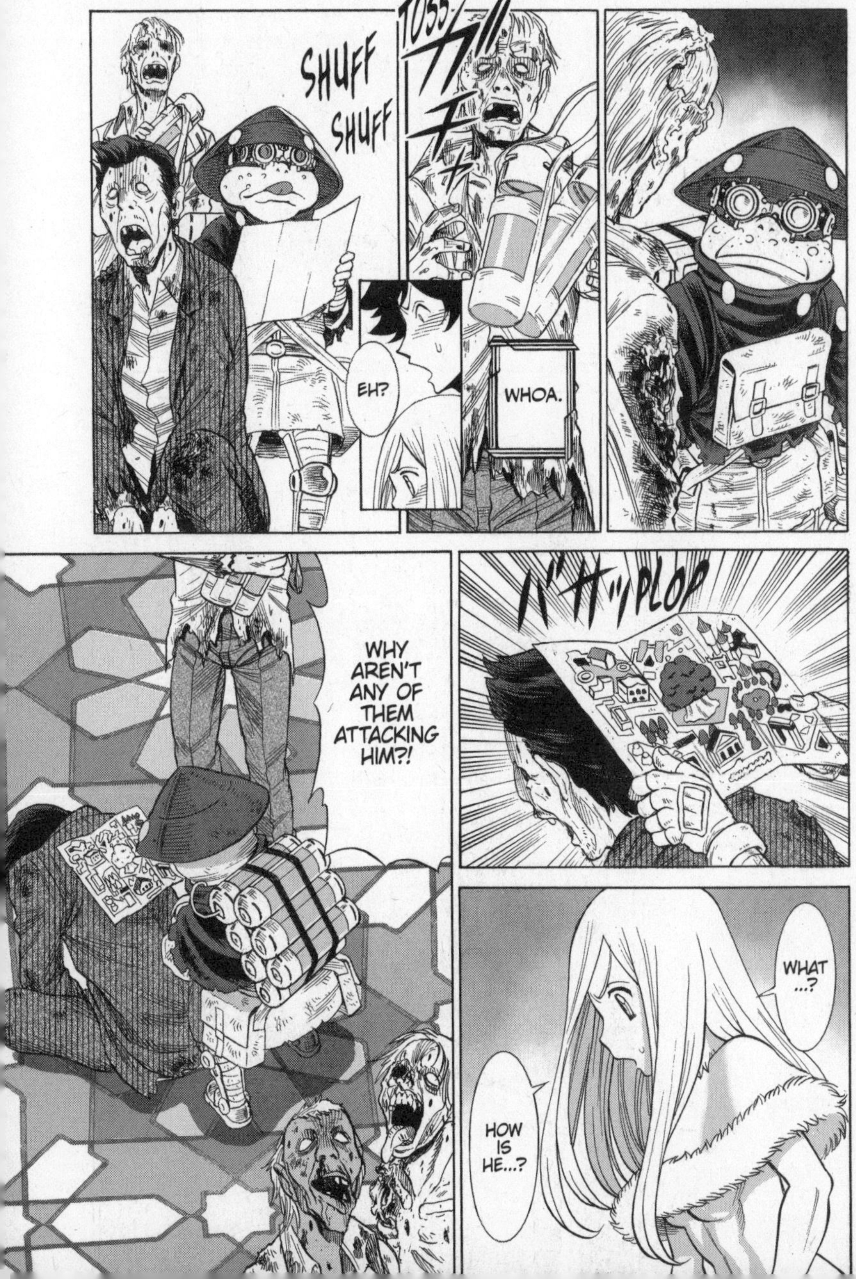
TOSS
WHOA.
EH?
SHUFF
SHUFF
PLOP
WHAT ...?
HOW IS HE...?
WHY AREN'T ANY OF THEM ATTACKING HIM?!

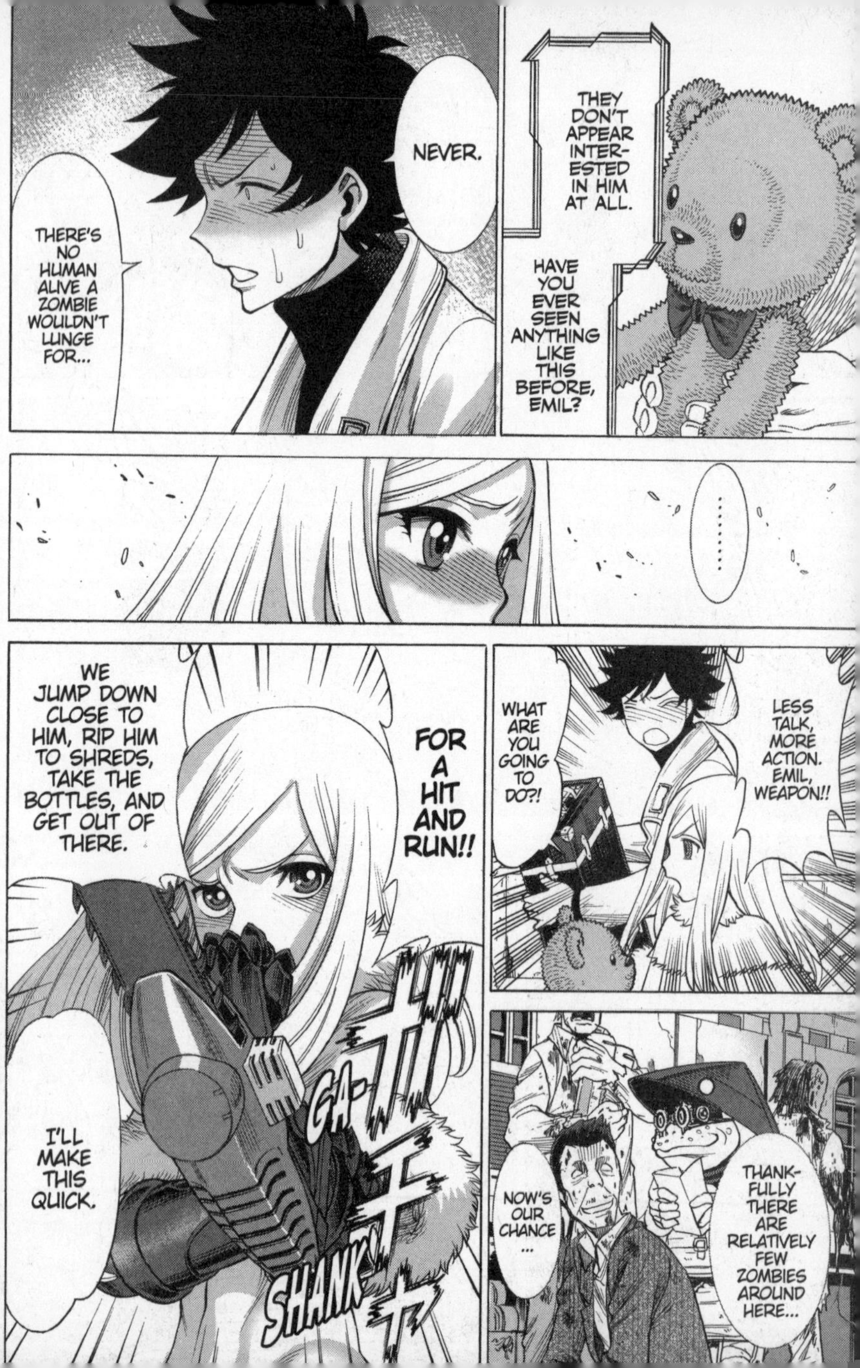
THEY DON'T APPEAR INTERESTED IN HIM AT ALL.
HAVE YOU EVER SEEN ANYTHING LIKE THIS BEFORE, EMIL?
NEVER.
THERE'S NO HUMAN ALIVE A ZOMBIE WOULDN'T LUNGE FOR...
......
LESS TALK, MORE ACTION. EMIL, WEAPON!!
WHAT ARE YOU GOING TO DO?!
THANKFULLY THERE ARE RELATIVELY FEW ZOMBIES AROUND HERE...
NOW'S OUR CHANCE...
FOR A HIT AND RUN!!
WE JUMP DOWN CLOSE TO HIM, RIP HIM TO SHREDS, TAKE THE BOTTLES, AND GET OUT OF THERE.
I'LL MAKE THIS QUICK.
GA-SHANK

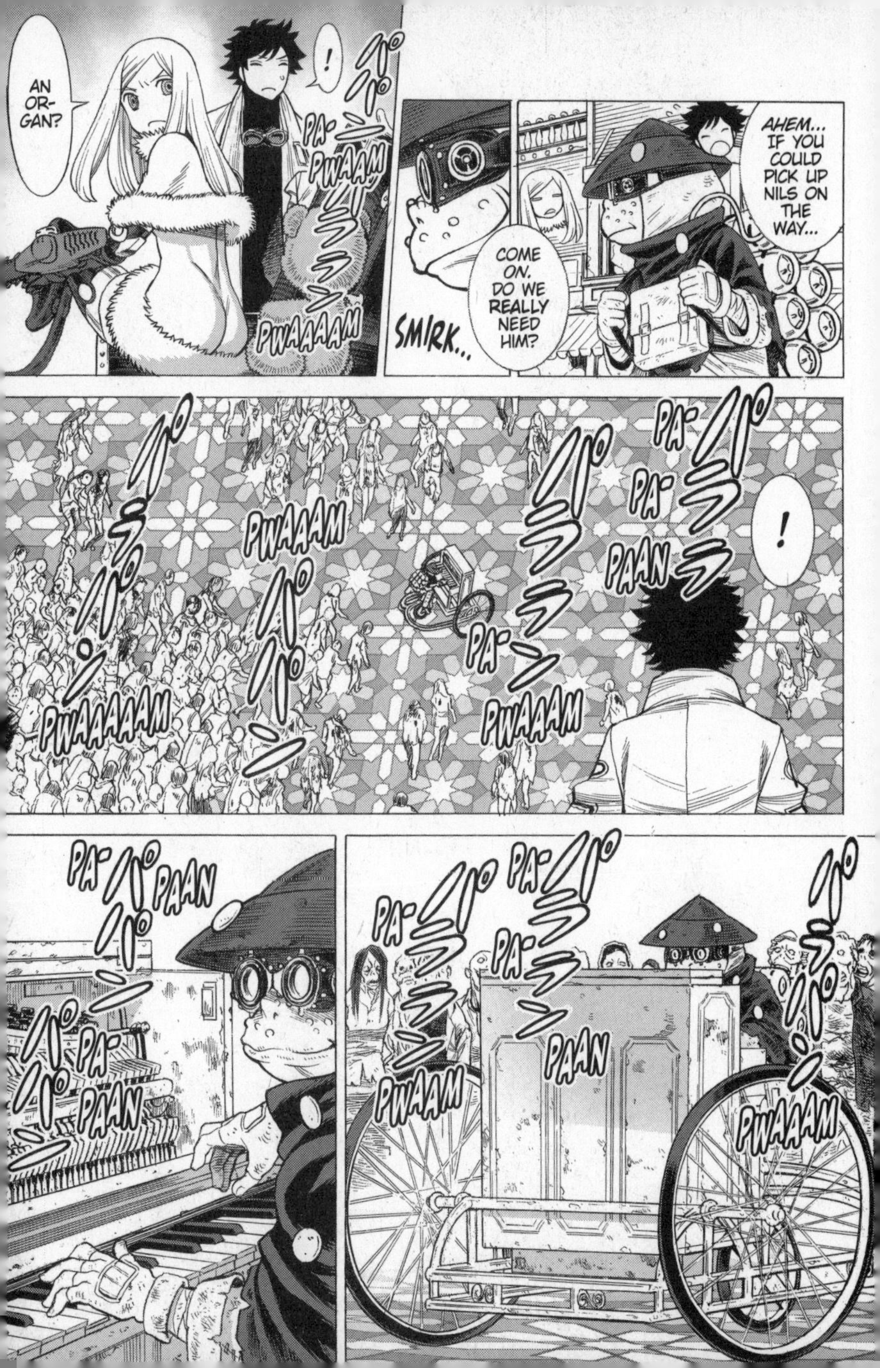
AHEM... IF YOU COULD PICK UP NILS ON THE WAY...
COME ON. DO WE REALLY NEED HIM?
SMIRK...
!
PA-PWAAM
PWAAAAM
AN ORGAN?
PA-PA-PAAN
!
PA-PWAAAM
PWAAAM
PWAAAAAM
PA-PA-PAAN
PA-PWAAM
PWAAAM
PA-PAAN
PA-PAAN

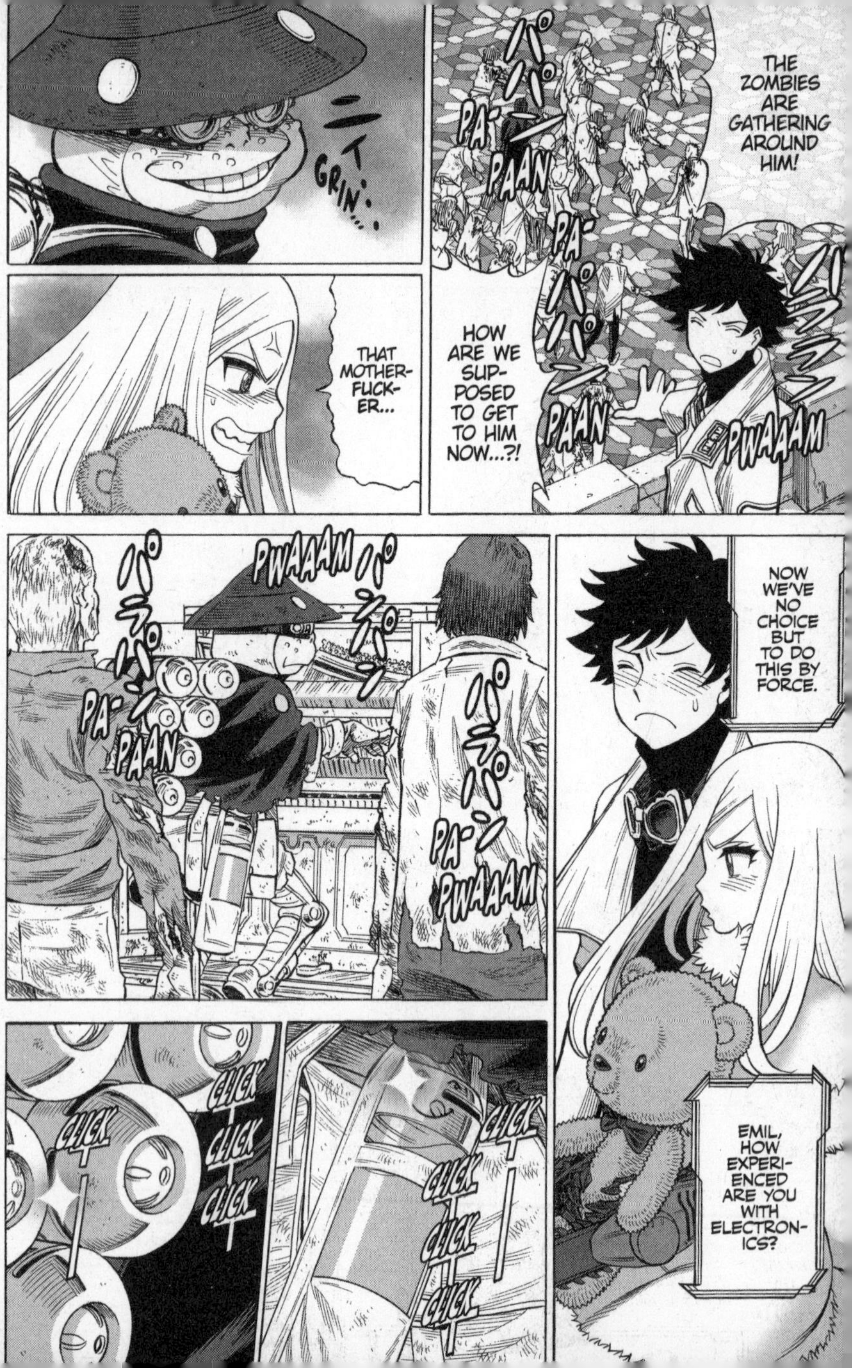
PA-
PAAN
THE ZOMBIES ARE GATHERING AROUND HIM!
PA-
PAAN
PWAAAM
HOW ARE WE SUP-POSED TO GET TO HIM NOW...?!
GRIN...
THAT MOTHER-FUCK-ER...
NOW WE'VE NO CHOICE BUT TO DO THIS BY FORCE.
EMIL, HOW EXPERI-ENCED ARE YOU WITH ELECTRON-ICS?
PWAAAM
PA-
PWAAAM
PA-
PAAN
CLICK
CLICK
CLICK
CLICK
CLICK
CLICK
CLICK
CLICK

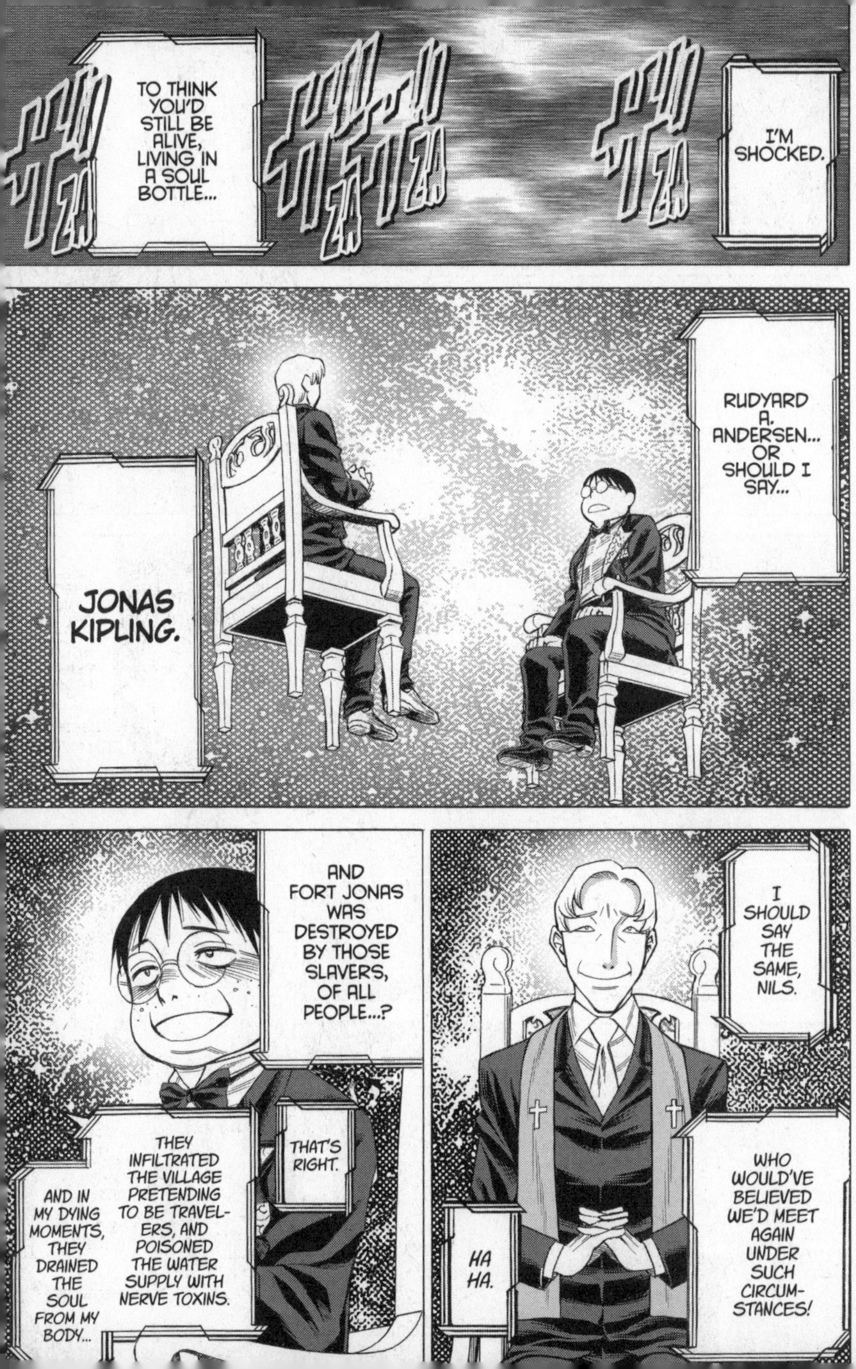
I'M SHOCKED.
TO THINK YOU'D STILL BE ALIVE, LIVING IN A SOUL BOTTLE...
RUDYARD A. ANDERSEN... OR SHOULD I SAY...
JONAS KIPLING.
I SHOULD SAY THE SAME, NILS.
WHO WOULD'VE BELIEVED WE'D MEET AGAIN UNDER SUCH CIRCUMSTANCES!
HA HA.
AND FORT JONAS WAS DESTROYED BY THOSE SLAVERS, OF ALL PEOPLE...?
THAT'S RIGHT.
THEY INFILTRATED THE VILLAGE PRETENDING TO BE TRAVEL-ERS, AND POISONED THE WATER SUPPLY WITH NERVE TOXINS.
AND IN MY DYING MOMENTS, THEY DRAINED THE SOUL FROM MY BODY...

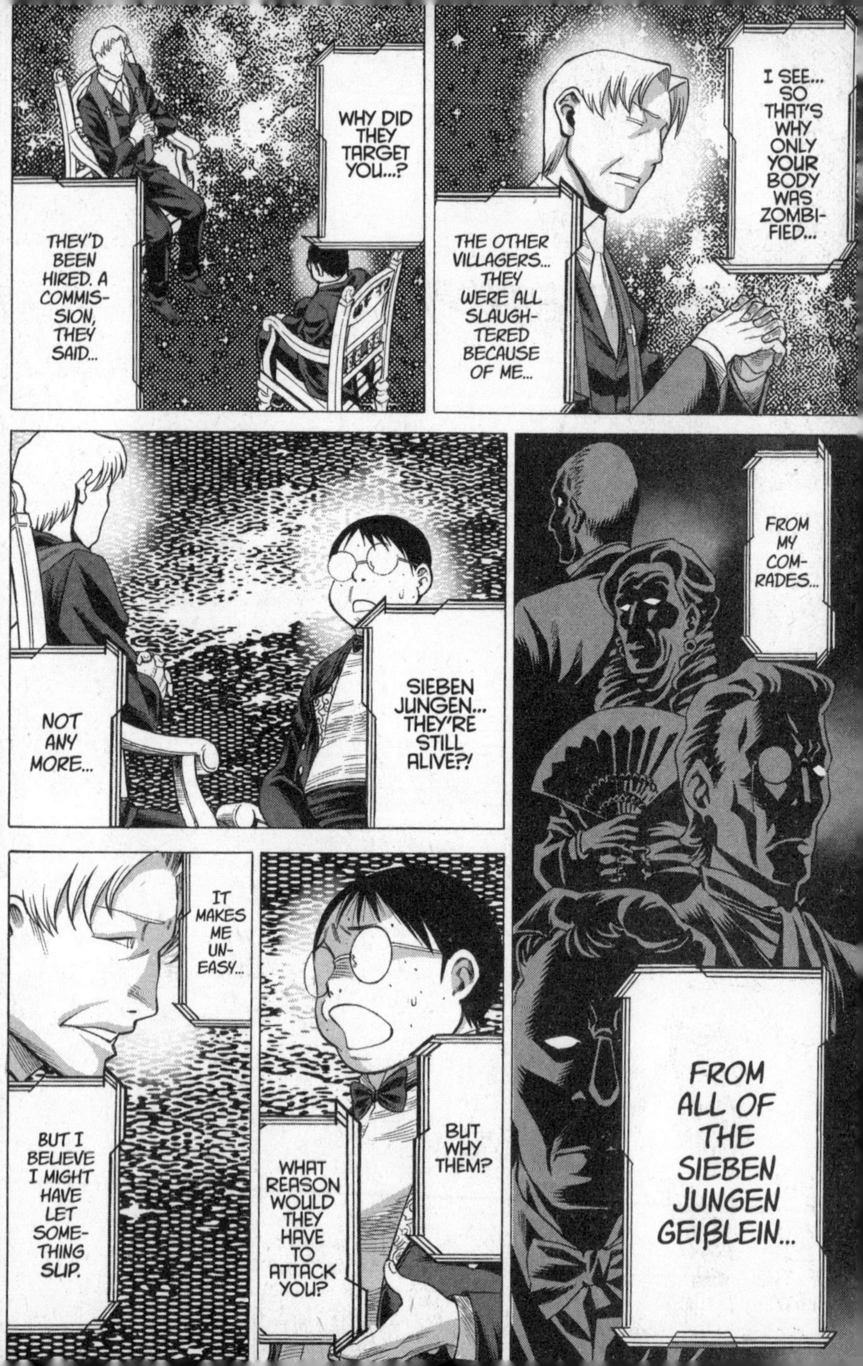
I SEE... SO THAT'S WHY ONLY YOUR BODY WAS ZOMBIFIED...
THE OTHER VILLAGERS... THEY WERE ALL SLAUGHTERED BECAUSE OF ME...
WHY DID THEY TARGET YOU...?
THEY'D BEEN HIRED. A COMMISSION, THEY SAID...
FROM MY COMRADES...
FROM ALL OF THE SIEBEN JUNGEN GEIßLEIN...
SIEBEN JUNGEN... THEY'RE STILL ALIVE?!
NOT ANY MORE...
BUT WHY THEM?
WHAT REASON WOULD THEY HAVE TO ATTACK YOU?
IT MAKES ME UNEASY...
BUT I BELIEVE I MIGHT HAVE LET SOMETHING SLIP.

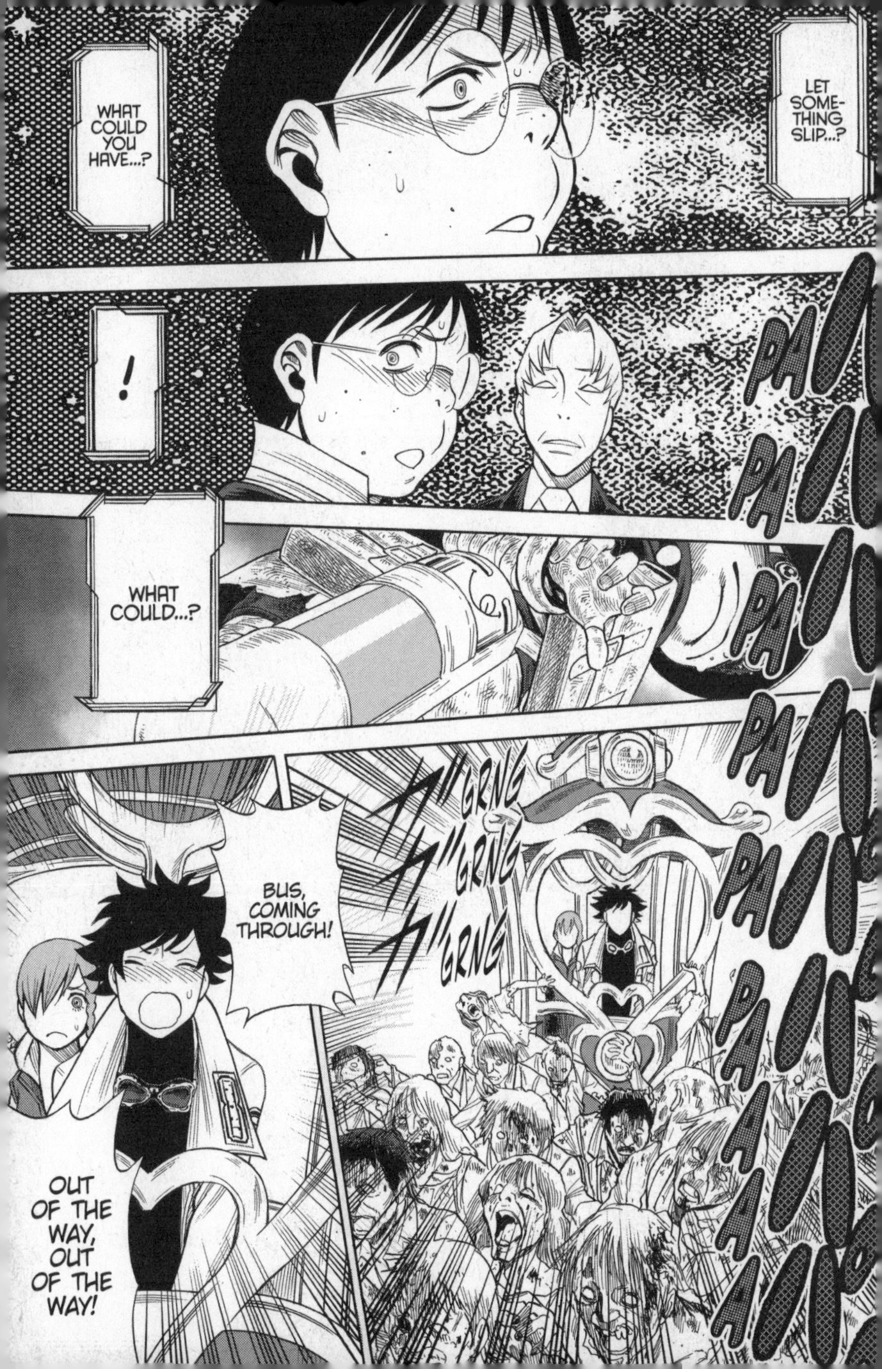
LET SOME-THING SLIP...?
WHAT COULD YOU HAVE...?
!
WHAT COULD...?
PA PA PA PA PA PA PA
GRNG GRNG GRNG
BUS, COMING THROUGH!
OUT OF THE WAY, OUT OF THE WAY!

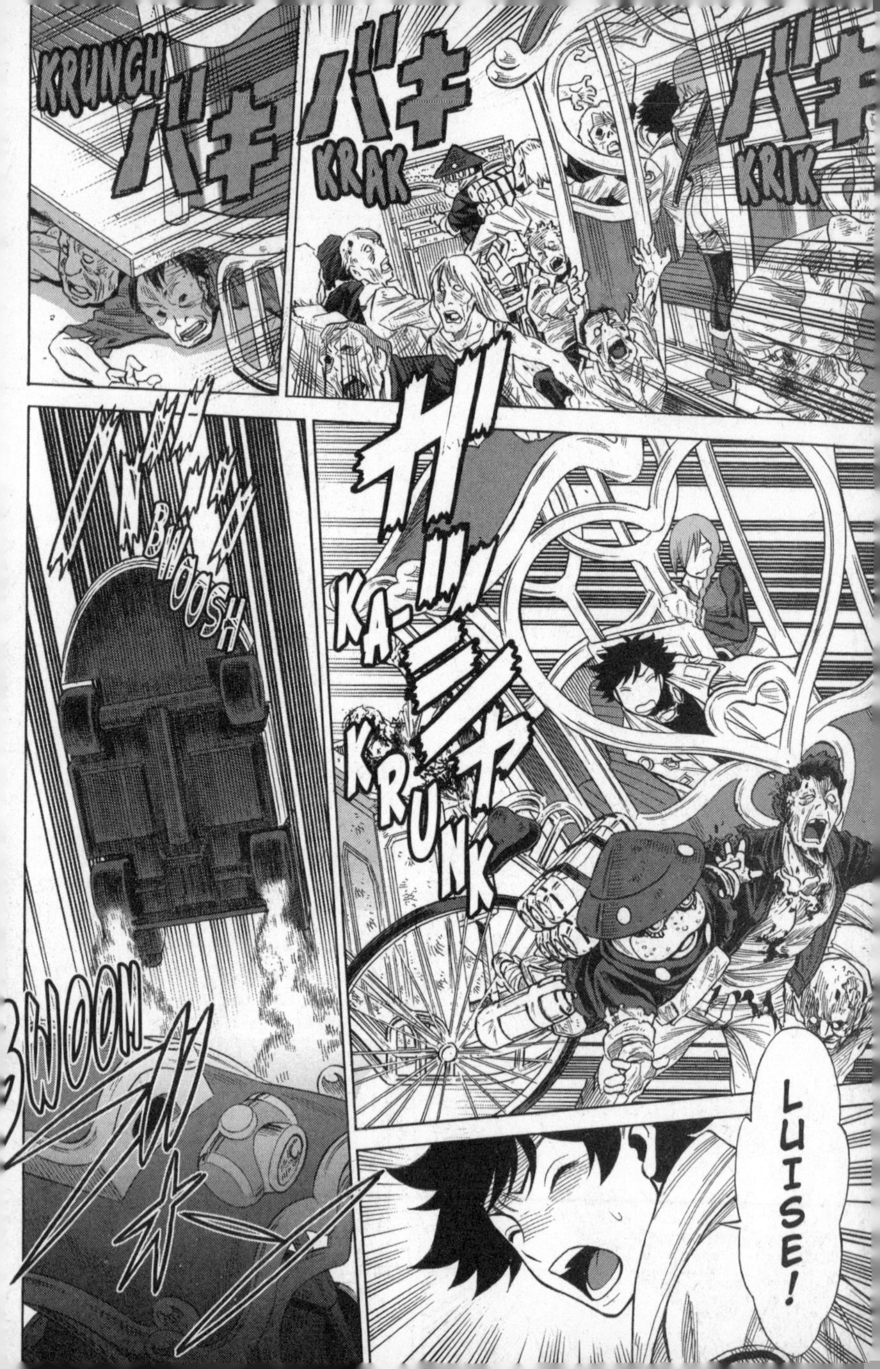

バキ
KRIK
バキ
KRAK
KRUNCH
バキ
ガシャ
KA-KRUNK
LUISE!
BWOOSH
BWOOM

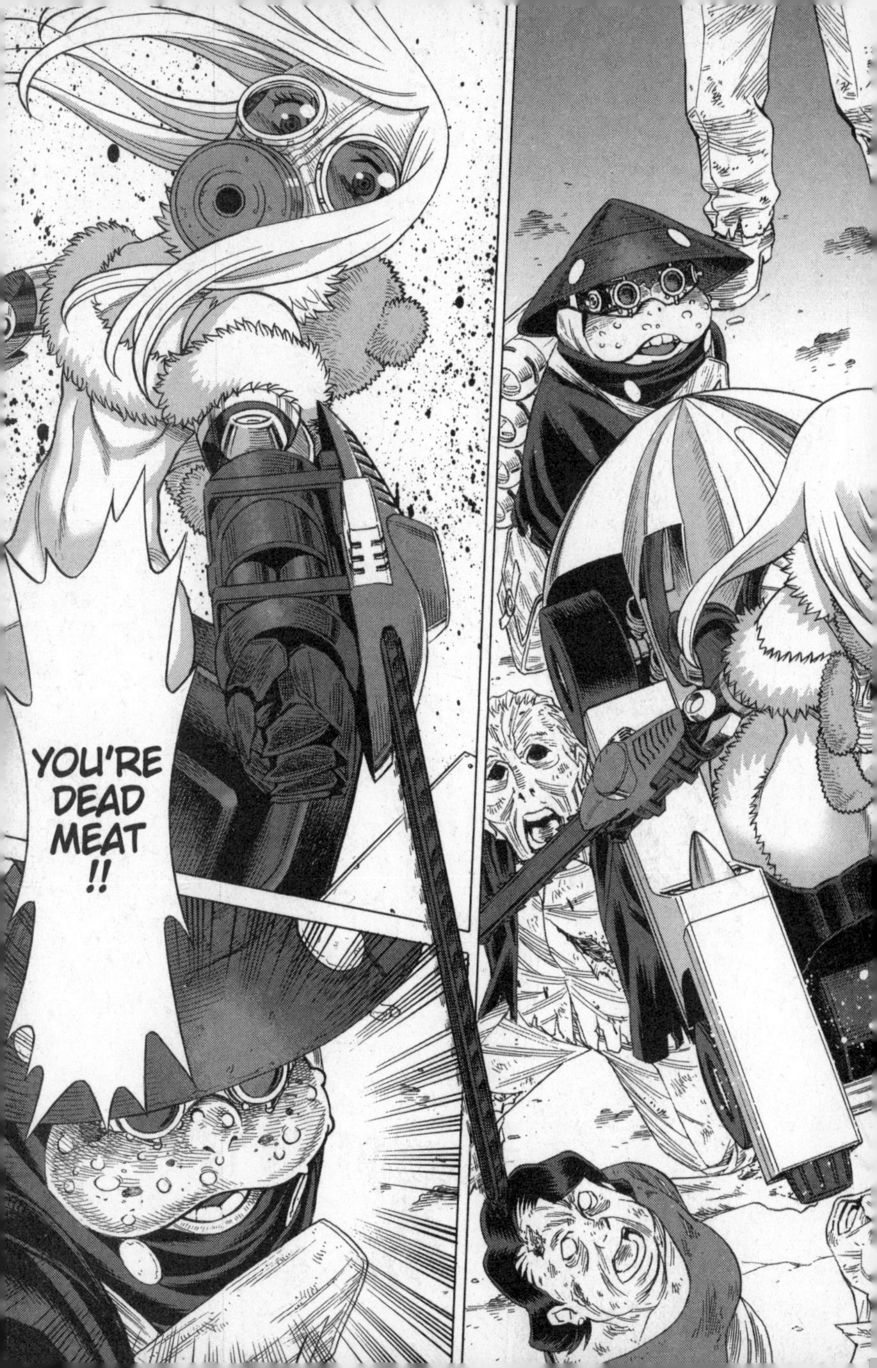
YOU'RE DEAD MEAT !!

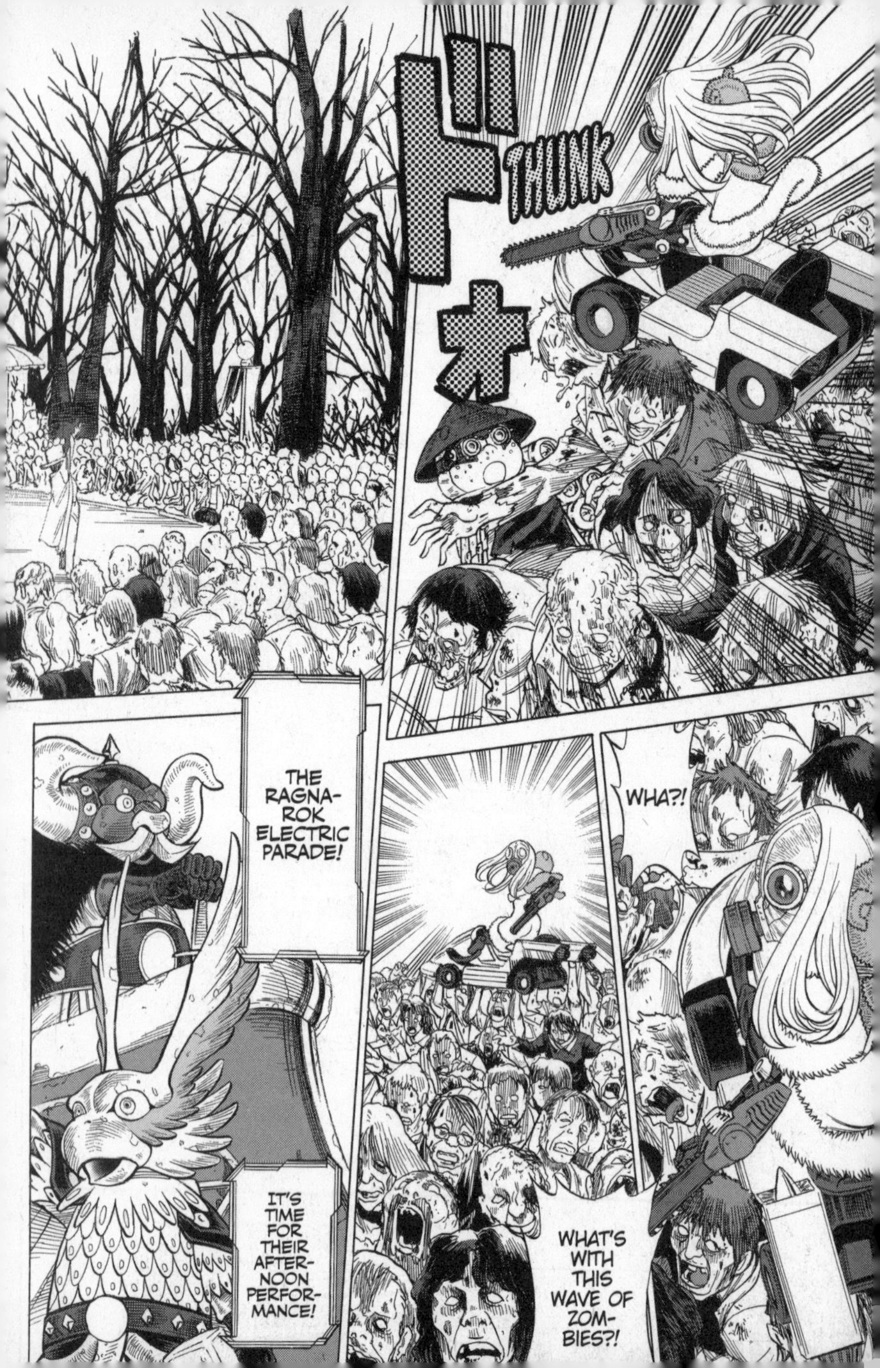
THUNK
WHA?!
WHAT'S WITH THIS WAVE OF ZOM-BIES?!
THE RAGNA-ROK ELECTRIC PARADE!
IT'S TIME FOR THEIR AFTER-NOON PERFOR-MANCE!

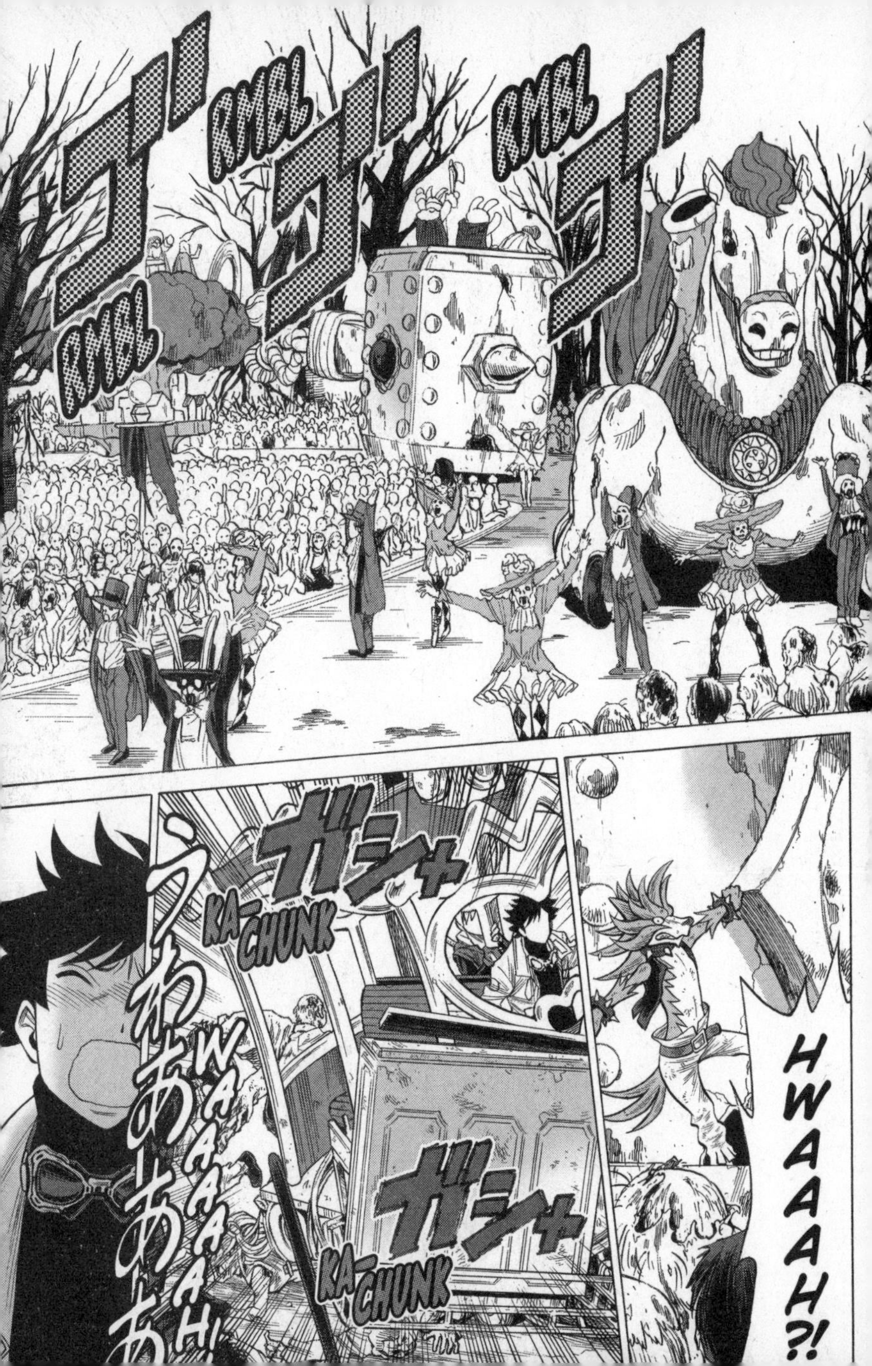
ゴ
RMBL
ゴ
RMBL
ゴ
RMBL
HWAAAAH?!
ガシャ
KA-CHUNK
ガシャ
KA-CHUNK
うわあああ
WAAAAAH!

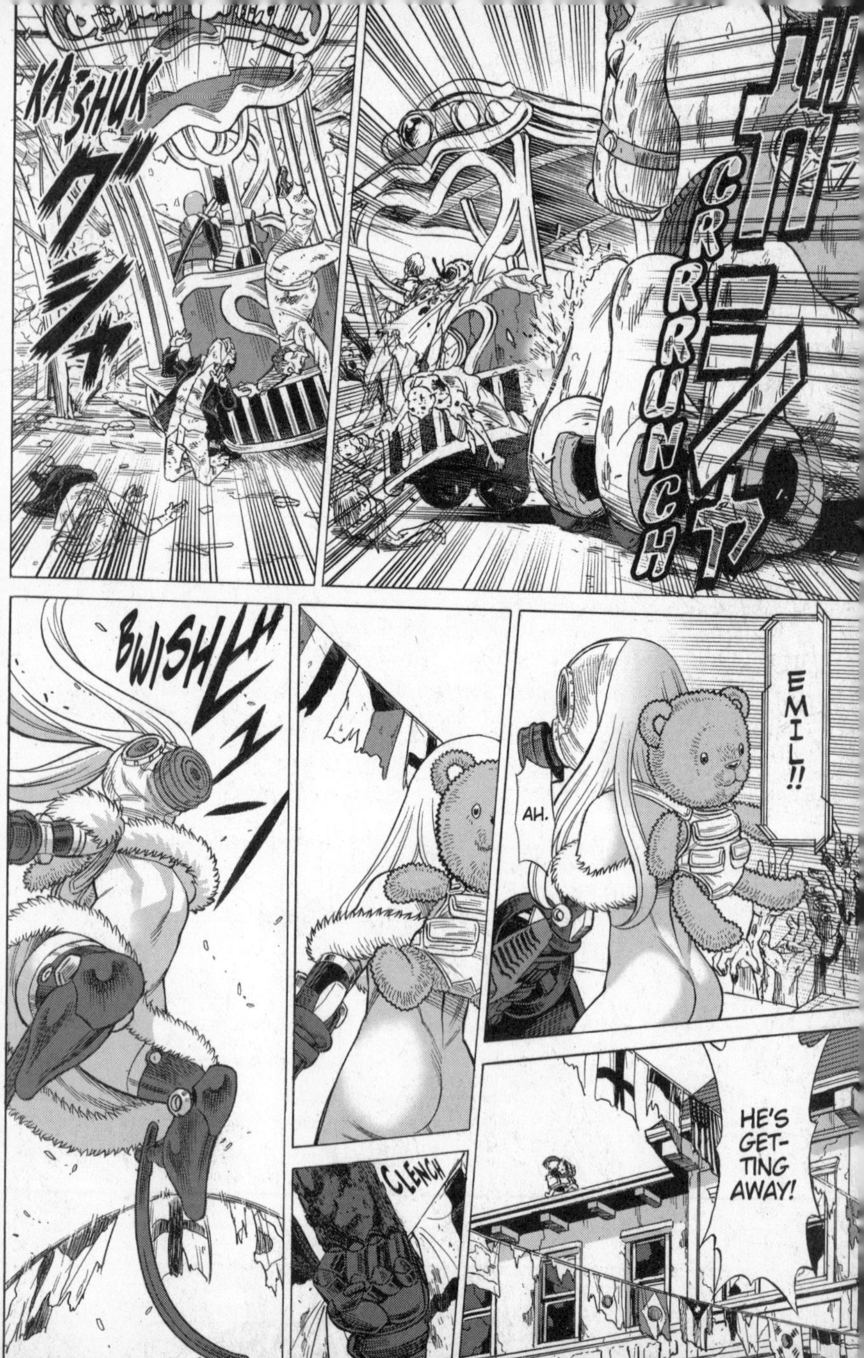
CRRRUNCH
KA-SHUK
EMIL!!
AH.
HE'S GET-TING AWAY!
CLENCH
BWISH

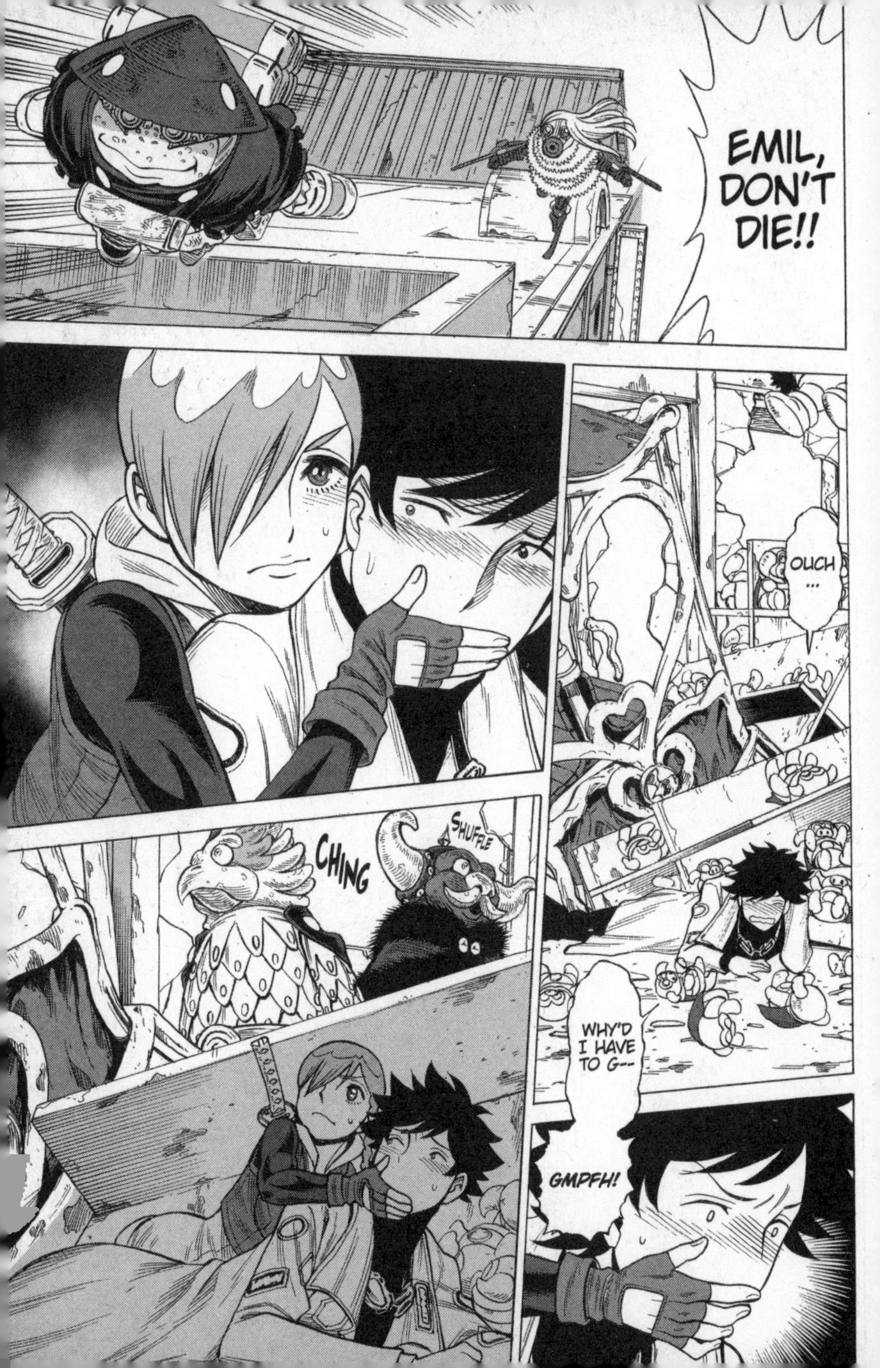
EMIL, DON'T DIE!!
OUCH ...
WHY'D I HAVE TO G--
SHUFFLE
CHING
GMPFH!

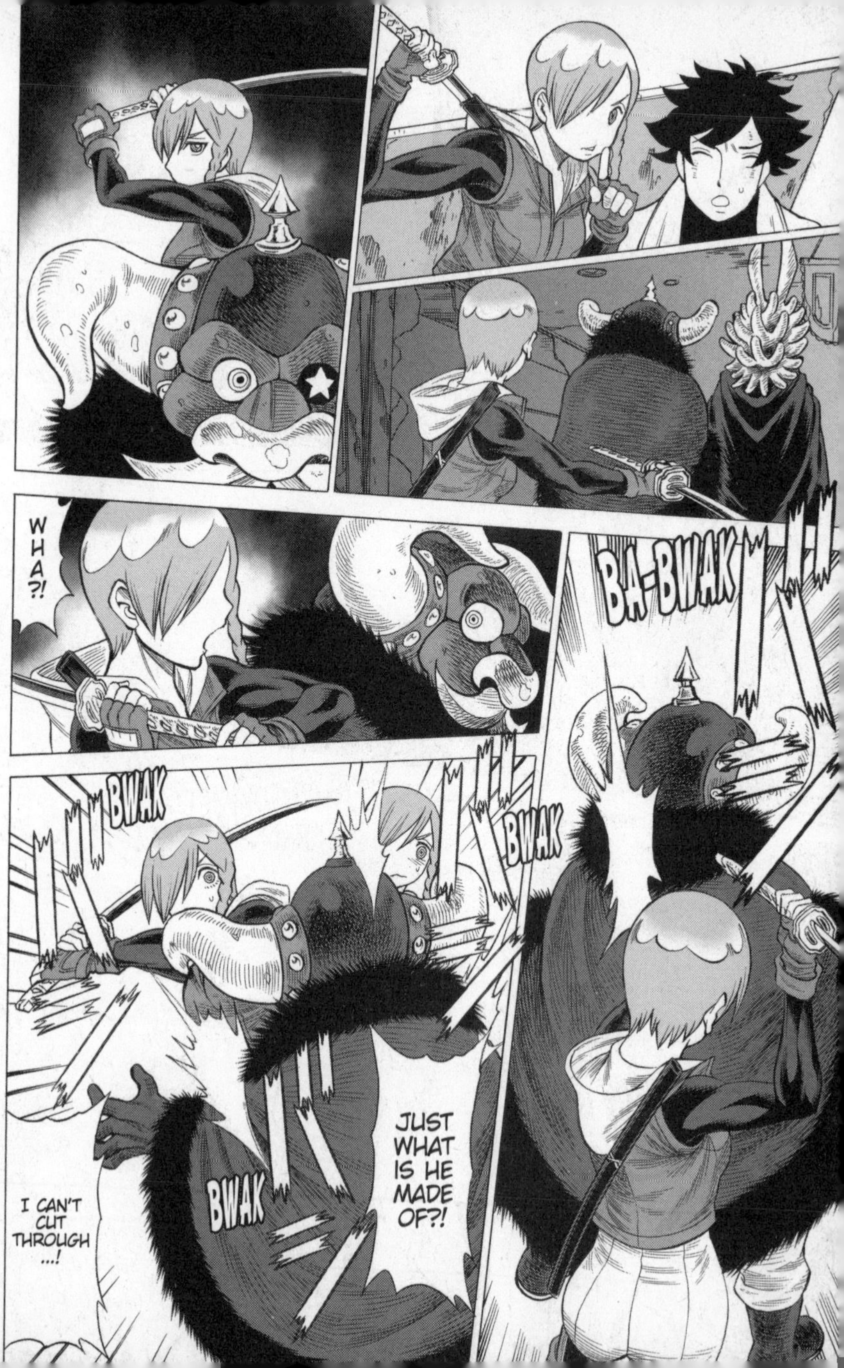
BA-BWAK
WHA?!
BWAK
BWAK
JUST WHAT IS HE MADE OF?!
BWAK
I CAN'T CUT THROUGH ...!

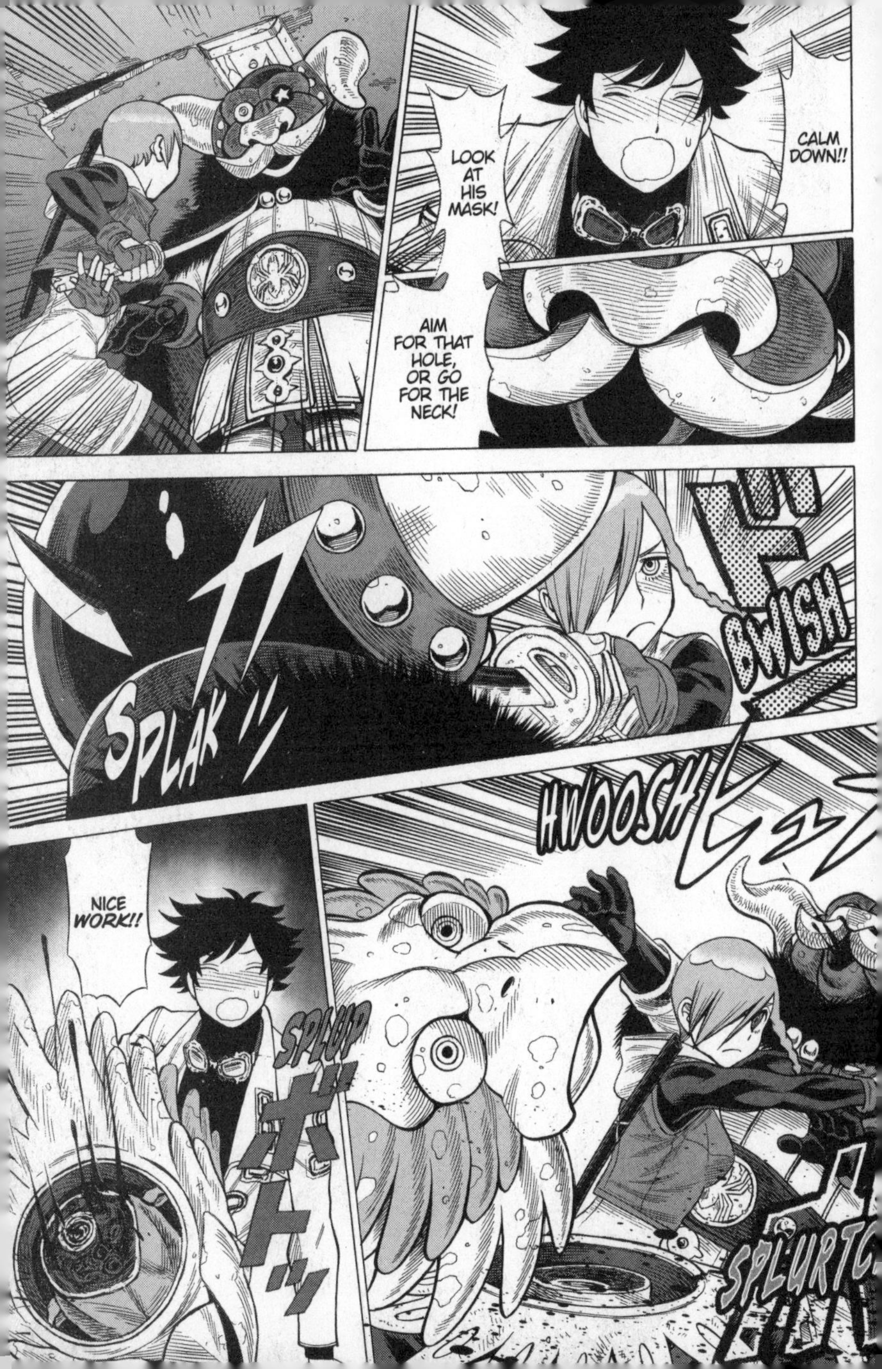
CALM DOWN!!
LOOK AT HIS MASK!
AIM FOR THAT HOLE, OR GO FOR THE NECK!
SWISH
SPLAK!!
HWOOSH
SPLURTC
NICE WORK!!
SPLUUP

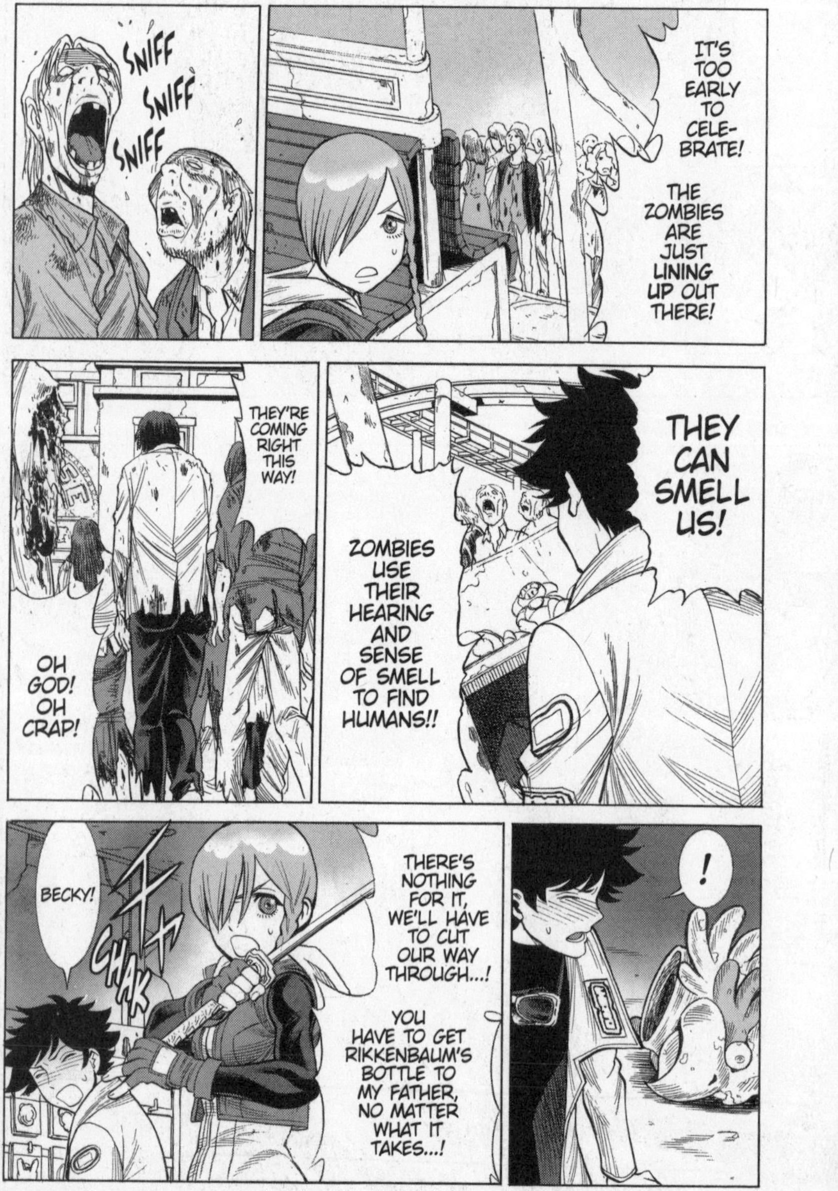
IT'S TOO EARLY TO CELE- BRATE!
THE ZOMBIES ARE JUST LINING UP OUT THERE!
SNIFF
SNIFF
SNIFF
THEY CAN SMELL US!
ZOMBIES USE THEIR HEARING AND SENSE OF SMELL TO FIND HUMANS!!
THEY'RE COMING RIGHT THIS WAY!
OH GOD! OH CRAP!
!
THERE'S NOTHING FOR IT, WE'LL HAVE TO CUT OUR WAY THROUGH...!
YOU HAVE TO GET RIKKENBAUM'S BOTTLE TO MY FATHER, NO MATTER WHAT IT TAKES...!
BECKY!
CHAK

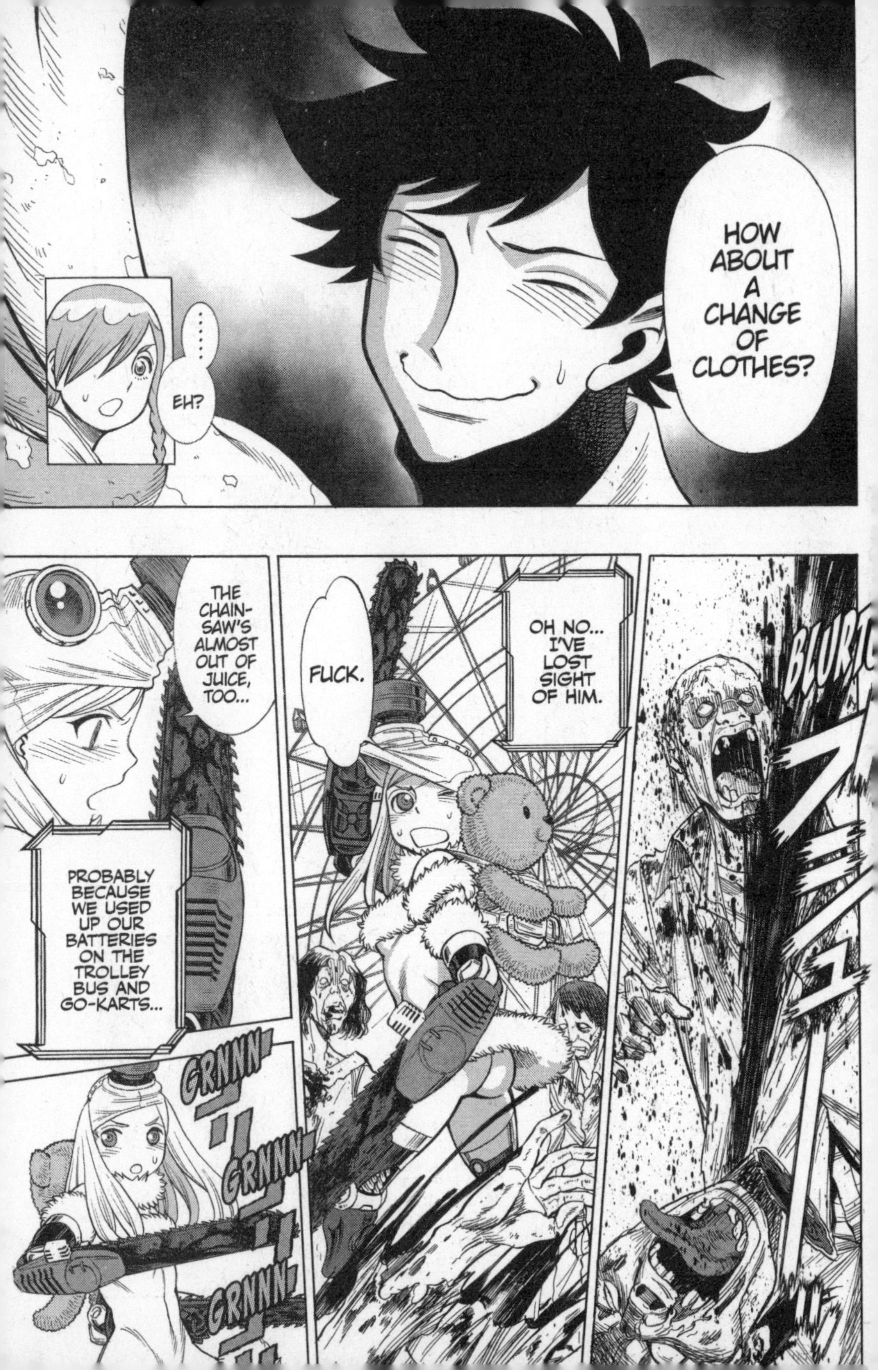
HOW ABOUT A CHANGE OF CLOTHES?
......
EH?
OH NO... I'VE LOST SIGHT OF HIM.
FUCK.
THE CHAIN-SAW'S ALMOST OUT OF JUICE, TOO...
PROBABLY BECAUSE WE USED UP OUR BATTERIES ON THE TROLLEY BUS AND GO-KARTS...
GRNNN
GRNNN
GRNNN

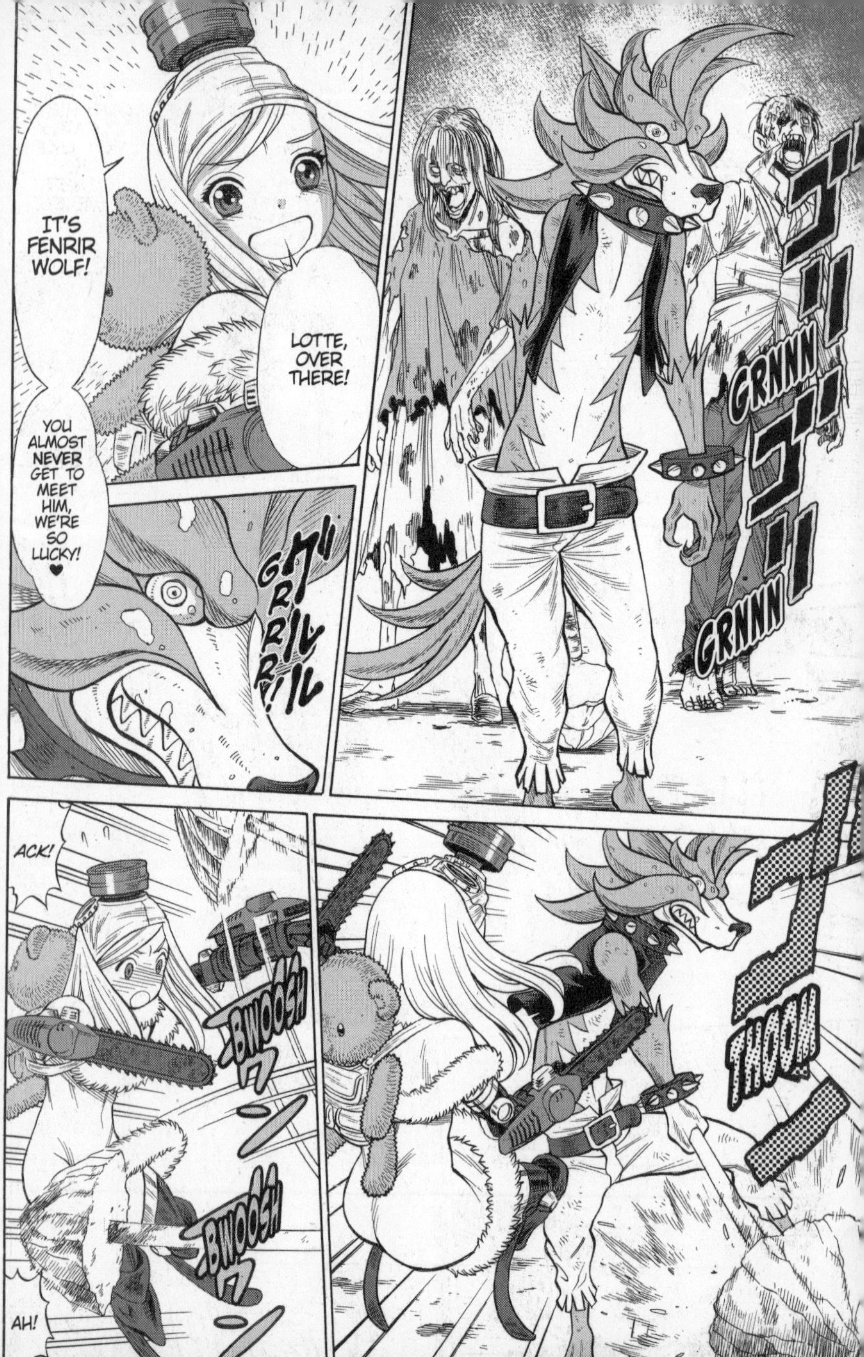
GRNNN
GRNNN
LOTTE, OVER THERE!
IT'S FENRIR WOLF!
YOU ALMOST NEVER GET TO MEET HIM, WE'RE SO LUCKY! ♥
GRRRR!
THOOM
ACK!
BWOOSH
BWOOSH
AH!

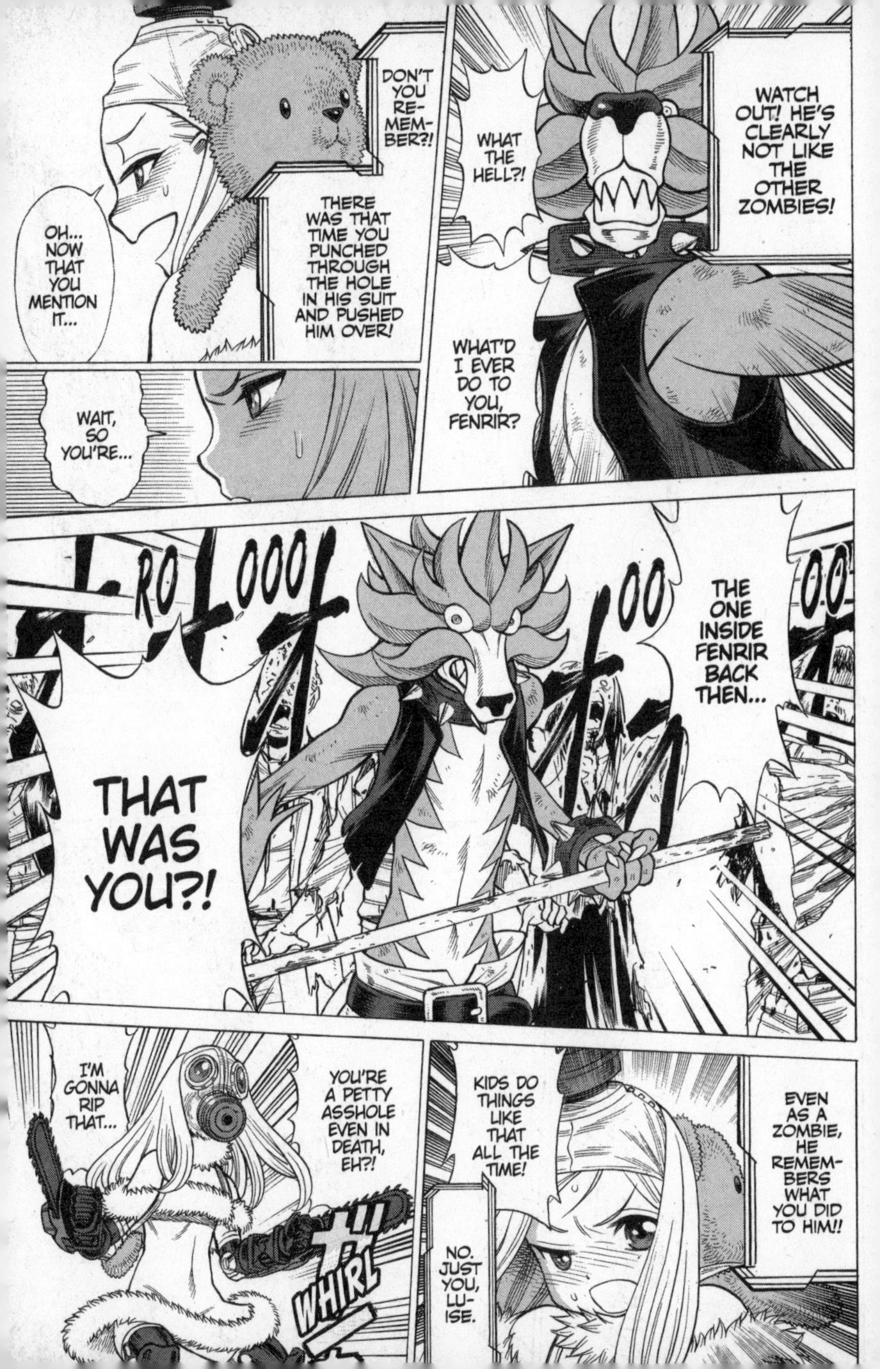
WATCH OUT! HE'S CLEARLY NOT LIKE THE OTHER ZOMBIES!
WHAT THE HELL?!
WHAT'D I EVER DO TO YOU, FENRIR?
DON'T YOU RE-MEMBER?!
THERE WAS THAT TIME YOU PUNCHED THROUGH THE HOLE IN HIS SUIT AND PUSHED HIM OVER!
OH... NOW THAT YOU MENTION IT...
WAIT, SO YOU'RE...
THE ONE INSIDE FENRIR BACK THEN...
ROOOOOOOO
THAT WAS YOU?!
EVEN AS A ZOMBIE, HE REMEM-BERS WHAT YOU DID TO HIM!!
KIDS DO THINGS LIKE THAT ALL THE TIME!
NO. JUST YOU, LU-ISE.
YOU'RE A PETTY ASSHOLE EVEN IN DEATH, EH?!
I'M GONNA RIP THAT...
WHIRL

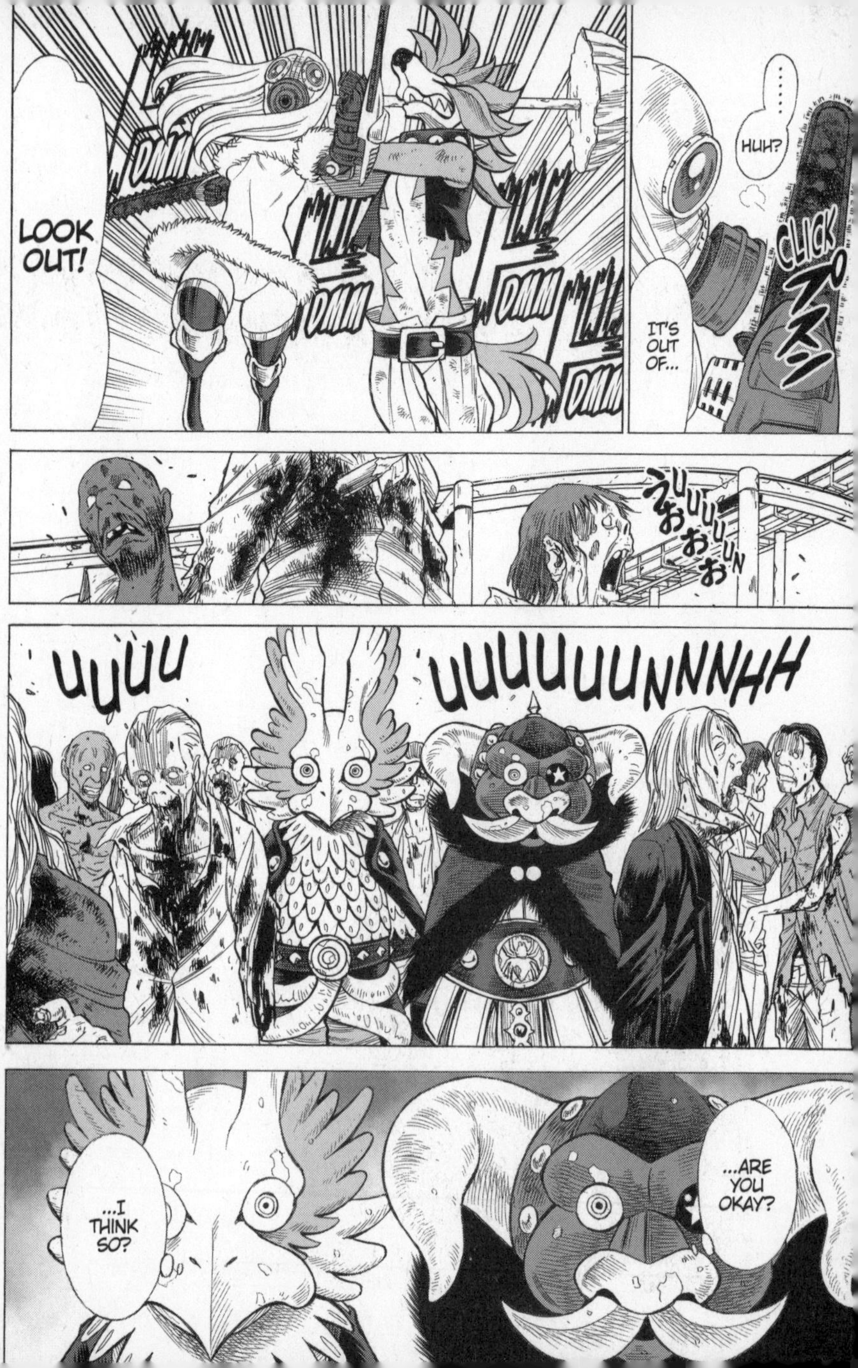
......
HUH?
CLICK
IT'S OUT OF...
LOOK OUT!
UUUUUUUN
UUUUUUUNNNHH
UUUU
...ARE YOU OKAY?
...I THINK SO?

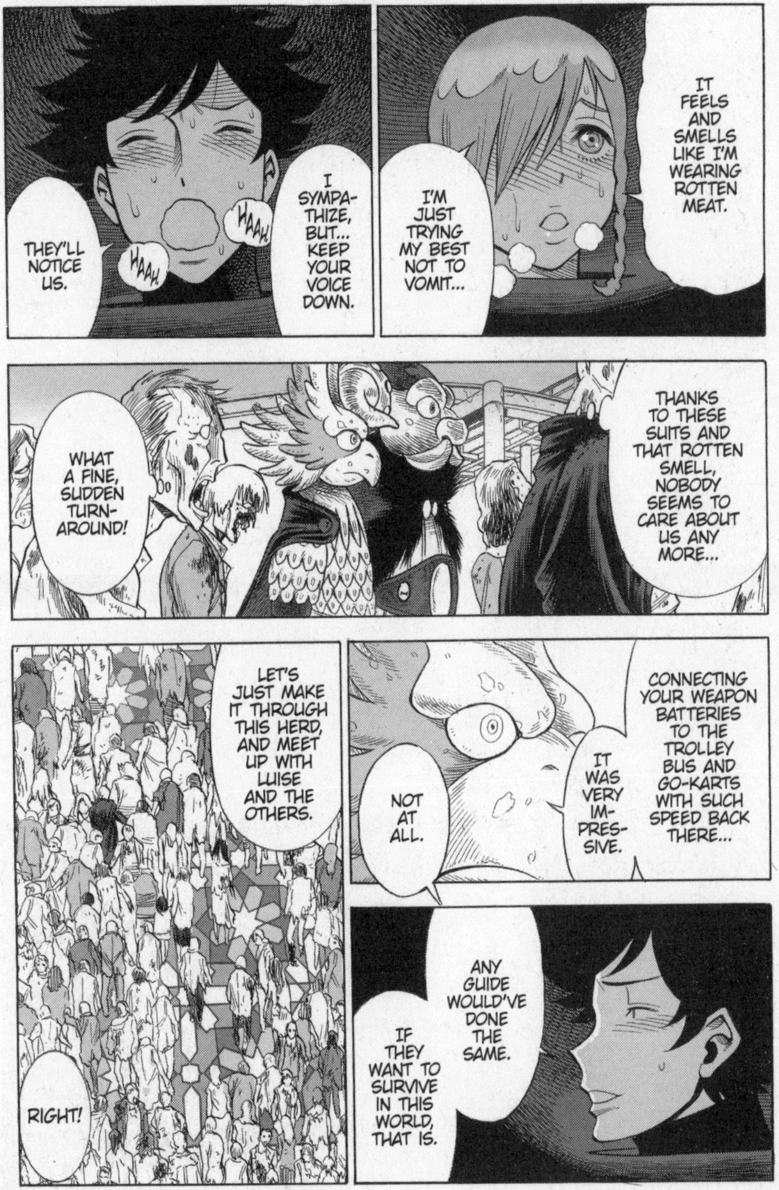
IT FEELS AND SMELLS LIKE I'M WEARING ROTTEN MEAT.
I'M JUST TRYING MY BEST NOT TO VOMIT...
I SYMPATHIZE, BUT... KEEP YOUR VOICE DOWN.
HAAH
HAAH
THEY'LL NOTICE US.
THANKS TO THESE SUITS AND THAT ROTTEN SMELL, NOBODY SEEMS TO CARE ABOUT US ANY MORE...
WHAT A FINE, SUDDEN TURN-AROUND!
CONNECTING YOUR WEAPON BATTERIES TO THE TROLLEY BUS AND GO-KARTS WITH SUCH SPEED BACK THERE...
IT WAS VERY IMPRESSIVE.
NOT AT ALL.
ANY GUIDE WOULD'VE DONE THE SAME.
IF THEY WANT TO SURVIVE IN THIS WORLD, THAT IS.
LET'S JUST MAKE IT THROUGH THIS HERD, AND MEET UP WITH LUISE AND THE OTHERS.
RIGHT!

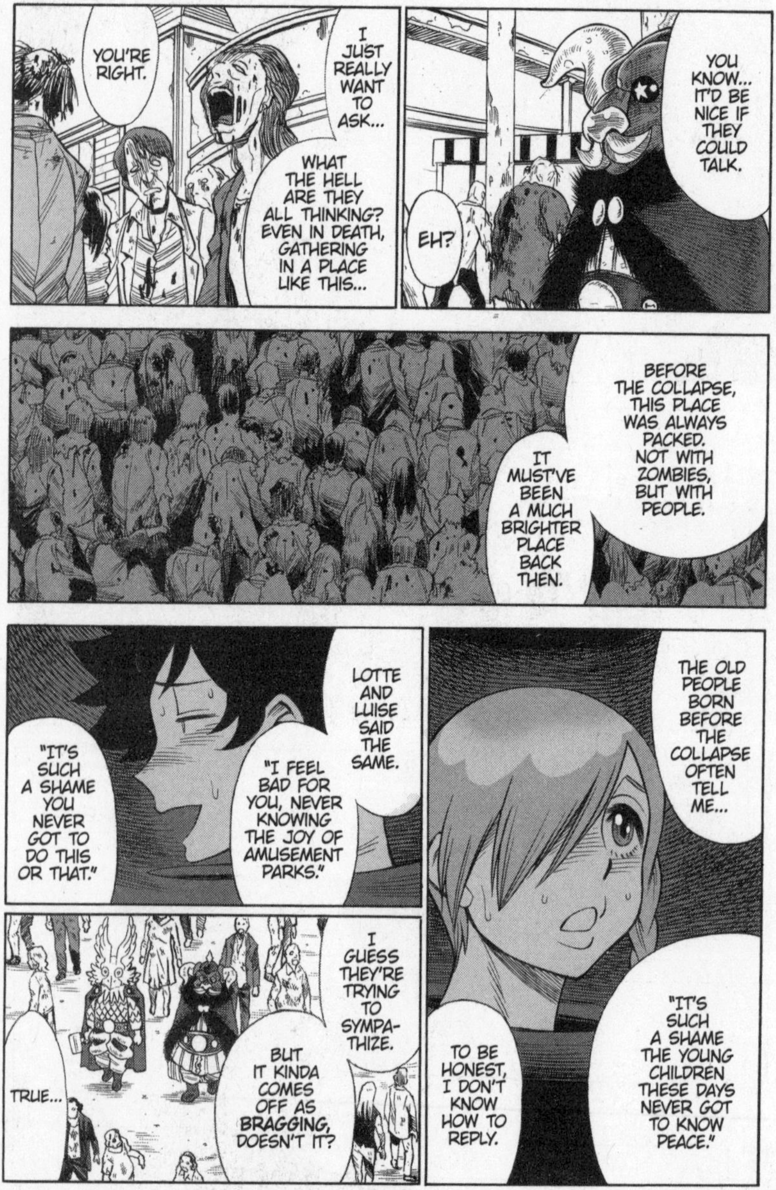
YOU KNOW... IT'D BE NICE IF THEY COULD TALK.
EH?
I JUST REALLY WANT TO ASK...
WHAT THE HELL ARE THEY ALL THINKING? EVEN IN DEATH, GATHERING IN A PLACE LIKE THIS...
YOU'RE RIGHT.
BEFORE THE COLLAPSE, THIS PLACE WAS ALWAYS PACKED. NOT WITH ZOMBIES, BUT WITH PEOPLE.
IT MUST'VE BEEN A MUCH BRIGHTER PLACE BACK THEN.
THE OLD PEOPLE BORN BEFORE THE COLLAPSE OFTEN TELL ME...
"IT'S SUCH A SHAME THE YOUNG CHILDREN THESE DAYS NEVER GOT TO KNOW PEACE."
TO BE HONEST, I DON'T KNOW HOW TO REPLY.
LOTTE AND LUISE SAID THE SAME.
"I FEEL BAD FOR YOU, NEVER KNOWING THE JOY OF AMUSEMENT PARKS."
"IT'S SUCH A SHAME YOU NEVER GOT TO DO THIS OR THAT."
I GUESS THEY'RE TRYING TO SYMPA-THIZE.
BUT IT KINDA COMES OFF AS BRAGGING, DOESN'T IT?
TRUE...

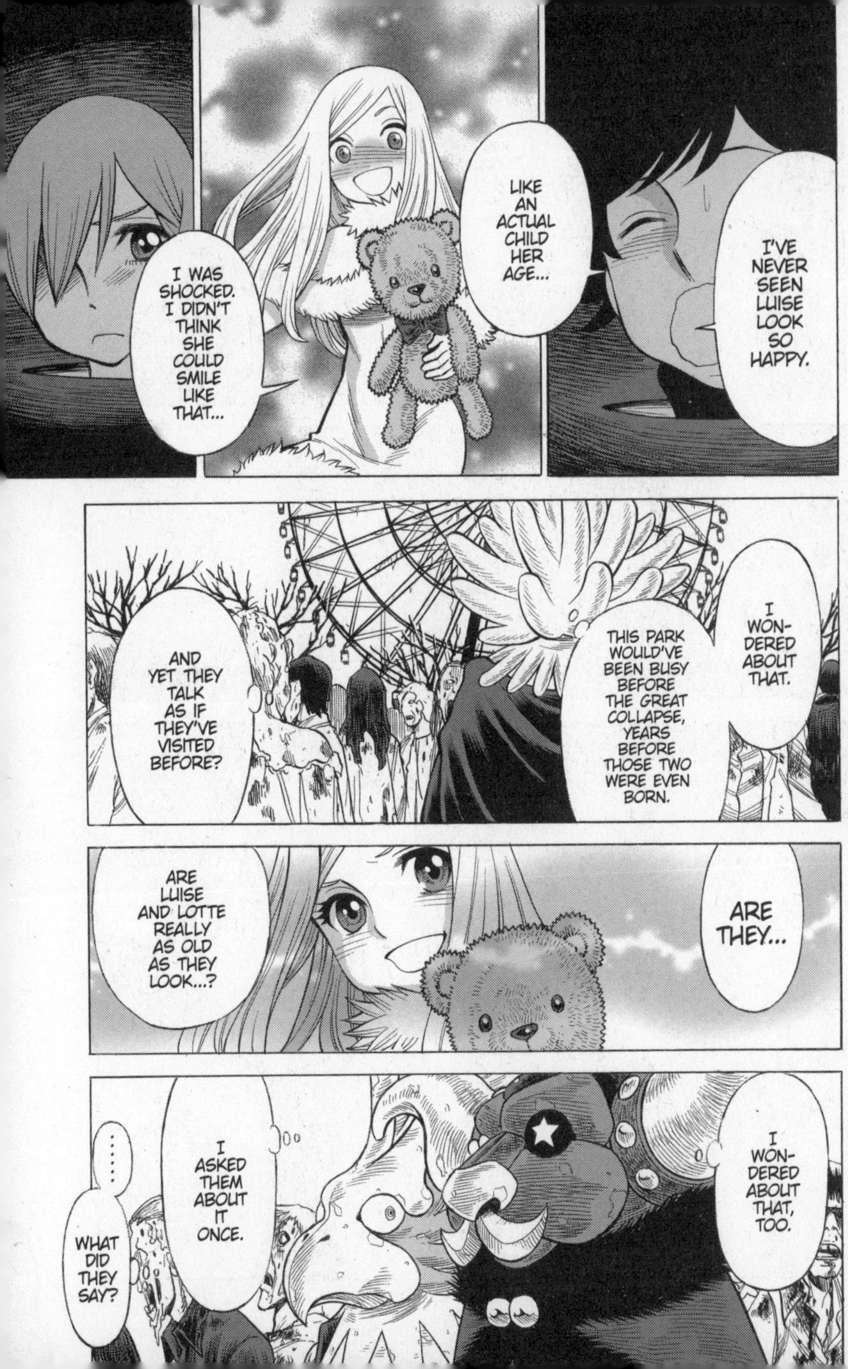
I'VE NEVER SEEN LUISE LOOK SO HAPPY.
LIKE AN ACTUAL CHILD HER AGE...
I WAS SHOCKED. I DIDN'T THINK SHE COULD SMILE LIKE THAT...
I WONDERED ABOUT THAT.
THIS PARK WOULD'VE BEEN BUSY BEFORE THE GREAT COLLAPSE, YEARS BEFORE THOSE TWO WERE EVEN BORN.
AND YET THEY TALK AS IF THEY'VE VISITED BEFORE?
ARE THEY...
ARE LUISE AND LOTTE REALLY AS OLD AS THEY LOOK...?
I WONDERED ABOUT THAT, TOO.
I ASKED THEM ABOUT IT ONCE.
......
WHAT DID THEY SAY?

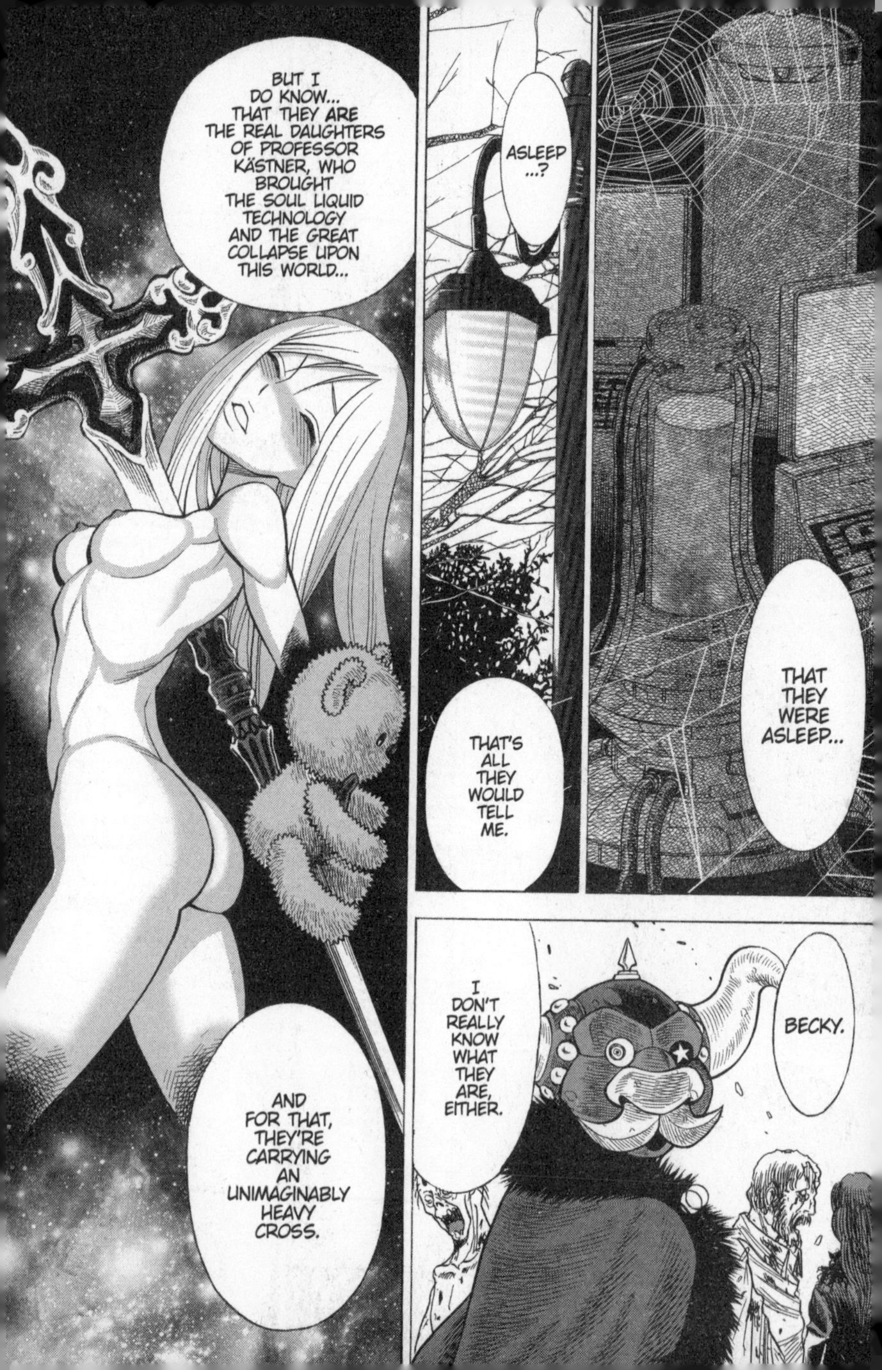
THAT THEY WERE ASLEEP...
ASLEEP ...?
THAT'S ALL THEY WOULD TELL ME.
BECKY.
I DON'T REALLY KNOW WHAT THEY ARE, EITHER.
BUT I DO KNOW... THAT THEY ARE THE REAL DAUGHTERS OF PROFESSOR KÄSTNER, WHO BROUGHT THE SOUL LIQUID TECHNOLOGY AND THE GREAT COLLAPSE UPON THIS WORLD...
AND FOR THAT, THEY'RE CARRYING AN UNIMAGINABLY HEAVY CROSS.

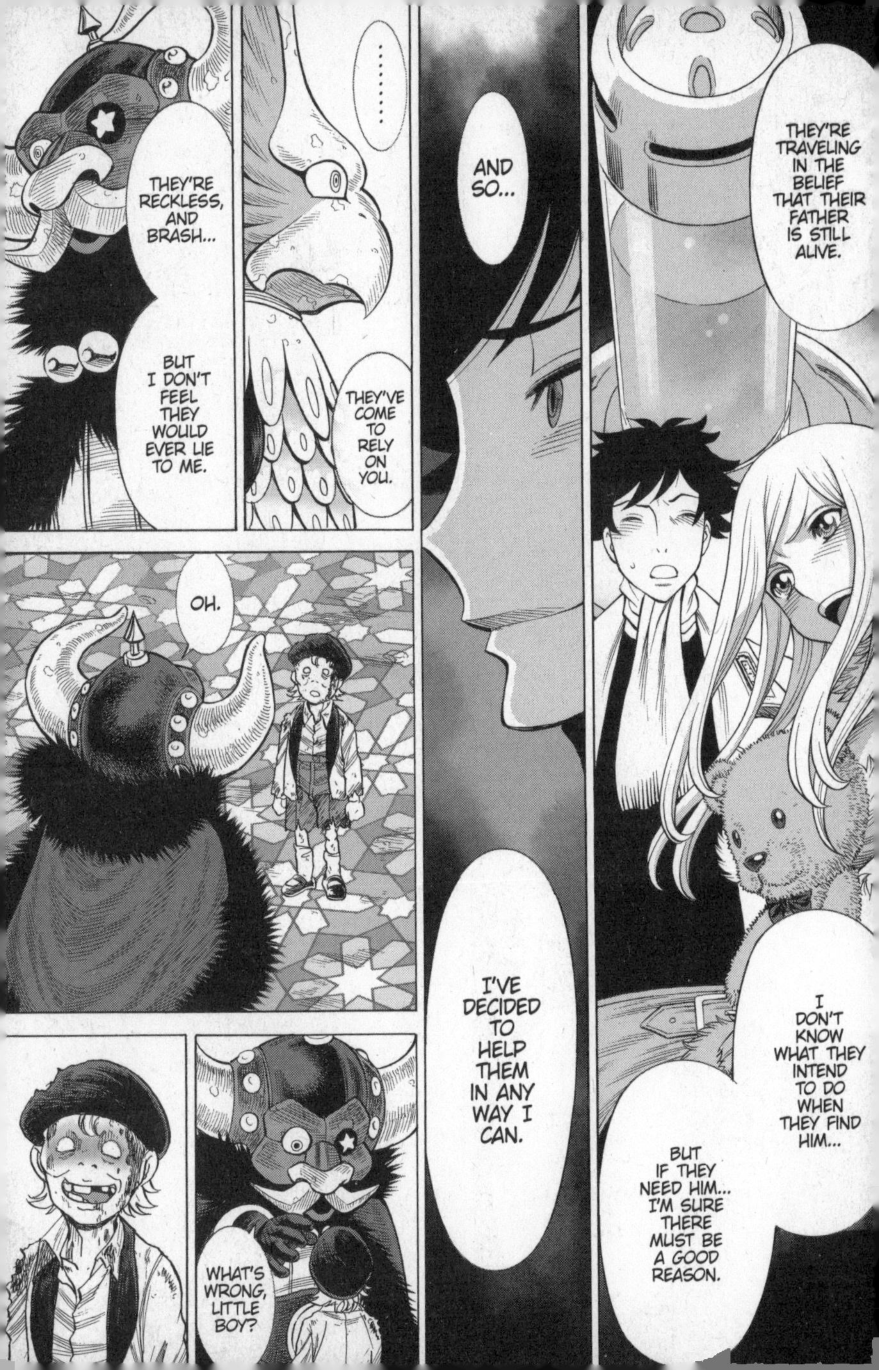
THEY'RE TRAVELING IN THE BELIEF THAT THEIR FATHER IS STILL ALIVE.
I DON'T KNOW WHAT THEY INTEND TO DO WHEN THEY FIND HIM...
BUT IF THEY NEED HIM... I'M SURE THERE MUST BE A GOOD REASON.
AND SO...
I'VE DECIDED TO HELP THEM IN ANY WAY I CAN.
......
THEY'VE COME TO RELY ON YOU.
THEY'RE RECKLESS, AND BRASH...
BUT I DON'T FEEL THEY WOULD EVER LIE TO ME.
OH.
WHAT'S WRONG, LITTLE BOY?

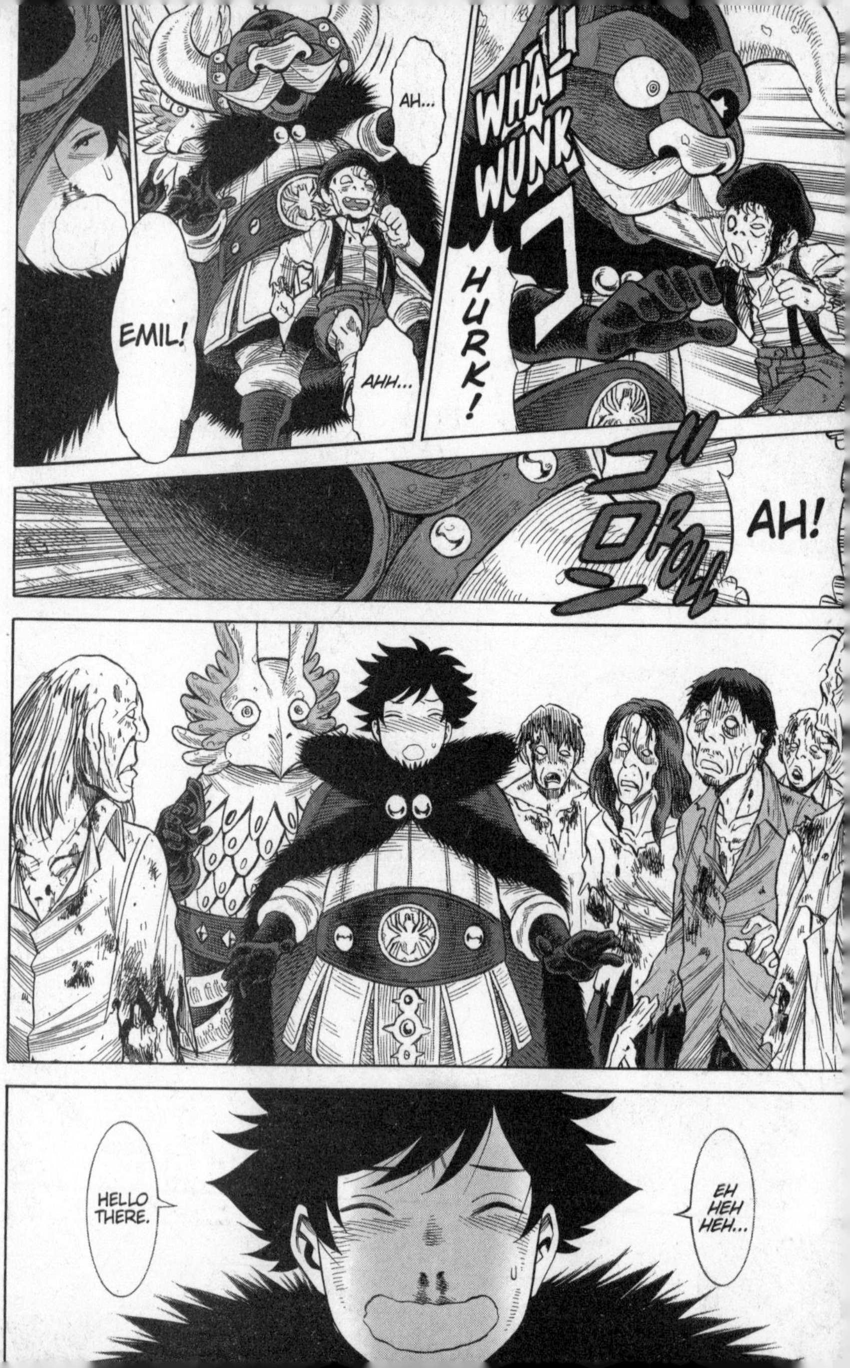
WHA-!!
WUNK
HURK!
AH...
EMIL!
AHH...
AH!
EH HEH HEH...
HELLO THERE.

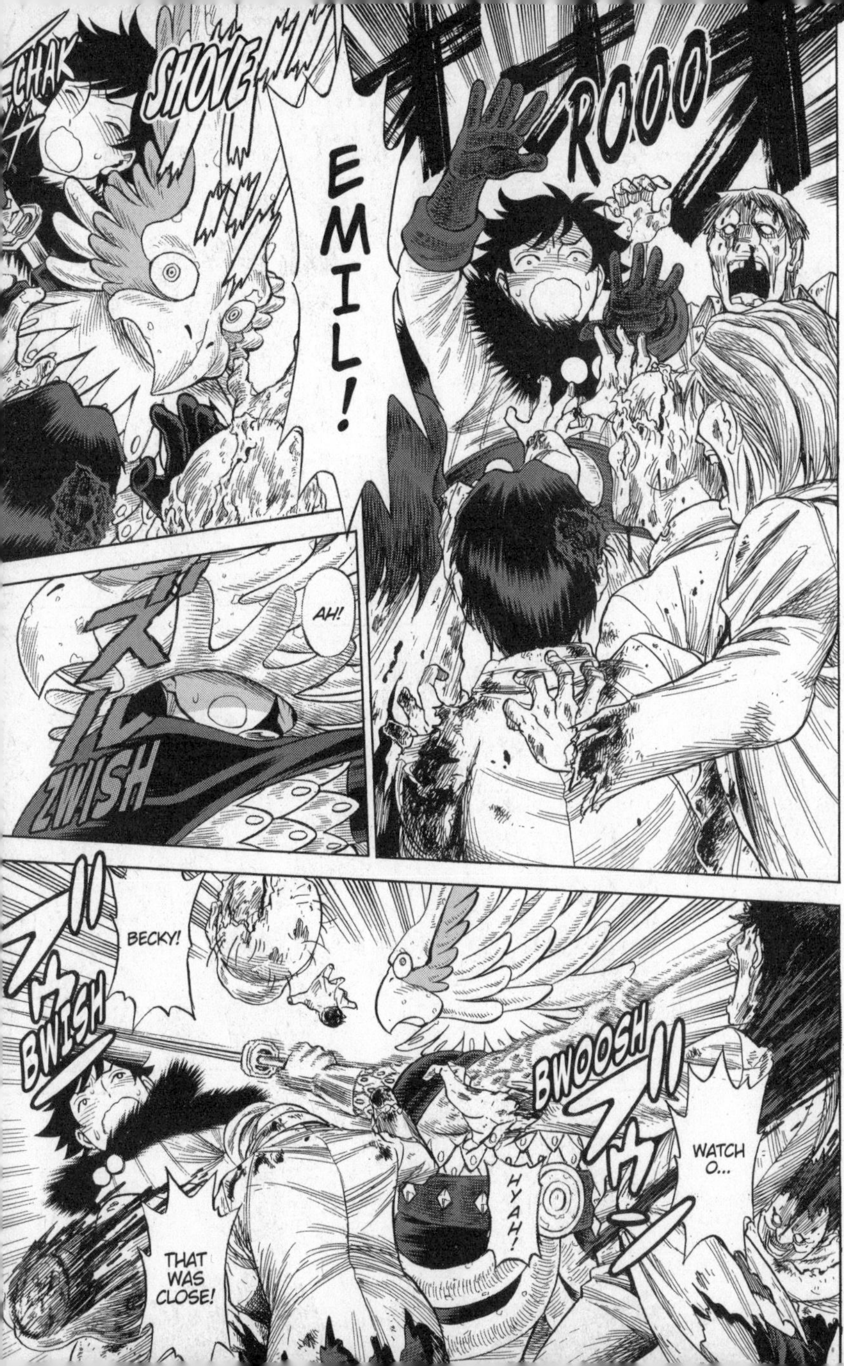
ROOO
EMIL!
CHAK
SHOVE
AH!
ZWISH
WATCH O...
BWOOSH
HYAH!
BECKY!
BWISH
THAT WAS CLOSE!

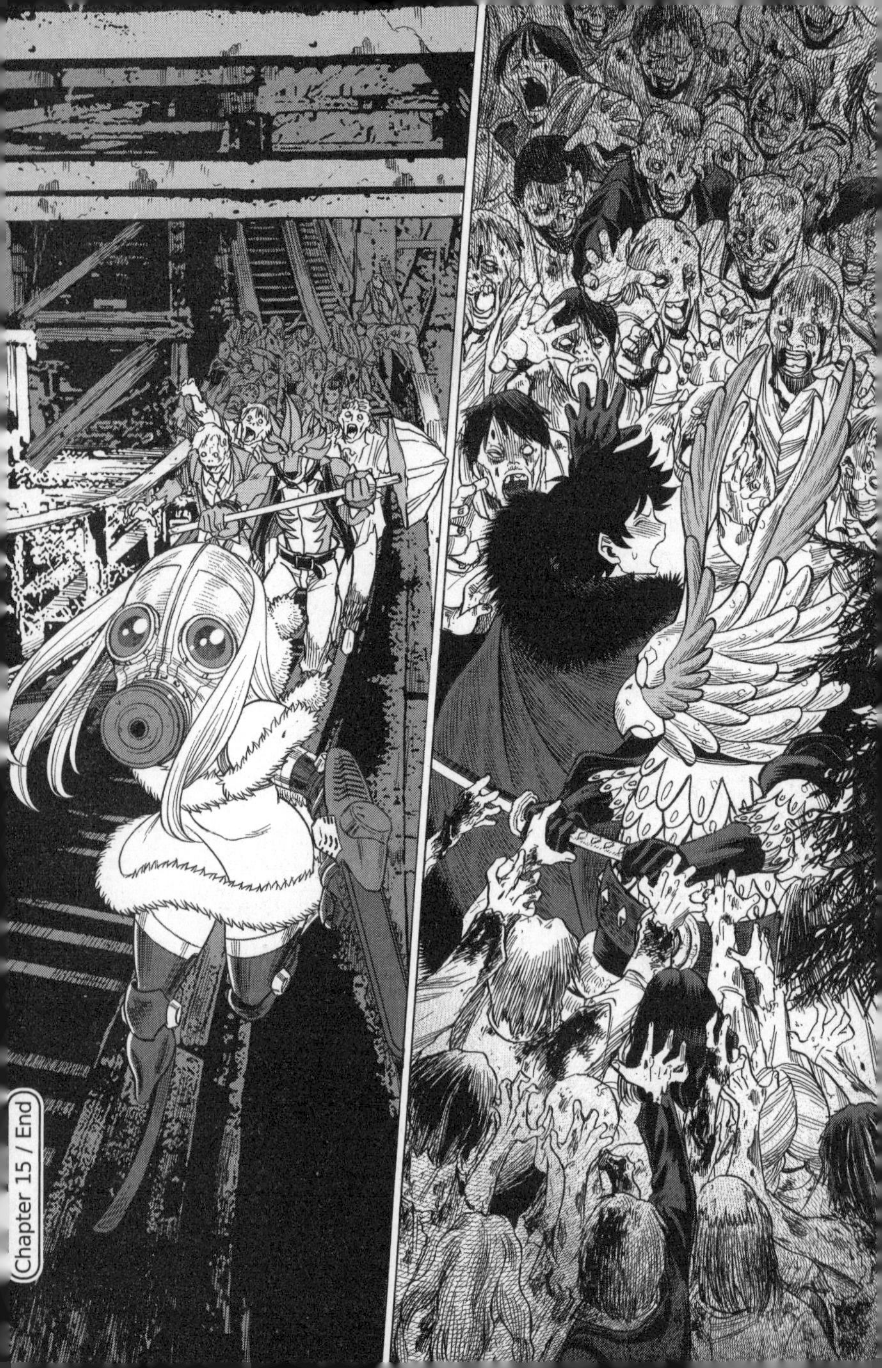
Chapter 15 / End

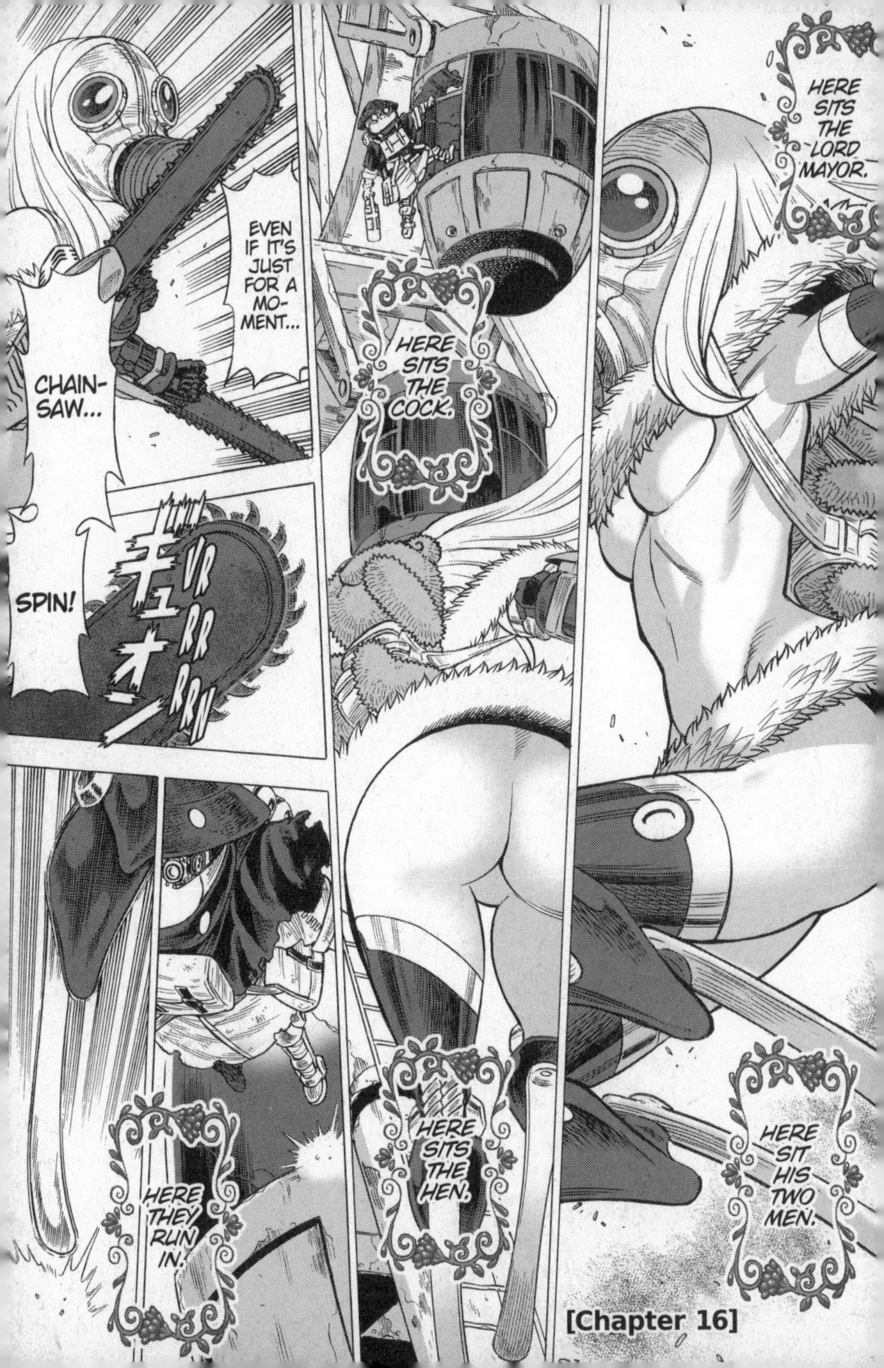

HERE SITS THE LORD MAYOR.
HERE SIT HIS TWO MEN.
HERE SITS THE COCK.
HERE SITS THE HEN.
EVEN IF IT'S JUST FOR A MO-MENT...
CHAIN-SAW...
SPIN!
VRRRRRN
HERE THEY RUN IN.
[Chapter 16]

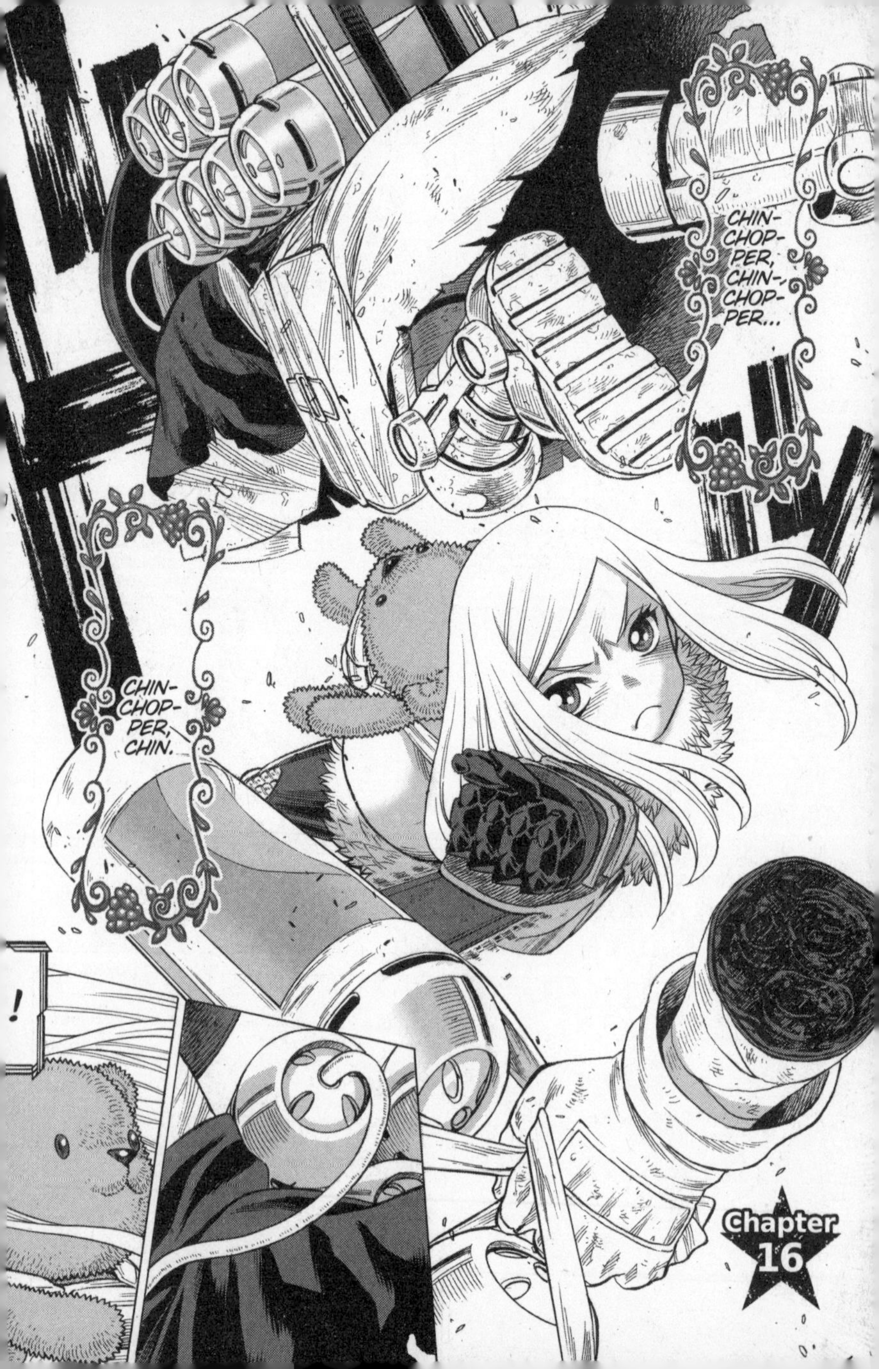
CHIN-CHOPPER, CHIN-CHOPPER...
CHIN-CHOPPER, CHIN.
!
Chapter 16

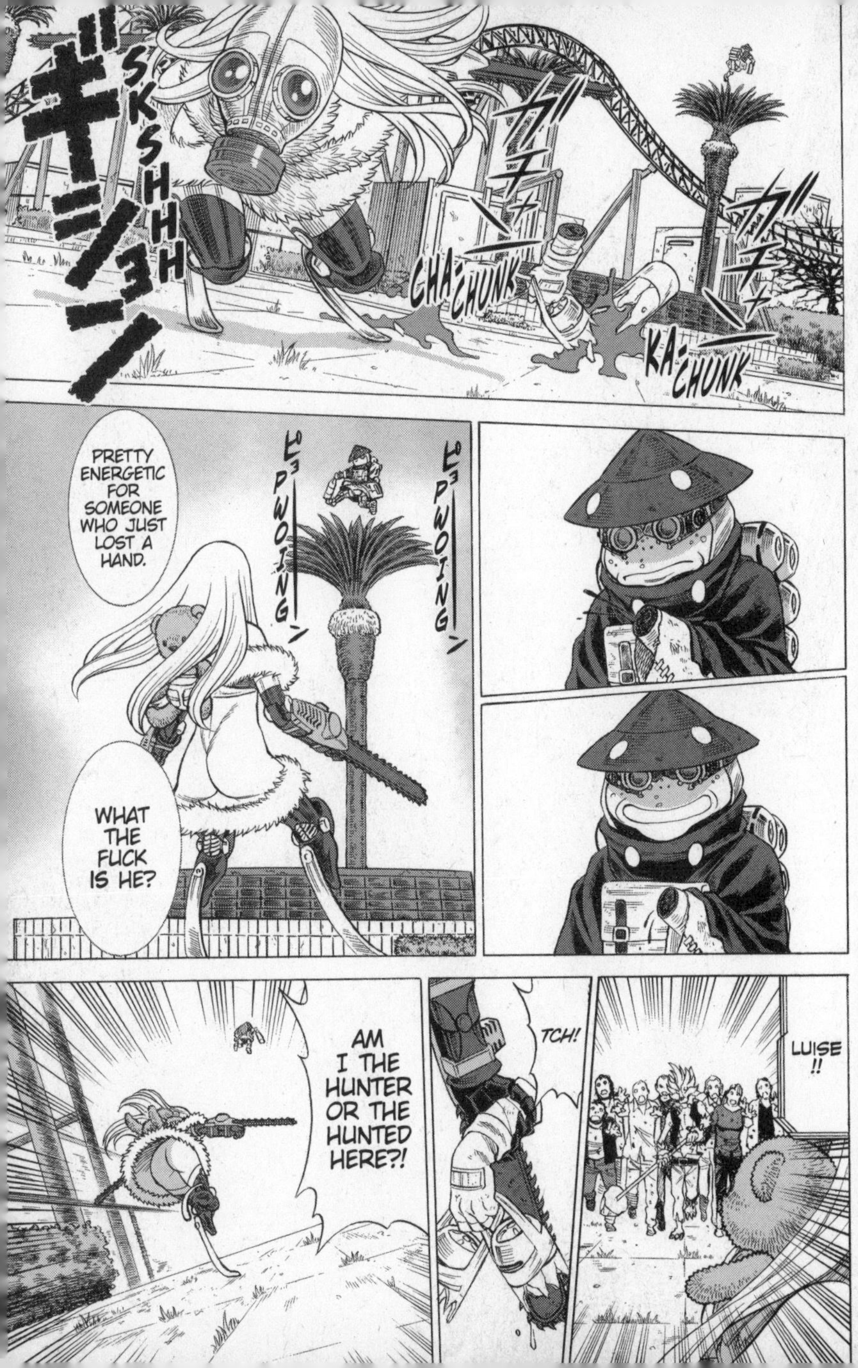
SKSHHHHH
KA-CHUNK
CHA-CHUNK
PWOING
PWOING
PRETTY ENERGETIC FOR SOMEONE WHO JUST LOST A HAND.
WHAT THE FUCK IS HE?
LUISE!!
TCH!
AM I THE HUNTER OR THE HUNTED HERE?!

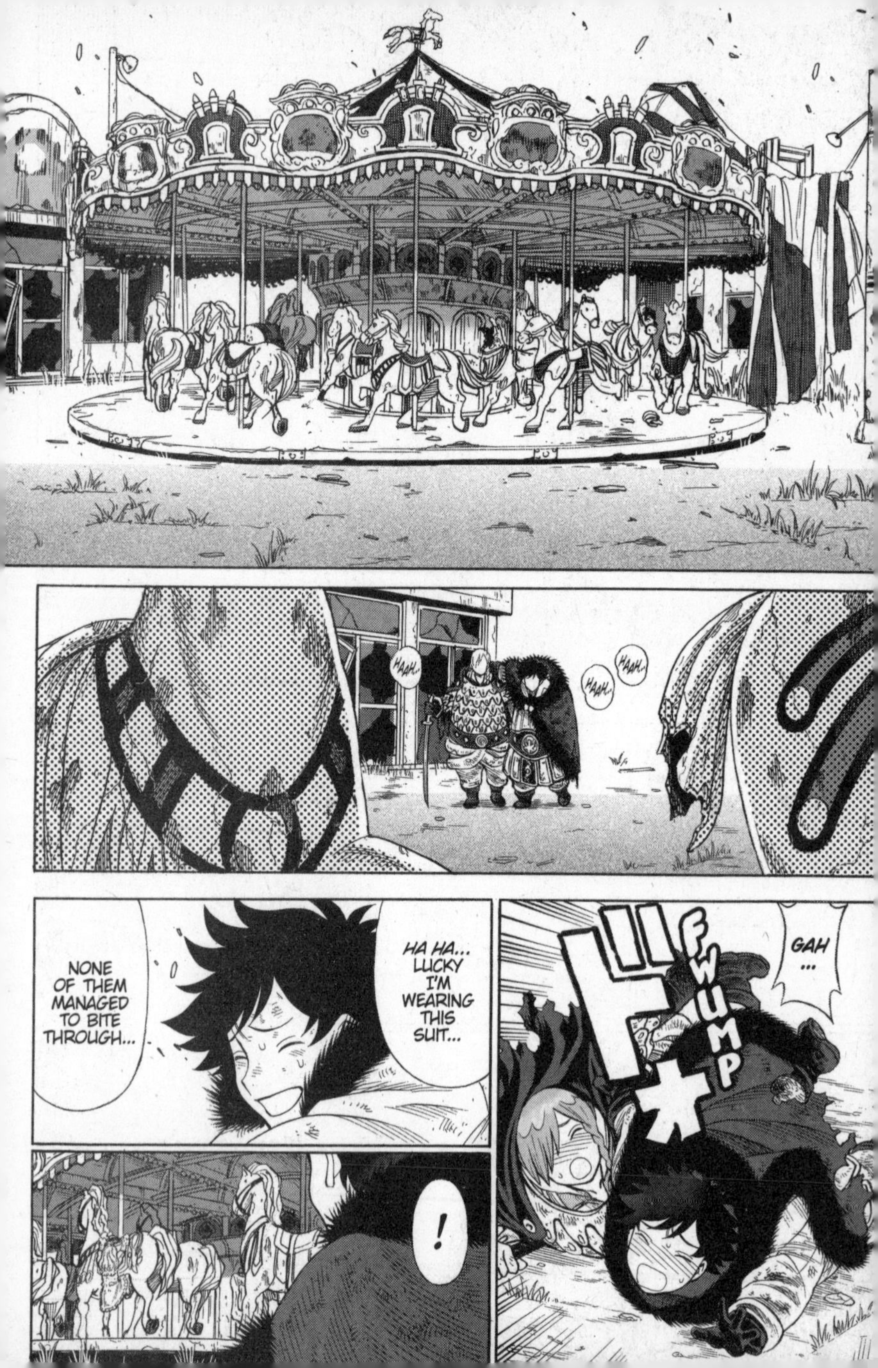
HAAH...
HAAH...
HAAH...
GAH...
FWUMP
HA HA... LUCKY I'M WEARING THIS SUIT...
NONE OF THEM MANAGED TO BITE THROUGH...
!

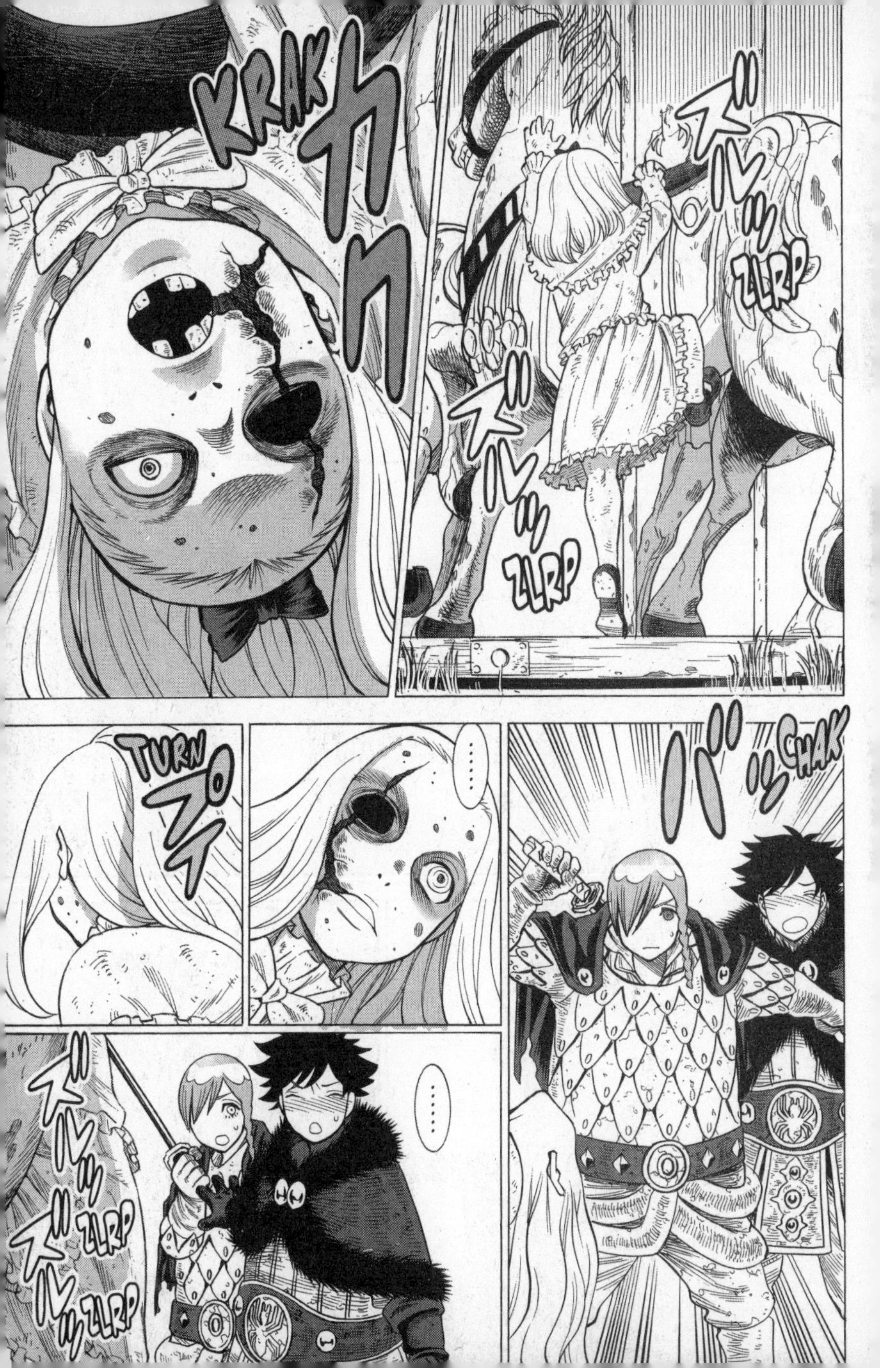
ZLRP
ZLRP
KRAK
CHAK
......
TURN
......
ZLRP
ZLRP

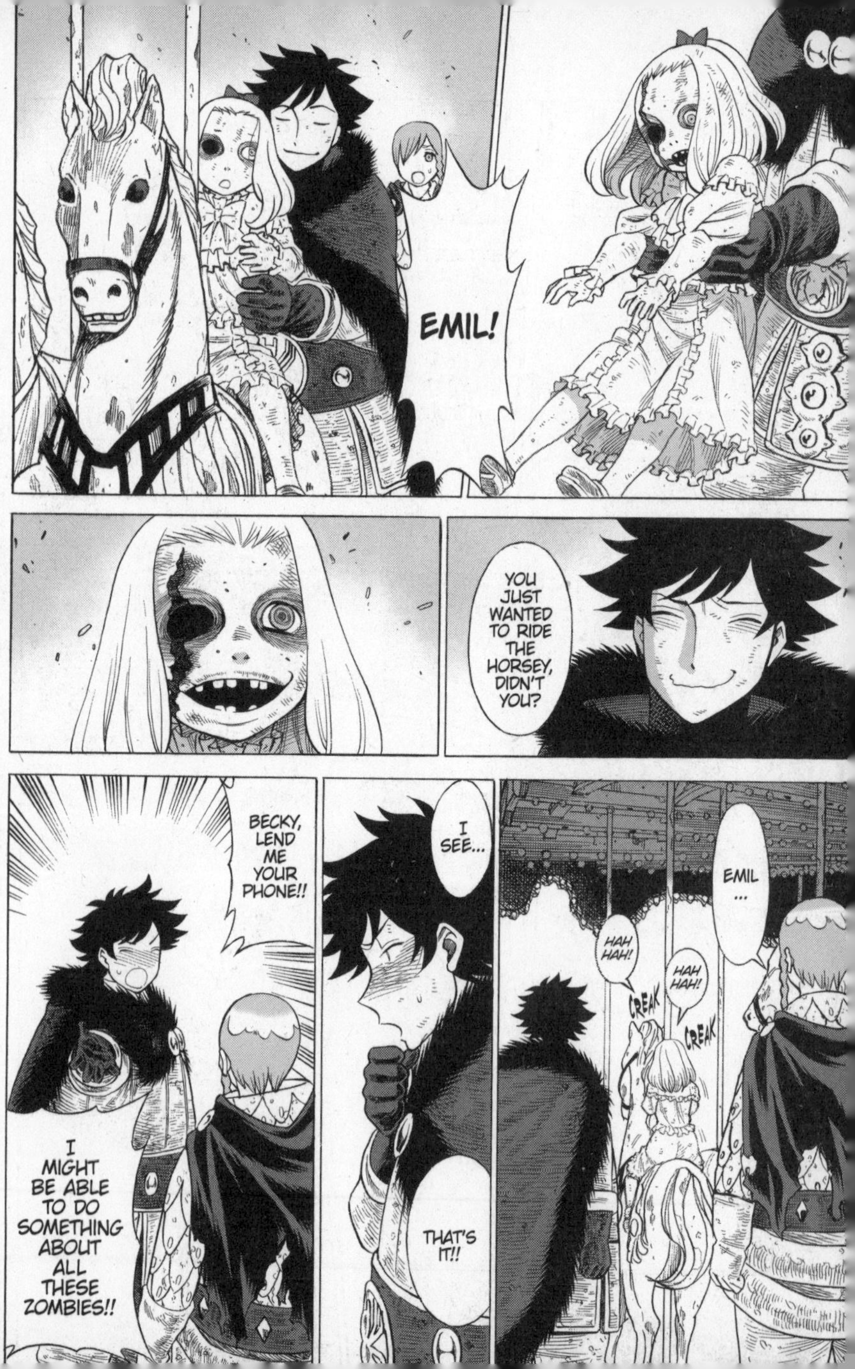
EMIL!
YOU JUST WANTED TO RIDE THE HORSEY, DIDN'T YOU?
EMIL ...
HAH HAH!
HAH HAH!
CREAK
CREAK
I SEE...
THAT'S IT!!
BECKY, LEND ME YOUR PHONE!!
I MIGHT BE ABLE TO DO SOMETHING ABOUT ALL THESE ZOMBIES!!

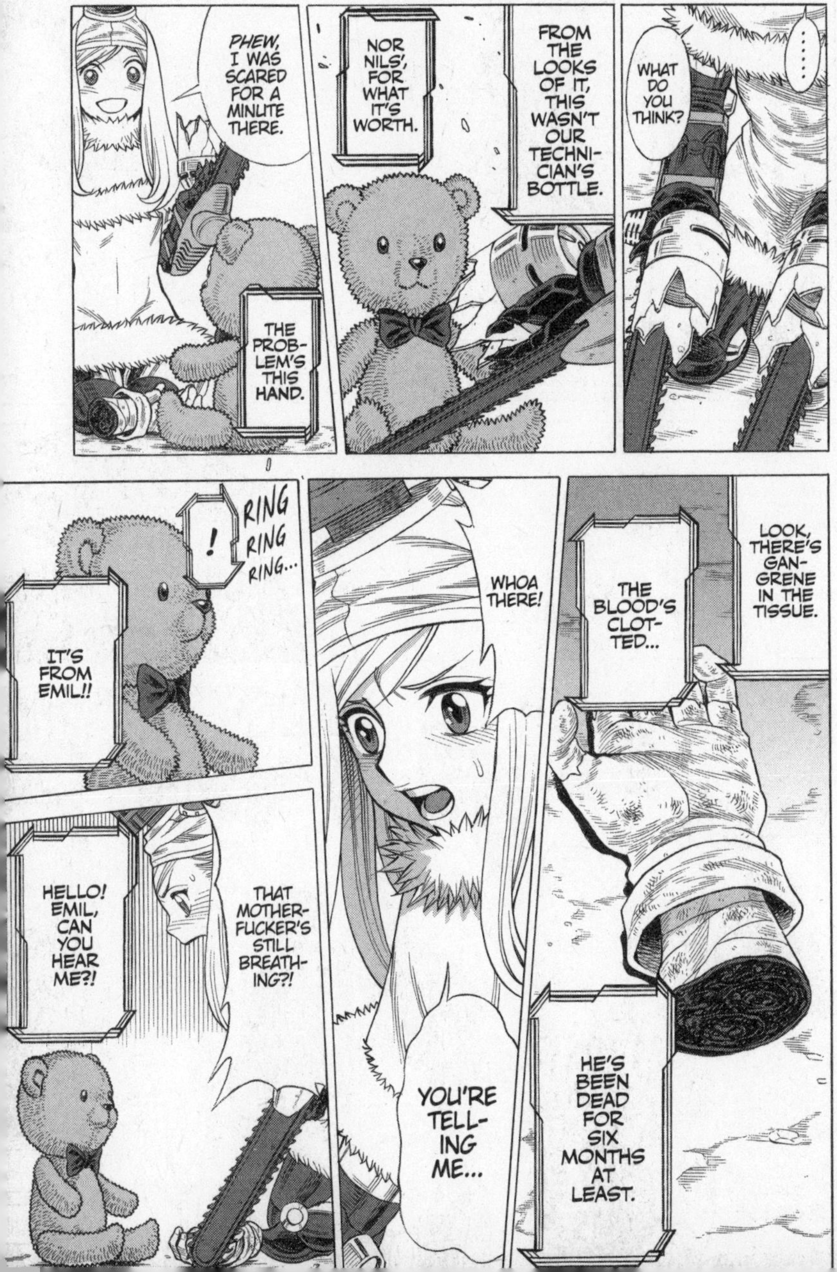
……
WHAT DO YOU THINK?
FROM THE LOOKS OF IT, THIS WASN'T OUR TECHNICIAN'S BOTTLE.
NOR NILS', FOR WHAT IT'S WORTH.
PHEW, I WAS SCARED FOR A MINUTE THERE.
THE PROBLEM'S THIS HAND.
LOOK, THERE'S GANGRENE IN THE TISSUE.
THE BLOOD'S CLOTTED...
HE'S BEEN DEAD FOR SIX MONTHS AT LEAST.
WHOA THERE!
YOU'RE TELLING ME...
RING RING RING...
!
IT'S FROM EMIL!!
THAT MOTHERFUCKER'S STILL BREATHING?!
HELLO! EMIL, CAN YOU HEAR ME?!

YOU WANT TO KNOW WHERE THE CONTROL ROOM IS...?

EH...?

?

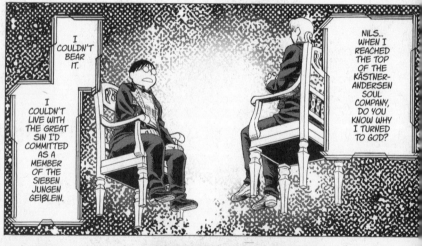

NILS... WHEN I REACHED THE TOP OF THE KÄSTNER-ANDERSEN SOUL COMPANY, DO YOU KNOW WHY I TURNED TO GOD?

I COULDN'T BEAR IT.

I COULDN'T LIVE WITH THE GREAT SIN I'D COMMITTED AS A MEMBER OF THE SIEBEN JUNGEN GEIßLEIN.

ARE YOU IMPLYING THE SPREAD OF SOUL LIQUID TECHNOLOGY CAUSED THE GREAT COLLAPSE?

IT WAS JUST AN UNFORTUNATE COINCIDENCE! WE MIGHT'VE HAD SOME UNDERHANDED INTENTIONS, BUT NOBODY COULD POSSIBLY ASSIGN DIRECT BLAME TO...

THAT'S NOT TRUE.

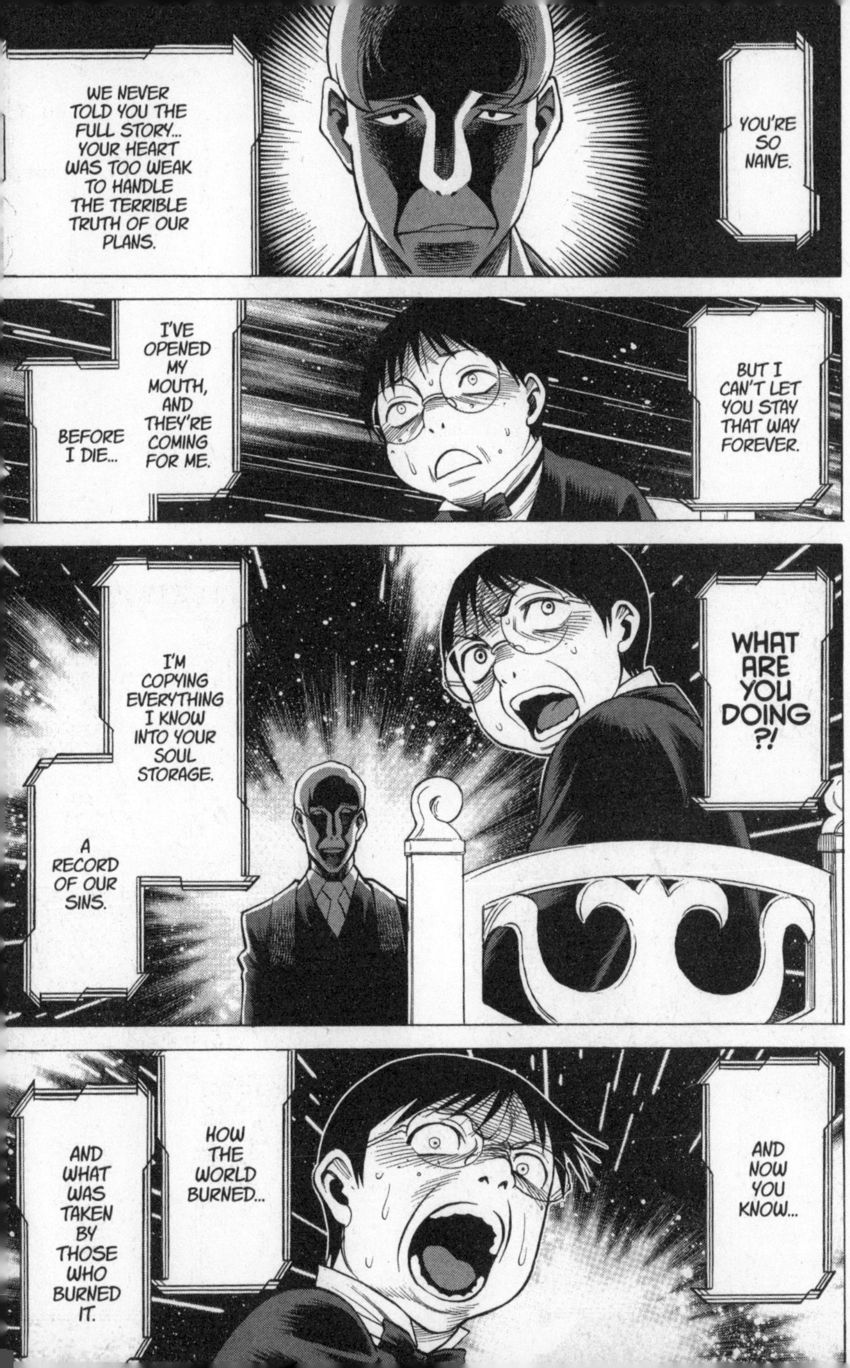
YOU'RE SO NAIVE.
WE NEVER TOLD YOU THE FULL STORY... YOUR HEART WAS TOO WEAK TO HANDLE THE TERRIBLE TRUTH OF OUR PLANS.
BUT I CAN'T LET YOU STAY THAT WAY FOREVER.
I'VE OPENED MY MOUTH, AND THEY'RE COMING FOR ME.
BEFORE I DIE...
WHAT ARE YOU DOING?!
I'M COPYING EVERYTHING I KNOW INTO YOUR SOUL STORAGE.
A RECORD OF OUR SINS.
AND NOW YOU KNOW...
HOW THE WORLD BURNED...
AND WHAT WAS TAKEN BY THOSE WHO BURNED IT.

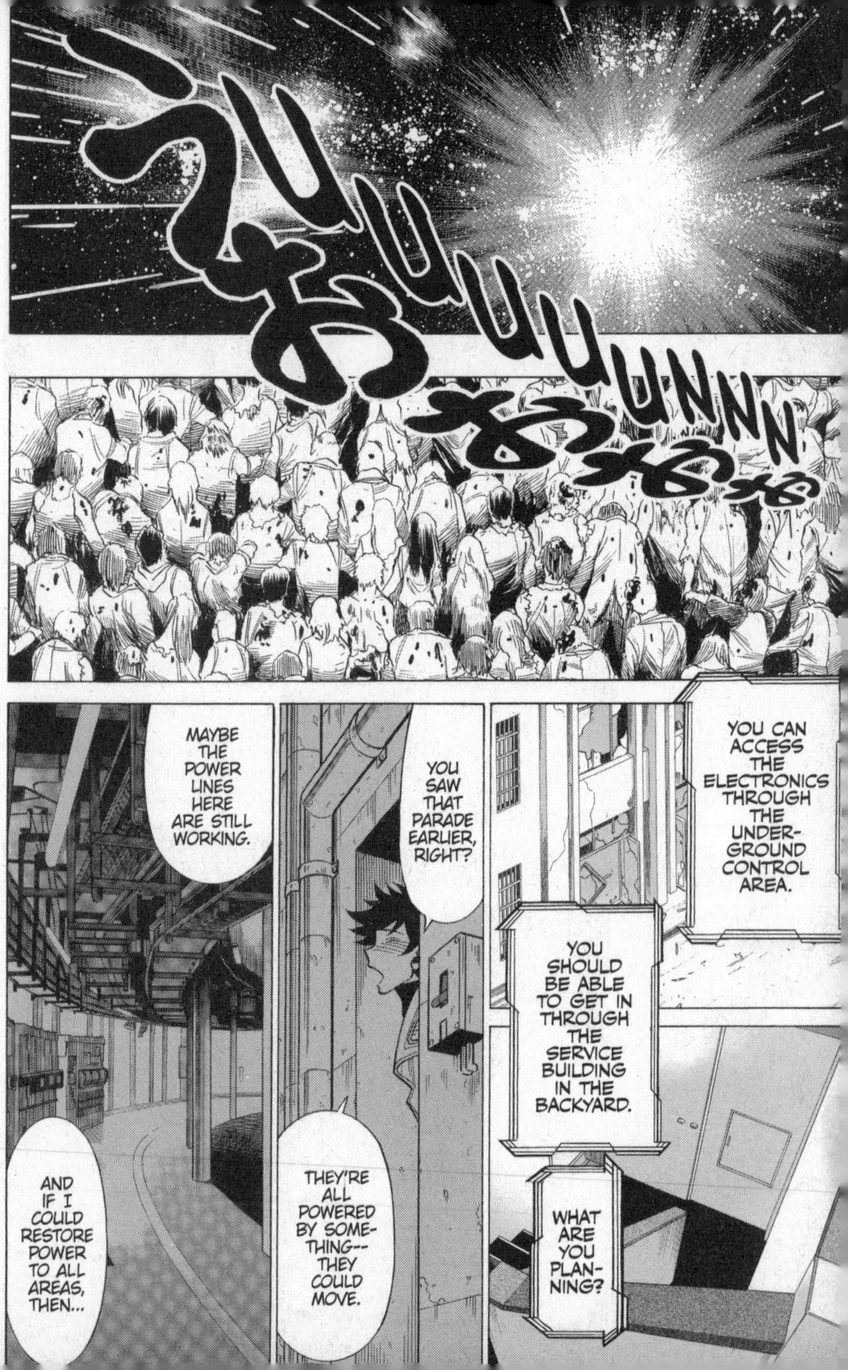
UUUUUUNNNN
YOU CAN ACCESS THE ELECTRONICS THROUGH THE UNDER-GROUND CONTROL AREA.
YOU SHOULD BE ABLE TO GET IN THROUGH THE SERVICE BUILDING IN THE BACKYARD.
WHAT ARE YOU PLAN-NING?
YOU SAW THAT PARADE EARLIER, RIGHT?
THEY'RE ALL POWERED BY SOME-THING-- THEY COULD MOVE.
MAYBE THE POWER LINES HERE ARE STILL WORKING.
AND IF I COULD RESTORE POWER TO ALL AREAS, THEN...

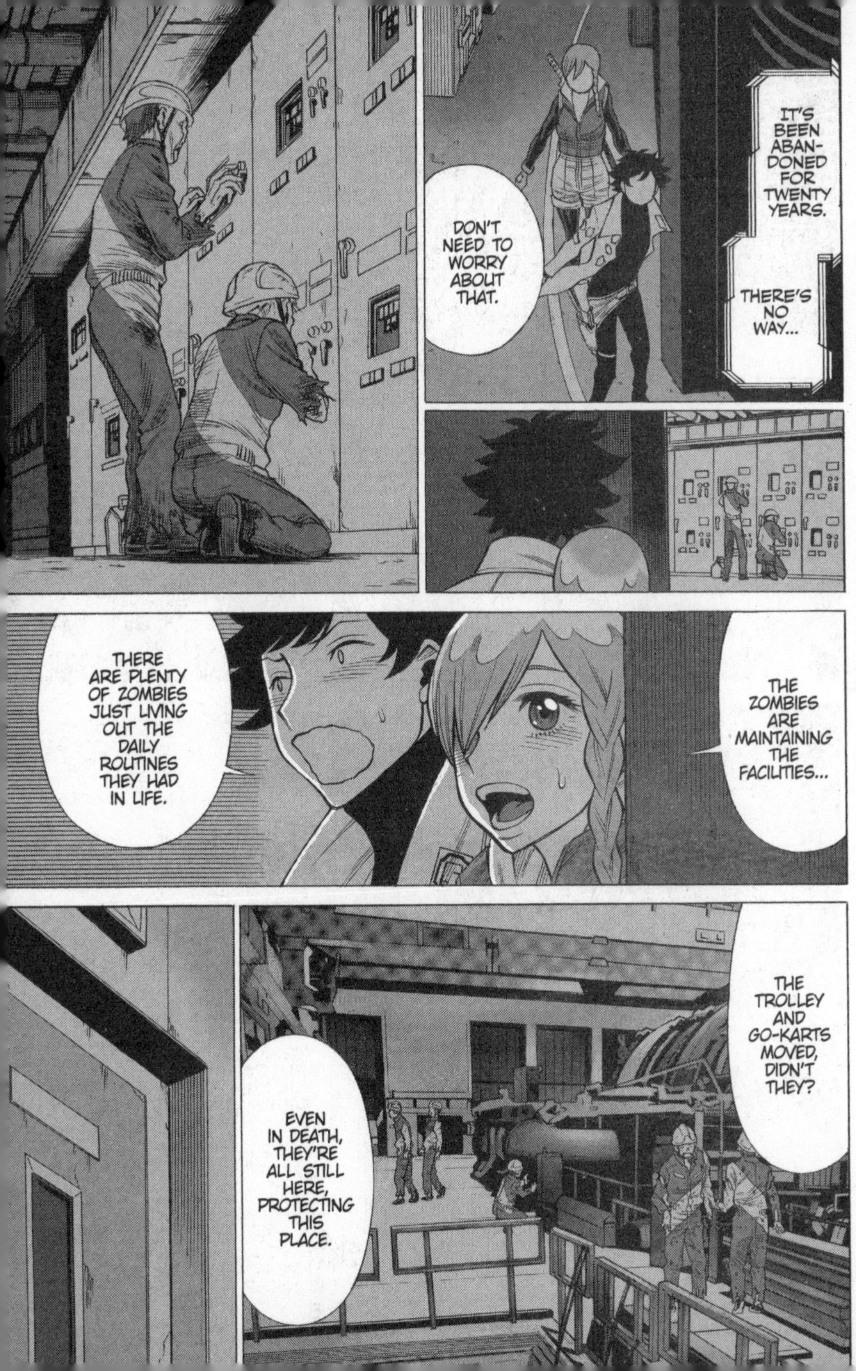
IT'S BEEN ABANDONED FOR TWENTY YEARS.
THERE'S NO WAY...
DON'T NEED TO WORRY ABOUT THAT.
THE ZOMBIES ARE MAINTAINING THE FACILITIES...
THERE ARE PLENTY OF ZOMBIES JUST LIVING OUT THE DAILY ROUTINES THEY HAD IN LIFE.
THE TROLLEY AND GO-KARTS MOVED, DIDN'T THEY?
EVEN IN DEATH, THEY'RE ALL STILL HERE, PROTECTING THIS PLACE.

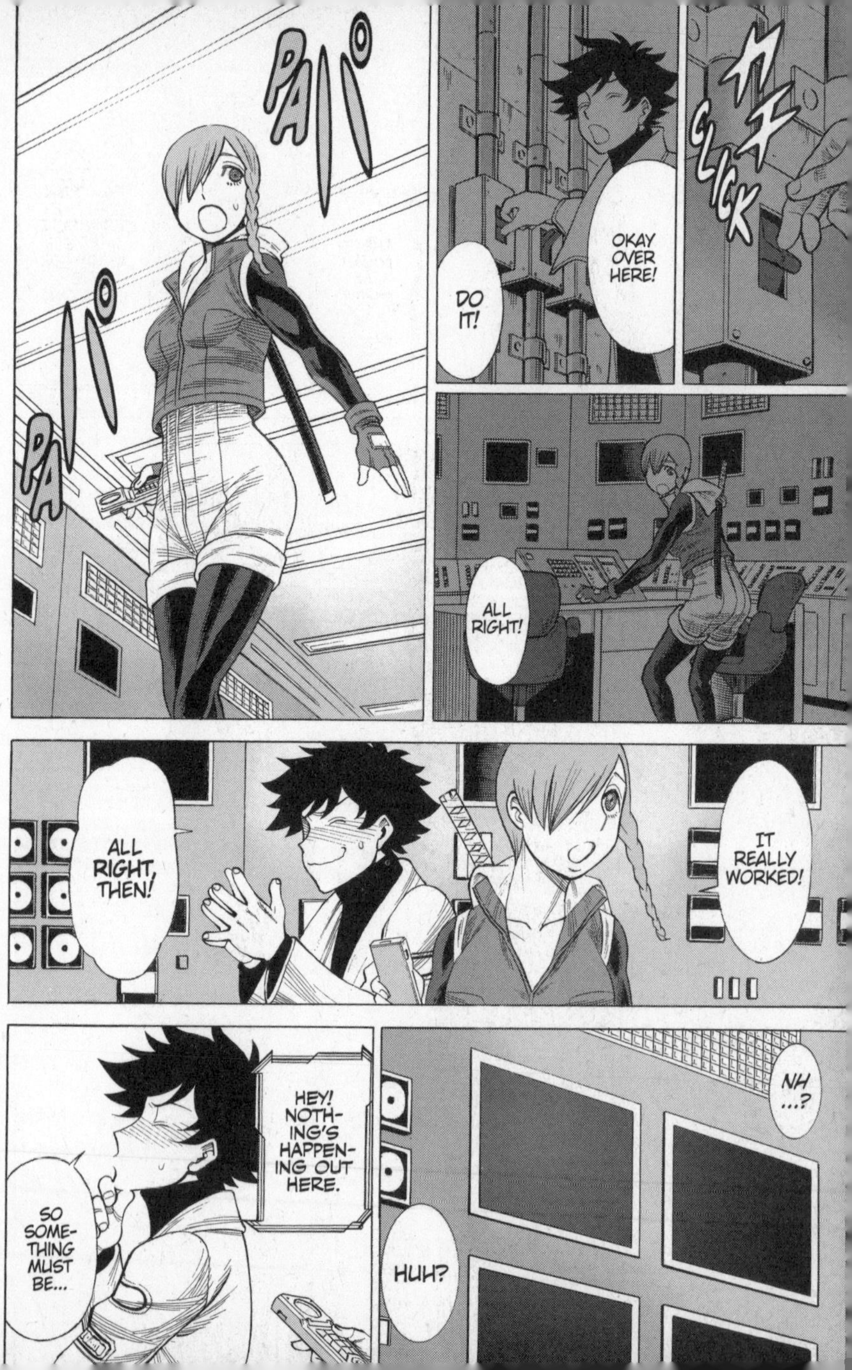
CLICK
OKAY OVER HERE!
DO IT!
ALL RIGHT!
PA
PA
IT REALLY WORKED!
ALL RIGHT, THEN!
NH ...?
HUH?
HEY! NOTHING'S HAPPENING OUT HERE.
SO SOMETHING MUST BE...

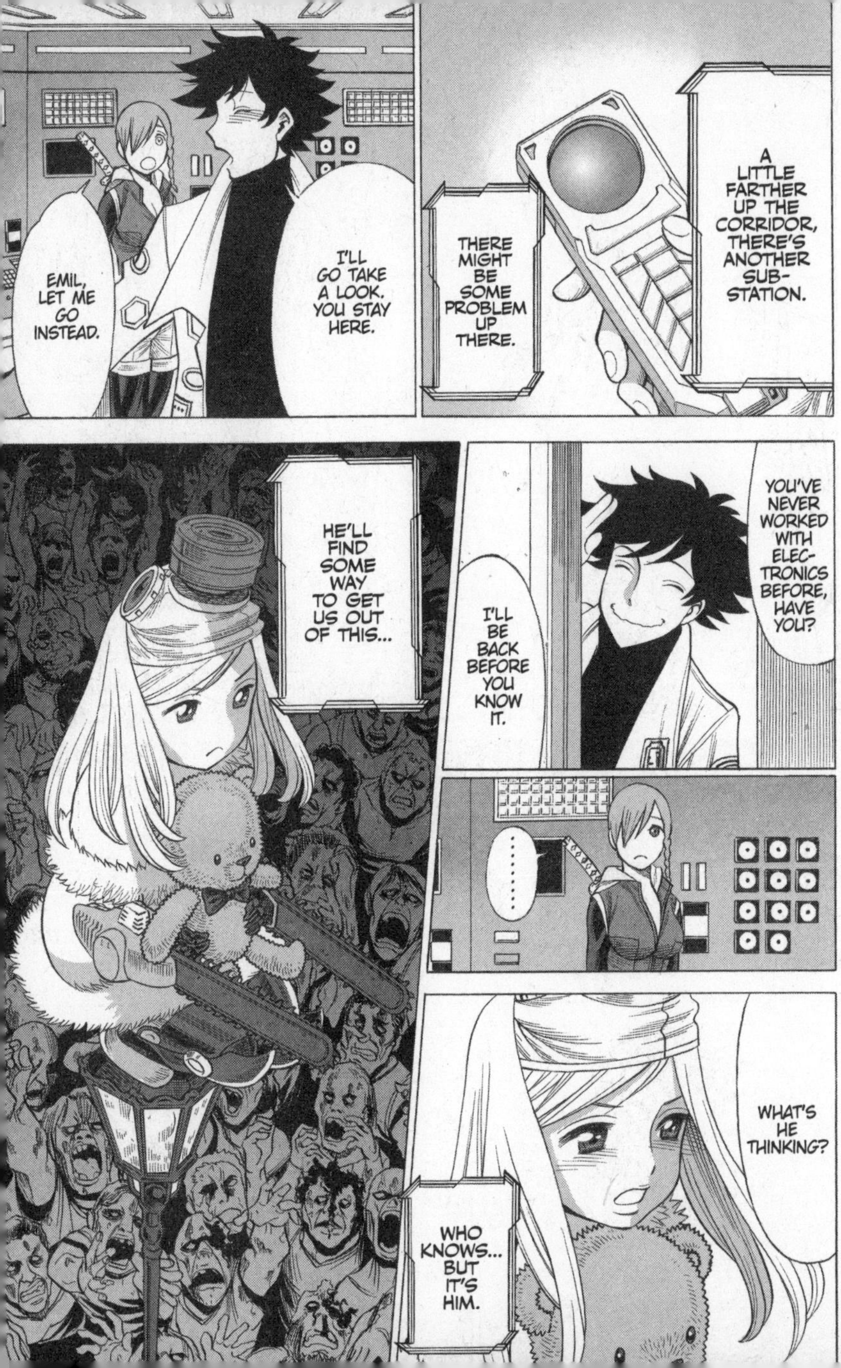
A LITTLE FARTHER UP THE CORRIDOR, THERE'S ANOTHER SUB-STATION.
THERE MIGHT BE SOME PROBLEM UP THERE.
I'LL GO TAKE A LOOK. YOU STAY HERE.
EMIL, LET ME GO INSTEAD.
YOU'VE NEVER WORKED WITH ELEC-TRONICS BEFORE, HAVE YOU?
I'LL BE BACK BEFORE YOU KNOW IT.
......
WHAT'S HE THINKING?
WHO KNOWS... BUT IT'S HIM.
HE'LL FIND SOME WAY TO GET US OUT OF THIS...

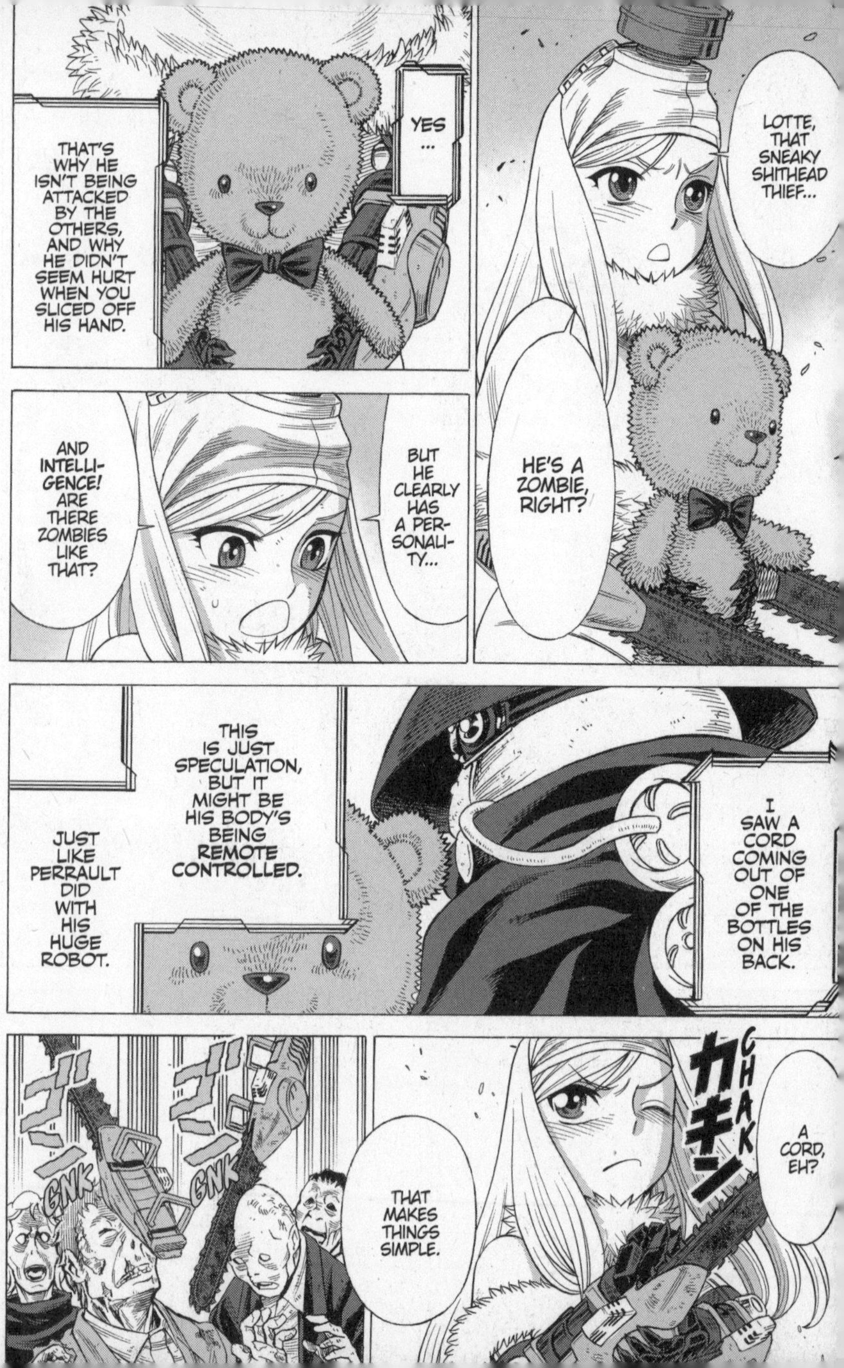

LOTTE, THAT SNEAKY SHITHEAD THIEF...
HE'S A ZOMBIE, RIGHT?
YES ...
THAT'S WHY HE ISN'T BEING ATTACKED BY THE OTHERS, AND WHY HE DIDN'T SEEM HURT WHEN YOU SLICED OFF HIS HAND.
BUT HE CLEARLY HAS A PERSONALITY...
AND INTELLIGENCE! ARE THERE ZOMBIES LIKE THAT?
I SAW A CORD COMING OUT OF ONE OF THE BOTTLES ON HIS BACK.
THIS IS JUST SPECULATION, BUT IT MIGHT BE HIS BODY'S BEING REMOTE CONTROLLED.
JUST LIKE PERRAULT DID WITH HIS HUGE ROBOT.
CHAK
A CORD, EH?
THAT MAKES THINGS SIMPLE.
GNK
GNK

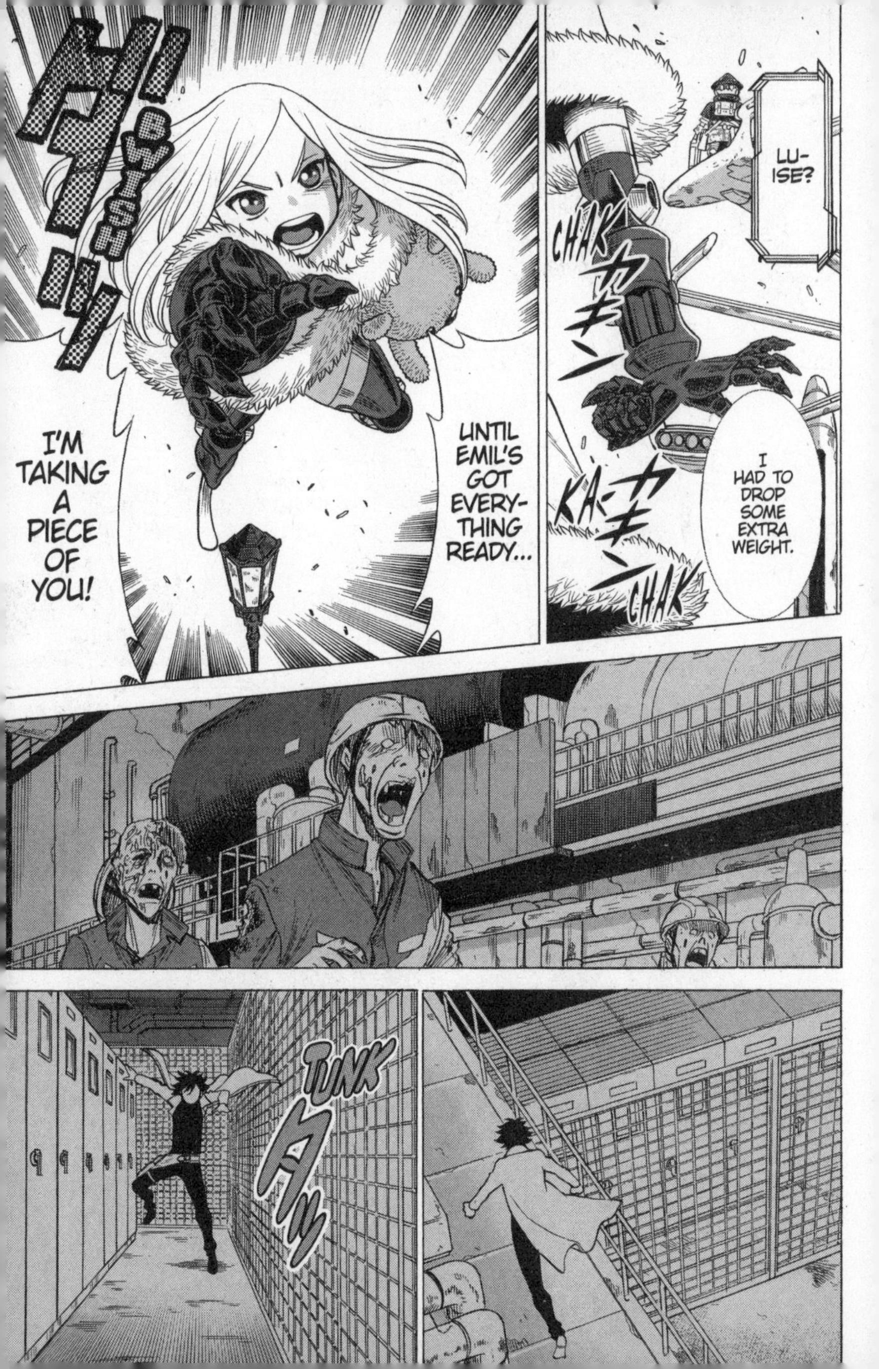
LU-ISE?
CHAK
KA-CHAK
I HAD TO DROP SOME EXTRA WEIGHT.
BWISH
UNTIL EMIL'S GOT EVERYTHING READY...
I'M TAKING A PIECE OF YOU!
TUNK

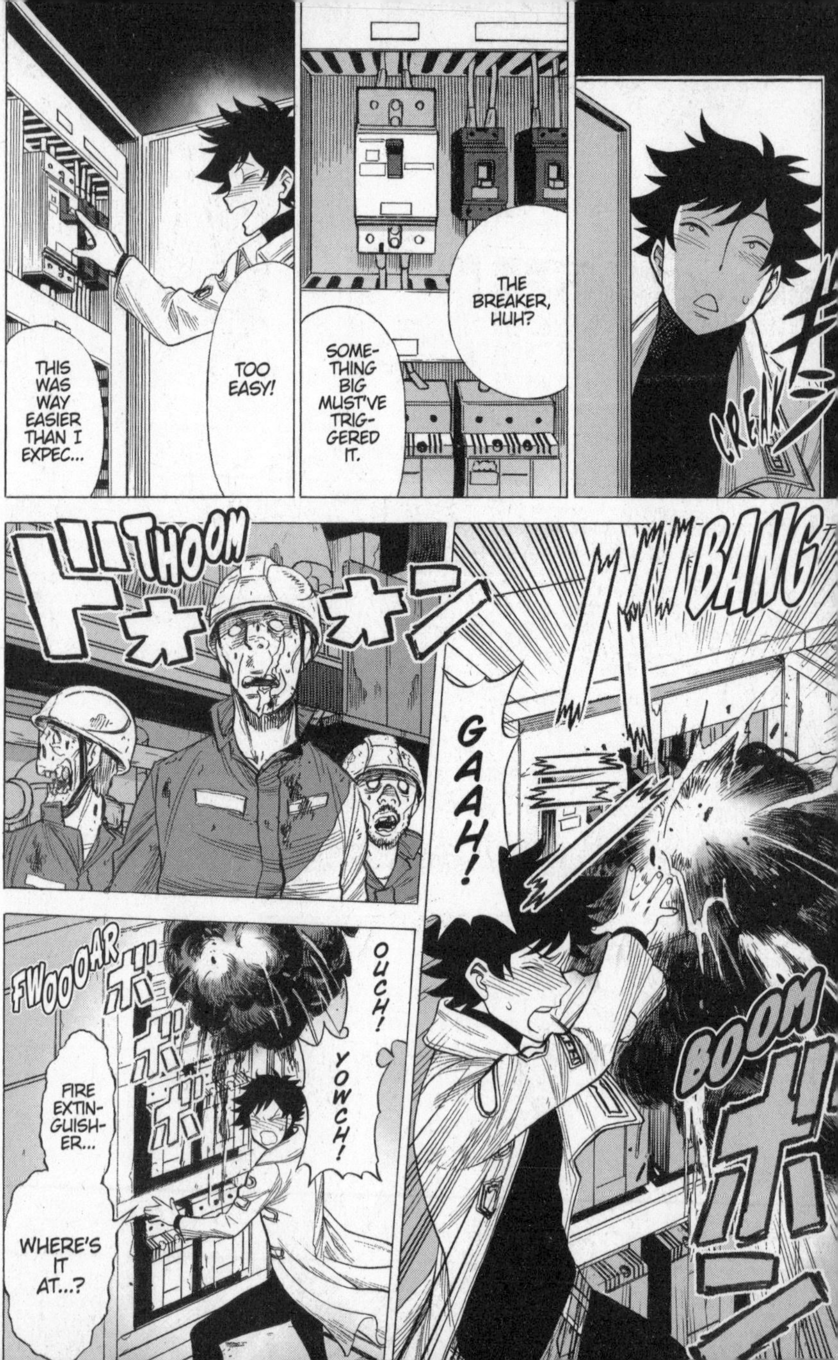
CREAK
THE BREAKER, HUH?
SOMETHING BIG MUST'VE TRIGGERED IT.
TOO EASY!
THIS WAS WAY EASIER THAN I EXPEC...
BANG
GAAAH!
BOOM
THOOM
FWOOOAR
OUCH! YOWCH!
FIRE EXTINGUISHER...
WHERE'S IT AT...?

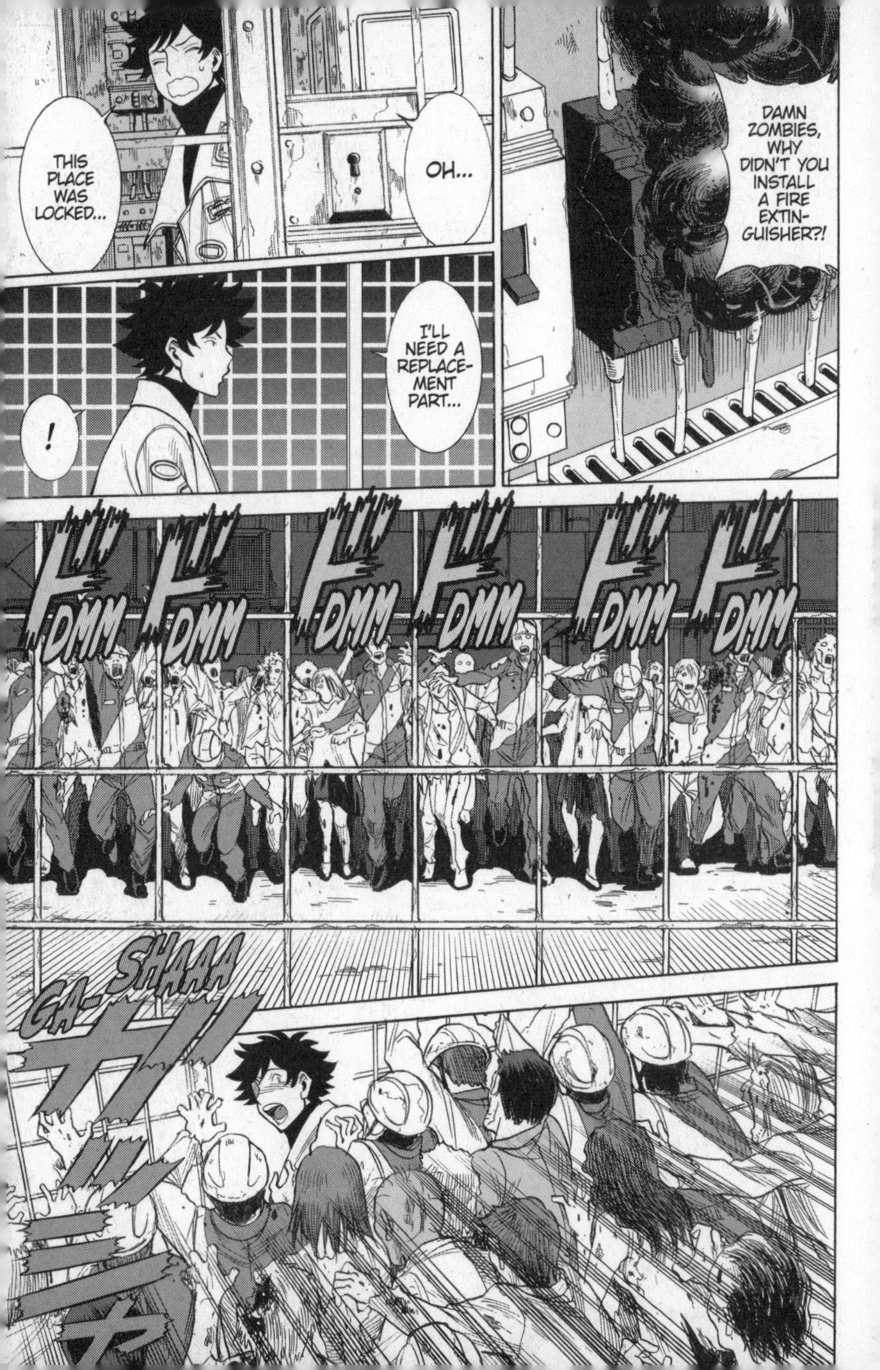
DAMN ZOMBIES, WHY DIDN'T YOU INSTALL A FIRE EXTIN-GUISHER?!
OH...
THIS PLACE WAS LOCKED...
I'LL NEED A REPLACE-MENT PART...
!
DMM
DMM
DMM
DMM
DMM
DMM
GA-SHAAA

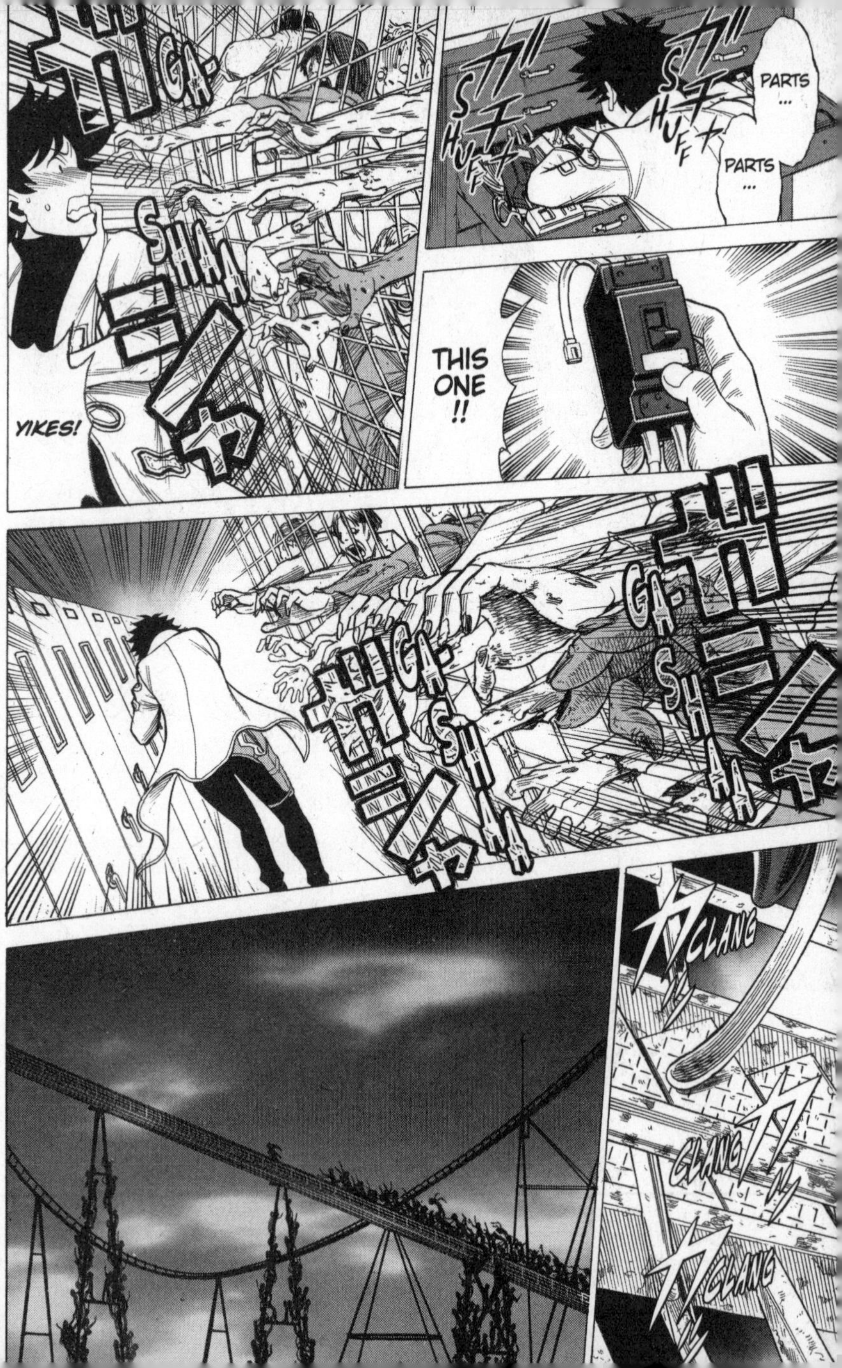
PARTS...
HUFF
HUFF
PARTS...
THIS ONE!!
GA-
SHAA
YIKES!
GA-SHAA
GA-SHAA
CLANG
CLANG
CLANG

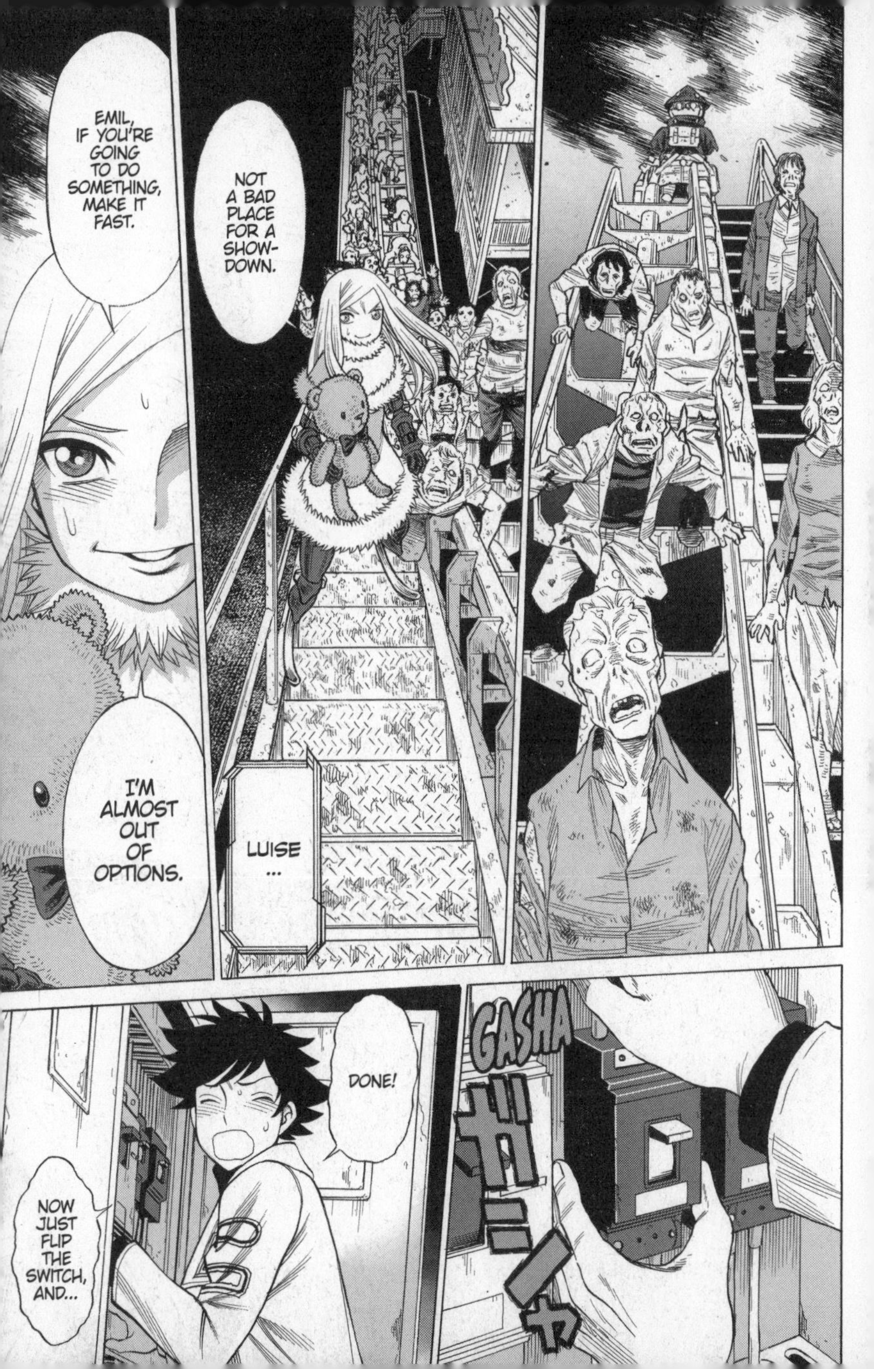
NOT A BAD PLACE FOR A SHOW-DOWN.
LUISE...
EMIL, IF YOU'RE GOING TO DO SOMETHING, MAKE IT FAST.
I'M ALMOST OUT OF OPTIONS.
GASHA
DONE!
NOW JUST FLIP THE SWITCH, AND...

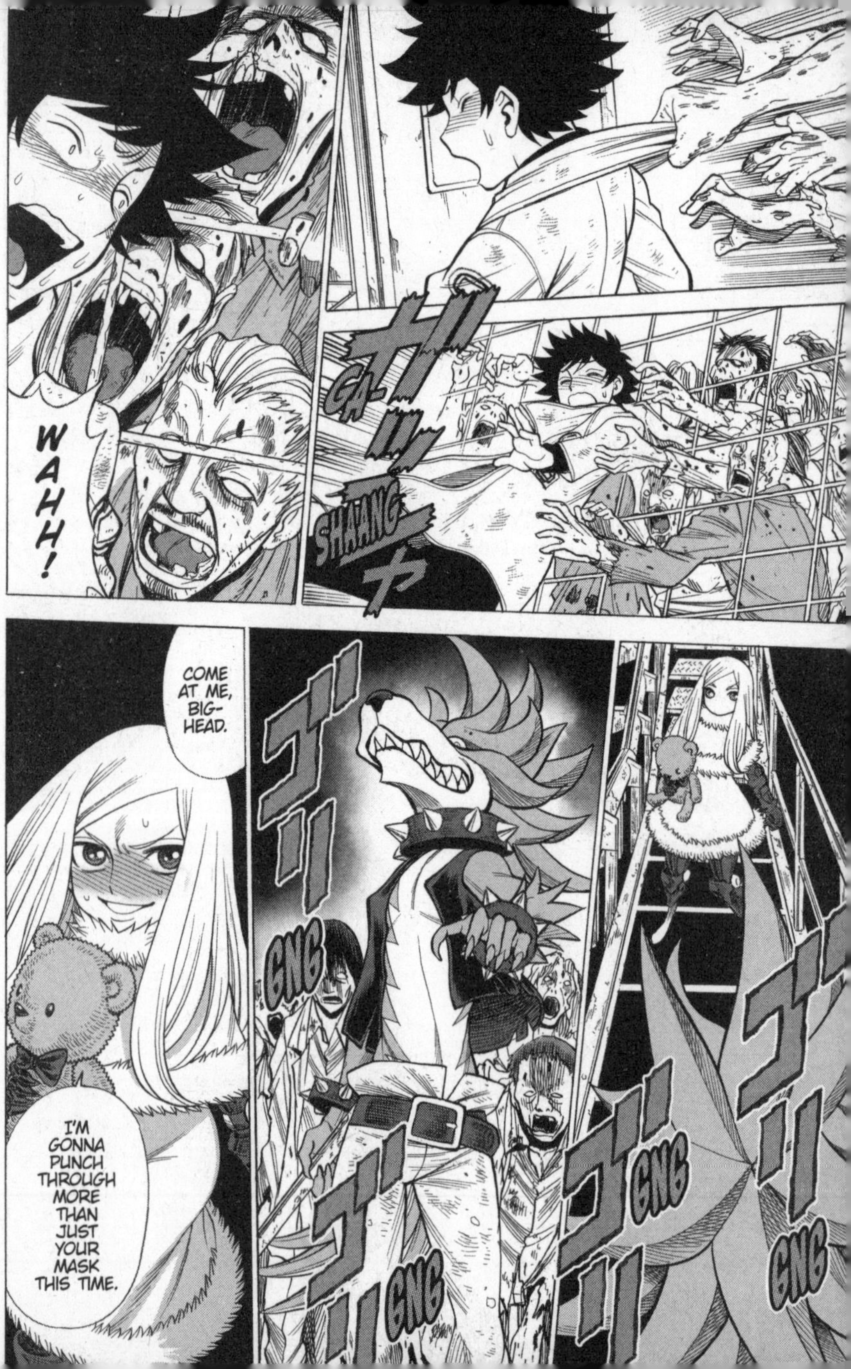
GA-
SHAANG
WAHH!
GNG
GNG
GNG
GNG
GNG
COME AT ME, BIG-HEAD.
I'M GONNA PUNCH THROUGH MORE THAN JUST YOUR MASK THIS TIME.

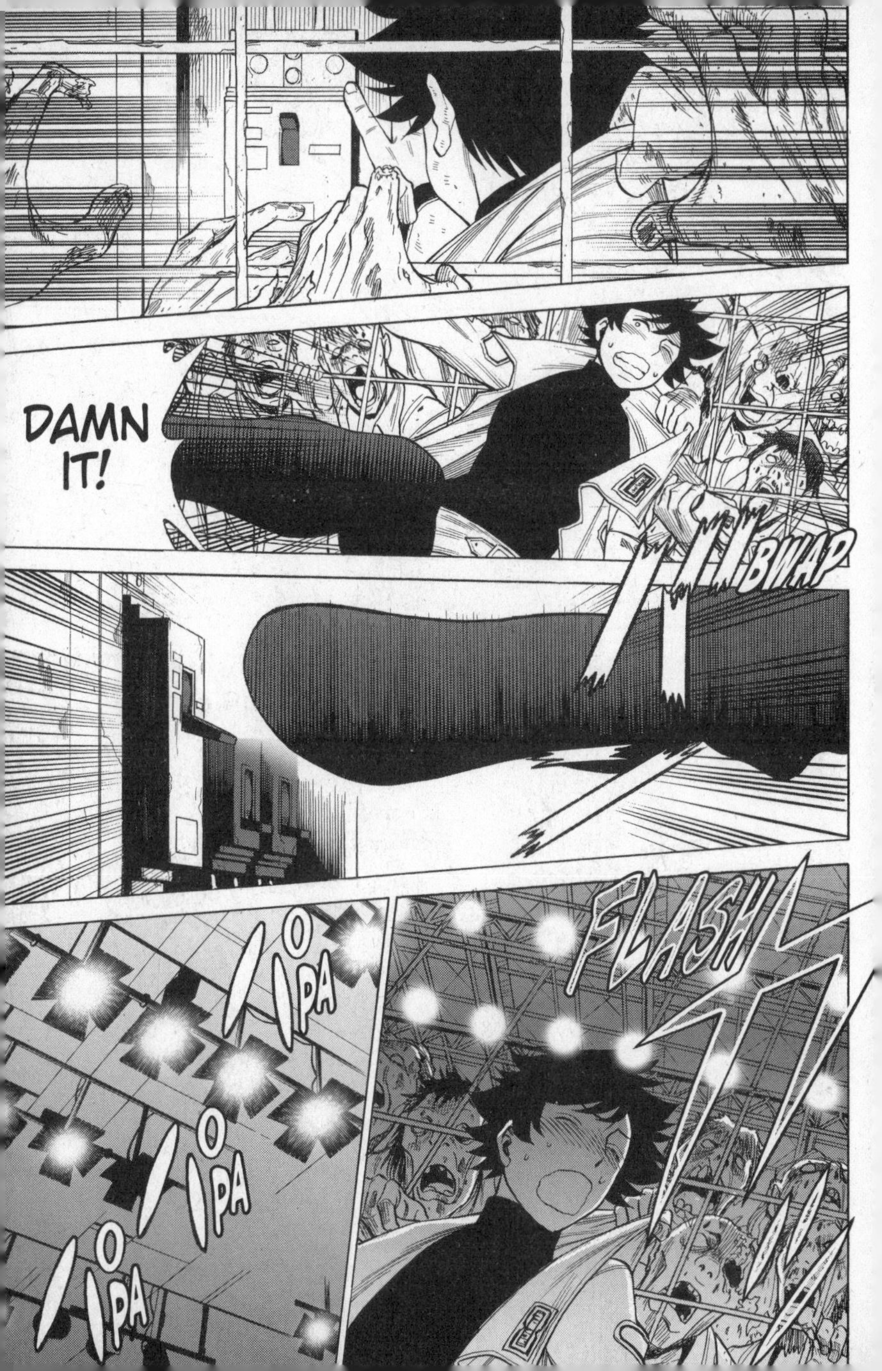
DAMN IT!
BWAP
FLASH
PA
PA
PA

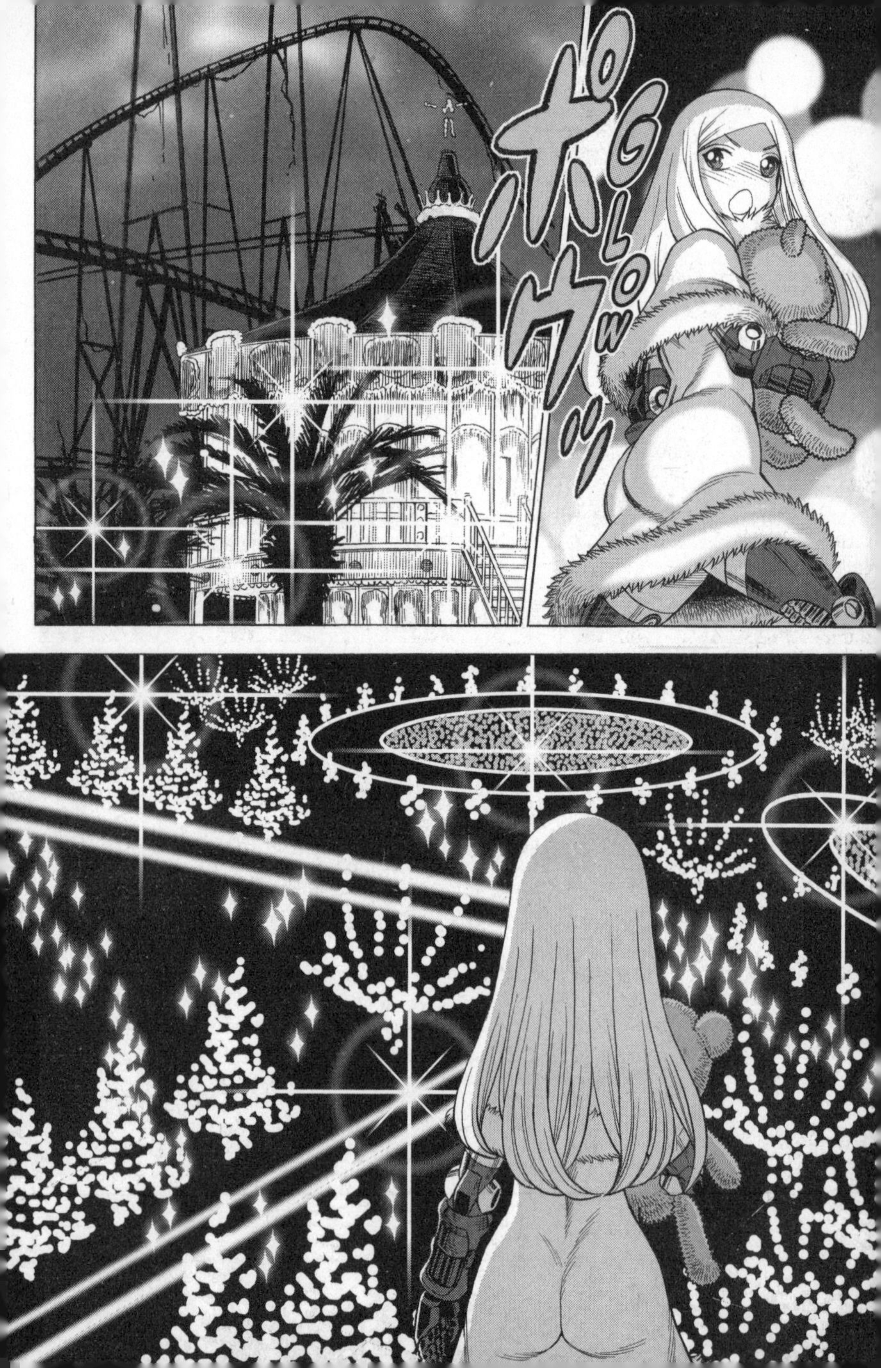
GLOW

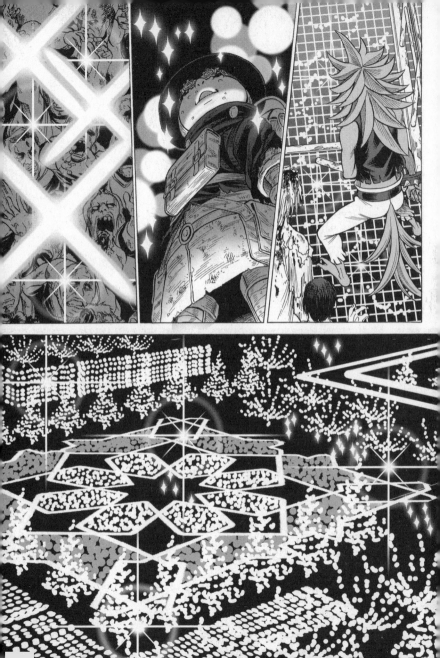

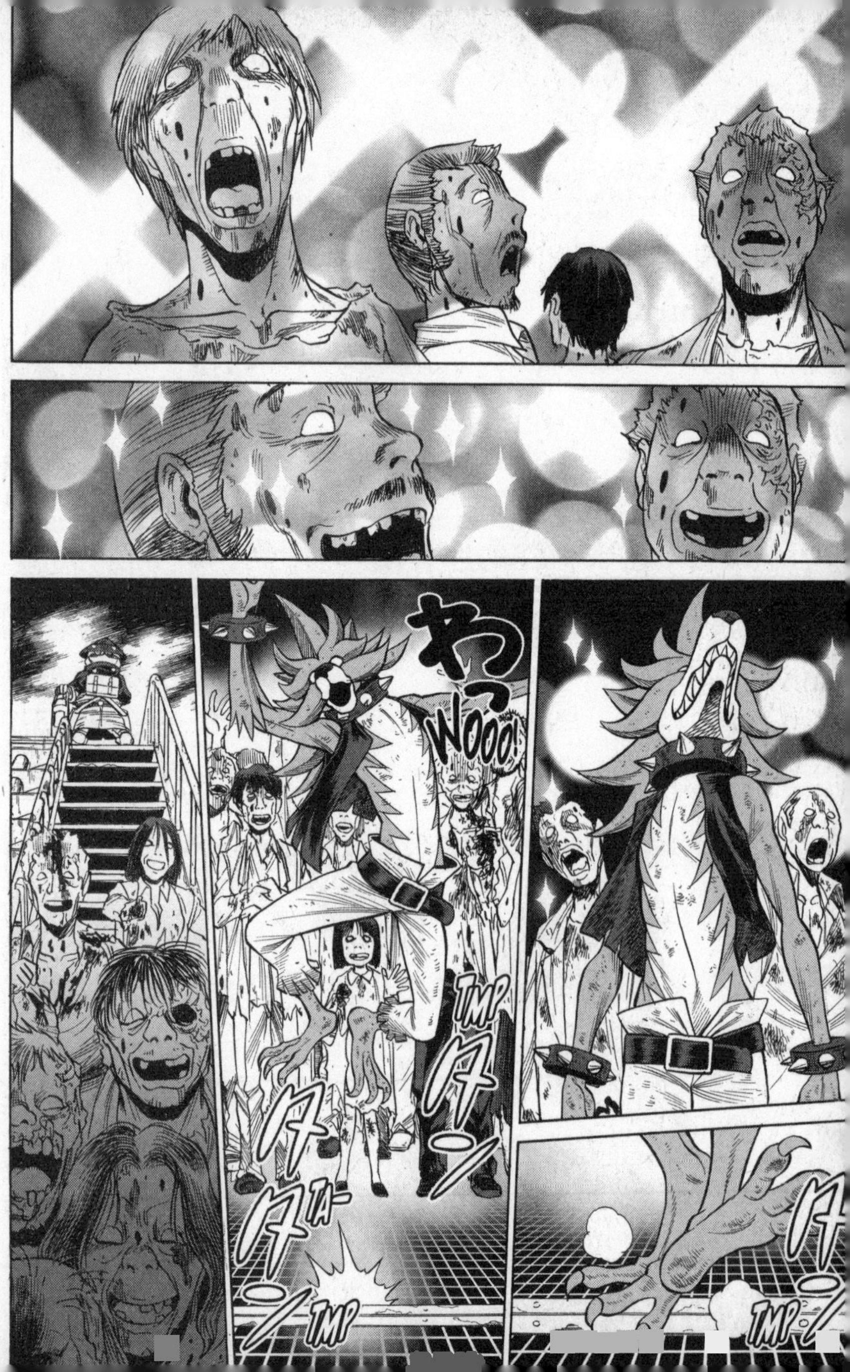

TMP
わっ
WOOO!
TMP
TA-
TMP

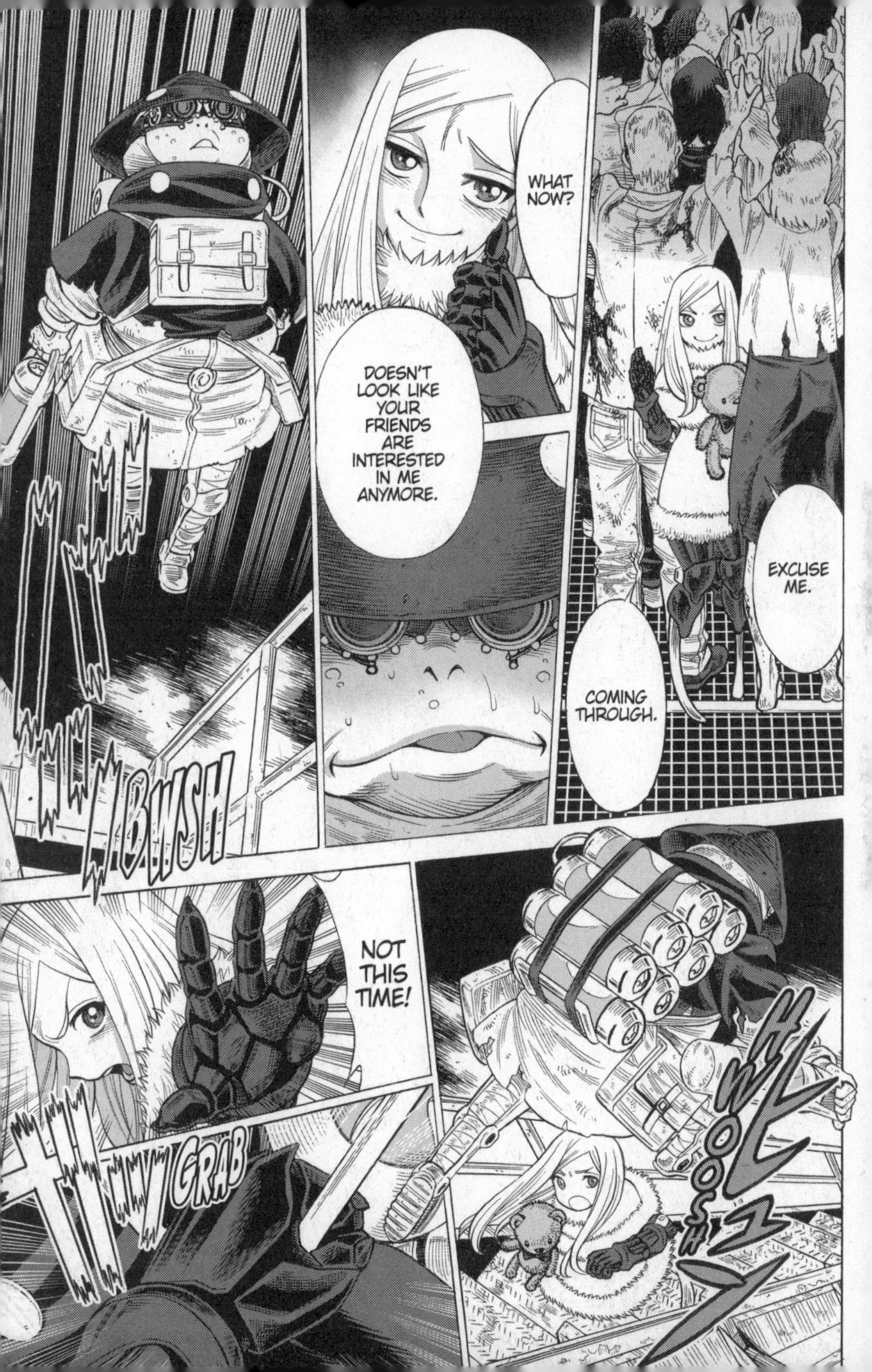
EXCUSE ME.
COMING THROUGH.
WHAT NOW?
DOESN'T LOOK LIKE YOUR FRIENDS ARE INTERESTED IN ME ANYMORE.
NOT THIS TIME!
GRAB

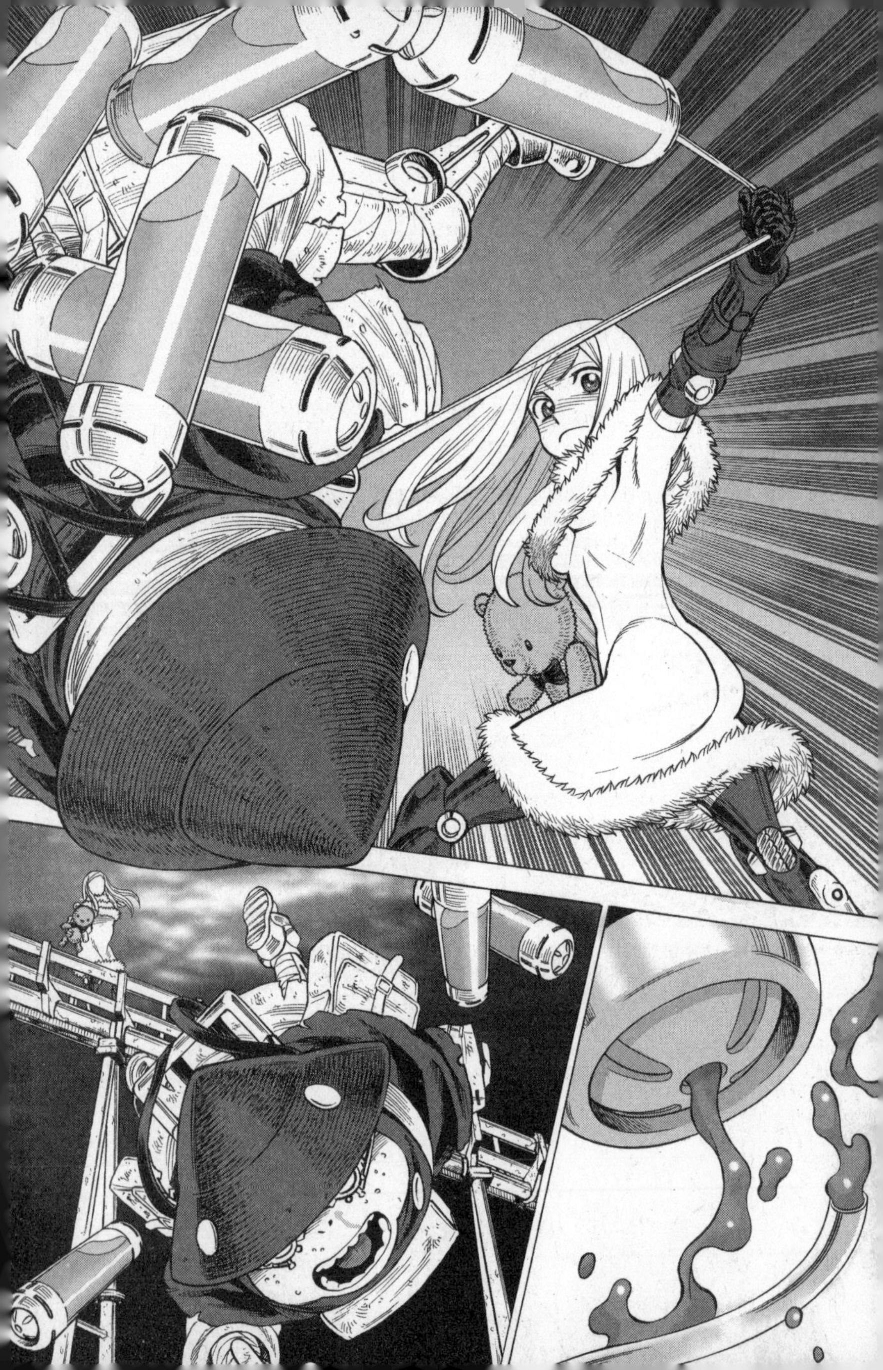

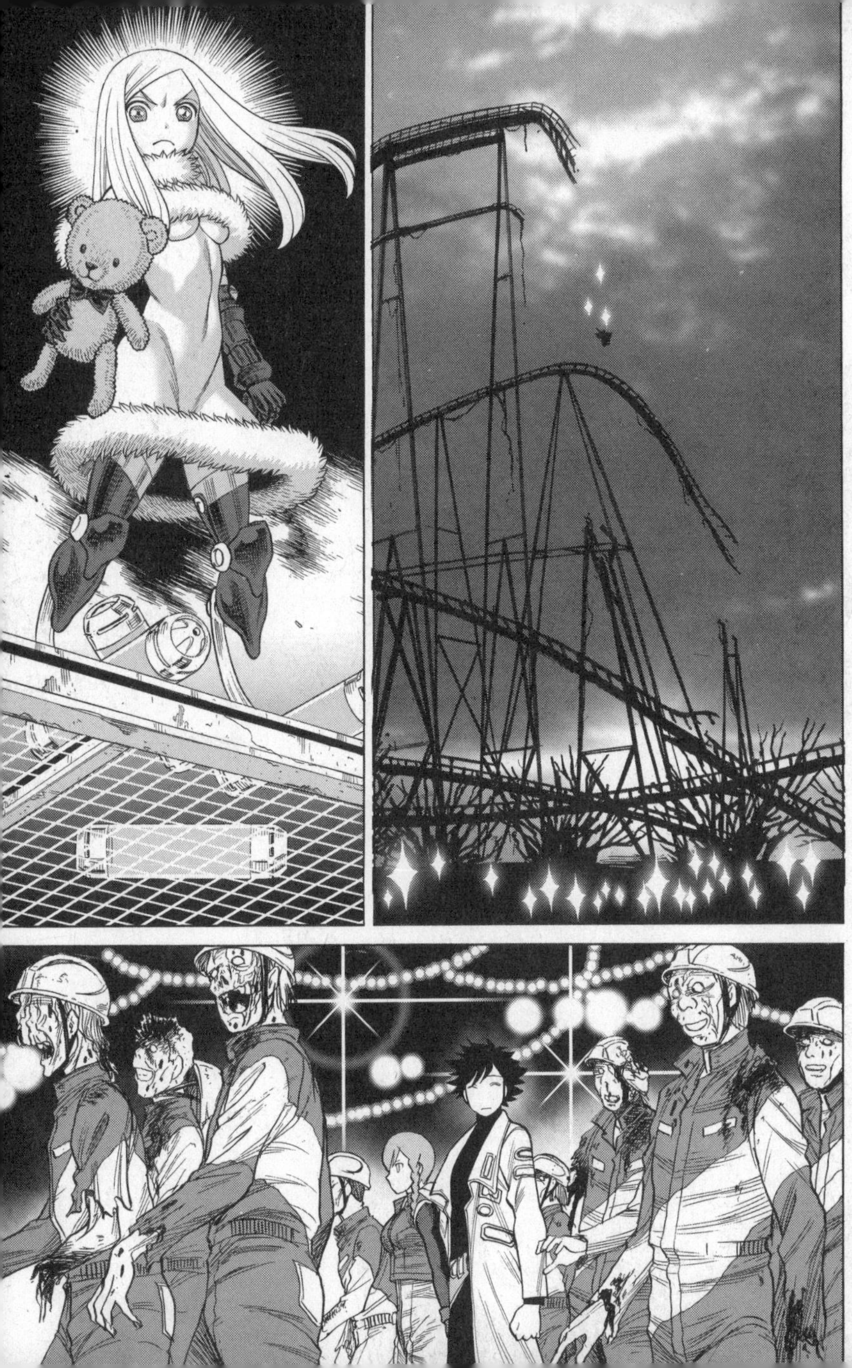

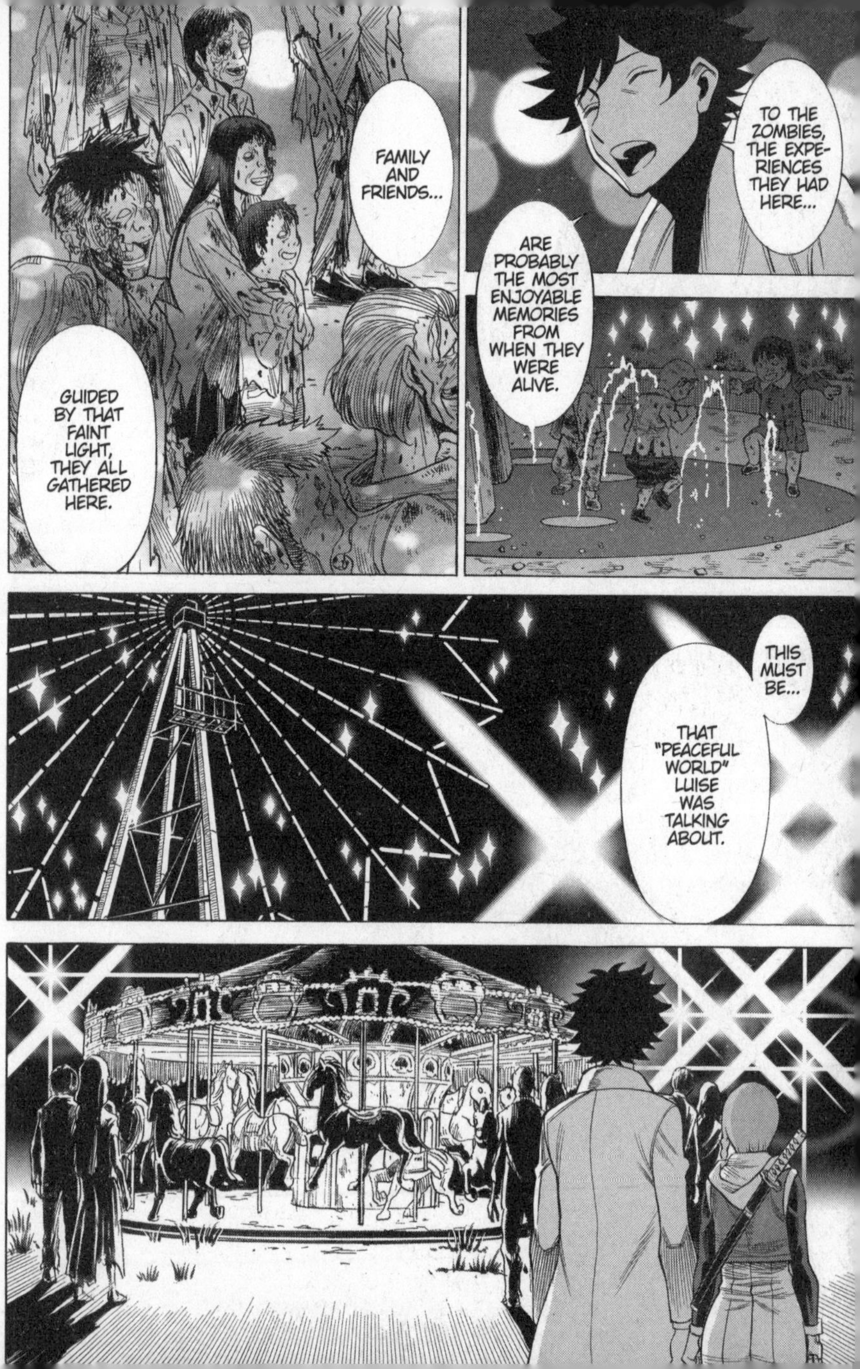
TO THE ZOMBIES, THE EXPE-RIENCES THEY HAD HERE...
ARE PROBABLY THE MOST ENJOYABLE MEMORIES FROM WHEN THEY WERE ALIVE.
FAMILY AND FRIENDS...
GUIDED BY THAT FAINT LIGHT, THEY ALL GATHERED HERE.
THIS MUST BE...
THAT "PEACEFUL WORLD" LUISE WAS TALKING ABOUT.

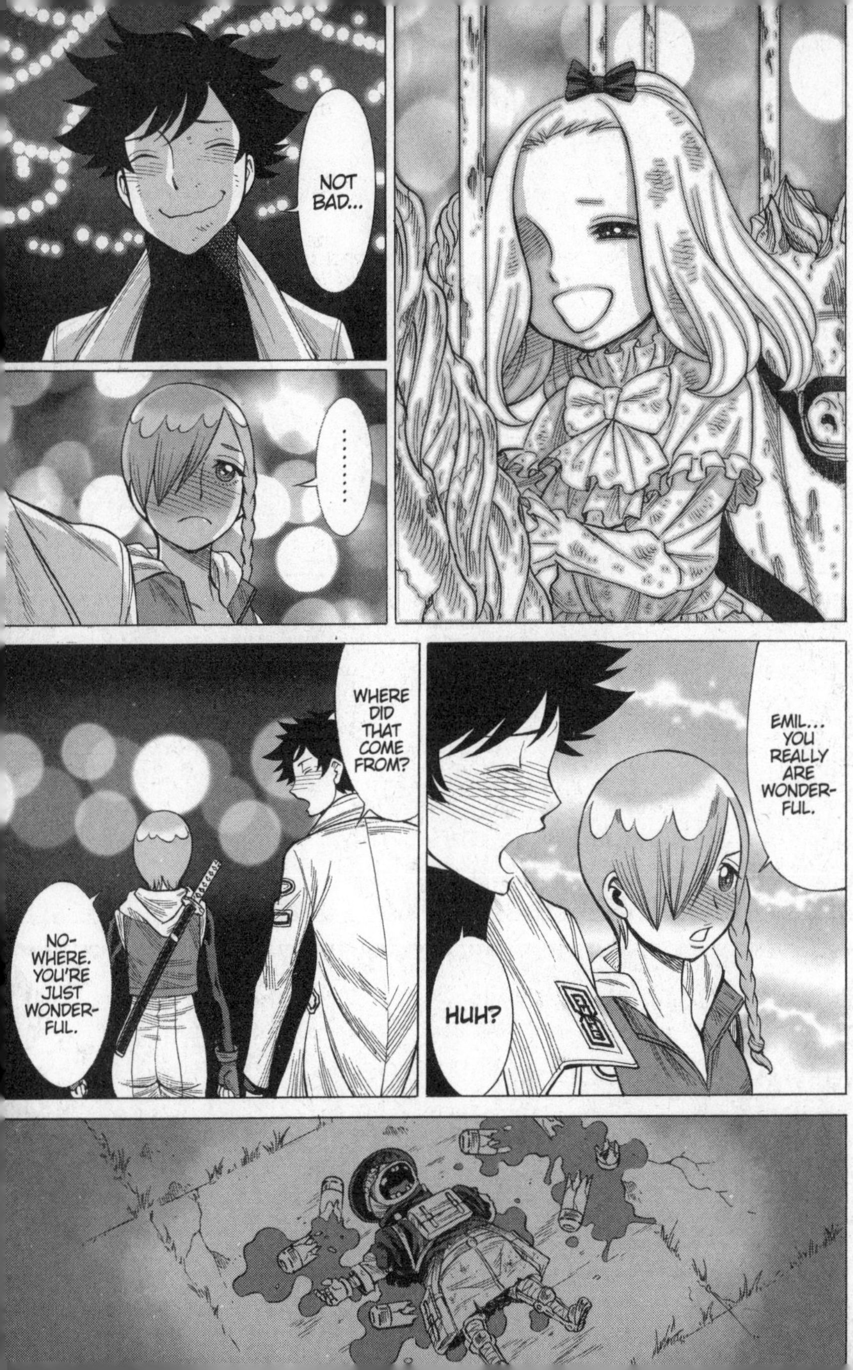
NOT BAD...
......
EMIL... YOU REALLY ARE WONDER-FUL.
HUH?
WHERE DID THAT COME FROM?
NO-WHERE. YOU'RE JUST WONDER-FUL.

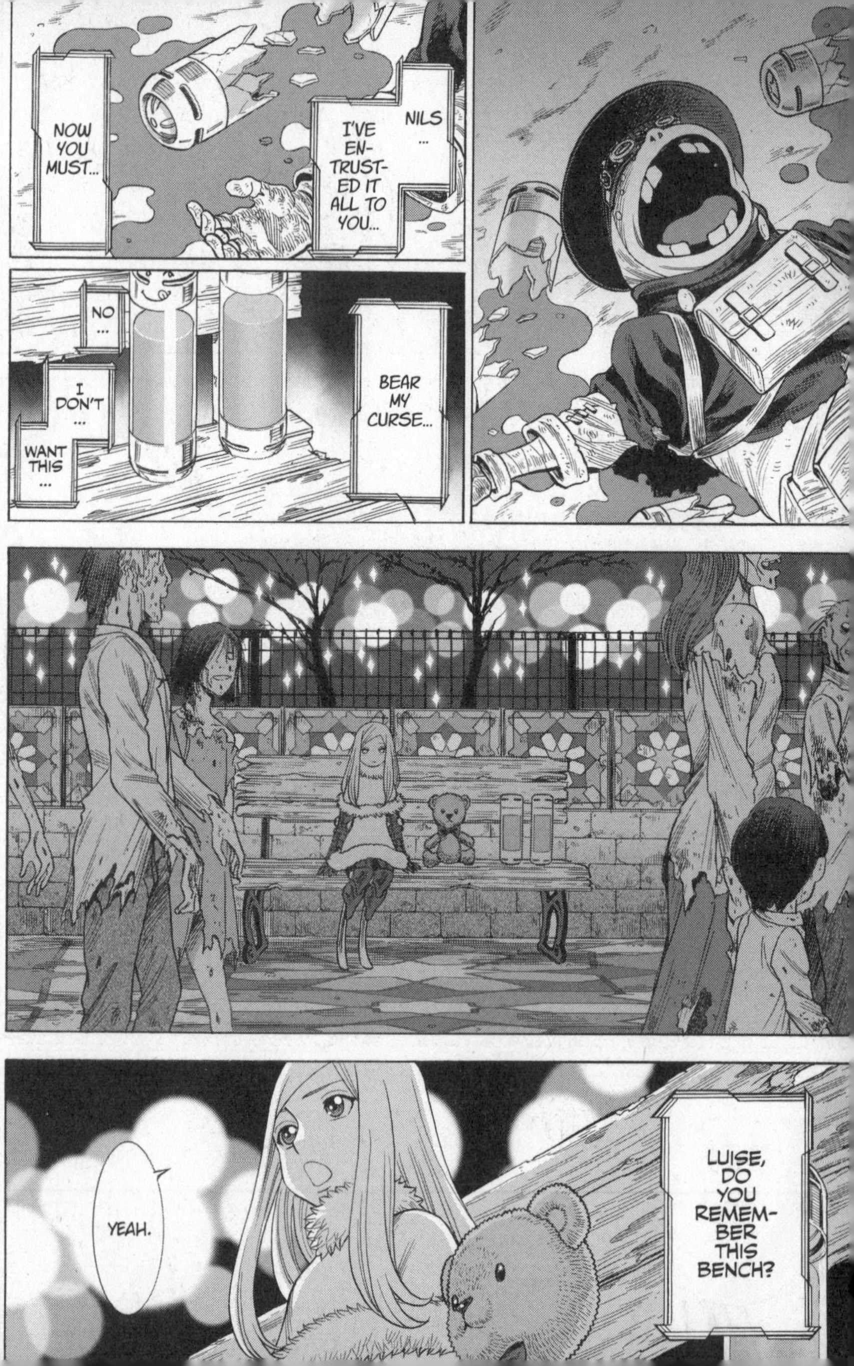
NILS ...
I'VE EN-TRUST-ED IT ALL TO YOU...
NOW YOU MUST...
BEAR MY CURSE...
NO ...
I DON'T ...
WANT THIS ...
LUISE, DO YOU REMEMBER THIS BENCH?
YEAH.

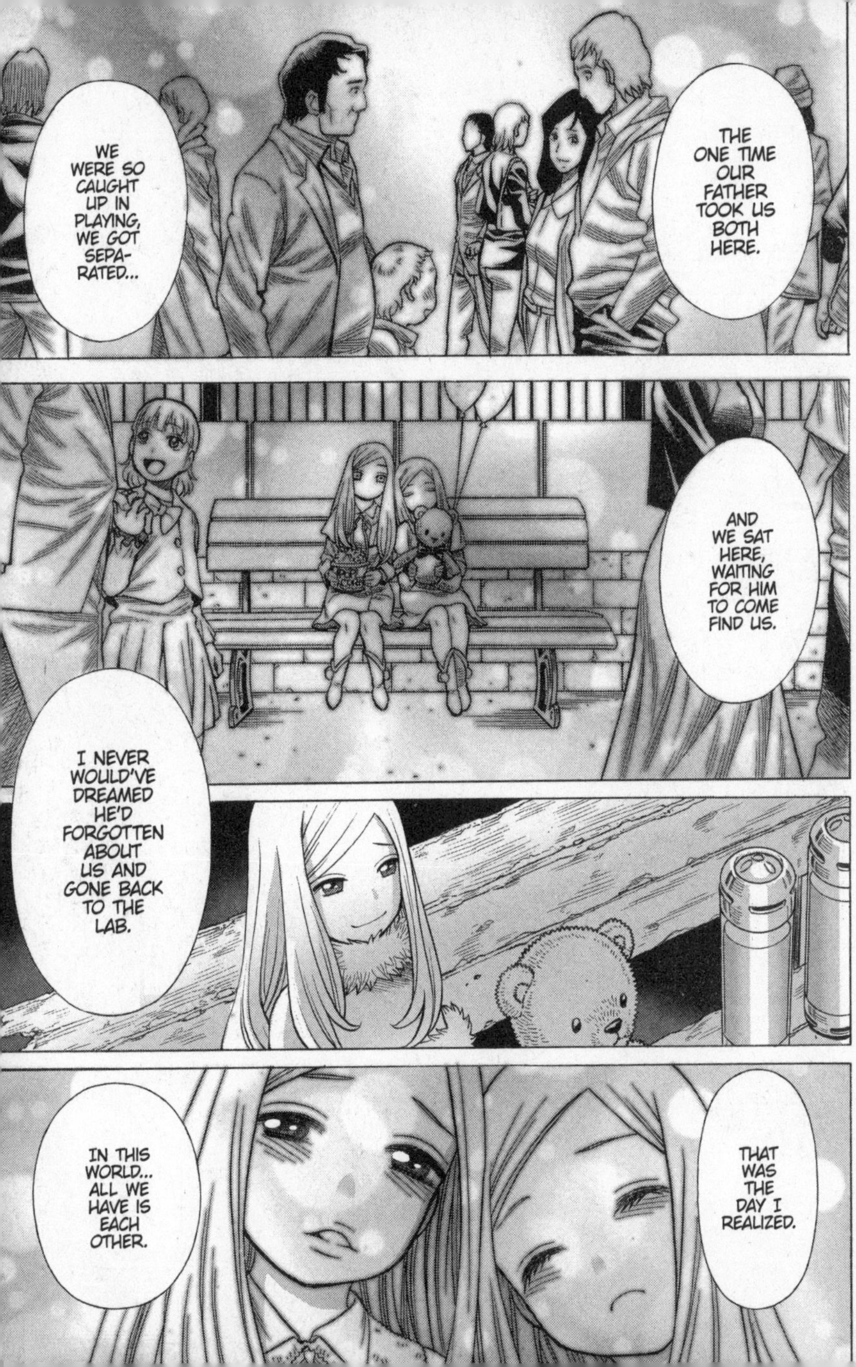
THE ONE TIME OUR FATHER TOOK US BOTH HERE.
WE WERE SO CAUGHT UP IN PLAYING, WE GOT SEPA-RATED...
AND WE SAT HERE, WAITING FOR HIM TO COME FIND US.
I NEVER WOULD'VE DREAMED HE'D FORGOTTEN ABOUT US AND GONE BACK TO THE LAB.
THAT WAS THE DAY I REALIZED.
IN THIS WORLD... ALL WE HAVE IS EACH OTHER.

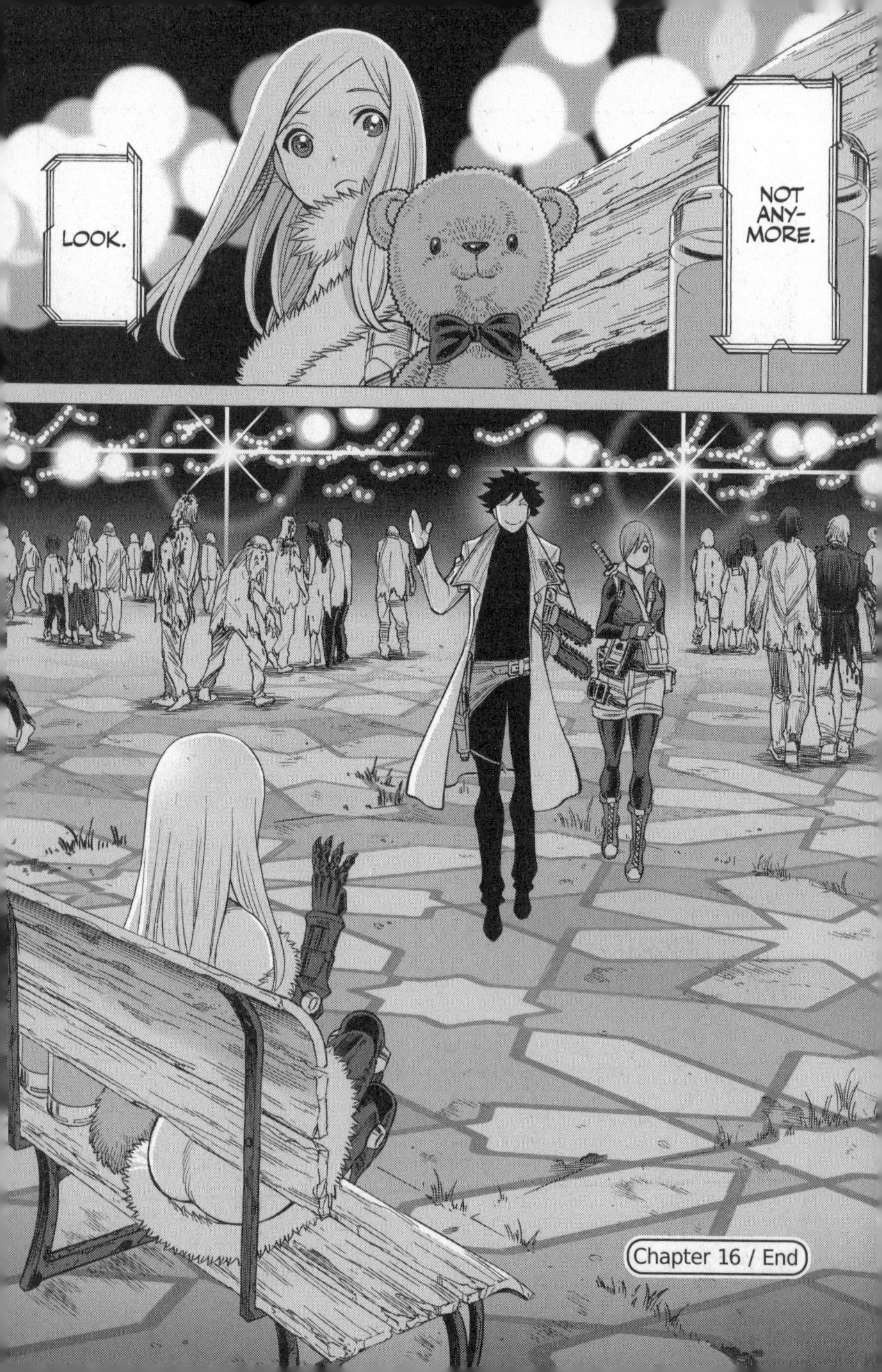
NOT ANY-MORE.
LOOK.
Chapter 16 / End

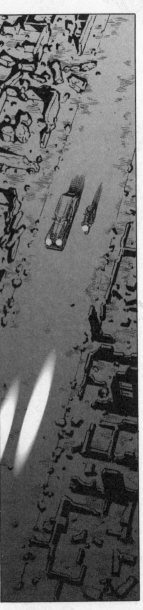

THAT'S... THE SOUL BOTTLE FROM THAT ZOMBIE WHO ATTACKED US?

HEY!

LICK

JUST... WHAT WAS HE?

SNIFF

SNIFF

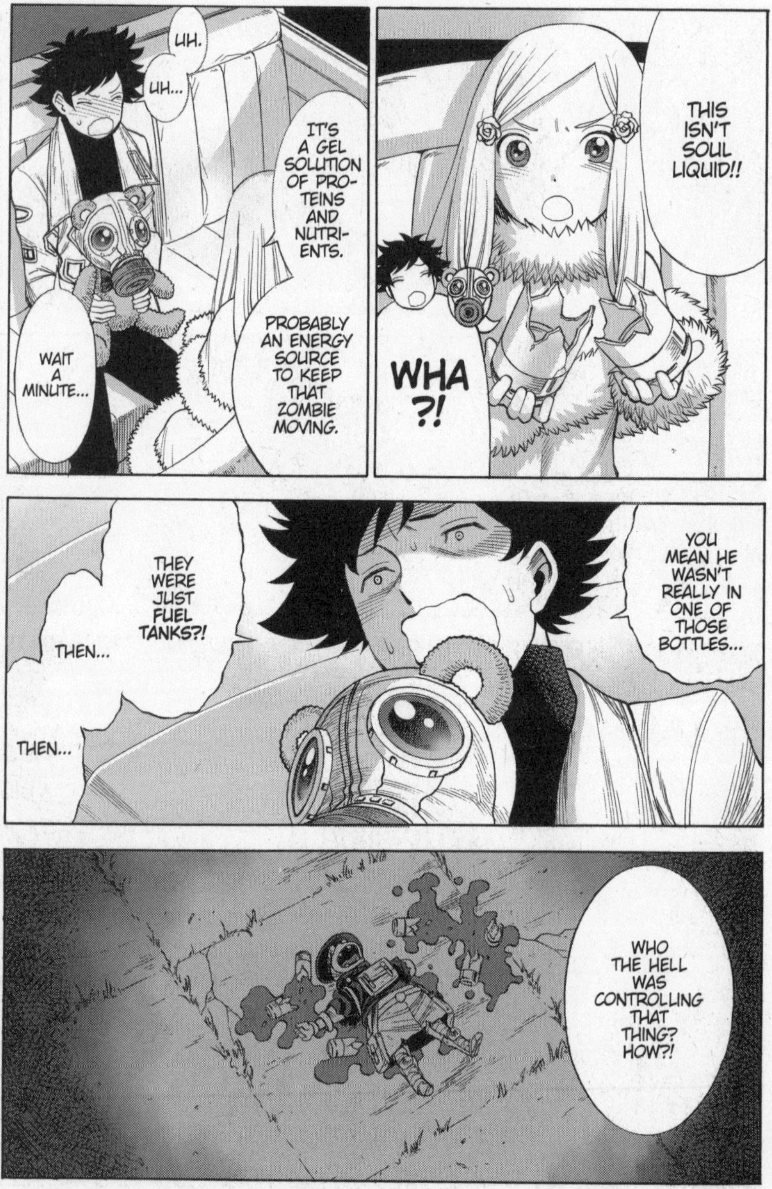
THIS ISN'T SOUL LIQUID!!
WHA ?!
IT'S A GEL SOLUTION OF PRO- TEINS AND NUTRI- ENTS.
PROBABLY AN ENERGY SOURCE TO KEEP THAT ZOMBIE MOVING.
UH.
UH...
WAIT A MINUTE...
YOU MEAN HE WASN'T REALLY IN ONE OF THOSE BOTTLES...
THEY WERE JUST FUEL TANKS?!
THEN...
THEN...
WHO THE HELL WAS CONTROLLING THAT THING? HOW?!

RUSTLE ボコ
RUSTLE ボコ
STRETCH
ズル ZLRP

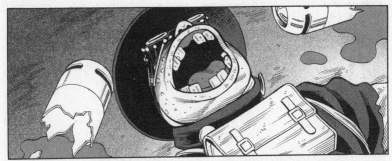

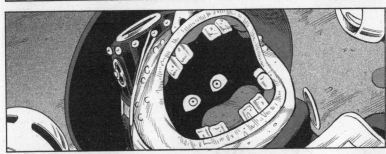

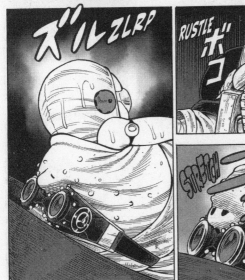

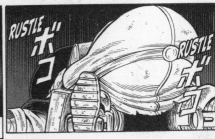

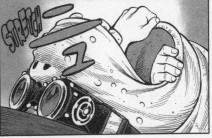

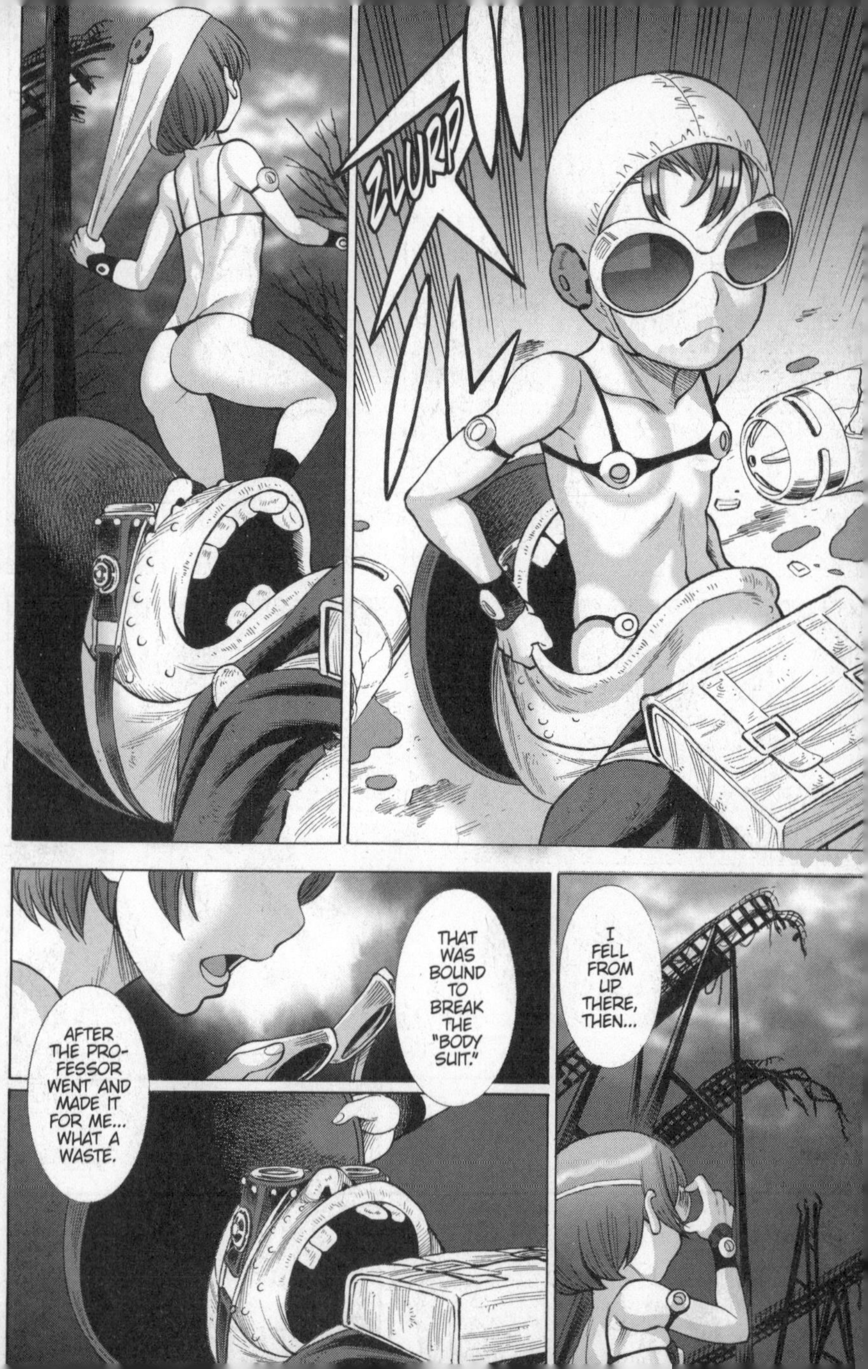
ZLURP
I FELL FROM UP THERE, THEN...
THAT WAS BOUND TO BREAK THE "BODY SUIT."
AFTER THE PRO-FESSOR WENT AND MADE IT FOR ME... WHAT A WASTE.

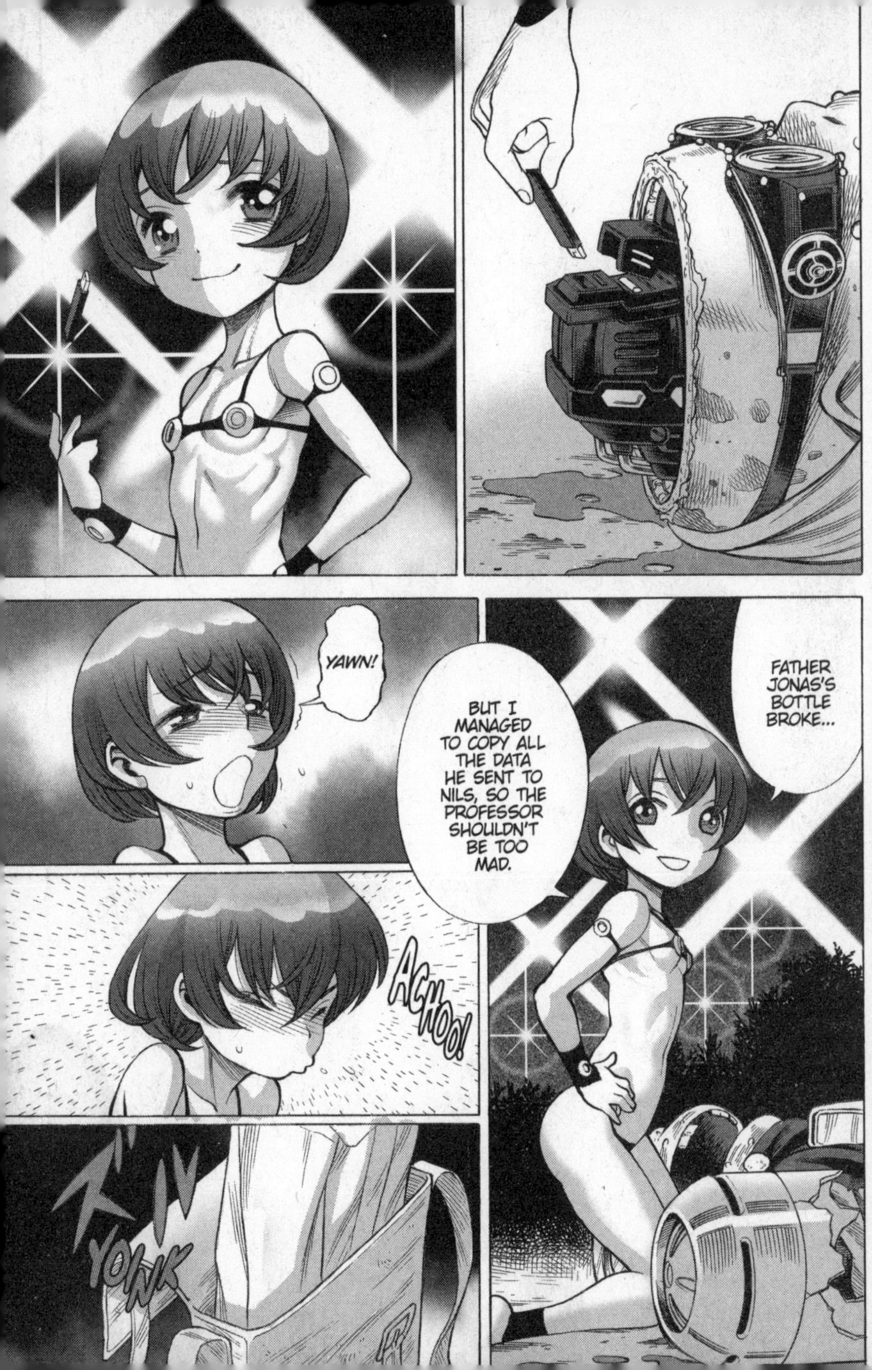
FATHER JONAS'S BOTTLE BROKE...
BUT I MANAGED TO COPY ALL THE DATA HE SENT TO NILS, SO THE PROFESSOR SHOULDN'T BE TOO MAD.
YAWN!
ACHOO!
YONK

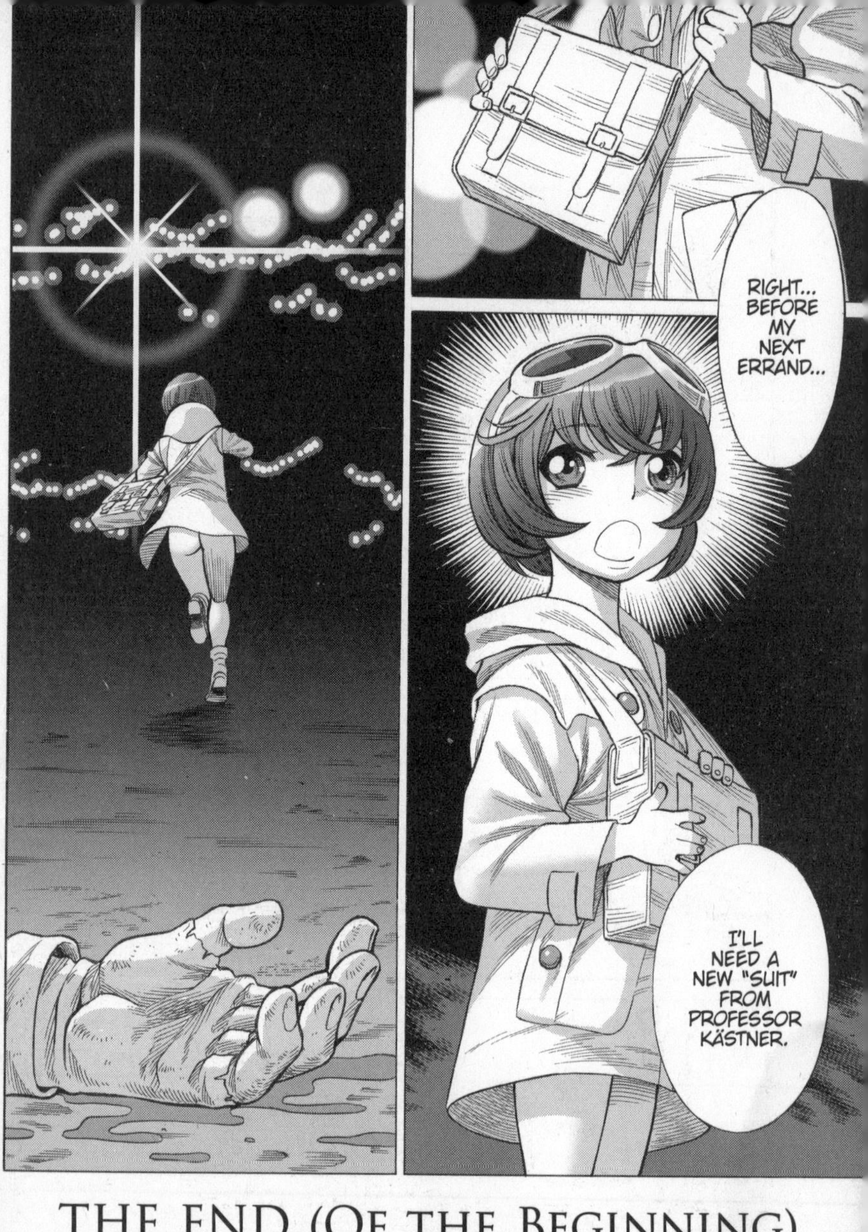
RIGHT... BEFORE MY NEXT ERRAND...
I'LL NEED A NEW "SUIT" FROM PROFESSOR KÄSTNER.

THE END (OF THE BEGINNING)

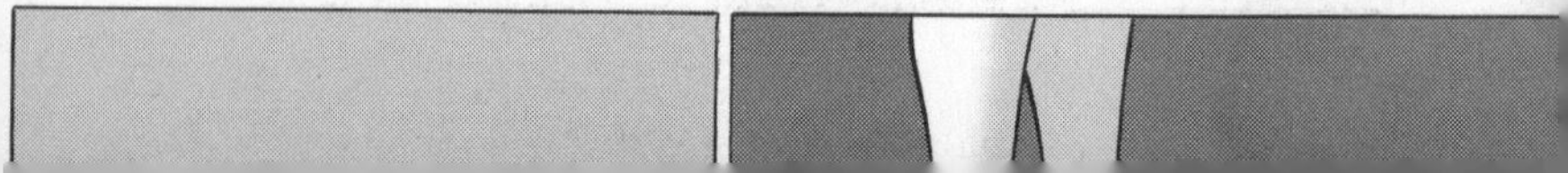

UUUH... UUUH...

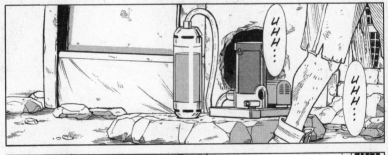

UHH... UHH...

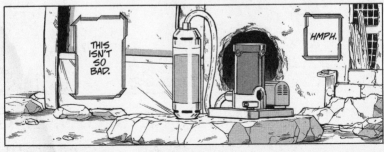

THIS ISN'T SO BAD.

HMPH.

SEVEN SEAS ENTERTAINMENT PRESENTS

SOUL LIQUID CHAMBERS

story and art by NOZOMU TAMAKI

VOLUME 3

TRANSLATION
Shane Hager

LETTERING AND RETOUCH
Ludwig Sacramento

COVER DESIGN
Karis Page

PROOFREADER
Janet Houck
Brett Hallahan

EDITOR
J.P. Sullivan

PRODUCTION ASSISTANT
CK Russell

PRODUCTION MANAGER
Lissa Pattillo

EDITOR-IN-CHIEF
Adam Arnold

PUBLISHER
Jason DeAngelis

SOUL LIQUID CHAMBERS VOL. 3
© Nozomu Tamaki 2016
Originally published in Japan in 2016 by SHONENGAHOSHA Co., Ltd., Tokyo.
English translation rights arranged through TOHAN CORPORATION, Tokyo.

Seven Seas books may be purchased in bulk for promotional, educational, or business use. Please contact your local bookseller or the Macmillan Corporate and Premium Sales Department at 1-800-221-7945, extension 5442, or by e-mail at MacmillanSpecialMarkets@macmillan.com.

Seven Seas and the Seven Seas logo are trademarks of Seven Seas Entertainment, LLC. All rights reserved.

ISBN: 978-1-626929-26-5

Printed in Canada

First Printing: January 2019

10 9 8 7 6 5 4 3 2 1

FOLLOW US ONLINE: *www.sevenseasentertainment.com*

READING DIRECTIONS

This book reads from *right to left*, Japanese style. If this is your first time reading manga, you start reading from the top right panel on each page and take it from there. If you get lost, just follow the numbered diagram here. It may seem backwards at first, but you'll get the hang of it! Have fun!!

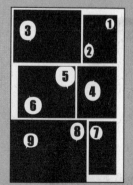